eight broads in the kitchen

8 Broads in the Kitchen

eightbroads.com

WINTERS PUBLISHING

winterspublishing.com
812-663-4948

Eight Broads in the Kitchen

© 2014 Eight Broads in the Kitchen ™

Published by:
Winters Publishing
P.O. Box 501
Greensburg, IN 47240
812-663-4948
www.winterspublishing.com

All photos courtesy of Jumping Rocks Photography and Christian Giannelli Photography.

ISBN 10: 1-883651-76-X
ISBN 13: 978-1-883651-76-3

Library of Congress Control Number: 2014918833

Printed in the United States of America.

dedication

With love and gratitude to our families, friends, colleagues, and enthusiastic guests, who for many years have requested our recipes ... here they are!

acknowledgments

There are many who have helped us on the journey to publishing this cookbook. We first thank Jay Karen, CEO extraordinaire of the innkeeping industry, who has always been enthusiastic about the endless possibilities of the Eight Broads and where we could take our vision. We thank Joan and Dane Wells, professional colleagues and friends, who welcomed us into their home for our first photo shoot. To Mark Smith and Matthew Lovette, Jumping Rocks Photography, and to Christian Giannelli, Christian Giannelli Photography, whose keen eyes and technical prowess created the artful photographs seen in this book. Thank you all!

contents

introduction

One cold spring day, somewhere between Lancaster, Pennsylvania, and Lenox, Massachusetts, Eight Broads in the Kitchen was born. Wouldn't it be great, Deb and Kathryn thought, to pool the collective resources of our foodie innkeeper friends and create a blog! Our guests would love it, and we would have fun. Fun was the operative word, and it still is!

Our little seed of an idea blossomed in a way that continues to amaze us. Some of us had never even met face-to-face, yet we all took the plunge and made a commitment to develop a fun, innovative blog devoted to breakfast foodies.

The Eight Broads in the Kitchen believe in sustainable local foods prepared with creativity and flair, with an accent on flavor and freshness. We are committed to sourcing locally as much as we can. Regional specialties frequently highlight our breakfast menus with happy eggs from happy chickens, pork from humanely-raised pigs, fruit grown right next door, and fresh herbs from our own gardens.

We have worked together, helping each other hone our culinary skills, taking them to new heights. As we jelled as a group, we started giving cooking classes at national innkeeping conferences, as well as locally, loving the ability to share what we have learned, to share our passion for breakfast.

Take eight innkeepers with more than 150 years combined experience. Add more than 184,200 breakfasts served to and enjoyed by happy guests. Factor in at least a half-million cookies munched by guests—though not the innkeepers (we probably only ate about 25,000 cookies). Stir in a creative streak and daring vision.

Over time, we cight innkeepers have become fast friends, sharing the joys of creative food along with the blessings and challenges of innkeeping and life. Shared cyberspace and in-person hugs, tears, and laughter have cemented the friendship for us Eight Broads.

And now the time has come for the first *Eight Broads in the Kitchen* cookbook. We hope you will savor our recipes, since we all live by the credo that beautiful, freshly prepared food from the finest ingredients is best shared with fabulous friends. Creating colorful and memorable breakfasts is an extension of our hospitality where our guests are central. The universal language of food opens doors, inspires conversation, calms restless souls, and often is just a good reason to laugh. Food bridges divides, connects opposite philosophies, and in the words of author John Gunther, "All happiness depends on a leisurely breakfast."

a word to our ingredients

Brown sugar:
light brown, unless otherwise noted.

Butter:
unsalted. We do not recommend margarine as it will not produce the same high-quality result.

Eggs:
large unless otherwise noted. We recommend that for pregnant, auto-immune-challenged people, and small children, that you use pasteurized eggs, found in the dairy section of your grocery store, in recipes calling for overnight storage as well as custards, which do not cook at high temps.

Flour:
unbleached all-purpose, unless otherwise noted.

Lukewarm water:
under 110 degrees or it will kill the yeast.

Muffins:
a standard muffin pan contains 12 cups.

Oats:
quick-cooking oats, never instant. If a recipe calls for rolled oats, they need to be rolled oats, not quick or instant.

Oil:
can be canola, rapeseed, or corn oil, unless we specify olive oil.

Salt:
We recommend using kosher and sea salt—kosher for baking, sea salt for cooking and finishing.

Sugar:
granulated, unless otherwise noted.

Size matters!
Pans are whatever size the recipe calls for. Other sizes will give different results. A 9-inch pie shell, for instance, will take 1½ times the amount of filling than an 8-inch pie shell.

8 fruit

an *apple* a day

baked apples

The Beechmont Inn Bed and Breakfast

SERVES 6

6 to 8	Honey Crisp, Fuji, or Granny Smith apples
6 tablespoons	brown sugar
2 tablespoons	butter, cut into small bits
	cinnamon
	nutmeg
	heavy cream

Preheat the oven to 350 degrees.

Grease 6 (3-inch) ramekins with butter or spray.

Peel, quarter, and remove seeds from each apple. Thinly slice each quarter. Place slices in ramekin, and when about half full, sprinkle with brown sugar, cinnamon, and nutmeg. Place a couple of bits of butter on the slices. Repeat with additional apple slices until they are just above the rim. Sprinkle with more brown sugar, cinnamon, nutmeg, and butter.

Place the ramekins on a baking sheet and bake for 30 minutes.

Splash each with a tablespoon of heavy cream and serve.

Note: The amount of apples needed to fill each ramekin will vary, depending upon the size of the apple. A large apple should fill the ramekin, but more will be needed if the apples used are small.

baked apricots

The White Oak Inn

SERVES 4

½ cup	almonds
6 tablespoons	brown sugar
3 tablespoons	butter
20	apricot halves (can also use plum halves or peach quarters), fresh or canned

Preheat the oven to 350 degrees.

In a food processor, combine the almonds, brown sugar, and butter. Pulse 8 to 10 times until crumbled.

Butter a 9-inch square baking dish.

Arrange the fruit in the bottom.

Top with almond/sugar mixture and bake for 15 minutes.

birchermuesli

Swiss Woods Bed & Breakfast Inn

SERVES 12

This classic Swiss dish was created by Dr. Bircher in the early 1900s as a health food. He believed that a raw diet would cure many ills, and over time, this dish has become synonymous with healthy living. Today the recipes are as varied as the people making it. Yogurt, oats, and grated apples are the constant ingredients.

1 cup	rolled oats
1½ cups	plain, low-fat yogurt
1	large apple, cored and grated
1	large peach, peeled and sliced
½ cup	red grapes, halved
1 (6-ounce) can	mandarin oranges, with their juice
1 (6-ounce) can	pineapple tidbits, with their juice
1 cup	strawberries, quartered
½ cup	walnuts, roughly chopped
¼ cup	golden raisins
2 tablespoons	lemon juice
1 teaspoon	vanilla
1 tablespoon	honey, adjust to taste

In a large bowl, combine all ingredients.

Mix just until blended and serve immediately.

blueberry yogurt parfait

Brampton Bed and Breakfast Inn

SERVES 4

We try to use blueberries in as many recipes as we can when they are in season. It is a very pretty fruit course. We use 8-ounce straight-sided wine glasses to serve the parfait.

12 ounces	fresh blueberries, rinsed
4 tablespoons	agave syrup, divided
1 cup	fat-free Greek yogurt
1	small ripe, but firm banana, quartered lengthwise and cut into ½-inch pieces
½ teaspoon	freshly grated lemon zest (less than ½ lemon)
½ cup	granola (see recipe on page 128)

In a medium bowl, mix blueberries and 2 tablespoons of agave syrup. Set aside.

In another medium bowl, mix yogurt, banana, 2 tablespoons agave syrup, and lemon zest. Refrigerate for 10 minutes.

Starting with the blueberries, measure ¼ cup into each wine glass.

Top each with a dollop of yogurt mixture.

Repeat the layering one more time.

Refrigerate until ready to serve.

Sprinkle each parfait with granola before serving.

brampton citrus

Brampton Bed and Breakfast Inn

SERVES 2

A refreshing morning fruit dish that is very good for you. Make it ahead and refrigerate overnight for an easy and delicious treat.

1	large pink grapefruit (choose a firm one; they are usually juicier)
2	large navel oranges (again, pick firm fruit)
1 tablespoon	honey, or to taste

Peel the fruit with a sharp knife. Remove all the white pith and expose the segments. Hold each fruit over a medium-size bowl to catch the juice.

With a sharp knife, carefully cut between the membranes to separate the citrus segments. Let the segments fall into the bowl.

When done, add the honey, cover with plastic wrap, and refrigerate for at least an hour or overnight. At that point, gently mix the segments. The honey will have melded in with the juices.

Distribute between 2 glass dishes and serve cold.

This recipe can easily be made for a crowd by adjusting the ingredients.

broiled grapefruit

The Beechmont Inn Bed and Breakfast

SERVES 2 PER GRAPEFRUIT

1	grapefruit, halved
1 tablespoon	brown sugar
	cinnamon, to sprinkle
	nutmeg, to grate

Set the oven to broil, with the rack in its top position.

Line a small sheet pan with aluminum foil.

Set each half of grapefruit on the foil. Sprinkle with brown sugar (about ½ tablespoon for each half). Sprinkle cinnamon and freshly grated nutmeg on each.

Broil for about 4 minutes and serve.

Note: Maple syrup can be used instead of brown sugar.

chilled peach soup

The William Henry Miller Inn

SERVES 8

4 cups	peeled and sliced fresh peaches, or frozen peaches that have been thawed
1 cup	sour cream or vanilla yogurt, plus more for garnishing
8 ounces	peach nectar
	sugar, optional
	dash of cinnamon
	dash of salt
	fresh mint

Add sour cream or yogurt to the peaches. With an immersion or regular blender, blend until smooth.

Add peach nectar and a bit of sugar, to taste, if necessary. Add just a dash of cinnamon and a dash of salt.

Chill.

Serve in martini glasses with a drizzle of yogurt over the top and fresh mint.

ginger-lime melons

Chambered Nautilus Bed and Breakfast Inn

SERVES 8 TO 10

1	cantaloupe
1	honeydew
	honey
	lime juice (unsweetened, preferably fresh)
	crystallized ginger, finely chopped
	lime wedges

Cut fresh cantaloupe and honeydew melons into bite-size pieces (or use a melon baller). Put pieces into individual fruit bowls.

Drizzle lightly with honey.

Drizzle with lime juice.

Sprinkle finely chopped crystallized ginger on top.

Garnish with lime wedge.

grilled peaches or nectarines

Birchwood Inn

SERVES 4

2   ripe, but firm, peaches or nectarines
berries or berry syrup
sorbet and mint leaf, for garnish

Preheat your barbecue or grill to medium-high.

Slice the fruit in half and remove the pit.

Grease a barbecue basket or grill pan with cooking spray and add the fruit, pit-side down.

Place the basket on the barbecue and close the lid.

Grill the fruit for 5 to 8 minutes, until the fruit is warm, and there are grill marks on the top.

Turn the basket over, close the barbecue lid, and cook for another minute or two.

Serve, filled with berries or a berry syrup, and top with a tangy sorbet and mint leaf.

lemon brandied apples

Swiss Woods Bed & Breakfast Inn

SERVES 6

On a trip through Germany's Black Forest region, our meal in a spectacular old farmhouse ended with the chef preparing these amazing apples tableside. They are perfect over a cinnamon French toast or, as he served them, topped with whipped cream and toasted almonds. Leftovers can be used to make muffins.

4	large firm apples, peeled, cored, and thinly sliced
2 tablespoons	butter
3 tablespoons	honey
	zest and juice of 1 large lemon
3 tablespoons	brandy

In a large flameproof skillet, melt the butter and add the apple slices.

Sauté for 2 minutes, then add the lemon zest, lemon juice, and the honey.

Cover and allow to cook until just soft, for about 10 minutes, depending on the apple type.

Remove from the heat.

In a separate small flameproof pan, gently warm the brandy.

Carefully light it with a long match, being careful to stay away from drafts while doing so.

Pour the lighted brandy over the apples and allow the flame to burn out.

Stir and serve immediately.

mango tango

Birchwood Inn

SERVES 8

¼	seedless watermelon
2	mangoes, ripe, but not mushy
2	limes, juiced
	zest of 2 limes
	mint sprigs, for garnish

Cut the watermelon into bite-size chunks or use a melon baller to make watermelon balls. Transfer the watermelon pieces to a medium bowl.

Cut off the bottom of the mangoes so they will stand up straight. Use a sharp paring knife to remove the peel. Cut the mangoes into bite-size pieces. Add to the watermelon.

Use a microplane to grate the zest from the limes. Cover and set aside.

Add the lime juice to the fruit and toss. Cover and refrigerate.

Remove the fruit from the refrigerator 15 minutes before serving.

Serve the fruit in a martini glass or parfait dish. Sprinkle lightly with the lime zest. Add a sprig of mint and serve.

orange spiced baked pears

Chambered Nautilus Bed and Breakfast Inn

SERVES 6 TO 8 WITH ½ PEAR PER PERSON

3 to 4	pears (D'Anjou, Bartlett, and Comice work nicely)
4 tablespoons	brown sugar
½ cup	orange juice
¼ teaspoon	ground cloves
½ teaspoon	vanilla
½ teaspoon	cinnamon
	honey yogurt (plain yogurt mixed with your favorite honey, to taste)
¼ cup	toasted and chopped pecans

Preheat the oven to 350 degrees.

Grease a 9-inch glass pie plate or medium glass baking dish.

Peel, core, and cut pears in half. Arrange in pie plate or baking dish.

Combine all other ingredients, except yogurt and pecans, and pour mixture over pears.

Bake uncovered for 25 to 40 minutes (depending on how ripe the pears are), until pears are slightly tender when poked with a fork or sharp knife. Baste pears with liquid once or twice during baking. Do not overcook.

Serve hot on individual plates; top with a dollop of the honey yogurt, and sprinkle with the toasted pecans.

pineapple napoleon

The William Henry Miller Inn

SERVES 8

1	ripe pineapple
8 ounces	cream cheese, softened
½ cup	sour cream
4 tablespoons	spoonable pineapple ice cream topping, such as Smuckers
¾ cup	sifted confectioners' sugar, plus more for dusting on top
	dash of salt
	fresh berries, for garnish

Use any leftover pineapple for fruit salad or freeze for a fruit smoothie.

Remove top of pineapple and cut rind off so that you are forming a "square." Slice pineapple into thin square slices. Use an apple or pineapple corer to remove the tough center.

Using a sharp knife, carve out the good pineapple inside the rind of the pineapple to use as "center slices."

Mix cream cheese, sour cream, ice cream topping, confectioners' sugar, and salt, and stir until creamy.

Layer slices of pineapple with cream. Each serving uses 3 or 4 slices of pineapple. Top with fresh raspberries, strawberries, or your choice of berries, and a generous sprinkling of confectioners' sugar.

Note: Can prepare the cream cheese filling the day before.

pineapple surprise!

Chambered Nautilus Bed and Breakfast Inn

SERVES 1 PERSON PER ½" TO 1" SLICE

> fresh pineapple (we use about a ½ to 1-inch
> thick round slice per person)
> brown sugar
> coconut or pineapple coconut ice cream
> sprig of mint, optional
> fresh assorted berries (blueberries, raspberries,
> blackberries, or sliced strawberries)
> toasted coconut, optional

Preheat the oven to 400 degrees.

Grease ovenproof glass pan(s).

Peel and core pineapple; slice into ½ to 1-inch thick slices.

Place pineapple in glass pan. Sprinkle with brown sugar and bake for 15 minutes, or until slices are soft. You can layer the pineapple, but be sure and sprinkle each layer with the brown sugar. Note: This can be done the night before. Cover and refrigerate the pineapple till the morning. Pull out and reheat in the oven.

Place a slice of hot pineapple on individual plate, and put a small scoop of coconut ice cream in the center of the slice; top with sprig of mint (optional), and sprinkle plate and pineapple with fresh berries and toasted coconut.

raspberry poached pears

Swiss Woods Bed and Breakfast Inn

SERVES 6

Pears are plentiful in the fall and winter months and lend themselves to creative presentations. Drizzle this dish with some melted chocolate and sour cream, or serve with a side of vanilla sauce, garnished with fresh raspberries.

6	pears (Bartlett or Anjou)
3 tablespoons	water
1 cup	red raspberries, whole (frozen or fresh)
1 teaspoon	orange zest
3 tablespoons	sugar
2 tablespoons	orange liqueur

Peel the pears, then using a melon baller, remove the core from the bottom up into the pear, leaving the pear intact with the stem.

If you need to, cut a sliver off the bottom so that it sits level.

Place the pears in a saucepan and add 3 tablespoons of water, the raspberries, orange zest, and the sugar.

Cover and simmer until the pears test tender, about 10 to 15 minutes depending on ripeness and type of pear.

Gently remove the pears onto a plate. They will have a beautiful red blush from the bottom up.

Strain the remaining juice left in the pan and reduce if needed.

Add the orange liqueur.

Place a pear on a serving dish and pour a bit of the raspberry sauce over it.

ray's strawberry soup

Lookout Point Lakeside Inn

SERVES 8

Refreshing and light on a hot summer morning.

1½ quarts	strawberries, hulled and halved
4 cups	low-fat buttermilk, divided
¾ cup	sugar
⅔ cup	sour cream
3 tablespoons	peach schnapps or apple juice
	fresh mint sprigs

Blend strawberries, 1 cup buttermilk, and sugar in a food processor. Set aside.

Combine the remaining 3 cups buttermilk, sour cream, and peach schnapps or apple juice in a large bowl.

Pour the strawberry mixture into the sour cream mixture. Stir to combine. Cover and chill.

Serve chilled, and garnish with mint sprigs.

spiced peaches

Chambered Nautilus Bed and Breakfast Inn

SERVES 14 TO 15 (⅔ CUP PER PERSON)

1 (5-pound) bag	fresh frozen peaches (peaches only, no sugar added)
1 cup	water
1 cup	sugar
2 teaspoons	apple pie spice (2 parts cinnamon, 2 parts nutmeg, 1 part allspice)
½ teaspoon	ground ginger

For the best flavor, prepare this the night before for serving in the morning.

Put frozen peaches and water in a pot on the stove and start to cook. When syrup begins to form, add ½ cup of sugar. Stir, as peaches start to thaw. When more syrup forms and the peaches separate, add second ½ cup of sugar, the apple pie spice, and the ginger.

Cook until peaches are tender, stirring frequently.

Serve in individual dishes, and top with fresh raspberries (if in season), or dried cranberries for a great winter fruit dish.

stewed plums

Brampton Bed and Breakfast Inn

SERVES 4

For breakfast serve these over plain Greek yogurt with a sprinkle of granola, or for dessert serve over vanilla ice cream.

6	large ripe, red Italian plums, washed
¼ cup	water
½ cup	pure maple syrup (we like grade B for the flavor)
1 teaspoon	ground cinnamon

Pit each plum and cut into eighths.

Add plums to a 2-quart saucepan.

Add water, maple syrup, and cinnamon.

Gently simmer for 15 to 20 minutes, depending on how firm the plums are.

Remove from heat and let cool completely.

Cover with plastic wrap and refrigerate overnight.

summer fruit crumble

Birchwood Inn

SERVES 6

for the topping

½ cup	brown sugar, packed
½ cup	all-purpose flour
5 tablespoons	unsalted butter, very cold
½ cup	quick or old-fashioned oats
	fresh nutmeg

for the filling

2 to 3	large nectarines, ripe, but still firm
2 to 3	red plums
¾ cup	blueberries
¼ cup	honey
½	lemon, juiced

In the winter, you can substitute apples (firm), pears (Bosc), and cranberries (fresh or frozen).

to make the topping

Combine the brown sugar, flour, and cold butter, cut into large cubes, in a food processor, and transfer to a medium-size bowl. Add the oats.

Set aside or make this ahead of time and freeze. At Birchwood Inn, we make a quadruple batch and freeze so we always have the topping on hand.

to make the filling

Preheat the oven to 350–375 degrees. Butter a 2-quart baking dish or 8 individual small oven-proof dishes.

Slice the nectarines and plums—not too thin—and transfer to a medium-size bowl. Add the blueberries.

Drizzle honey on the fruit. Squeeze the lemon over the fruit. Toss the fruit gently. Add the fruit to the baking dish or dishes. Add the topping. Grate the fresh nutmeg on the top. Place in the oven.

Bake for 45 minutes for the baking dish and 30 minutes for the individual dishes, or until the fruit is tender.

Serve warm, room temperature, or cold. Add a dollop of ice cream or crème anglaîse if you are serving the crumble as a dessert.

8 muffins, scones, and breads

batter up

applesauce date muffins

The White Oak Inn

MAKES 36 MUFFINS

This recipe can be halved.

3 cups	chopped dates
2 teaspoons	baking soda
1½ cups	boiling water
6 cups	flour
3 tablespoons	baking powder
1½ teaspoons	salt
1 tablespoon	cinnamon
4	eggs
2½ cups	brown sugar, lightly packed
1½ cups	applesauce
1 cup	vegetable oil

Preheat the oven to 375 degrees.

Mix dates and baking soda and pour boiling water over the top. Let sit.

Separately mix flour, baking powder, salt, and cinnamon together.

In another bowl, beat eggs with brown sugar. Beat in applesauce and vegetable oil. Mix in date mixture.

Add liquids to dry ingredients and fold in gently. Pour batter into greased or paper-lined muffin tins ¾ filled. Bake for 15 to 20 minutes or until top bounces back when touched lightly with your finger.

apricot walnut muffins

The White Oak Inn

MAKES 12 MUFFINS

2 cups	all-purpose flour
1 cup	quick-cooking oats
½ cup	brown sugar, lightly packed
1 tablespoon	baking powder
2 teaspoons	cinnamon
½ teaspoon	salt
2	large eggs
1 cup	milk
¼ cup	vegetable oil
½ cup	chopped apricots, canned or fresh
½ cup	chopped walnuts

This recipe also works well with dried cherries and chopped almonds.

Preheat the oven to 375 degrees and grease a muffin tin.

Measure flour, oats, brown sugar, baking powder, cinnamon, and salt into a large bowl and mix well. Make a well in the center.

Beat eggs, milk, and oil together. Pour into the well. Add the apricots and walnuts, and with a spatula fold dry ingredients into liquid just until combined.

Fill greased muffin tins about ¾ full. Bake for 15 to 18 minutes or until golden brown and firm to the touch.

Let stand in pan for about 5 minutes before removing.

asiago muffins

The White Oak Inn

MAKES 12 MUFFINS

2	cups flour
1 cup	Asiago cheese, divided into 2 (½-cup) portions
1 tablespoon	baking powder
1 teaspoon	parsley flakes
1 teaspoon	dried minced onion or 1 tablespoon minced fresh onion
1 teaspoon	dried basil
1 teaspoon	dried oregano
½ teaspoon	salt
1	large egg
1½ cups	milk
1 tablespoon	lemon juice
¼ cup	melted butter
1 tablespoon	sugar

Preheat the oven to 375 degrees.

Measure flour, ½ cup Asiago cheese, baking powder, parsley, onion, basil, oregano, and salt into a large bowl. Make a well in the center.

Beat egg with milk. Add lemon juice, melted butter, and sugar. Add to dry ingredients and stir until moistened. Spoon batter into 12 greased muffin cups. Sprinkle remaining Asiago cheese over batter.

Bake for about 15 minutes or until top is golden brown and springs back when touched.

blueberry buttermilk muffins

Chambered Nautilus Bed and Breakfast Inn

MAKES 12 MUFFINS

6 tablespoons	butter, softened (melted is okay)
⅔ cup	sugar
2	eggs
1 cup	buttermilk
2 teaspoons	vanilla
2¼ cups	all-purpose flour
½ teaspoon	salt
1 teaspoon	baking soda
2 teaspoons	baking powder
½ teaspoon	nutmeg
1½ cups	frozen blueberries

Preheat the oven to 400 degrees.

Grease muffin tins. Cream butter and sugar until light and fluffy. Add eggs, buttermilk, and vanilla. Lightly beat until blended.

In another bowl, stir flour, salt, baking soda, baking powder, and nutmeg. Add dry mixture to liquid and stir just until flour disappears.

Gently stir blueberries into batter and fill muffin cups to the top.

Bake for 20 minutes and serve warm or at room temperature.

blueberry coffee cake

Swiss Woods Bed & Breakfast Inn

SERVES 12

Goes well with a lemon sauce.

2 cups	flour
1 cup	sugar
½ teaspoon	baking soda
1 tablespoon	baking powder
¾ teaspoon	salt
⅔ cup	butter, cold
1 cup	milk
2	large eggs
	zest and juice of 1 lemon
1 teaspoon	vanilla
1½ cups	blueberries, fresh or frozen

for the streusel topping

⅓ cup	brown sugar, firmly packed
⅓ cup	sugar
½ cup	almonds, finely chopped
2 tablespoons	butter, softened
	zest of 1 lemon

Preheat the oven to 350 degrees. Spray a 9 x 13-inch baking pan with nonstick spray.

In a food processor bowl, combine flour, sugar, baking soda, baking powder, and salt. Add the ⅔ cup butter by chunks and process until it resembles coarse crumbs. Transfer to mixing bowl.

In a small bowl, whisk together the milk and eggs. Add lemon zest, the lemon juice, and vanilla. Add liquid ingredients to dry ingredients and stir until just moistened.

Fold the blueberries into the batter and pour into prepared baking pan.

Prepare the streusel by combining the brown sugar, sugar, almonds, 2 tablespoons butter, and the lemon zest, mixing with your hands to make crumbs. Sprinkle evenly over the batter.

Bake for 45 to 50 minutes or until a tester comes out clean. Serve warm.

cheddar dill scones

The White Oak Inn

MAKES 16 LARGE SCONES

2½ cups	flour
1 tablespoon	parsley flakes (or 2 tablespoons fresh parsley, chopped)
1 tablespoon	baking powder
1 teaspoon	dried dill weed
½ teaspoon	salt
¾ cup	butter
1 cup	shredded cheddar cheese
2	eggs
½ cup	half-and-half

This recipe can be halved.

Preheat the oven to 400 degrees.

In a food processor, combine flour, parsley, baking powder, dill weed, and salt. Cut butter into ¼-inch slices and drop in bowl. Pulse until mixture resembles fine crumbs. Transfer to medium-size bowl. Mix in cheddar cheese. Beat eggs with half-and-half. Stir into flour mixture and mix with a fork. Turn onto a lightly-floured surface and knead 7 or 8 times.

Roll or pat to ½-inch thickness and cut as desired into larger or smaller triangles. Bake until golden brown. (Large scones take about 15 minutes to bake, smaller ones 10 minutes.)

Note: For 16 large triangles: Divide dough in half and pat each half out into an 8-inch circle. Cut each circle into 8 wedges.

For mini-triangles: Roll dough out and cut with largest size biscuit cutter. Cut each biscuit into 4 pieces.

coffee cake muffins

The White Oak Inn

MAKES ABOUT 30 MUFFINS

for the filling

2 cups	chopped pecans
½ cup	melted butter
½ cup	white sugar
⅔ cup	brown sugar, lightly packed
2 teaspoons	cinnamon

for the muffins

6 cups	flour
3 tablespoons	baking powder
1 teaspoon	salt
2 cups	sugar
3	eggs
1½ cups	milk
2 cups	sour cream
1 cup	melted butter

Preheat the oven to 375 degrees.

Mix filling ingredients together and set aside.

Combine flour, baking powder, salt, and 2 cups sugar.

Beat the eggs with milk and sour cream. Mix in the 1 cup melted butter. Make a well in the dry ingredients and pour liquids in. Fold together just until all the flour is moistened.

Grease muffin tins generously. Put a generous tablespoon of batter in each tin. Top with about a teaspoon of the pecan filling mixture. Spoon more batter over top, until tins are about ¾ full. Put another teaspoon of pecan mixture on top. Bake for 15 to 20 minutes or until golden brown and top springs back when touched.

cranberry-orange bread

Chambered Nautilus Bed and Breakfast Inn

MAKES 1 LOAF

2 tablespoons	butter, at room temperature
1 cup	sugar
1	egg
¾ cup	orange juice
¼ teaspoon	orange extract
2 cups	all-purpose flour
1 teaspoon	baking powder
½ teaspoon	baking soda
½ teaspoon	salt
2 cups	whole fresh cranberries (or frozen, thaw before using)
½ cup	chopped walnuts

Preheat the oven to 350 degrees.

Grease a 9 x 5-inch loaf pan.

In a large bowl, combine butter and sugar. Mix well. Add egg, orange juice, and orange extract. In separate bowl, whisk together the flour, baking powder, baking soda, and salt. Add to liquid ingredients and stir until just moistened. Fold in cranberries and nuts.

Bake in prepared loaf pan for 60 to 70 minutes, until bread tests done.

cranberry sticky buns

The Beechmont Inn Bed and Breakfast

MAKES 12 ROLLS

for the roll dough

2 tablespoons	active dry yeast
¼ cup	warm water (90 degrees)
1 teaspoon	sugar
⅔ cup	whole milk (90 degrees)
6 tablespoons	unsalted butter
4 tablespoons	sugar
2	large eggs, lightly beaten
1 teaspoon	salt
4 cups	unbleached flour

In a large bowl, add warm water to yeast and sugar. Stir until the yeast is dissolved. Let it sit for a few minutes so it starts to bubble.

In a saucepan over medium-low heat, add milk, butter, and sugar. As the butter melts, stir to combine the ingredients. Remove the saucepan from the heat. Place the eggs and salt in a small bowl or 4-cup measuring cup. Add the warm milk mixture and stir to combine.

Add this liquid to the yeast. Stir in the flour 1 cup at a time. The dough will become stiffer as the flour is added. Remove the dough when it becomes too stiff to stir and place on a well-floured surface to begin kneading. Rinse the large bowl and butter it to use for rising the dough.

Knead the dough for about 5 to 7 minutes, adding flour as necessary to keep it from sticking to the work surface. The dough will become elastic and smooth. Place it in the buttered bowl, cover with a clean towel, and let it rise in a warm place for about 1½ hours. It may take longer, depending upon how warm your kitchen is.

for the filling

1 cup	chopped pecans (walnuts or almonds may be used)
½ cup	chopped cranberries
½ cup	sugar
2 teaspoons	cinnamon
½ teaspoon	grated nutmeg
4 tablespoons	unsalted butter, softened (used to spread on dough before adding filling)

Combine the pecans, cranberries, sugar, cinnamon, and nutmeg in a small bowl. Set aside.

for the topping

8 tablespoons	unsalted butter, melted
½ cup	brown sugar, packed
1 teaspoon	vanilla
1 teaspoon	grated lemon zest
1 cup	chopped pecans (or walnuts or almonds)

In a small pan, melt butter and brown sugar over low heat. Remove from heat. Stir in the vanilla and lemon zest, and then add pecans. Spread this topping in the bottom of a 9 x 13-inch baking pan that has been prepared with baking oil or butter.

Roll the dough into an 18 x 12-inch rectangle. Brush the 4 tablespoons of softened unsalted butter on top of the dough before sprinkling the cranberry pecan filling on top. Beginning with the 18-inch edge, roll up jelly roll-style. Cut the roll into 12 even slices. Place each slice face down in the baking pan, in rows of three. Cover and let rise until nearly doubled (or refrigerate overnight; in the morning bring to room temperature before baking). Preheat the oven to 350 degrees. Bake for 30 to 35 minutes or until the tops are nicely browned and the brown sugar topping is bubbling up between the rolls.

Remove from the oven and wait for about 5 minutes before inverting the pan of sticky buns onto a baking sheet.

english muffins

The William Henry Miller Inn

MAKES 16 TO 18 MUFFINS

2 packages	active dry yeast
2 cups	warm water
5 to 6 cups	flour
1 tablespoon	sugar
1 tablespoon	salt
½ cup	shortening (we use vegetable oil)
	cornmeal, for sprinkling

In a large bowl, dissolve yeast in warm water.

Add 3 cups flour, sugar, salt, and shortening to yeast mixture, stirring by hand until smooth.

Gradually add remaining 2 to 3 cups flour to form a stiff dough.

On a floured surface, gently knead dough 5 to 6 times until no longer sticky. Roll dough to ¼-inch thickness and cut with a 3-inch round cutter.

Evenly sprinkle cornmeal over 2 ungreased cookie sheets. Place cut-out dough on cornmeal and sprinkle each muffin with additional cornmeal.

Cover loosely with plastic wrap and towel. Let rise for 30 to 45 minutes.

Heat an ungreased electric griddle to 350 degrees and place each muffin cutout on the griddle.

Cook for 5 to 6 minutes on each side or until golden brown.

honey oat bread

The William Henry Miller Inn

MAKES 2 LOAVES

1¾ cups	warm water, divided
1 tablespoon	dry yeast
¾ cup	quick-cooking oats
⅓ cup	honey
3 tablespoons	vegetable oil
2½ teaspoons	salt
about 5 cups	flour
1	egg, beaten
	additional quick-cooking oats

Stir ¼ cup warm water and yeast in a small bowl. Let stand for 10 minutes to dissolve the yeast.

Use a stand mixer with dough hook. Place yeast mixture in bowl. Stir in the remaining water, oats, honey, oil, and salt.

Stir in enough flour to form soft dough.

Coat another large bowl with oil. Transfer dough to the oiled bowl and turn to coat.

Cover with plastic wrap and then a kitchen towel, and let rise at room temperature until dough is doubled in volume, for roughly 1 hour.

Oil 2 (5 x 7-inch) loaf pans. Punch down dough, and then shape into 2 loaves. Place 1 loaf in each pan. Cover and let rise in warm, draft-free area until almost doubled in volume, for about 20 minutes.

Preheat the oven to 350 degrees.

Brush the tops of the loaves with beaten egg. Sprinkle additional oats on top.

Bake for about 40 minutes, until brown on top and a tester inserted into the center comes out clean.

Serve toasted with your favorite jam.

lemon ginger rolls

Swiss Woods Bed & Breakfast Inn

MAKES 18 ROLLS

6 cups	flour
1	packet yeast (or 1 tablespoon)
¼ cup	sugar
1 tablespoon	salt
	zest of 1 lemon
8 tablespoons	butter
1 cup	hot water
1 cup	milk
½ cup	candied ginger, minced
1	egg, beaten
	zest and juice of 1 large lemon
1 cup	powdered sugar

Mix the dry ingredients, plus first lemon zest, together in a bowl.

Put the butter into the hot water and allow to melt. Add the milk to the water and butter. Cool until just warm.

Add to the dry ingredients, and in a standing mixer, mix with the dough hook. Mix for 2 to 3 minutes, or until the dough appears smooth. If sticky, add more flour little by little until it pulls away from the side of the bowl. Add the minced candied ginger and knead for a minute longer.

Place dough in large oiled bowl. Cover and allow to double in size.

Shape into 2-inch balls and place on a baking sheet. Cover with a light towel and allow to double in size.

Preheat the oven to 350 degrees. Brush the tops of the rolls with the beaten egg. Bake for 30 minutes or until golden brown. Remove from the oven and cool.

for the glaze
Mix the lemon juice, second lemon zest, and powdered sugar to make a glaze. When almost cool, glaze the rolls and serve with honey butter.

matthew's buttermilk biscuits

Brampton Bed and Breakfast Inn

MAKES 14 (2½-INCH) BISCUITS

Matthew Lovette and his partner, Mark Smith, make up the very talented duo of Jumping Rocks Photography. They are responsible for many of the beautiful pictures in this cookbook. In a former life, they were innkeepers. Hailing from the South, Matthew knows a thing or two about good biscuits, and he shared this wonderful recipe with us. When we serve these, we get "oohs and aahs" from all our guests.

3½ cups	white flour (White Lily would be the best!)
½ cup	whole wheat flour
4 teaspoons	baking powder
1 teaspoon	baking soda
1 teaspoon	salt
1 cup	cold, unsalted butter, cut into small pieces
1½ cups	buttermilk
½ cup	melted, unsalted butter

Preheat the oven to 450 degrees.

Combine all the dry ingredients in a large bowl and whisk together. Cut in the cold butter lightly, using a pastry cutter, leaving pea-size lumps.

Pour in the buttermilk and mix together quickly, just until it starts to stick together.

Spread a little extra flour on your work surface, and transfer biscuit dough to it. Knead together maybe 1 or 2 times, and then pat together, using your hands. Do not overwork.

Roll out to about ¾-inch and cut with a round biscuit cutter or cut into squares. Place on a sheet pan lined with parchment paper and brush tops with the melted butter.

Bake for about 15 to 20 minutes or until just starting to brown.

Serve warm with butter and jam.

melodious poppy seed bread

Lookout Point Lakeside Inn

MAKES 2 OR 3 LOAVES

for the bread

3 cups	flour
1½ teaspoons	salt
1½ teaspoons	baking powder
3	eggs, lightly beaten
1½ tablespoons	poppy seeds
1½ cups	milk
1 cup	oil
2½ cups	sugar
1½ teaspoons	vanilla
1½ teaspoons	almond extract
1½ teaspoons	butter extract

for the glaze

¼ cup	orange juice
¾ cup	sugar
½ teaspoon	vanilla
½ teaspoon	almond extract
½ teaspoon	butter extract

Preheat the oven to 350 degrees.

Mix all bread ingredients together well. Pour into 2 or 3 greased (9 x 5-inch) loaf pans. Bake loaves until done, for approximately 50 minutes. Let bread cool for 5 to 10 minutes.

Mix together glaze ingredients. Drizzle glaze over loaves while the bread is still in the pan and warm. Let cool before serving.

oat bran muffin mix

The White Oak Inn

MAKES 4 BATCHES OF 12 MUFFINS

for the dry mix

4 cups	oat bran
3 cups	oatmeal
6 cups	flour
2½ cups	brown sugar, lightly packed
5 tablespoons	baking powder
2 teaspoons	salt
2 tablespoons	cinnamon

Mix all together and store in a large container.

for 1 batch of 12 muffins

2	cups milk
2	eggs
¾ cup	vegetable oil
4	cups dry mix
1 cup	chopped nuts, such as pecans, walnuts, or almonds
1½ to 2 cups	dried fruit (I like apricots, Craisins, and raisins)

Unused batter can be stored in the refrigerator up to a week. You will need to add more milk before using it.

Preheat the oven to 350 degrees. Grease a 12-cup muffin tin or use paper liners.

Beat the milk, eggs, and vegetable oil together. Pour into the dry mix ingredients and add the nuts and dried fruit. Mix to combine. Let stand for at least 15 minutes before using. Don't worry if it seems runny, this mixture will absorb the liquid both as it sits and as it bakes.

Fill greased muffin tins ¾ full and bake for about 20 minutes.

oatmeal granola muffins

The William Henry Miller Inn

MAKES 12 MUFFINS

1 cup	flour
1 cup	quick oats
¾ cup	granola
½ cup	sugar
1 tablespoon	baking powder
1½ teaspoons	cinnamon
1 teaspoon	salt
½ cup	raisins (dried cranberries, apricots, cherries, or other dried fruit will also work)
1	egg
1 cup	water
¼ cup	vegetable oil

Preheat the oven to 400 degrees. Grease a 12-cup muffin pan or use paper liners.

In a medium bowl, whisk together the flour, oats, granola, sugar, baking powder, cinnamon, and salt. Add the raisins and blend with a rubber spatula or large spoon.

Mix the egg, water, and oil with a whisk. Pour the wet ingredients over the flour mixture and stir with a large spoon or rubber spatula until just moist. Do not overblend.

Fill muffin cups or greased muffin pan ¾ full. Bake for 20 minutes for large muffins or 14 to 15 minutes for mini-muffins.

pear pecan cardamom bread

Birchwood Inn

SERVES 20 (MAKES 2 LOAVES)

1 cup	canola oil
2 cups	sugar
3	eggs
1 cup	sour cream
2½ cups	Bosc pears, chopped
1 cup	pecans, coarsely chopped
½ teaspoon	orange zest
2 teaspoons	vanilla extract
3 cups	all-purpose flour
½ teaspoon	salt
1 teaspoon	baking soda
1 teaspoon	cinnamon
½ teaspoon	nutmeg
½ teaspoon	cardamom

Preheat the oven to 350 degrees.

In a medium mixing bowl, combine the oil, sugar, eggs, and sour cream. Blend well. Stir in pears, pecans, orange zest, and vanilla extract.

In another bowl, combine the remaining ingredients.

Stir the dry ingredients into the pear mixture. Stir to combine.

Grease 2 (9 x 5-inch) loaf pans with cooking spray.

Spoon the batter into the loaf pans. You may wish to add a sprinkle of sugar mixed with a little nutmeg on the top.

Bake for 1 hour or until tester comes out clean.

Cool for 10 minutes. Remove the bread loaves from the pans and cool on a wire rack.

pomegranate ginger muffins

Birchwood Inn

MAKES 12 MUFFINS

Christmas is a great time for this festive muffin. But why wait until Christmas?

2 cups	all-purpose flour
⅔ cup	sugar
1 tablespoon	baking powder
½ teaspoon	salt
⅓ cup	crystallized ginger, minced
1 teaspoon	lemon zest
1¼ cups	pomegranate seeds
1 cup	milk
1	egg, beaten
¼ cup	butter, melted
	sugar, for topping

Preheat the oven to 425 degrees.

Grease 12 muffin cups with cooking spray.

Mix the dry ingredients (flour, sugar, baking powder, and salt) in a large bowl.

Mix the wet ingredients (ginger, lemon zest, pomegranate seeds, milk, egg, and melted butter) in a medium bowl.

Make a well in the dry ingredients and pour in the wet ingredients. Stir until just mixed. Spoon the batter into the muffin cups. Sprinkle the muffin tops with sugar.

Bake for 15 to 20 minutes, until the muffins are puffed and golden, and a tester comes out clean.

Let the muffins cool in the pan for 5 to 10 minutes. Remove the muffins from the pan and serve.

pumpkin bread

Chambered Nautilus Bed and Breakfast Inn

MAKES 3 LOAVES

3 cups	flour
3½ cups	sugar
1½ teaspoons	cinnamon
1½ teaspoons	nutmeg
1½ teaspoons	salt
2 teaspoons	baking soda
1 cup	corn oil
⅔ cup	water
4	eggs
1 (15-ounce) can	pumpkin (slightly less than 2 cups)
1½ cups	chopped walnuts

Preheat the oven to 350 degrees.

Mix together flour, sugar, cinnamon, nutmeg, salt, and baking soda. Add corn oil, water, eggs, and pumpkin. Mix with hand mixer. Stir in chopped nuts.

Pour into 3 (9 x 5-inch) loaf pans which have been well-greased and floured.

Bake for 1 hour. Insert a tester; it should come out clean.

Let cool for 1 hour. These loaves freeze well.

raspberry streusel muffins

The Beechmont Inn Bed and Breakfast

MAKES 12 MUFFINS

2 cups	flour, plus ¼ cup flour
½ cup	sugar
1 tablespoon	baking powder
½ teaspoon	salt
1 (8-ounce) container	plain yogurt
½ cup	vegetable oil
2	large eggs
1 teaspoon	vanilla
	zest of 1 lemon, grated
1 cup	fresh or frozen raspberries

for the streusel topping

2 tablespoons	flour
4 tablespoons	sugar
2 tablespoons	cold butter, diced

Preheat the oven to 375 degrees. Grease a regular muffin pan or line with muffin papers.

In large bowl, combine 2 cups flour, sugar, baking powder, and salt. Whisk to combine.

In smaller bowl, blend together the yogurt, oil, and eggs. Stir in the vanilla and lemon zest. Add to the dry ingredients and stir until just blended. Toss the raspberries with ¼ cup flour and fold into the batter. Spoon batter into muffin tins, about ⅔ full.

to make the streusel topping

Combine flour and sugar, and cut butter into the mixture with a pastry blender or fingers until thoroughly mixed and crumbly. Spoon topping over muffins.

Bake for 20 to 25 minutes until muffins are done. Remove muffins from pan after 5 minutes and cool on wire racks.

shoofly pie muffins

Swiss Woods Bed & Breakfast Inn

MAKES 12 MUFFINS

Growing up in Pennsylvania Dutch Country, Shoofly Pie was a staple, and my mom made the best around. Using her recipe, these muffins have the same flavor and moistness of the pie and are much more versatile.

2 cups	flour
1 cup	brown sugar, lightly packed
½ cup	butter/shortening
1 cup	boiling water
½ cup	baking molasses
1 teaspoon	baking soda
¼ teaspoon	salt
½ teaspoon	vanilla
½ teaspoon	cinnamon

Preheat the oven to 350 degrees.

Mix together flour, brown sugar, and shortening into crumbs.

Save 1 cup of these crumbs to put on top of muffins before baking.

Mix boiling water, molasses, and baking soda.

Mix the wet and dry ingredients (including salt, vanilla, and cinnamon) together (except the reserved dry crumbs for topping).

Fill 12 muffin cups lined with muffin papers.

Add the dry crumbs on top of the 12 muffins.

Bake for 40 to 45 minutes or until a tester comes out clean.

strawberry cornmeal muffins

The Beechmont Inn Bed and Breakfast

MAKES 12 MUFFINS

1 cup	cornmeal
1 cup	flour
⅓ cup	sugar
2½ teaspoons	baking powder
¼ teaspoon	salt
2 cups	strawberries (cut in small pieces)
1 cup	vanilla yogurt
¼ cup	canola oil
1	egg, slightly beaten

Preheat the oven to 350 degrees.

Grease muffin pan or line with paper cups.

In a large bowl, whisk together the cornmeal, flour, sugar, baking powder, and salt. Add strawberries and toss gently to coat with the flour mixture.

In a small bowl, whisk together the yogurt, oil, and egg.

Add yogurt mixture to flour mixture and combine until dry ingredients are just combined. Do not overmix.

Fill muffin cups about ⅔ full and bake for 20 to 25 minutes.

strawberry rhubarb coffee cake

Swiss Woods Bed & Breakfast Inn

SERVES 12

Make this cake in the spring when strawberries are plentiful and rhubarb is fresh at the Farmers' Market. It makes a large coffee cake and can easily be baked in 2 smaller pans—freeze one for another time!—adjusting the baking time accordingly.

for the fruit mixture

5 cups	rhubarb, chopped
¼ cup	water
5 cups	strawberries, quartered
	zest and juice of 1 lemon
½ cup	cornstarch
1½	cups sugar

for the batter

3 cups	flour
1 cup	sugar
2 teaspoons	baking powder
1 teaspoon	salt
1 cup	butter, softened
1 cup	buttermilk
2	large eggs
1 teaspoon	vanilla
½ teaspoon	almond extract

for the topping

¾ cup	sugar
½ cup	flour
¼ cup	butter, softened

Cook rhubarb in a large saucepan with ¼ cup water until just tender. Add the strawberries and juice of lemon.

Combine the cornstarch and 1½ cups sugar. Add to the strawberries and rhubarb, mix to combine, and then bring just to a boil, stirring constantly until thickened. Set aside.

Spray a 9 x 13-inch baking pan with nonstick spray. Preheat the oven to 375 degrees.

In a large bowl, combine the 3 cups flour, 1 cup sugar, baking powder, salt, and lemon zest. Add the 1 cup butter, and with your hands, work it into the flour until crumbly.

In a separate bowl, combine the buttermilk, eggs, vanilla, and almond extract.

Pour the wet ingredients into the dry ingredients and stir until well combined.

Pour half of the batter into the prepared pan.

Spread the strawberry rhubarb mixture on top of the batter and then spread the remainder of the batter on top of the fruit mixture.

Combine the ¾ cup sugar, ½ cup flour, and ¼ cup butter into crumbs and sprinkle on top of the batter.

Bake for 45 to 50 minutes or until a tester comes out clean. Allow to cool before cutting into squares. Serve with sweetened Greek yogurt.

sunflower pumpkin bread (vegan)

The William Henry Miller Inn

MAKES 2 LOAVES

2½ cups	flour
2 cups	sugar
2 teaspoons	baking soda
½ teaspoon	cinnamon
½ teaspoon	ginger
½ teaspoon	allspice
½ teaspoon	salt
1½ cups	pumpkin
½ cup	vegetable oil
½ cup	sunflower seeds
½ cup	finely chopped walnuts
2 cups	dried cranberries, coarsely chopped

Preheat the oven to 350 degrees. Grease and flour 2 (8½ x 4½ x 2½-inch) loaf pans.

Put the flour, sugar, baking soda, cinnamon, ginger, allspice, and salt in a medium bowl. Blend to combine.

Mix the pumpkin and vegetable oil in a large bowl. Add the dry ingredients. Mix in the sunflower seeds, chopped walnuts, and dried cranberries. The batter will be stiff.

Divide the batter between the 2 prepared loaf pans. Bake for 55 minutes or until a tester comes out clean.

upside-down sour cherry muffins

Swiss Woods Bed & Breakfast Inn

MAKES 10 MUFFINS

2 cups	frozen sour cherries, thawed and drained (the darker red, the better)
½ cup	sugar
¼ cup	melted butter
1½ cups	flour
1½ teaspoons	baking powder
⅛ teaspoon	salt
½ cup	sugar
1	egg
¾ cup	milk
¼ cup	melted butter
1 teaspoon	vanilla

Serve to rave reviews!

Preheat the oven to 375 degrees. Spray 10 muffin tins with coating.

Mix cherries, ½ cup sugar, and ¼ cup melted butter together well and divide evenly. Fill only 10 of the muffin slots.

Mix dry ingredients together. Then mix the wet ingredients together and add them all at once to the dry ingredients. Gently stir to a batter and spoon onto the cherries in the muffin tins. They will appear full.

Bake for 20 minutes or until the cake part bounces back when touched. Remove from the oven, run a knife around each muffin to loosen.

Place a cookie sheet on top of the muffins, then grasp the sides of the muffin tin and in one quick motion, turn the whole thing over, being careful to turn it away from yourself.

Allow to rest several seconds to loosen, then gently raise the muffin tin, allowing the little upside-down muffins to fall out.

white chocolate and cranberry tea scones

The White Oak Inn

MAKES ABOUT 12 TO 14 SCONES

2 cups	flour
2 tablespoons	sugar
4 teaspoons	baking powder
½ teaspoon	salt
⅓ cup	butter
2	eggs
½ cup	half-and-half or heavy cream
½ cup	white chocolate chips
½ cup	dried cranberries

Perfect for dessert or as an accompaniment to breakfast.

Preheat the oven to 425 degrees.

Mix together flour, sugar, baking powder, and salt. Cut in butter, using either the pulse setting on a food processor or by hand with a pastry blender. Mixture should resemble coarse crumbs, with no visible chunks of butter.

Separate one of the eggs, setting the white aside. Beat the yolk with the other whole egg and the half-and-half. Add this to the dry mixture, along with the white chocolate chips and cranberries. Stir with a fork until barely mixed.

Turn dough onto a floured board and knead gently, about 6 to 8 times. Roll or pat dough out to ½-inch thickness. Cut into rounds with a biscuit cutter.

Place on an ungreased baking sheet about an inch apart and brush the tops with the reserved egg white. Bake for 10 to 12 minutes or until top is golden brown.

zopf or braided bread

Brampton Bed and Breakfast Inn

MAKES 1 LARGE BRAIDED BREAD

The Sunday morning bread of Switzerland is called "Zopf," which means braid. To make this bread correctly, please use a scale to measure the flour and butter.

2.2 pounds	white bread flour
1½ tablespoons	granulated yeast
1 teaspoon	sugar
1 tablespoon	salt
2½ to 3 cups	whole milk, lukewarm
4.4 ounces	unsalted butter, melted
1	small egg, diluted with 1 teaspoon of milk for the egg wash

The braid tastes best when served slightly warm with sweet butter and jams.

Mix flour, yeast, sugar, and salt in a large bowl.

In a 4-cup measuring cup, mix together 2½ cups of milk and the melted butter. Make a well in the dry ingredients. Pour liquid into the well and start slowly mixing it together.

Make sure the dough is not too dry; add more milk if necessary. The dough should be soft and slightly sticky. Turn dough onto a clean and lightly floured surface. Knead dough for 8 to 10 minutes.

Lightly butter a bowl before returning the dough. Cover with plastic wrap, let rest in a warm place until double in size. Punch down and cut into 3 equal parts. Roll each part into an 18-inch cylinder. Braid.

Preheat the oven to 375 degrees.

Transfer braid onto a baking sheet lined with parchment paper. Cover with a clean dish towel and let rise again for about 30 minutes. Before baking, brush with the egg wash.

Bake for about 15 minutes before turning the oven down to 350 degrees. Bake for 30 to 40 minutes more, until braid is golden and sounds hollow when tapped on the back.

Let cool on a wire rack for 30 minutes before cutting into slices.

8 sweet breakfast

guilty pleasures

baked oatmeal

Swiss Woods Bed & Breakfast Inn

SERVES 4

Serve with milk.

½ cup	oil (canola, corn, not olive oil)
1 cup	sugar
2	eggs
1½ cups	quick-cooking oats (not instant)
1½ cups	rolled oats
2 teaspoons	baking powder
1 teaspoon	salt
1 cup	milk
1 teaspoon	vanilla
1 teaspoon	cinnamon
1½ cups	mixed berries (blackberries, strawberries, blueberries)

Preheat the oven to 350 degrees. Grease an 8 x 8-inch square baking pan.

Cream oil, sugar, and eggs together in a small bowl.

Add all other ingredients, except berries, and mix.

Pour half of the batter into the greased baking dish.

Divide the mixed berries evenly across the batter.

Top with the remaining batter.

Bake for 30 minutes.

banana sour cream pancakes

The William Henry Miller Inn

SERVES 4 TO 6

2 cups	all-purpose flour
2 teaspoons	baking powder
1 teaspoon	baking soda
2 tablespoons	sugar
½ teaspoon	cinnamon
2 cups	sour cream or yogurt
2	eggs
⅓ cup	oil
2 to 3	ripe bananas, mashed

Preheat the electric griddle to 350 degrees. Use oil or butter to grease the griddle.

In a medium bowl, whisk together the flour, baking powder, baking soda, sugar, and cinnamon. In a separate bowl, combine the sour cream, eggs, and oil. Pour the liquid ingredients into the dry and mix until just combined. Stir in mashed bananas with a rubber spatula.

Place about ⅓ to ½ cup of mixture on the griddle for each pancake. Cook until the bottom of the pancake is golden brown and the bubbles on top pop and stay open. Flip each pancake to finish cooking, for about 2 to 3 minutes. Serve immediately.

blueberry cornmeal pancakes

The Beechmont Inn Bed and Breakfast

MAKES 16 (4-INCH) PANCAKES

2 cups	flour, plus 1 tablespoon flour for blueberries
1 cup	ground cornmeal
⅓ cup	sugar
2 teaspoons	baking powder
½ teaspoon	baking soda
¾ teaspoon	cinnamon
½ teaspoon	salt
1 cup	plain yogurt
1½ cups	milk
4	large eggs
6 tablespoons	unsalted butter, melted
1 teaspoon	vanilla
2 tablespoons	grated orange zest
2 cups	blueberries

In large bowl, combine the 2 cups of flour, cornmeal, sugar, baking powder, baking soda, cinnamon, and salt. Use a whisk to blend.

In separate smaller bowl, blend the yogurt, milk, eggs, melted butter, vanilla, and orange zest.

Pour the liquid ingredients into the flour mixture and blend, being careful not to overmix. Lightly coat the blueberries with a tablespoon of flour and add blueberries to mixture.

Preheat an electric griddle to 350 degrees. Cook pancakes on hot griddle until done.

Serve with warm syrup and your favorite bacon or sausage.

blueberry sour cream pancakes with lemon sauce

The William Henry Miller Inn

SERVES 4 TO 6

for the pancakes

2 cups	all-purpose flour
2 teaspoons	baking powder
1 teaspoon	baking soda
2 tablespoons	sugar
2	eggs
2 cups	sour cream or yogurt
⅓ cup	oil
2 cups	blueberries

Preheat an electric griddle to 350 degrees. Use oil or butter to grease the griddle.

In a medium bowl, whisk together the flour, baking powder, baking soda, and sugar. In a separate bowl, combine eggs, sour cream, and oil. Pour the sour cream mixture into the dry ingredients and stir until just combined.

Drop about ½ cup of batter on griddle for each pancake. Drop blueberries onto each pancake. Cook until the bottom of the pancake is golden brown and the bubbles on top pop and stay open. Flip each pancake to finish cooking, for about 2 to 3 minutes. Serve immediately.

for the lemon sauce

½ cup	sugar
1 cup	hot water
1 tablespoon	cornstarch
2 tablespoons	butter
1 teaspoon	lemon zest

In a medium saucepan, combine the sugar, hot water, and cornstarch. Add the butter and lemon rind. Cook until the mixture thickens to a syrup consistency. Makes 1½ cups of sauce.

caramel peach bread pudding

The White Oak Inn

SERVES 12

4 cups	sliced peaches (frozen or fresh)
12	large eggs
1 cup	evaporated milk
½ cup	2% milk
1 teaspoon	vanilla
1 teaspoon	almond extract
2 tablespoons	sugar
About 10 slices	Italian or French bread, cut into ¾-inch cubes (you may need more or less, depending on the size of the loaf of bread)

for the topping

¼ cup	butter
2 tablespoons	corn syrup
1 cup	brown sugar, lightly packed
¾ cup	chopped pecans

Preheat the oven to 350 degrees. Spray a 9 x 13-inch pan and place peaches in a single layer on bottom.

Mix eggs, evaporated milk, 2% milk, vanilla, almond extract, and sugar, and beat well.

Mix bread cubes into the egg batter. You want to use just enough cubes so that they are saturated and you have some liquid left. Spoon bread mixture over peaches.

Meanwhile, in a medium saucepan, melt the butter, mix in corn syrup and brown sugar, and bring to a simmer over medium heat, stirring constantly. Remove from heat and stir in pecans. Drizzle evenly over bread mixture.

Cover with foil and bake for about 40 minutes. Remove foil and continue baking until center is set. (Test with a knife—if no egg batter runs out, it is done.)

chocolate chip
buttermilk pancakes

Chambered Nautilus Bed and Breakfast Inn

SERVES 6 (2 PANCAKES PER PERSON)

> Makes a great basic buttermilk pancake.

2¼ cups	unbleached, all-purpose flour
1½ teaspoons	baking powder
½ teaspoon	baking soda
½ teaspoon	salt
1 tablespoon	sugar, plus 1 teaspoon sugar
2 tablespoons	butter, melted
2	eggs
2½ cups	buttermilk
⅓ to ½	semisweet chocolate chips
	fresh strawberries, tossed with sugar, to taste
	powdered sugar, for garnish

Mix all ingredients, except the chocolate chips, fresh strawberries, and powdered sugar, together in a large mixing bowl. Separately toss strawberries with sugar to bring out the juice, and reserve to top the pancakes.

Preheat electric griddle to 350 degrees. Grease the griddle with butter. Water droplets that dance briefly before disappearing mean the heat is right. Ladle ⅓ to ½ cup of batter per pancake onto griddle. Drop chocolate chips into each pancake. Flip the pancakes when they are covered with bubbles. Check the underside to make sure it is nicely browned before flipping. Cook the other side for half as long.

Sprinkle with powdered sugar and top with strawberries.

Variations: Use frozen or fresh blueberries instead of chocolate chips.

cranberry french toast

The Beechmont Inn Bed and Breakfast

SERVES 8

for the cranberry sauce

1 (12-ounce) bag	fresh cranberries
1 cup	sugar
½ cup	orange juice
1 teaspoon	cinnamon
½ cup	sweet orange marmalade

Place cranberries, sugar, orange juice, and cinnamon in saucepan and bring to a boil. Reduce heat and simmer until cranberries start to pop. Remove from heat and add marmalade. Mix and set aside.

for the french toast

8 tablespoons	butter
1¼ cups	brown sugar, lightly packed
4 tablespoons	light corn syrup
1 (1-pound) loaf	Italian bread (or other thick-sliced bread)
8 ounces	cream cheese
8	eggs
1½ cups	half-and-half
2 tablespoons	orange juice
1 teaspoon	vanilla

Serve French toast with a side of the remaining cranberry sauce, maple syrup, and your favorite bacon or sausage.

Preheat the oven to 350 degrees (if baking immediately). Grease a 9 x 13-inch baking dish.

In saucepan, melt butter, brown sugar, and corn syrup together over low heat. Stir to blend. Add 1 to 1½ cups of the cranberry sauce to the brown sugar mixture. Set aside.

Slice bread and spread cream cheese on one slice, covering with another piece of bread (like a sandwich).

Beat eggs and add half-and-half, orange juice, and vanilla. Blend.

Spread the cranberry/brown sugar mixture in baking dish. Layer the cream cheese sandwiches on top.

Pour egg mixture over the bread. Refrigerate overnight or bake immediately for 45 to 60 minutes. Bake covered with aluminum foil for 30 minutes, then remove foil and bake for 30 minutes more (bread should be nicely browned).

decadent chocolate french toast with strawberry syrup

Birchwood Inn

SERVES 4 (3 TRIANGLES PER PERSON)

This is the perfect breakfast for Valentine's Day!

for the strawberry syrup

¼ cup	sugar
	zest and juice of 1 lemon
1 cup	strawberries
2 tablespoons	Grand Marnier

for the french toast

3	eggs
½ cup	vanilla sugar (or ½ cup sugar, plus 1 teaspoon vanilla)
2 tablespoons	cocoa powder
½ cup	milk
2 tablespoons	butter
6 slices	challah, 1-inch each, and cut on the diagonal into 12 triangles

for the garnish

	cocoa
	whipped cream
4	strawberries, dipped in chocolate
	confectioners' sugar

to make the strawberry syrup

Add syrup ingredients to blender and purée.

to make the french toast

In a large bowl, whisk the eggs.

In a small bowl, combine the vanilla sugar (or sugar and vanilla) and cocoa until well blended.

Whisk the sugar/cocoa mixture into the eggs. Whisk in the milk.

Using a frying pan or griddle, melt the butter over medium heat.

Dip the triangles into the egg mixture until well moistened, but not soggy.

Place the triangles in the pan or on the griddle.

Cook until golden, for about 2 to 3 minutes per side, turning once. (This batter browns very quickly, so watch that the triangles don't burn.)

for the presentation

Dust 4 plates with cocoa.

Place one triangle flat on the plate. Place the second triangle on the plate, overlapping the first triangle. Repeat with third triangle.

Drizzle with the strawberry syrup. Add a dollop of whipped cream on the French toast.

Top with a chocolate-dipped strawberry.

Sprinkle with confectioners' sugar and serve.

ginger spice pancakes

Chambered Nautilus Bed and Breakfast Inn

SERVES 6 (2 PANCAKES PER PERSON)

2½ cups	all-purpose flour
5 teaspoons	baking powder
1½ teaspoons	salt
1 teaspoon	baking soda
1 teaspoon	cinnamon
½ teaspoon	ginger
¼ cup	molasses
2 cups	milk
2	eggs
6 tablespoons	butter, melted
1 cup	raisins
	powdered sugar, for garnish

Preheat electric griddle to 350 degrees.

In a large bowl, combine the dry ingredients. Add the remaining ingredients, except raisins, and beat with an electric mixer until well blended. Stir in raisins.

Ladle about ½ cup of batter onto hot griddle. Turn the pancakes when the edges are dry and bubbles rise to the surface.

Sprinkle with powdered sugar and serve with warm syrup.

granola pancakes

Swiss Woods Bed & Breakfast Inn

SERVES 6

2 cups	milk
1 cup	granola
1 cup	rolled oats
2	large eggs, beaten
¼ cup	butter, melted
½ cup	flour
2 tablespoons	sugar
2 teaspoons	baking powder
¼ teaspoon	nutmeg
¼ teaspoon	cinnamon
¼ teaspoon	salt
	butter, for the griddle

Combine milk, granola, and rolled oats. Allow to stand in the refrigerator overnight.

The next morning, mix eggs and butter together and add to granola mixture. Blend the remaining dry ingredients in a small bowl and stir into the granola mixture.

Combine until smooth, but do not overmix.

Preheat an electric griddle to 350 degrees. Butter the griddle.

With a ¼-cup measure, pour the batter onto the buttered griddle.

Bake until bubbles appear on the surface, then flip and bake until done, for about 2 minutes.

Serve warm with lemon brandied apples (see recipe on page 19).

griess schnitten (cream of wheat squares)

Swiss Woods Bed & Breakfast Inn

SERVES 8

In Switzerland, we used leftover cream of wheat to make these fabulous squares for a light supper. They were usually served with applesauce.

4¼ cups	milk
1 tablespoon	butter
1 cup	cream of wheat
½ teaspoon	salt
1 teaspoon	vanilla
1 tablespoon	butter, for the griddle

Serve hot with a fruit compote and cinnamon/sugar.

Scald the milk, being careful not to boil. Add 1 tablespoon butter to the milk.

While constantly whisking, add the cream of wheat in a slow stream. Stir in the salt. Remove from the heat and stir in the vanilla.

Grease a 9 x 13-inch sheet pan.

Pour the cream of wheat mixture into the pan while still hot.

Cover and chill for 2 hours, until cold and set. At this point, it can be refrigerated overnight to use the next day.

Remove from the refrigerator and cut into 3-inch squares.

Heat a large skillet until a drop of water bounces on the surface.

Add 1 tablespoon butter and as soon as it has melted, but before it browns, arrange the squares on the skillet.

Fry squares for 5 to 10 minutes, or until golden brown on the bottom.

Flip and fry on the other side until golden brown.

lemon ricotta pancakes

Brampton Bed and Breakfast Inn

SERVES 4 TO 5 (MAKES ABOUT 14 [3½-INCH] PANCAKES)

This is one decadent pancake—yet light and airy—and the flavor of lemon is always welcome at breakfast.

¾ cup	unbleached flour
1 teaspoon	baking powder
4 tablespoons	granulated sugar
½ teaspoon	salt
6	large eggs, separated
1½ cups	ricotta cheese
2 tablespoons	unsalted butter, melted
2 tablespoons	grated lemon zest (2 to 3 large lemons)

Preheat griddle to medium hot.

In a medium bowl, mix flour, baking powder, sugar, and salt. Set aside.

Separate eggs and mix yolks in a large bowl with ricotta cheese, melted butter, and lemon zest.

Slowly add dry ingredients to egg mixture and fold in gently.

Whip egg whites with an electric mixer until soft peaks form. Carefully fold egg whites into batter.

Spray griddle with nonstick coating.

Ladle a scant ½ cup of batter for each pancake. Cook until lightly browned on bottom, flip and repeat on other side. Cook for approximately 4 minutes on each side. Keep an eye on them, as different griddles will have varied results.

Serve immediately with fresh strawberries or raspberries and lemon curd (see recipe on page 149) on the side.

mixed berry bread pudding with orange-scented custard

Swiss Woods Bed & Breakfast Inn

SERVES 6

1½ cups	mixed berries (red raspberries, strawberries, blackberries, currants—can be frozen or fresh)
2 tablespoons	orange liqueur (triple sec, Grand Marnier)
8 slices	white bread, cubed
8 ounces	cream cheese, cubed
1½ cups	milk
8	eggs
¼ cup	honey
1 teaspoon	orange zest
¼ cup	butter, melted, optional (but really, really good!)

Mix the berries in a bowl and add the orange liqueur. Toss.

Butter a 9 x 9-inch baking dish. Place half of the cubed bread in the bottom of the baking dish. Layer with the half of the marinated berries and half of the cubed cream cheese.

Cover with half of the remaining bread cubes, the rest of the berries, and the cream cheese cubes, finishing with the last of the bread cubes.

Mix the milk, eggs, honey, and orange zest in a bowl and pour over the bread layers. Bake immediately, or cover and refrigerate overnight.

Remove from the refrigerator half an hour before baking. Drizzle with the melted butter.

Preheat the oven to 350 degrees. Cover with foil and bake for 30 minutes. Uncover and bake for an additional 15 to 20 minutes or until a tester comes out clean.

Cut and serve with the orange-scented custard (recipe follows) and lightly sweetened fresh berries, drizzled with a bit of orange liqueur.

for the orange-scented custard

2 cups	milk
1	whole egg
1	egg yolk
¼ cup	sugar
1 tablespoon	cornstarch
1 teaspoon	orange zest
1 teaspoon	vanilla extract
	pinch of salt

Scald 2 cups of milk in a small saucepan.

In a small bowl, beat the egg and egg yolk, sugar, and cornstarch until there are no lumps.

When the milk is hot, add half to the egg mixture, stirring until smooth.

Slowly pour the egg/milk mixture into the remaining hot milk in the saucepan and return to the burner.

Cook over medium heat, stirring constantly, until you see it starting to thicken.

The custard is finished when it thickens, coats a spoon, but has not boiled.

Remove from the heat, add the orange zest, vanilla, and a pinch of salt.

Stir at intervals until the custard has cooled, but is still warm.

Serve with the warm bread pudding. Makes 2 cups of custard.

orange blintz bake

The White Oak Inn

SERVES 8 TO 12

for the filling

8 ounces	cream cheese, at room temperature
1 cup	small curd cottage cheese (may substitute ricotta)
1	egg
1 tablespoon	sugar
1 teaspoon	vanilla
2 tablespoons	frozen orange juice concentrate, optional
½ cup	orange marmalade (microwave for a few seconds)
1½ cups	blueberries, fresh or frozen

for the batter

½ cup (1 stick)	butter, at room temperature
⅓ cup	sugar
4	eggs
1 cup	all-purpose flour, sifted
2 teaspoons	baking powder
1 cup	plain or vanilla yogurt
½ cup	sour cream

Preheat the oven to 350 degrees. Grease a 9 x 13-inch pan.

In one bowl, beat together cream cheese, cottage cheese, egg, sugar, vanilla, and orange juice concentrate, and set aside.

In a second bowl, make the batter. Cream butter and sugar together. Add eggs one at a time, beating well. Add the rest of the ingredients one at a time, mixing well and scraping the bowl down.

Pour half of batter mixture into the prepared pan. Pour the cream cheese mix over the batter. Dot with orange marmalade, and sprinkle blueberries over. Cover this with the remainder of the batter. Bake for about 40 minutes until set in the center, or until golden brown on top.

Let cool for at least 10 minutes before cutting and serving.

peach-nectarine upside-down french toast

Birchwood Inn

SERVES 8

½ cup	unsalted butter
1 cup	brown sugar, firmly packed
2 tablespoons	light corn syrup
2 to 3	ripe, but firm peaches, cut into ½-inch slices
2 to 3	ripe, but firm nectarines, cut into ½-inch slices
1 loaf	challah (egg bread)
4	eggs
1 cup	whole milk
1 tablespoon	vanilla extract
	cinnamon/sugar
	melon slices or berries, for garnish

Over medium-low heat, melt the butter in a saucepan. Stir in the brown sugar and corn syrup, until the sugar has dissolved. Cook for 3 to 5 minutes, until the mixture is thick and bubbly.

Remove the pan from the heat, and add the peaches and nectarines, stirring gently, until all of the fruit is coated.

Grease a 9 x 13-inch glass pan with cooking spray. Add the fruit mixture and spread evenly in the pan.

Slice the crust off the challah and cut the challah into 8 (1-inch) slices.

Place the slices in one layer on top of the fruit. Cover and refrigerate overnight.

Preheat the oven to 375 degrees. Whisk the eggs, milk, and vanilla together and pour over the bread slices. Sprinkle with cinnamon/sugar.

Bake for 50 minutes, until the top is golden brown and crisp. Remove the French Toast from the oven and let it sit for 5 minutes before cutting.

Cut the French Toast into 8 servings, inverting each serving on individual plates, fruit side up. Spoon the pan liquid over the top and serve with colorful melon slices or berries.

puff pancakes

Brampton Bed and Breakfast Inn

SERVES 8

This is one of the easiest breakfast dishes we serve at the inn, yet it is also one of the prettiest. If you have a hot oven, an ovenproof dish, and pot holders, you are good to go.

> This is an unbelievably versatile dish and a showstopper.

4	large eggs, at room temperature
1 cup	half-and-half
1 cup	unbleached flour
¼ cup	unsalted butter

Preheat the oven to 450 degrees.

In a large bowl, whisk together eggs and half-and-half very well. Sift flour over egg mixture and whisk until smooth. Refrigerate for 10 minutes.

Spray 8 ramekin dishes or one 8 x 8-inch ovenproof dish with nonstick spray.

Add ½ tablespoon of butter to each ramekin dish (2 tablespoons to the large dish), and put into hot oven to melt for 1 minute. Be careful, the hot oven will burn the butter if you leave it in too long.

Be careful not to burn yourself when you do the next step. The oven will be very hot.

As soon as the butter is melted and hot, add batter (approximately ⅓ cup to each ramekin dish), and bake small dishes for 10 to 15 minutes, and large dish for 20 to 30 minutes. The pancakes should be puffed up and have crispy and lightly browned edges. Serve at once with a topping of your choice.

sweet toppings
Fresh slightly sweetened berries of any kind, sliced peaches, puréed peaches with a bit of maple syrup, fried bananas, warm applesauce, sautéed apples, lemon juice, toasted nuts, etc., sprinkled with powdered sugar.

savory toppings
Chopped tomatoes with pesto, wilted spinach with a poached egg, caramelized onion and grated smoked Gouda.

pumpkin-ginger pancakes

Chambered Nautilus Bed and Breakfast Inn

SERVES 4 (2 LARGE PANCAKES EACH)

for the pancakes

1 cup	flour
¼ teaspoon	salt
2 tablespoons	brown sugar
1 teaspoon	baking powder
½ teaspoon	baking soda
½ teaspoon	cinnamon
½ teaspoon	nutmeg
½ teaspoon	ground ginger
1	egg, beaten
½ cup	plain yogurt
¾ cup	milk
¾ cup	canned pumpkin
2 tablespoons	melted butter

In a medium-size bowl, sift together the flour, salt, brown sugar, baking powder, baking soda, cinnamon, nutmeg, and ground ginger. In a separate bowl, combine the remaining ingredients. Add the flour mixture and stir until just blended.

Heat electric griddle to 350 degrees and grease with butter. Use about ½ cup of batter per pancake. Cook on both sides until pancakes are done. Serve with gingered butter and warm maple syrup.

for the gingered butter

2 tablespoons	finely chopped candied ginger
¼ cup	softened butter

Beat ginger and butter together. This keeps well in the refrigerator.

raised waffle

Brampton Bed and Breakfast Inn

MAKES ABOUT 8 WAFFLES

Light as air, crispy on the outside and soft on the inside. We have been serving this waffle to our guests for 20 years. It is best made with a Belgian waffle maker.

¼ cup	whole milk
1 tablespoon	dry yeast
2 cups	unbleached flour
2 tablespoons	ground cornmeal
1 teaspoon	salt
1 tablespoon	granulated sugar
2 cups	whole milk, lukewarm
1 stick	unsalted butter, melted (4 ounces)
2	large eggs, lightly beaten

The batter will keep refrigerated for up to 3 days. Whisk vigorously before each use.

Put the ¼ cup milk into a large mixing bowl and sprinkle yeast on top. Let stand for 5 minutes. Yeast will dissolve and start to bubble.

In a separate large bowl, mix flour, cornmeal, salt, and sugar. Set aside.

To another large bowl, add the 2 cups warmed milk (make sure milk is less than 110 degrees or it will kill the yeast), melted butter, eggs, and bubbly yeast mixture, and whisk until everything is well incorporated. Add flour mixture ½ cup at a time, whisking vigorously after each addition. The batter should be smooth.

Cover with plastic wrap and set bowl on a large rimmed cookie tray to catch the overflow if necessary, as the batter will double in volume. Refrigerate overnight.

In the morning, preheat the waffle iron to high.

Whisk batter; it will deflate; let batter rest for 15 minutes at room temperature.

Pour about ¾ cup of batter per waffle onto hot waffle iron. Bake until waffles are golden and edges are crisp.

Serve topped with warm maple syrup, any berries of your choice, or lightly sweetened fresh pineapple.

spice pancakes with lemon sauce

The Beechmont Inn Bed and Breakfast

SERVES 4

2	large eggs, separated
2½ cups	buttermilk
2 tablespoons	melted butter
1 tablespoon	sugar
2 teaspoons	dark molasses
2 cups	flour
½ cup	oats (quick or regular)
2 teaspoons	baking powder
1 teaspoon	baking soda
2 teaspoons	ginger
1 teaspoon	ground cinnamon
½ teaspoon	ground nutmeg
¼ teaspoon	ground cloves
	pinch of salt

For lighter pancakes, separate eggs and beat egg whites in a deep bowl on high speed until they hold moist peaks.

Beat egg yolks in a large bowl with buttermilk, melted butter, sugar, and molasses. Add flour, oats, baking powder, baking soda, ginger, cinnamon, nutmeg, cloves, and salt. Beat until well mixed. Add whipped egg whites to the mixture by folding them gently into the batter until combined.

Preheat electric griddle to 350 degrees and butter griddle. Cook by pouring out enough batter to form pancakes about 4 to 5 inches in diameter. Cook until the tops are full of bubbles and then flip and cook for another 1 to 2 minutes until golden brown.

Serve with warm lemon sauce.

for the lemon sauce

1 cup	sugar
2 to 3 tablespoons	cornstarch
2 cups	water
4 tablespoons	butter
2 to 3 tablespoons	grated lemon zest
¼ cup	lemon juice

In a small pan, mix sugar with cornstarch.

Add water and bring to a boil over high heat.

Remove from heat and add butter, grated lemon zest, and lemon juice.

Stir until the butter melts. Serve.

whole wheat pancakes with roasted pecans

Lookout Point Lakeside Inn

MAKES 12 PANCAKES

¾ cup	all-purpose flour
¾ cup	whole wheat flour
3 tablespoons	sugar
1½ teaspoons	baking powder
½ teaspoon	baking soda
½ teaspoon	salt
1½ cups	buttermilk (low-fat is fine)
1 tablespoon	vegetable oil
1	large egg
1	large egg white, beaten
¾ cup	maple syrup
½ cup	chopped pecans, roasted
	dollop of whipped cream

Serve with maple syrup, roasted pecans, and a dollop of whipped cream.

Lightly spoon flours into dry measuring cups, level with a knife. Combine flours, sugar, baking powder, baking soda, and salt in a large bowl, stirring with a whisk. Combine buttermilk, oil, and egg. Stir until well blended, then gently fold in beaten egg white. Add liquid to flour mixture, stirring just until moist.

Heat griddle over medium-low heat, with a light coating of oil. Spoon about ¼ cup batter per pancake onto griddle. Turn pancakes over when tops are covered with bubbles and edges look cooked.

Note: These pancakes are thick, so be patient and do not cook too fast.

8 savory breakfast

get *crackin'*

artichoke frittata

The William Henry Miller Inn

SERVES 8

1 cup	salsa (such as the breakfast salsa on page 127)
1 (14-ounce) can	artichoke hearts, drained and chopped into bite-size pieces
1½ cups	Monterey Jack cheese
1½ cups	sharp cheddar, shredded
6	eggs
1 cup	sour cream

Preheat the oven to 350 degrees.

Spray a 9 x 13-inch glass baking dish with nonstick spray. Spread salsa evenly in bottom of dish and sprinkle with artichokes and cheeses.

In a medium bowl, beat eggs and sour cream. Pour egg mixture over artichokes and cheese.

Bake for 30 to 40 minutes or until set and slightly brown.

asparagus goat cheese quiche

The Beechmont Inn Bed and Breakfast

SERVES 6

Goat cheese is smooth and creamy, and I love the combination of goat cheese and fresh asparagus. Quiche, as I know all of you know, should have a flaky pastry crust, but I make mine without. Maybe it's the extra few minutes to make the crust, and maybe it's that it cuts a few calories, but I don't miss the crust. Add one, if you prefer.

12 ounces	fresh asparagus, trimmed
2 tablespoons	olive oil
½ teaspoon	Herbes de Provence
4 ounces	goat cheese, crumbled
8	large eggs
1¼ cups	half-and-half
	pinch of salt (I use kosher)
¼ teaspoon	freshly ground pepper

Preheat the oven to 375 degrees. Spray a 9-inch pie plate with nonstick spray.

Prepare asparagus by cutting the stems into ½-inch pieces.

In medium skillet, heat the olive oil over medium heat and add the asparagus. Sauté for 2 minutes.

Place the asparagus in the bottom of pie plate. Sprinkle Herbes de Provence over the asparagus and add crumbled goat cheese.

In a large bowl, whisk the eggs until light. Stir in the half-and-half. Season with salt and pepper, to taste. Pour over the asparagus and cheese.

Bake until quiche is puffed and lightly brown, for about 40 to 45 minutes. Serve warm.

caramelized onion omelet

Brampton Bed and Breakfast Inn

SERVES 4

2	large sweet onions, such as Vidalia
2 tablespoons	good olive oil
1 tablespoon	unsalted butter
1 (3-inch)	twig of fresh rosemary
8	large eggs
	sea salt and a few grindings
	of black pepper, to taste
2 tablespoons	heavy cream
4 teaspoons	unsalted butter
1 cup	smoked Gouda, coarsely grated

> Caramelizing onions takes time, but is well worth the effort, and it is a task you can do a day ahead.

Dice the onions into ¼-inch pieces (approximately 5 cups).

Melt olive oil and 1 tablespoon butter in a large frying pan over medium high heat until the butter and olive oil start foaming.

Add diced onion, turn the heat to low and cook slowly for 45 minutes to an hour, stirring every 5 minutes or so to make sure the onions don't burn. Onions have a high sugar content and what gives them their incredible flavor when cooked slowly can also be their demise when cooked too fast and they burn. The onions should have a dark golden color when done. Remove from heat and set aside.

Remove the rosemary leaves from the stem and chop very finely. Add to the caramelized onion and mix well.

In a 2-cup measuring cup, vigorously whisk 2 eggs, salt and pepper, to taste and add ½ tablespoon of heavy cream.

Melt 1 teaspoon butter in an 8-inch nonstick omelet pan over medium-high heat. When the butter stops foaming, add whisked eggs and let set for 30 seconds before using a heatproof spatula to lift the eggs from the side to the center to ensure that the eggs are cooked evenly without drying out.

Distribute a quarter of the caramelized onions/rosemary mixture on half the omelet. Sprinkle with ¼ cup grated cheese.

Fold omelet in half and keep warm. Repeat the same procedure for the other 3 omelets and serve immediately.

crab and artichoke egg puff

Chambered Nautilus Bed and Breakfast Inn

SERVES 6

5	eggs, beaten
¼ cup	flour
½ teaspoon	baking powder
8 ounces	cottage cheese
2 cups	Monterey Jack cheese, grated
4 ounces	crabmeat, shredded
6 ounces	artichoke hearts, chopped
	salt and pepper, to taste
6 drops	Tabasco sauce

Preheat the oven to 350 degrees. Spray 6 individual (6-ounce) ramekins with cooking spray.

In a medium bowl, combine eggs, flour, and baking powder until well mixed. Add remaining ingredients to eggs and mix well.

Divide mixture equally between ramekins.

Bake for approximately 30 minutes or until golden brown.

This is wonderful when topped with a little of your favorite hollandaise (see recipe on page 148) and served with roasted asparagus.

eggs florentine

Swiss Woods Bed & Breakfast Inn

SERVES 8

Fresh spinach is a must here, as are the fresh leeks. Leaving the leeks in rings gives this dish great texture and appearance.

6	eggs
12 ounces	cottage cheese
8 ounces	cream cheese
8 ounces	sour cream
2 tablespoons	flour
⅛ teaspoon	pepper
2 cups	aged sharp cheddar, shredded
1	large leek (can use an onion or spring onions)
3 cups	fresh spinach, stems removed, and somewhat chopped

In a mixing bowl, mix the first 7 ingredients (through the cheddar) until blended. Do not overmix, as you do not want to lose the consistency of the cottage cheese.

At this point, you can cover and hold overnight in the refrigerator to bake in the morning.

When ready to bake, preheat the oven to 350 degrees.

Slice the leek, leaving the rings whole (or if using onions, dice them). Use up through the white part until the leek starts to turn a darker green.

Fold the spinach and leeks into the egg and cheese mixture, and pour into a 2-quart baking dish that has been greased, sprayed, or buttered.

Bake for about 45 minutes. The finished casserole should be somewhat puffed and a tester inserted should come out clean. The edges will be brown. At this stage, it will hold in a warm oven until you are ready to serve it. Close the door and turn the oven off.

Serve hot.

fondue florentine soufflé

Birchwood Inn

SERVES 8

5 cups	French bread cubes (½ to ¾-inch cubes)
2 pounds	Swiss chard, or 10 ounces frozen, chopped spinach, thawed, and squeezed to get most of the moisture out
2 quarts	salted water to boil Swiss chard
2 tablespoons	unsalted butter
2	large shallots, minced, or 1 large onion, chopped, or 1 leek, grated
1 teaspoon	kosher salt
	freshly ground black pepper
¼ pound	Gruyère cheese, coarsely grated
⅛ pound	Emmentaler (Swiss cheese), coarsely grated
⅛ pound	Appenzeller cheese, coarsely grated, optional
15	large eggs
3 cups	whole milk
1 teaspoon	Maggi Seasoning (found in most supermarkets, used by Europeans for flavor, often instead of salt)
¼ cup	kirsch, optional
2 tablespoons	Dijon mustard

the day before serving
Grease 8 (8-ounce) ramekins.

Toast the bread cubes in the oven for 15 minutes, until crunchy, but not brown.

Wash the Swiss chard and tear off the leaves, removing the stem and large veins. Bring salted water to a boil, and add the chard for a minute or two. Drain. Squeeze as much water out of the chard as possible. If you are using frozen spinach instead of Swiss chard, squeeze as much water out of the thawed spinach as possible.

Melt the butter in a skillet over medium heat, and sauté the shallots, onions, or leeks until somewhat translucent.

Add the chard or spinach. Salt and pepper, to taste.

Grate the cheese.

Spread half of the cubed bread on the bottom of each ramekin.

Add 1 heaping tablespoon of the onion-chard/spinach mixture on top of the bread.

Sprinkle half of the grated cheese (Gruyère/Emmantaler or may use Parmesan/cheddar) on top of the onion-chard/spinach mixture.

Add the other half of the bread, then the onion-chard/spinach mixture, and the remaining cheese.

In a large bowl, crack the eggs. Add the milk, Maggi Seasoning, kirsch (if desired), Dijon mustard, and pepper, to your taste. Whisk well.

Pour the egg mixture into each ramekin, filling just about to the top.

Cover the ramekins with plastic wrap and refrigerate overnight or freeze for up to 2 weeks.

the day you are serving the soufflé
An hour before you are ready to serve the soufflé, preheat the oven to 400 degrees.

Place the ramekins in the oven, directly on the rack, and cook for 45 minutes or until lightly browned.

Serve immediately before the soufflé deflates.

garden baked eggs

Chambered Nautilus Bed and Breakfast Inn

SERVES 6

2	eggs, per person
½ cup	half-and-half
	salt and pepper, to taste
	thyme (dried or fresh), to taste
2 cups	vegetables, chopped, fresh and seasonal (suggestions are green and red peppers, asparagus, broccoli, zucchini, yellow squash, mushrooms, green onions, sundried tomatoes soaked in olive oil [pat dry and chop], or dried sundried tomatoes that have been rehydrated)
½ cup	cheddar cheese, shredded (to sprinkle on top)
	chives, chopped

Serve with your favorite muffins, sweet breads, or potatoes.

Preheat the oven to 350 degrees. Spray 6 (6-ounce) ramekins with cooking spray.

Blend eggs, half-and-half, salt, pepper, and thyme (a 4-cup measuring cup with pouring spout is useful).

Fill ramekins with ⅓ cup chopped vegetables.

Put egg mixture in ramekins over the vegetables. Top with cheddar cheese and chives.

Bake for 20 to 30 minutes or until set.

ham and cheese rolled omelet

Birchwood Inn

SERVES 6

4 ounces	cream cheese, softened
¾ cup	whole milk
2 tablespoons	all-purpose flour
¼ teaspoon	kosher salt
12	large eggs

for the filling

2 tablespoons	Dijon mustard
2 cups	cheddar cheese, grated, divided
1½ cups	cooked ham, diced
½ cup	green onion, sliced

This is just one suggested filling. We often use cheddar and apples, sautéing the apples before adding to the omelet. Or use your favorite omelet fillings. Be creative!

Preheat the oven to 375 degrees.

Grease the bottom of a jelly roll pan (15 x 10 x 1-inch) with cooking spray. Line the bottom of the jelly roll pan with parchment paper, making sure to have the paper going up the sides. Use cooking spray to grease the parchment paper.

In a blender, blend the cream cheese and milk until smooth. Add the flour and salt and blend to combine.

Beat the eggs until well blended. Add the eggs to the cream cheese mixture in the blender. Blend well.

Place the prepared pan on the middle rack of the oven to preheat (for about 5 minutes).

Carefully pour the egg mixture into the pan and bake for 15 to 20 minutes or until the eggs are set and puffed.

Remove the pan from the oven and immediately spread the top of the eggs with mustard. Sprinkle with 1¾ cups of cheese. Then sprinkle with the ham and green onions.

Roll up the omelet from the short side, peeling the parchment paper away while rolling.

Sprinkle the top with the remaining ¼ cup cheese. Return the omelet to the oven for 3 to 4 minutes to melt the cheese.

Slice the omelet into 6 slices and serve.

ham baked eggs

Chambered Nautilus Bed and Breakfast Inn

SERVES AS MANY AS NEEDED

1 slice	Black Forest ham, per serving
2	eggs, per serving
	cheddar, Swiss, or Parmesan cheese, grated
	parsley or chives, chopped, for garnish

Preheat the oven to 400 degrees.

Grease 1 ramekin per person.

Lay 1 slice of ham on top of the ramekin and gently press it down into the well. Crack 2 eggs into the well created by the ham, and top the eggs with cheddar cheese (or your choice of Swiss or Parmesan).

Bake in the oven for about 15 to 18 minutes or until the eggs are set. A greased regular muffin tin can be used instead of a ramekin, with 1 slice of ham and 1 egg in each.

Lift the baked ham and eggs from each ramekin and sprinkle with chopped parsley or chives.

Serve with roasted potatoes and fresh fruit.

huevos trifecta

Lookout Point Lakeside Inn

SERVES 2

2 tablespoons	butter, melted
½ cup	cream
4	eggs
	dash of cayenne pepper
2 tablespoons	cheddar cheese, grated
1 piece	prosciutto, thinly sliced
4	English muffins, halved and toasted
	dash of Mediterranean sea salt
4	sausage links, cooked
	tomato and rosemary, for garnish

In a 10-inch skillet, melt butter over high heat; immediately add cream.

Slide eggs into butter and cream. When egg whites begin to set, flip eggs over. Add dash of cayenne pepper. Sprinkle with cheese.

Finish cooking until desired level of egg yolk doneness is reached.

Place prosciutto atop toasted English muffin halves. Slide eggs on muffin halves with some of the hot cream and butter. Sprinkle Mediterranean sea salt on the eggs.

Serve with sausage links on the side.

Garnish with a slice of tomato and rosemary.

kiss my grits!

Birchwood Inn

SERVES 8

4½ cups	water
1 cup	stone-ground yellow grits
1 teaspoon	salt
2 tablespoons	unsalted butter
1 pound	Italian turkey sausage (½ lb. sweet and ½ lb. hot)
1	large onion, chopped
4 tablespoons	unsalted butter
2	eggs, lightly beaten
2 cups	cheddar cheese, grated or
	Parmesan cheese, grated
¼ cup	parsley or basil, minced

Mix the water, grits, salt, and butter in a large saucepan or pot. Bring to a boil over medium heat. Reduce the heat to low; cover and simmer for 45 minutes or until thick. If the grits become too thick, add more water.

Grease a 9 x 13-inch pan or individual "long boats." Preheat the oven to 400 degrees.

Sauté the sausage, breaking it into small pieces. Remove sausage. Sauté the onion in the fat from the sausage. Drain. Add the onion to the sausage.

Add the butter, eggs, cheese, and parsley or basil to the grits. Combine the grits with the sausage and onions.

Pour into the prepared pan or dishes. At this point, you can refrigerate the grits for up to 2 days before baking. It freezes well.

Bake for 1 hour until brown (for 45 minutes, if using individual dishes).

maryland blue crab quiche

Brampton Bed and Breakfast Inn

SERVES 8 FOR BREAKFAST, 6 FOR LUNCH

for the pastry

1¼ cups	unbleached flour
8 tablespoons	cold unsalted butter, cut into ½-inch cubes
¼ teaspoon	salt
3 to 4 tablespoons	ice water

for the filling

4	large eggs
2 cups	half-and-half
2 tablespoons	finely chopped fresh chives
2 tablespoons	finely chopped fresh parsley
1 tablespoon	finely chopped fresh lovage
½ teaspoon	Old Bay seasoning
½ teaspoon	salt
¼ teaspoon	freshly ground black pepper
⅛ teaspoon	freshly grated nutmeg
1 pound	lump crabmeat, picked over to remove shells
4 ounces	fontina, Monterey Jack, or any other mild cheese, grated

to make the pastry

Preheat the oven to 375 degrees.

In a food processor, pulse together flour, butter, and salt until mixture resembles coarse meal.

Drizzle with 3 tablespoons ice water and pulse 3 to 4 times until incorporated.

Squeeze a small handful. If it doesn't hold together, add more ice water, ½ tablespoon at a time, pulsing until just incorporated; test again. Do not overwork mixture or the pastry will be tough.

Turn mixture out onto a work surface and divide into 4 portions. With heel of your hand, smear each portion once or twice in a forward motion to help distribute fat. Gather dough together with a scraper and press into a ball, then flatten into a 4-inch disk. Wrap dough with plastic wrap and chill, until firm, for about 1 hour.

Roll out dough into a round (approximately 12 inches) on a lightly floured surface.

Line a deep-dish pie plate with the pastry.

Fold overhang under pastry and press against rim of pie plate to reinforce edge. Crimp edge. Prick bottom and side of pastry with a fork. Freeze until firm, for about 20 minutes.

Line pie shell with foil and fill with pie weights. Bake until pastry is set underneath foil, for about 15 minutes. Remove foil and weights and continue baking shell until bottom and sides are lightly golden, for about 10 minutes more. Remove from oven and cool completely in glass dish on a wire rack.

to make the filling
Reduce the oven temperature to 350 degrees.

Whisk together eggs, half-and-half, herbs, Old Bay seasoning, salt, pepper, and nutmeg.

Place pie plate on a rimmed baking sheet. Layer crust with crabmeat and cheese.

Pour egg mixture on top and bake until filling puffs, for 40 to 50 minutes. It should no longer be wobbly in center.

Remove from oven and cool on rack for at least 15 minutes before serving warm.

mediterranean quiche

Chambered Nautilus Bed and Breakfast Inn

SERVES 12 (USING 6-OUNCE ROUND RAMEKINS)

10	eggs
½ cup	flour
1 teaspoon	baking powder
2 ounces	butter, melted
3 cups	cottage cheese
1 cup	cheddar cheese, shredded
1 (10-ounce) box	frozen leaf spinach, thawed and squeezed dry
1 cup	roasted red pepper, chopped
1 tablespoon	oregano, dried
	Tabasco sauce, to taste
	salt and black pepper, to taste
1 cup	crumbled feta cheese

Preheat the oven to 375 degrees.

Beat eggs and mix in flour, baking powder, and melted butter. Mix well; there will still be a few lumps from the flour, which is okay.

Stir in cottage cheese, cheddar cheese, spinach, roasted red pepper, oregano, and other seasonings. Pour into greased (6-ounce round) individual ramekins, and sprinkle the top with feta cheese.

Bake for 30 minutes. Tops should be lightly browned.

mini corn cakes

The White Oak Inn

SERVES 12 TO 16 (APPROXIMATELY 3 MINI CAKES PER PERSON)

1½ cups	flour
1½ teaspoons	baking soda
1½ tablespoons	sugar
¾ teaspoon	salt
1¾ cups	milk, soured with
	2 tablespoons lemon juice
2	eggs
3 tablespoons	melted butter
4 cups	fresh or frozen corn kernels
½ cup	very finely diced red pepper
3 tablespoons	chopped fresh parsley
2 tablespoons	chopped fresh chives or
	2 teaspoons dried chives
½ teaspoon	pepper
	sour cream

Preheat griddle over medium heat and grease.

Combine flour, baking soda, sugar, and salt in mixing bowl. Mix with fork.

Whisk together soured milk, eggs, and melted butter. Add flour mixture to liquids and stir well. Mix in corn, red pepper, parsley, chives, and pepper.

Drop by generous tablespoons onto a hot griddle and cook about 3 to 4 minutes. Flip and cook until lightly brown on both sides.

Serve warm with a dollop of sour cream.

mushroom sausage bread pudding

Swiss Woods Bed & Breakfast Inn

SERVES 8

There are just some dishes that rise to the top as perennial favorites. This is hands down, far and away, my family's favorite breakfast dish. As the girls married and left home, this was the recipe they made sure to have ready for company. Grate the cheeses and freeze for quick use. Use a mild salt-and-pepper sausage.

5 to 6 cups	day-old bread, cubed
1 pound	sausage, removed from the casing
2 tablespoons	butter
12 ounces	mushrooms, sliced thin
3 tablespoons	flour
2½ cups	milk, divided
½ teaspoon	dry mustard
6	eggs
½ teaspoon	salt
	pepper, to taste
½ cup	Emmentaler cheese, grated
½ cup	Gruyère cheese, grated

Spray a 9 x 13-inch baking dish with nonstick spray.

Spread the cubed bread evenly in the pan and set aside.

In a skillet, brown the sausage. Set aside. Using the same skillet, melt butter, add the sliced mushrooms, and sauté until tender and slightly brown.

Add the flour and combine.

Pour in 1 cup of the milk a little at a time, stirring constantly, to make a creamy mushroom sauce. Set aside.

In a bowl, mix the 1½ cups milk, mustard, eggs, salt, and pepper.

Evenly distribute the cooked sausage on top of the bread.

Pour the egg mixture over the sausage and bread.

Mix the grated cheese into the cooled mushroom sauce and then spread over top of the sausage layer.

Cover and refrigerate overnight or for a minimum of 1 hour.

Remove from the refrigerator, remove the cover, and allow to stand for 30 minutes to lose some of the chill.

Preheat the oven to 350 degrees.

Bake the sausage soufflé for 45 minutes to 1 hour or until it puffs a bit and a tester comes out clean.

northwest salmon breakfast pie

Chambered Nautilus Bed and Breakfast Inn

SERVES 6

1	pie crust
12 ounces	fully cooked salmon
1	large onion, chopped (1 cup)
1	clove garlic, minced
3 tablespoons	butter
5	eggs, beaten
¼ cup	all-purpose flour
2¼ cups	sour cream
1½ cups	Swiss cheese, shredded, divided
1 teaspoon	dried dill

Preheat the oven to 400 degrees. Bake pie crust for 8 minutes and remove from oven. Reduce oven temperature to 375 degrees.

Remove any skin and bones from salmon; flake into small pieces.

In a medium skillet, over low-medium heat, sauté onion and garlic in butter until tender. Then add to the salmon and mix well.

In a bowl, whisk the eggs and flour. Add sour cream and mix well.

Add salmon and the onion mixture and stir until blended. Add 1 cup of Swiss cheese and the dill. Blend.

Pour mixture into partially baked crust. Sprinkle with the remaining cheese. Bake uncovered for 30 minutes, and then cover with foil. Bake for another 15 minutes or until mixture is set.

omelet with variations

The Beechmont Inn Bed and Breakfast

SERVES 1

for the basic omelet

2 to 3	eggs
1 tablespoon	water
1 tablespoon	butter
	salt and pepper, to taste

Break eggs into a small bowl and break the yolks with a whisk or fork. Add water and whisk until just blended.

Heat a nonstick 8-inch skillet with sloped sides over medium heat, then add the butter and melt. The butter should sizzle slightly. Pour the eggs into the skillet, and in 15 seconds, using a heat-proof spatula, pull the set eggs to the center of the skillet. This allows the unset eggs to cook. Watch carefully and lower the heat, if necessary, to prevent the eggs from burning.

Add herbs, cheese, or fillings when the top thin layer of eggs is still moist. Using the spatula, fold the omelet in half (or fold one-third over the middle, and then the other third over the middle). Slide the omelet out of the pan by tilting it over the plate.

suggested variations

for bacon, apple, and cheddar omelet
Cook 2 slices of bacon until crisp. Drain on a paper towel. Wipe out the bacon drippings and add ½ tablespoon of butter. Sauté half an apple that has been peeled, cored, and thinly sliced. After cooking for about 3 minutes, until tender, place apples in a small dish and set aside. Follow directions for the basic omelet. Add bacon and apple as a filling, and spread with 2 tablespoons of grated sharp cheddar cheese. Fold and serve.

for spinach and mushroom omelet

Sauté ¼ cup sliced mushrooms in lightly coated nonstick skillet. After 2 minutes, add ½ cup spinach and cook until the spinach wilts. Remove from the skillet and set aside. Follow directions for the basic omelet, then add the spinach and mushroom filling. Add ¼ cup grated Gruyère; fold and serve.

Other combinations include asparagus and crumbled goat cheese, zucchini and tomato, and broccoli and carmelized onions in combination with feta, Parmigiano-Reggiano, Swiss, or cheddar cheese.

Roasted red peppers, squash, and other veggies can be used.

Chopped parsley, thyme, scallions, garlic, and rosemary are flavorful additions.

potato veggie pancakes

Swiss Woods Bed & Breakfast Inn

SERVES 8 (MAKES 14 TO 16 PANCAKES)

4 cups	potatoes, cooked and coarsely shredded
¼ cup	onion, diced
¼ cup	red peppers, diced
¼ cup	zucchini or yellow squash, in julienne strips
½ cup	mushrooms, coarsely chopped
¼ cup	sliced leeks or scallions (green onions)
1	bunch parsley (⅛ cup, chopped)
2 tablespoons	flour
2	large eggs, beaten
2 tablespoons	water
2 tablespoons	butter, melted
¼ cup	grated sharp cheddar cheese, optional
½ teaspoon	salt
⅛ teaspoon	freshly grated pepper
	oil or butter, for the griddle

Boil and cool potatoes. (This can be done the day before.)

Preheat a griddle or frying pan to medium high. Add some oil or butter or a combination of both.

Prepare vegetables. Peel and grate potatoes with a coarse grater. Add the prepared vegetables, flour, eggs, water, melted butter, cheese, salt, and pepper. Mix gently with a spoon or spatula until combined.

Drop onto hot griddle, using a medium ice cream scoop that holds about ¼ cup. Do not pack or form, as these are better if they are somewhat loosely connected. Press only enough to shape and hold together.

Fry until golden brown, flipping once.

Serve hot.

savory breakfast strudel

Lookout Point Lakeside Inn

SERVES 6 TO 8

1 sheet	puff pastry, thawed according to package directions
6	eggs
	salt and pepper, to taste
¼ cup	chopped bell peppers
¼ cup	chopped green onions
	butter, to sauté peppers and onions
¼ cup	cheddar cheese, shredded
1 tablespoon	freshly grated Parmesan cheese
1	egg, for egg wash
1 tablespoon	water, for egg wash

Preheat the oven to 400 degrees.

Thaw puff pastry according to package directions. While preparing other ingredients, keep thawed puff pastry on parchment paper-lined baking sheet, covered with plastic wrap, in the refrigerator.

Whisk eggs; add salt and pepper. Sauté bell peppers and green onions in butter until tender. I prefer the red peppers for color.

Prepare egg wash by whisking 1 egg, and adding 1 tablespoon of water to dilute.

Remove puff pastry from refrigerator, and prepare the pastry. The pastry appears to be in thirds. With a sharp knife or pizza cutter, cut a series of approximately eight "wings" at an angle on each outer third of the puff pastry, leaving a ½-inch tail at the bottom of the pastry. Looking at the pastry, the appearance reminds me of an arrowhead.

Over high heat, scramble eggs, along with the bell pepper and onion mixture, until soft-scrambled. Spread the eggs over the center third of the puff pastry. Spread the cheddar cheese over the eggs.

Starting at the top of the pastry, wrap the eggs with the puff pastry, overlapping the cut "wings" of the pastry to hold the eggs. Tuck the pastry "tail" under the last wings to seal the pastry. Brush egg wash over the puff pastry. Sprinkle with grated Parmesan.

Bake for 15 to 20 minutes, until puffed and golden brown. Serve hot.

Note: This recipe is written for puff pastry sheets purchased from the grocer refrigerator case. I use commercial sheets, which are larger and easier to use. With commercial sheets, adapt the recipe using 12 eggs and ½ cup of each vegetable, serving 10 persons.

This strudel is a great vegetarian entrée. If you prefer, consider adding chopped, cooked bacon or diced ham to the eggs.

southwest breakfast bake

The White Oak Inn

SERVES 12

1 pound	ground sausage (your choice of chorizo, turkey, hot or mild Italian)
4 small cans	chopped green chilies
8	small tortillas (corn or wheat), cut in ½-inch strips
2 cups	shredded cheddar cheese
1 (14-ounce) can	diced tomatoes, drained
12	eggs
1½ cups	milk
½ teaspoon	salt
½ teaspoon	black pepper
2 cloves	garlic, chopped
1 teaspoon	ground cumin
2 teaspoons	dried onion flakes
2 cups each	sour cream and salsa
	chopped cilantro, for garnish, optional

Can be assembled the night before, refrigerated, and baked in the morning, after bringing to room temperature for about 30 minutes.

Scramble fry the sausage and drain off the fat.

Preheat the oven to 350 degrees. Grease either a 9 x 13-inch baking dish or 2 (9-inch) deep-dish pie plates.

Put 2 cans of chopped chilies in the bottom of prepared dish(es).

Layer with half the tortillas, then half of the sausage, and half of the cheese. Repeat layers. Arrange diced tomatoes on top.

Beat eggs, milk, salt, pepper, garlic, cumin, and onion flakes together. Pour carefully over the tortilla mix. Allow to sit for at least 30 minutes before baking, to allow the tortillas to absorb the liquid.

Bake uncovered for about 45 minutes or until a knife inserted in the center comes out clean.

Serve with sour cream, salsa, and chopped cilantro.

spinach brownies

Birchwood Inn

SERVES 12

4 tablespoons	unsalted butter
20 ounces	chopped frozen spinach, thawed and squeezed, to remove moisture
3	eggs
1 cup	milk
1 cup	all-purpose flour
1 teaspoon	salt
1 teaspoon	baking powder
1 pound	aged cheddar cheese, grated

Preheat the oven to 350 degrees.

Grease a 9 x 13-inch baking dish.

Melt the butter in the baking dish.

Thaw spinach and drain well. Squeeze the spinach to remove as much moisture as possible.

In a mixing bowl, beat the eggs and add the milk.

Mix the flour, salt, and baking powder together and add to the egg/milk mixture.

Add the cheese and spinach. Mix well. Spoon the mixture into the baking dish.

Bake for 35 to 45 minutes, until the top is lightly brown. (If the mixture is chilled, bake for 50 to 60 minutes.]

Cool slightly before cutting into squares or triangles.

spring strata

Swiss Woods Bed & Breakfast Inn

SERVES 8

5 cups	day-old French bread, cubed
4 cups	asparagus spears, sliced in 1-inch diagonal slices (about 2 pounds)
	water, to cook asparagus
1 cup	roasted red peppers, diced
2 cups	fresh spinach leaves, cleaned and stems discarded
2	large spring onions, sliced in thin rings
½ pound	Gruyère cheese, grated
6	eggs
2 cups	milk
½ cup	Greek-style yogurt or ricotta
¼ cup	parsley, chopped
	salt and pepper, to taste
1 tablespoon	grainy mustard
3 tablespoons	dried bread crumbs
2 tablespoons	Parmesan cheese
2 tablespoons	sesame seeds, black and white
3 tablespoons	melted butter

Prepare a 9 x 13-inch baking dish with nonstick cooking spray.

Cook the asparagus just until tender. Drain.

Layer half of the cubed bread, cooked asparagus, red peppers, spinach, and onions alternately, followed by the second half of the bread cubes, cooked asparagus, red peppers, onions, and Gruyère cheese.

Blend the eggs, milk, yogurt, parsley, salt, pepper, and mustard. Pour over the layered bread and veggies. Sprinkle the top with the bread crumbs, Parmesan cheese, and sesame seeds.

Drizzle with the butter. Refrigerate overnight.

Next day, remove the strata from the refrigerator and allow to stand for 10 to 15 minutes.

Preheat the oven to 350 degrees. Bake for 45 to 55 minutes or until golden brown on top.

summer veggie crustless quiche

The White Oak Inn

SERVES 6

2 tablespoons	butter
1 cup	diced onion
1	large yellow or green zucchini, sliced into ¼-inch slices
1 teaspoon each	dried basil and oregano
5	eggs
¾ cup	milk
¼ cup	flour
1 teaspoon	baking powder
1 cup	fresh diced tomatoes
½ cup	cheddar cheese, shredded
1 cup	feta cheese, crumbled

Preheat the oven to 350 degrees. Spray a 9-inch pie plate with cooking spray.

Melt butter in a skillet and sauté the onion until translucent.

Add the zucchini. Sprinkle with basil and oregano. Sauté for about 3 or 4 minutes.

Combine the eggs, milk, flour, and baking powder in a blender or food processor.

Spread the onion/zucchini mixture in the bottom of the pie plate. Spread the diced tomatoes, cheddar and feta cheeses evenly over top. Gently pour the egg batter over all.

Bake for about 40 minutes or until set in the middle. Let sit for 10 minutes before slicing into 6 wedges.

Note: If fresh herbs are in season, substitute 2 tablespoons shredded basil and 2 teaspoons fresh oregano leaves for the dried.

texas eggs

Lookout Point Lakeside Inn

SERVES 6

6	large eggs
¼ cup	all-purpose flour
½ teaspoon	baking powder
	pinch of salt
2 cups	Monterey Jack cheese, shredded
1 cup	nonfat cottage cheese
¼ cup	butter, melted
1 can	chopped green chilies, drained

Spray a 9-inch glass pie plate with nonstick spray.

In a large bowl, whisk eggs until smooth. In a small bowl, whisk together dry ingredients of flour, baking powder, and salt. Add to eggs and stir well. The batter will appear lumpy.

Stir in the cheeses, melted butter, and green chilies, and mix thoroughly.

Pour into the prepared pie plate. Cover and refrigerate overnight.

The next day, preheat the oven to 350 degrees. Take the pie plate out of the refrigerator 15 minutes prior to putting in the oven. Bake until the top just starts to turn golden brown, for about 40 to 45 minutes. Allow to sit for about 5 minutes before serving.

tomato basil tart

Birchwood Inn

SERVES 6

3 to 4	large tomatoes
½ teaspoon	kosher salt
¼ teaspoon	freshly ground black pepper
1 cup	fresh basil
¾ cup	ricotta cheese
4	large eggs, lightly beaten
1 cup	grated Parmesan cheese
	additional salt and freshly ground black pepper, to taste
1	(9-inch) unbaked pie shell

Serve hot or at room temperature.

the day before serving

Slice the tomatoes about ¼-inch thick, saving the ends as well as the slices. Place the slices and ends on a cookie sheet lined with a double layer of paper towels.

Sprinkle the tomatoes lightly with kosher salt and pepper. Cover with a double layer of paper towels. Cover with plastic wrap and refrigerate overnight.

In a food processor, purée the basil and ricotta. Add the eggs and blend. Pour the mixture into a bowl. Add the Parmesan cheese, additional salt, and pepper to taste, and combine. Refrigerate mixture covered overnight.

the day you are serving

Preheat the oven to 400 degrees. Remove the pie crust from the refrigerator. Prick the sides and bottom of the pie shell with a fork. Spray a sheet of foil with cooking spray and place sprayed side down on the pie shell. Fill the pie shell with baking beans. Prebake the pie shell for 20 minutes. Remove the pie shell from the oven. Remove the beans and foil. Line the bottom of the pie crust with the leftover end pieces of tomato. Pour the ricotta mixture over the tomatoes.

Arrange the tomato slices on top of the ricotta mixture in one overlapping layer. Sprinkle a bit more Parmesan cheese on the tomatoes. Spray the pie lightly with nonstick cooking spray.

Protect the edges of the pie with a pie crust saver or aluminum foil. Bake for 1 hour or until set and lightly browned.

Remove from the oven and let sit for 5 to 10 minutes before slicing into 6 servings.

Note: This recipe is also great as individual tarts!

tomato benedict

The White Oak Inn

SERVES 6

This is a versatile side dish that can be used several different ways. This particular recipe uses it under poached eggs; however, we sometimes serve it over scrambled eggs, and have even served it as a hot appetizer dish with crostini.

This dish goes very well with ham.

about 6	large fresh plum tomatoes
¼ cup	mayonnaise
2 teaspoons	dried basil
1½ cups	shredded cheddar cheese
½ cup	shredded Asiago or Parmesan cheese
12	eggs
6	English muffins
	chopped fresh parsley, for garnish

Preheat the oven to 350 degrees. Spray a 9-inch pie plate.

Dice the plum tomatoes into ½-inch cubes. Drain off any excess liquid and combine tomatoes with mayonnaise, basil, cheddar, and Asiago cheese.

Pour into pie plate and bake for about 25 to 30 minutes, until top is golden brown.

While tomato is baking, poach the eggs and toast the English muffins.

Place 2 muffin halves on each plate. Divide the tomato mixture between the muffins. Top each muffin half with a poached egg. Sprinkle each egg with fresh parsley and serve.

tortilla strata

Lookout Point Lakeside Inn

SERVES 12

1 cup	salsa (see recipe on page 127)
1 cup	black beans, rinsed and drained
12	corn tortillas, cut into 1-inch thick strips
1½ cups	Monterey Jack cheese, shredded
1 cup	sour cream
1 cup	milk
6	large eggs, beaten
¼ cup	green onions, sliced
¼ cup	green chilies, diced
1 teaspoon	salt
1 tablespoon	fresh cilantro
1 tablespoon	dried onion flakes

Mix salsa and black beans together. In a greased 9 x 13-inch casserole dish, layer tortilla strips on bottom, bean/salsa mix, and cheese; then tortilla strips, bean/salsa mix, cheese, and tortilla strips on top.

Mix the sour cream, milk, eggs, green onions, green chilies, salt, cilantro, and onion flakes. Pour over tortilla layers. Cover with foil and refrigerate overnight.

Preheat the oven to 375 degrees. Bake covered for 45 minutes. Uncover and sprinkle with more cheese. Bake uncovered for another 15 to 20 minutes, until casserole appears set and cheese is bubbly.

Serve with sour cream and picante sauce.

veggie frittata

Lookout Point Lakeside Inn

SERVES 6 TO 8

Serve with salsa, if desired.

12	large eggs
2 tablespoons	half-and-half
½ teaspoon	salt
⅛ teaspoon	pepper
⅓ cup	Parmesan cheese
3 tablespoons	olive oil
⅓ cup	artichoke hearts, quartered
⅓ cup	diced green onions
⅓ cup	diced red bell pepper
⅓ cup	diced asparagus
¾ cup	Monterey Jack cheese and/or cheddar cheese, grated, divided
1 teaspoon	parsley

Preheat oven to broil. Set rack so pan will be approximately 5 inches below the broiler.

Whisk eggs, half-and-half, salt, pepper, and Parmesan cheese.

Coat the bottom of a 10-inch skillet generously with olive oil. With the heat on high, sauté the vegetables until tender. Pour the eggs over the vegetables. Add half of the grated cheese. Lift edges of the eggs to allow liquid eggs to run underneath; continue to lift the edges until the eggs are firm, but still wet on top. Sprinkle remaining grated cheese on top, and then sprinkle with parsley.

Place the pan under broiler for 4 to 5 minutes until lightly golden brown.

Slide frittata off pan onto cutting surface. Allow to rest for 1 minute, then cut and serve.

Any combination of ingredients may be used. Lookout Point veggie frittatas usually include bell peppers, chopped asparagus, green onions, and artichokes. Any veggies in season work perfectly for this dish!

8 side dishes ————

sidekicks

apple sausage bake

The Beechmont Inn Bed and Breakfast

SERVES 12

⅓ cup	finely chopped onions
	oil, to sauté onions
3 pounds	sausage
2¼ cups	herbed bread stuffing
3	eggs, lightly beaten
¾ cup	milk
1	finely diced large apple
½ teaspoon	dried sage
	salt and pepper, to taste

Preheat the oven to 350 degrees.

Sauté onions in a small amount of olive oil in a skillet over low heat until translucent in color.

In a large bowl, place loose sausage meat. Add onion, stuffing, eggs, milk, apple, and seasonings. Mix together until blended well.

Line a baking sheet with quick release aluminum foil (or use regular foil and spray lightly with oil). Form sausage mixture into round log-like form and position on baking sheet. Bake for 55 minutes.

Slice to serve.

brampton breakfast salsa

Brampton Bed and Breakfast Inn

MAKES APPROXIMATELY 2¾ CUPS

We serve this mild salsa with soft scrambled eggs and corn chips. It is a welcome change from more traditional breakfast fare and a perfect dish during the hot summer months when tomatoes, peppers, and herbs are fresh out of the garden.

1 cup	diced tomatoes (small)*
1 cup	diced green pepper (small)*
½ cup	diced sweet onion (small)*
1 medium	garlic clove, finely minced
1	fresh lime, juice only
2 tablespoons	good extra-virgin olive oil
¼ teaspoon	ground cumin
2 tablespoons	chopped fresh cilantro
	salt, freshly ground black pepper, and hot sauce, to taste

Mix all the ingredients in a medium-size bowl. Cover with plastic wrap and refrigerate for at least an hour, preferably overnight.

*I prefer to dice the tomatoes, peppers, and onion by hand for this dish. It looks much better on the plate.

The salsa is also delicious on top of non-dairy polenta with slices of avocado for a vegan option, or in an omelet with thin slices of ripe avocado, or as a side to any eggs.

brampton granola

Brampton Bed and Breakfast Inn

MAKES ABOUT 7 CUPS

This is our favorite granola.

3 cups	old-fashioned rolled oats (we use gluten-free oats)
1½ cups	nuts (we use half pistachios and half chopped pecans)
1 cup	raw pumpkin seeds, hulled
1 cup	shredded unsweetened coconut
½ teaspoon	ground cinnamon
½ teaspoon	ground cardamom
½ cup	extra-virgin olive oil
¾ cup	pure maple syrup
1½ teaspoons	coarse sea salt
¾ cup	dried apricots, chopped into ¼-inch pieces

Preheat the oven to 300 degrees.

Line a rimmed cookie sheet with a piece of parchment paper.

In a large bowl, combine oats, nuts, pumpkin seeds, shredded coconut, cinnamon, and cardamom.

Mix well with a spoon to distribute evenly.

In a small bowl, whisk together olive oil, maple syrup, and sea salt. Pour over dry ingredients and mix really well.

Spread mixture onto the baking sheet in an even layer, and bake for 45 minutes, stirring every 10 minutes, until golden brown and well toasted.

Transfer granola to a large bowl and add apricots, tossing to combine.

Can be frozen for up to a month. It never lasts that long, though!

corned beef hash

Birchwood Inn

SERVES 4 TO 6

2 pounds	Yukon Gold potatoes, with peel on, diced into 1-inch pieces
	cold water, to cover potatoes
3 tablespoons	unsalted butter
2	large onions, diced
2	bell peppers, any color or a combination of colors
1½ to 2 pounds	lean, cooked corned beef, diced into 1-inch pieces
½ to ¾ cup	milk
½ cup	chopped parsley
¼ cup	chopped chives
	salt and pepper, to taste
4 to 6 tablespoons	canola oil

In a medium saucepan, add the potatoes and enough cold water to cover. Bring to a boil over high heat and then reduce the heat to medium. Cook until just tender.

Melt the butter in a frying pan over medium heat. Add the onions and peppers and sauté until tender, but still crisp.

Drain the potatoes and place in a bowl. Add the onions and peppers. Set the unwashed frying pan aside.

Add the corned beef, milk, parsley, and chives to the potatoes/onions/ peppers, and carefully toss. Season and toss again.

Heat the oil in the frying pan over medium. Add the potato mixture and reduce heat to medium-low. Cook, gently stirring occasionally, until the potatoes are uniformly crispy and lightly browned.

Spoon the hash onto the plates and serve topped with fried eggs.

creamy polenta

The Beechmont Inn Bed and Breakfast

SERVES 8

3 cups	water
1 cup	uncooked regular polenta (I use gluten-free)
⅓ cup	heavy cream
4 tablespoons	butter
8 ounces	grated sharp cheddar cheese
2	eggs, lightly beaten
1 teaspoon	salt
½ teaspoon	freshly ground black pepper
1 tablespoon	chopped parsley

In a large pot, boil the water. Very slowly add the polenta in a steady stream, and stir constantly for several minutes to avoid lumps. Lower the heat and cook the polenta for 30 minutes. It will thicken as it cooks.

Add the heavy cream, butter, grated cheese, and eggs. Stir until blended. Add salt, pepper, and parsley and cook for another 5 minutes. Remove from the heat and serve immediately as a side to eggs and bacon.

Or pour the mixture into a 9 x 13-inch pan and cool. Cover and refrigerate. The polenta can be sliced and used in place of English muffins in Eggs Benedict, or sliced and layered with spinach, tomatoes, and/or cheese and topped with poached eggs for a gluten-free breakfast entrée.

Chopped green onions or scallions can be used to garnish polenta for a bit of zip.

dressed-up taters

Lookout Point Lakeside Inn

SERVES 6

6	medium potatoes
	water, to cook potatoes
½ pound	bacon, cut in pieces
1	large onion, sliced
8 ounces	creamy Italian dressing or
	creamy cucumber dressing
½ cup	Swiss cheese, grated

Peel potatoes and chop into chunks. Boil for 20 minutes. Drain and cool.

Fry bacon and onion together until bacon is crisp and onion is soft.

Preheat the oven to 325 degrees. Spray a 2-quart casserole dish with nonstick spray.

Layer potatoes with bacon and onion mixture. Pour dressing over all. Sprinkle with cheese and bake for an hour or until bubbly.

glazed bacon

Lookout Point Lakeside Inn

SERVES 4

1 pound	bacon, thick-sliced
¼ cup	Dijon mustard
½ cup	brown sugar, lightly packed

Preheat the oven to 375 degrees.

Lay bacon strips on foil-lined rimmed cooking sheet (15 x 10 x 1-inch). Bake until approximately 50% cooked.

Remove from oven and brush each bacon slice with Dijon mustard. Sprinkle with brown sugar. Bake for approximately 15 more minutes or until desired crispness of bacon.

Remove bacon to serving plate and keep warm until serving.

gourmet granola

Chambered Nautilus Bed and Breakfast Inn

MAKES ABOUT 1 GALLON (36 ⅓-CUP SERVINGS)

6 cups	rolled oats
½ cup	chopped pecans
1 cup	chopped walnuts
½ cup	sesame seeds
¾ cup	sunflower seeds, raw
1 cup	dried coconut
½ cup	raisins
½ cup	dried cranberries
½ cup	light oil
½ cup	brown sugar, lightly packed
½ cup	honey
½ cup	maple syrup
¼ cup	molasses
1 tablespoon	vanilla extract
1½ teaspoons	cinnamon
½ teaspoon	salt

Preheat the oven to 350 degrees. On separate sheet pans (cookie sheets with rims work well), oven roast the oats (20 to 30 minutes), pecans and walnuts (8 to 10 minutes), and sesame and sunflower seeds (10 to 15 minutes) until lightly toasted. Cool. In a large bowl, combine all toasted ingredients with coconut, raisins, and dried cranberries. Set aside.

Combine oil, brown sugar, honey, maple syrup, molasses, vanilla, cinnamon, and salt in a saucepan. Stir over low heat until well combined and warm to the touch. (Do not boil!)

Pour the liquid mixture over the dry mixture and mix well. Turn out and flatten onto 2 greased cookie sheet pans and roast for about 30 minutes, stirring every 10 minutes.

Remove from oven, cool, and store in tightly-sealed containers in a cool, dry place.

ham, apple, and goat cheese breakfast toast

The Beechmont Inn Bed and Breakfast

SERVES 8

8 slices	Saloio bread or other dense bread
½ cup	apple butter
½ pound	thinly sliced ham (or prosciutto)
2	Granny Smith apples, peeled, cored, and thinly sliced
8 ounces	goat cheese
	pepper, to taste, optional
	finely chopped parsley, for garnish

Preheat the oven to 375 degrees.

Heat a griddle with a light covering of olive oil and place 8 slices of bread on grill. Toast each side, and place on a baking sheet.

Smooth apple butter on one side of each slice of bread. Place ham on top of apple butter, folding as necessary. Position apple slices on top of ham and then add slices of goat cheese over the apples. Add freshly ground pepper on the cheese, if desired.

Bake in the oven for about 15 minutes or until cheese melts. Remove from oven and sprinkle chopped parsley over the tops of the "toast."

Serve with scrambled eggs.

homemade turkey sausage

Brampton Bed and Breakfast Inn

MAKES APPROXIMATELY 16 PATTIES

2 pounds	ground turkey
½ cup	fresh lovage,* thyme, and sage (mostly lovage, though), chopped
½	large yellow onion, diced
½	large apple, diced
1 teaspoon	kosher salt
	coarsely ground pepper
2	whole cloves garlic, peeled and finely minced
1	large egg
3 tablespoons	good olive oil

In a large bowl, break up the ground turkey into small pieces.

In a food processor, add the herbs, onions, and apples and pulse 4 to 5 times. This mixture should be similar in consistency with the ground meat.

Add herb mixture, salt, pepper, minced garlic, egg, and olive oil to the ground meat.

It's a messy job, but best done wearing disposable plastic gloves. Mix well and form into somewhat loose 3 to 4-ounce patties.

On a medium hot griddle, cook patties on each side until done. The meat needs to be cooked through.

If you wish, you can freeze the sausage patties for up to a month.

*Lovage (Levisticum officinale) is a fragrant perennial plant. The leaves are used to flavor food, especially in South European cuisine. It is a tall (3 to 9-foot) perennial that vaguely resembles its cousin, celery, in flavor.

neapolitan potatoes

The White Oak Inn

SERVES 12

about 12	medium-size red or Yukon Gold potatoes
1 (14-ounce) can	diced tomatoes, liquid drained
3	cloves garlic, finely chopped
½ cup	olive oil
2 tablespoons	dried basil

Spray a 9 x 13-inch pan with nonstick coating and preheat the oven to 375 degrees.

Wash potatoes and dry. Cut each potato in half lengthwise, then in half lengthwise again, then in half through the middle, to give 8 pieces.

Combine tomatoes, garlic, olive oil, and basil. Toss with potatoes.

Pour potatoes into baking dish and cover with foil. Bake for about 45 minutes. Remove the foil and bake for an additional 30 minutes or until potatoes are soft when pierced with a fork.

parmesan heirloom cherry tomatoes

Swiss Woods Bed & Breakfast Inn

SERVES 6

In the summer when cherry tomatoes are plentiful and come in all kinds of colors, this is the perfect side to a savory breakfast. And easy!

2 pints	heirloom cherry tomatoes, red and yellow
½ cup	panko bread crumbs
¼ cup	coarsely grated Parmesan cheese
	cracked black pepper
	sea salt
¼ cup	chopped herbs (any combination of basil, parsley, and chives)
2 tablespoons	oil, to drizzle

Preheat the oven to 375 degrees.

Cut the cherry tomatoes in half lengthwise.

In a bowl, toss the tomatoes with the panko, Parmesan, cracked pepper, salt, and herbs.

Spoon into 6 ramekins. Drizzle with oil.

Bake until a slight brown shows on some of the tomatoes, for about 15 minutes.

Serve hot.

roasted fall root vegetables

Swiss Woods Bed & Breakfast Inn

SERVES 6

Whoever thought you could have veggies for breakfast and love them so? This is more of a process than a recipe, as you can use whatever veggies you have on hand. I love the color of beets and carrots, but mix and match as you please. Baby pattypan squash look especially appealing.

3	red-skinned potatoes
2	carrots, peeled
1	onion, peeled
2	summer squash
1	small zucchini
3 tablespoons	oil
	salt, to taste
	pepper, to taste
	optional add-ins: sweet potatoes, butternut squash, mushrooms, roasted garlic, red beets, parsnips
1 bunch	parsley, chopped, for garnish

Preheat the oven to 375 degrees.

Scrub the potatoes and carrots well. Cut into 1-inch pieces.

Slice the onion crosswise, not in rings. Slice the summer squash and zucchini lengthwise, and then into 2-inch sticks.

Heat the oil in a 10-inch ovenproof skillet.

Add the potatoes and carrots and sauté for several minutes. Add the onion, summer squash, and zucchini. Sprinkle with salt and pepper.

Place the skillet in the oven and roast for 15 minutes or until veggies are golden and they test tender. Some of the edges may begin to blacken. Remove from the oven, and add the chopped parsley.

Serve immediately.

strawberry salsa

The Beechmont Inn Bed and Breakfast

MAKES 3 TO 4 CUPS

6 tablespoons	olive oil
2 tablespoons	white balsamic vinegar
½ teaspoon	salt
1 pint	fresh strawberries, coarsely chopped
4	green onions, chopped
2 pints	cherry tomatoes, chopped
⅓ cup	chopped fresh cilantro (use up to ½ cup if you like cilantro)

In a large bowl, whisk together olive oil, vinegar, and salt.

Add strawberries, onions, tomatoes, and cilantro, and toss.

Chill for at least an hour before serving.

Serve about ¼ cup on the side with eggs or serve with corn chips.

Strawberry salsa is a wonderful accompaniment to egg dishes.

sweet potato hash

The Beechmont Inn Bed and Breakfast

SERVES 8

2	medium sweet potatoes, peeled, diced in ½-inch cubes (about 1½ pounds)
	water, to cook the sweet potatoes
2 tablespoons	olive oil
1 pound	ground sausage
½ cup	diced celery
½	chopped onion
1	Granny Smith apple, peeled, cored, and diced
½ teaspoon	ground sage
	salt and freshly ground pepper

In a saucepan, boil enough water to cover diced sweet potatoes. Drop the sweet potatoes into the water and cook until barely tender, for about 4 to 5 minutes.

In a large skillet, heat olive oil and add sausage. Brown until thoroughly cooked, for about 10 minutes. Remove sausage with a slotted spoon and drain on paper towels to remove grease.

Add celery and onion to same skillet and cook until just tender; add apples. Cook for another 3 to 4 minutes. Add sweet potatoes and sausage to mixture and season with sage, and salt and pepper, to taste.

to serve
Use as a side to scrambled eggs, or poach or fry eggs and place on top of hash.

8 sauces, toppings, and condiments

——oh, my!

arkansas chocolate gravy

Lookout Point Lakeside Inn

SERVES 6

This surprisingly tasty breakfast treat is an old southern country recipe from my son-in-law's family. What an extraordinary way for chocolate lovers to begin their day!

1 stick	butter
4 tablespoons	cocoa
4 tablespoons	flour
¾ cup	sugar
2 cups	milk

Melt the butter in a small saucepan. Add the cocoa and flour, whisking until well combined, and then stir in the sugar and milk. Cook over medium heat until thickened, whisking constantly. Serve over biscuits and enjoy every bite.

blueberry sauce

Birchwood Inn

SERVES 12

2 cups	blueberries, fresh or frozen (preferably, the small wild blueberries)
½ cup	sugar
	juice of ½ lemon, freshly squeezed
1 tablespoon	cornstarch
1½ tablespoons	orange juice

Combine the blueberries, sugar, and lemon juice in a medium-size saucepan.

Cook over medium heat until the sugar is dissolved and the mixture begins to bubble.

Mix the cornstarch and orange juice. Add this mixture to the blueberries and stir. Continue cooking, stirring frequently, until the sauce is thickened.

bourbon pecan syrup

Birchwood Inn

SERVES 12

1 cup	maple syrup
¼ to ⅓ cup	bourbon
¾ cup	pecans, lightly toasted

In a small saucepan, mix the maple syrup and bourbon.

Cook over medium heat until the syrup begins to bubble.

Add the pecans just before serving.

Pour over French toast, pancakes, or ice cream.

brampton simple syrups

Brampton Bed and Breakfast Inn

MAKES 1½ CUPS

A tablespoon or two of a flavored simple syrup can really add a bit of zing to any fruit dish. We use the mint syrup on a pineapple and kiwi fruit cup and decorate it with a mint leaf. The orange syrup replaces the Grand Marnier in the trifle recipe when we make it without alcohol. A tablespoon or two of lemon syrup added to sliced strawberries is wonderful served over Matthew's biscuits. The ginger syrup is amazing on a tropical fruit salad with mango, pineapple, star fruit, and papaya.

for the basic recipe

1 cup	granulated sugar
1 cup	water

Mix both ingredients in a small saucepan and bring to a quick boil over high heat. Remove from heat immediately. Stir to make sure sugar is completely dissolved.

While the sugar water is still hot, add one of the following and steep until cool:
The zest of 2 well-scrubbed lemons;
The zest of 2 well-scrubbed oranges;
1 inch of grated, fresh, peeled gingerroot;
A handful of chopped mint leaves; or
You can experiment with a combination of herbs of your choice.

When the syrup is cold, strain it into a jar fitted with an airtight screw top. Discard the solids.

The simple syrups can be kept in the refrigerator for up to 2 weeks.

caramel sauce

The Beechmont Inn Bed and Breakfast

MAKES 4 CUPS

½ pound	butter
2¼ cups	brown sugar, lightly packed
1 pint	heavy cream
1 teaspoon	vanilla

Place the butter and brown sugar in a saucepan and cook over medium heat. As the butter and brown sugar melt, whisk until thoroughly blended. Remove from heat and add the heavy cream slowly so it doesn't bubble over. Blend with the whisk, and then add the vanilla. Stir. Be careful! The caramel is very hot!

This is a great topping for French toast, pancakes, and ice cream. Dip apple slices into the sauce or drizzle over your favorite baked goods. It can even be stirred into morning coffee or latte.

The sauce can be stored in a glass jar and refrigerated for a week. To reheat, place the sauce in a saucepan over low heat until warmed.

cilantro butter

The William Henry Miller Inn

MAKES ¼ CUP

1 stick	unsalted butter, softened to room temperature
1 teaspoon	salt
2 tablespoons	cilantro leaves, chopped

Mix the butter, salt, and cilantro with a hand mixer on low.

Spoon onto a piece of plastic wrap and form into a log. Refrigerate for an hour. When ready to serve, slice into rounds. This can be prepared ahead and frozen for later use.

cinnamon syrup

Chambered Nautilus Bed and Breakfast Inn

MAKES 1⅓ CUPS

1 cup	sugar
½ cup	light corn syrup
¼ cup	water
¼ teaspoon	ground cinnamon (use a touch more for stronger flavor)
½ cup	whipping cream

In a small saucepan, stir together the sugar, corn syrup, water, and cinnamon. Stirring constantly, bring to a boil over a moderate heat and boil for 2 minutes. Remove from heat. Stir in the cream. Cool for at least 30 minutes. Syrup will thicken as it cools.

The syrup may be refrigerated for a week or two. Serve warm or at room temperature on French toast, waffles, or pancakes.

crème fraîche

Lookout Point Lakeside Inn

MAKES 1¼ CUPS

1 cup	sour cream
⅛ cup	heavy cream
⅛ cup	brown sugar
½ teaspoon	vanilla

Great on fruit and parfaits.

Mix ingredients together. Will keep up to 2 weeks in refrigerator.

A dollop of crème fraîche on a small bowl of berries, atop a slice of watermelon, or on poached pears provides a delicious finishing touch.

hot water hollandaise

Swiss Woods Bed & Breakfast Inn

MAKES 1¼ CUPS OR 10 SERVINGS

While searching for the perfect no-fail hollandaise recipe to teach to others, I came across this method, and I've never looked back. It is so easy, the result so silky smooth, creamy, and not runny—all but foolproof. Serve over poached salmon or allow to cool and fold into deviled egg filling.

	water for a double boiler
2	egg yolks
1 tablespoon	hot water
1 tablespoon	lemon juice
	pinch of salt
1 cup	cold, unsalted butter, cut into pieces
	pepper, to taste

In a double boiler, bring the water to a slow simmer. Whisk the egg yolks, hot water, lemon juice, and salt together. Put the top part of the double boiler over the simmering water and whisk. As the egg yolks warm, add 1 or 2 pieces of the cold butter and whisk until almost melted; then add another 2 pieces of butter, continuing to do so until all the butter is melted into the egg mixture and the whole mixture is creamy and opaque. With a spoon, taste to make sure the flavor is where you want it. Add salt and pepper, to taste. If you need more lemon, you can add a bit of lemon zest. It will be the consistency of heavy cream. Remove from the top of the double boiler and serve over Eggs Benedict or salmon filets.

Leftovers of this sauce will hold in a container in the refrigerator. It will solidify into what feels like a soft butter. To serve, gently warm over hot water and serve.

lemon curd

The White Oak Inn

MAKES 2 CUPS

3	eggs, beaten
1 cup	sugar
½ cup	fresh lemon juice
1 tablespoon	grated lemon rind
¼ cup	butter

In a medium-size heavy saucepan, combine all of the ingredients.

Cook on a low heat, stirring constantly, until thickened, for about 5 minutes of simmering.

Let cool. Store in a covered jar in the refrigerator.

Use within 2 weeks.

vanilla sauce

Swiss Woods Bed & Breakfast Inn

MAKES 1½ CUPS

Such a Plain Jane name for such an amazingly flavorful and versatile sauce. My childhood Christmas dinners always included a steamed plum pudding topped with this vanilla sauce. It was the crowning glory we all looked forward to every year. As an adult it dawned on me that I didn't have to wait until Christmas. Surely there was something else I could put it on during the year. Today it tops the likes of sticky bun bread pudding or bourbon pumpkin bread pudding, much to everyone's delight!

1 cup	water
⅔ cup	sugar
1 tablespoon	cornstarch
	pinch of salt
2 tablespoons	butter
2 teaspoons	vanilla

Bring water to a boil.

In a small bowl, combine the sugar, cornstarch, and salt.

Whisk the sugar/cornstarch mixture into the hot water.

Bring to a full boil, stirring constantly until thick.

Remove from the heat.

Add the butter and whisk until melted and incorporated.

Stir in the vanilla.

Serve warm over bread pudding.

8 sweet treats ———

finish your
breakfast, *first*

a peach of a blueberry pie

The William Henry Miller Inn

SERVES 8

1½ cups	flour
2 teaspoons	granulated sugar
1 teaspoon	salt
½ cup	vegetable oil
2 tablespoons	milk
½ cup	powdered sugar
⅓ cup	flour
2 cups	fresh blueberries
2 cups	fresh peaches, peeled and sliced
¾ cup	flour
½ cup	brown sugar, firmly packed
½ teaspoon	cinnamon
⅓ cup	butter, softened

Preheat the oven to 375 degrees.

Combine 1½ cups flour, granulated sugar, salt, oil, and milk, forming a soft pastry dough. Place dough evenly in a 9-inch pie pan.

Combine the powdered sugar, ⅓ cup flour, and fruit. Spoon over the pastry.

Combine ¾ cup flour, brown sugar, and cinnamon. Cut in the butter until crumbly. Spread over the fruit.

Bake for 45 minutes until the topping is golden brown.

almond cake with raspberry coulis

The White Oak Inn

SERVES 10 TO 12

for the cake

1 cup	butter
2 cups	sugar
2	eggs
2 cups	flour
½ cup	ground almonds
1½ teaspoons	baking powder
¼ teaspoon	salt
2 teaspoons	almond extract
1 cup	sour cream
¼ cup	blanched and sliced or slivered almonds
3 tablespoons	powdered sugar

for the raspberry coulis

1 (12-ounce) bag	frozen raspberries, thawed
¾ cup	sugar

Preheat the oven to 325 degrees.

Grease and flour a 9-inch or 10-inch round springform pan.

Cream butter and gradually beat in sugar. Beat in eggs, one at a time. In a separate bowl, combine flour, ground almonds, baking powder, and salt. Gently fold into the creamed mixture. Stir in the almond extract and sour cream. Batter will be very thick. Spoon the batter into the prepared cake pan. Level the top and sprinkle the almonds evenly over the top. Bake for about 45 minutes, or until a tester inserted in the center comes out clean. Allow to cool and remove from the pan. Sieve powdered sugar over the top.

to make the coulis

Combine raspberries and sugar in a blender or food processor and process on low until combined.

To serve, slice cake into 10 or 12 slices. Spoon about 2 tablespoons of raspberry sauce into a pool on the plate. Garnish with fresh mint if available.

almond ginger cookies

The Beechmont Inn Bed and Breakfast

MAKES 2 DOZEN LARGE COOKIES

2 cups	flour
1 teaspoon	salt
2 teaspoons	baking soda
1 teaspoon each	cinnamon and ginger
½ teaspoon	allspice
½ teaspoon	nutmeg
½ teaspoon	cloves
¾ cup	oil
1 cup	sugar
1	egg
4 tablespoons	molasses
1 teaspoon	vanilla
½ cup	sliced almonds

Preheat the oven to 350 degrees.

Sift together the flour, salt, baking soda, and spices. Set aside.

Beat together the oil and sugar until well blended. Add the egg, molasses, and vanilla. Blend. Stir in the dry ingredients and then the almonds. Dough will be fairly stiff.

Drop by tablespoons onto a greased cookie sheet. Bake for 10 minutes. Remove the cookies from the baking sheet and cool. Store in an airtight container with a slice of bread to preserve chewy texture.

applesauce jumbles

The Beechmont Inn Bed and Breakfast

MAKES 3 TO 4 DOZEN

2¾ cups	flour
1 teaspoon	cinnamon
1 teaspoon	salt
½ teaspoon	baking soda
¼ teaspoon	cloves
1½ cups	packed brown sugar
½ cup	unsalted butter, at room temperature
2	eggs
1 teaspoon	vanilla extract
¾ cup	unsweetened applesauce
2 cups	chocolate chips

Preheat the oven to 375 degrees. Grease a baking sheet or line with a Silpat.

In a small bowl, combine the flour, cinnamon, salt, baking soda, and cloves. Use a whisk to blend.

In a large mixing bowl, beat together the brown sugar and butter until well mixed. Add the eggs one at a time and blend. Add the vanilla and applesauce, and then the flour mixture. Mix. Then fold in the chocolate chips.

Drop by rounded tablespoons onto baking sheet. Bake for 10 minutes. Remove the cookies from sheet and cool. Ice the cookies with brown buster glaze (also known as "brown butter glaze").

for the brown buster glaze

⅓ cup	butter
2 cups	confectioners' sugar
1½ teaspoons	vanilla
2 to 4 tablespoons	hot water

Melt the butter in a small saucepan over low heat until golden brown. Remove from heat. Blend the confectioners' sugar and vanilla into butter. Stir in the hot water until you reach a spreading consistency. Ice the cooled cookies.

apricot chocolate crumb squares

The White Oak Inn

MAKES 24 (2-INCH) SQUARES

1 cup	butter or margarine, softened
½ cup	brown sugar, lightly packed
2 cups	flour
¼ teaspoon	salt
1 can	sweetened condensed milk
2 cups	semisweet chocolate chips, divided
¾ cup	apricot preserves

Preheat the oven to 350 degrees. Grease a 9 x 13-inch pan.

Cream the butter and brown sugar together. Fold in the flour and salt. Press 1¾ cups of this mixture into the prepared pan. Reserve the rest for the top.

Bake for about 10 minutes, until the edges are starting to brown.

Combine the sweetened condensed milk and 1 cup of the chocolate chips in a microwave-safe bowl. Microwave on high setting for 1 minute. Stir until the chocolate is melted. Spread this mixture over the baked crust.

Warm the apricot preserves in the microwave for about 15 seconds and then randomly drop by teaspoons over the chocolate mix. Sprinkle the remaining crumb mixture and chocolate chips over top.

Bake for about 25 minutes or until crumbs are golden and top is set. Cool and cut into squares.

aunt norma's brownies

Birchwood Inn

SERVES 12

4 ounces	unsweetened chocolate
½ pound	unsalted butter
4	eggs
2 cups	sugar
2 teaspoons	vanilla
1½ cups	all-purpose flour
1 teaspoon	baking powder
1 teaspoon	salt
1 cup	walnuts, roughly chopped
1 cup	raisins

Preheat the oven to 350 degrees.

Grease a 9 x 13-inch pan.

In a microwave-safe bowl, melt the chocolate and butter slowly in the microwave, stirring every 30 seconds until completely melted.

Pour the chocolate/butter mixture into the bowl of an electric mixer.

Add the eggs, sugar, and vanilla and blend.

Mix together the flour, baking powder, and salt.

Add the dry ingredients to the egg mixture and combine well.

Add the walnuts and raisins.

Bake for 30 to 35 minutes until cakey on the edges and firm, but still oozy and fudgy in the middle.

Cool. Cover with plastic wrap and refrigerate for an hour.

Cut the brownies into squares when ready to serve.

aunt norma's sour cream coffee cake

Birchwood Inn

SERVES 12

for the cake

¾ pound	unsalted butter, softened
1½ cups	sugar
3	eggs
1½ teaspoons	vanilla
2 cups minus 1 tablespoon	all-purpose flour
1½ teaspoons	baking powder
1⅛ teaspoons	baking soda
	pinch of salt
1 cup plus 1 tablespoon	sour cream

for the streusel topping

½ cup	walnuts
½ cup	packed brown sugar
1½ teaspoons	cinnamon

Preheat the oven to 375 degrees.

Grease and flour a 10-inch springform pan.

Beat the butter and sugar together. Add the eggs and vanilla and mix thoroughly.

Mix together the flour, baking powder, baking soda, and salt. Add half of the flour mixture. Blend. Then add half of the sour cream to the batter. Combine well. Add the rest of the flour and then the sour cream to the batter. Stir well.

For the streusel, in a separate bowl, mix together the walnuts, brown sugar, and cinnamon for topping.

Pour the batter into the prepared pan. Sprinkle the streusel topping on top of the batter. Bake for 45 minutes or until cake tester comes out clean.

Cool. Invert onto a plate. Invert that plate onto the serving plate.

brown betty

Brampton Bed and Breakfast Inn

SERVES 6

8 tablespoons	unsalted butter, melted (1 stick)
1½ tablespoons	granulated sugar
6 slices	thin white sandwich bread, crusts removed
4	large, somewhat firm apples (a mixture of Golden Delicious and Granny Smith works well), peeled, cored, and diced into ½-inch pieces (4 cups)
¼ to ½ cup	packed light brown sugar, more if apples are very tart
½ teaspoon	ground cinnamon
¼ teaspoon	freshly grated nutmeg
½ cup	fresh bread crumbs (1 slice of white bread, finely chopped)

Preheat the oven to 325 degrees. Spray six (4-inch) round ramekin dishes with cooking spray.

With a pastry brush, coat each dish with the melted butter and sprinkle each with ¼ teaspoon granulated sugar. Set aside.

With a rolling pin, flatten each piece of bread. Lightly brush each side with melted butter. Gently fit each piece of bread into a prepared dish.

In a medium-size bowl, stir together the apples, brown sugar, cinnamon, and grated nutmeg. Toss to coat. Add the fresh bread crumbs and the rest of the melted butter and mix to distribute evenly. Fill each bread cup with the apple mixture. Use all of the apple mixture, heaping if necessary.

Set the ramekins on a rimmed cookie sheet and cover with a large piece of aluminum foil. Bake for 30 minutes. Remove the foil and continue baking until the apples are tender, for about 10 to 20 minutes more. The baking time depends on the apples used. They should be soft when done. Let stand for 15 minutes before gently removing from dishes.

Serve warm with vanilla or maple custard (see recipe on page 186) on the side.

buttermilk pie

The Beechmont Inn Bed and Breakfast

SERVES 6 TO 8

1	(9-inch) pie crust
1¼ cups	sugar
3 tablespoons	flour
4	eggs, lightly beaten
¼ cup	butter, melted
1 cup	buttermilk
	zest of 1 lemon
1 tablespoon	fresh lemon juice
1 teaspoon	vanilla extract
2 teaspoons	freshly grated nutmeg

Preheat the oven to 425 degrees.

Make pie crust (see pastry dough recipe on page 174) or use a premade crust of your choice.

Combine the sugar and flour in a medium bowl and whisk to blend. Using a hand mixer, add the beaten eggs and mix well. Stir in the melted butter and buttermilk. Add the lemon zest, lemon juice, vanilla, and nutmeg. Mix on low until blended. Pour into the pie shell.

Place in the center of the oven and bake for 15 minutes. Lower the temperature to 350 degrees and bake for another 40 minutes or until the filling is set. It will be light golden brown in color.

Cool to room temperature and serve. The pie will keep in the refrigerator, if preferred. Bring to room temperature to serve.

The number of servings depends on the size of slices.

cherry crumble

The White Oak Inn

SERVES 8 TO 10

for the topping

1 cup	butter or margarine
2 cups	flour
1½ cups	brown sugar, lightly packed
1 cup	quick oats

for the filling

5 cups	pitted cherries, fresh or frozen
1 cup	sugar
¼ cup	cornstarch
1 teaspoon	vanilla extract
½ teaspoon	almond extract
½ teaspoon	salt

Preheat the oven to 350 degrees and grease a 9 x 13-inch baking dish or 10 individual ramekins.

to make the topping

Melt butter or margarine. Combine the flour, brown sugar, and oatmeal together and stir in the melted butter with a fork. Mixture should be crumbly.

to make the filling

Combine the cherries, sugar, cornstarch, vanilla, almond extract, and salt and spoon into the prepared baking dish(es).

Sprinkle the topping over the filling. Bake for about 40 to 45 minutes for a 9 x 13-inch dish or 30 minutes for ramekins, or until crumble topping is golden brown and the fruit juice is bubbling at the edges.

Note: For a quick version, you can substitute 2 cans of cherry pie filling for the filling ingredients. This recipe works with any fruit pie filling—apple, peach, or raspberry.

chocolate cream cheese bars

The William Henry Miller Inn

MAKES 48 BARS

½ cup	butter, at room temperature
4 ounces	cream cheese, at room temperature
1 cup	sugar
3	eggs
2 teaspoons	vanilla
1 cup	flour
6 tablespoons	cocoa
½ teaspoon	baking soda
1 cup	chocolate chips

Preheat the oven to 350 degrees.

In a medium bowl, use an electric mixer to beat together the butter and cream cheese until well blended. Add the sugar, eggs, and vanilla and beat until blended.

In a separate bowl, use a whisk to blend the flour, cocoa, and baking soda. Add the flour mixture to the cream cheese mixture and blend. Stir chocolate chips into the batter with a rubber spatula.

Spread the batter into a greased 9 x 13-inch baking dish and bake for about 25 minutes or until cake tester comes out clean. Do not overbake. Allow to cool in the pan.

for the sour cream chocolate frosting

½ cup	semisweet chocolate chips
⅓ cup	sour cream

Place the chocolate chips in a bowl and melt over a saucepan filled with hot, not boiling, water. Remove from heat and add the sour cream in three additions, stirring well after each addition. This will produce a thin layer of frosting for the bars.

When the bars are cool, spread with frosting.

coconut macaroons

Brampton Bed and Breakfast Inn

MAKES ABOUT 4 DOZEN

⅓ cup	unsalted butter, at room temperature
3 ounces	cream cheese, at room temperature
¾ cup	sugar
1	large egg yolk
2 teaspoons	pure almond extract
2 teaspoons	orange juice
1¼ cups	unbleached flour
2 teaspoons	baking powder
½ teaspoon	salt
4 cups	flaked, sweet coconut

Preheat the oven to 325 degrees.

Cream the butter, cream cheese, and sugar in a large mixing bowl until light and fluffy.

Add the egg yolk, almond extract, and orange juice and beat well.

Combine the flour, baking powder, and salt. Gradually add the flour mixture to the creamed mixture. Stir in 3 cups of coconut. Cover tightly and chill for 1 hour until firm.

Shape the dough into 1½-inch balls (we use a small ice cream scoop to do this) and roll in remaining coconut flakes.

Place the dough balls 1½ inches apart on a cookie sheet lined with a Silpat or parchment paper.

Bake for 12 to 15 minutes until barely golden.

Remove from the oven and cool for 5 minutes before transferring the macaroons to a cooling rack. When completely cooled, store in an airtight container.

cookie dough brownies

Lookout Point Lakeside Inn

SERVES 18

for the brownies

2 cups	granulated sugar
1½ cups	flour
½ cup	cocoa
½ teaspoon	salt
1 cup	vegetable oil
4	eggs
2 teaspoons	vanilla

for the filling

½ cup	butter
½ cup	brown sugar, lightly packed
¼ cup	sugar
2 tablespoons	milk
1 teaspoon	vanilla
1 cup	flour

for the glaze frosting

1 cup	chocolate chips
1 tablespoon	butter

to make the brownies

Preheat the oven to 350 degrees. In a mixing bowl, combine the granulated sugar, flour, cocoa, and salt. Add the oil, eggs, and vanilla. Beat at medium speed for 3 minutes. Pour into a greased 9 x 13-inch pan. Bake for 30 minutes. Cool completely.

to make the filling

Cream the butter and sugars in a mixing bowl. Add the milk and vanilla and mix well. Beat in the flour. Spread over the cooled brownies. Chill until firm.

to make the glaze

Melt the chocolate chips and butter in a saucepan. Spread over the filling.

cranberry–orange angel food cake

Brampton Bed and Breakfast Inn

MAKES 12 SLICES

1½ cups	egg whites (about 1 dozen egg whites), at room temperature
1¼ teaspoons	cream of tartar
½ teaspoon	salt
1½ cups	sugar, divided
1 cup	sifted unbleached flour
⅛ cup	cornstarch
1 teaspoon	pure vanilla extract
2 teaspoons	pure orange extract
	zest of 2 oranges
1 cup	Craisins, chopped into small pieces
	powdered sugar, for garnish

Preheat the oven to 375 degrees.

Whip the egg whites in the bowl of a stand-up mixer with the whisk attachment until foamy. Add the cream of tartar and salt and keep whipping until soft peaks form. With the mixer running, gradually add 1 cup of the sugar and continue whipping until the egg whites are stiff and the sugar has dissolved. This will take about another 45 seconds.

Sift the remaining ½ cup sugar with the flour and cornstarch 3 times. Carefully fold the flour into the egg whites. You want to do this very gently. Towards the end, add the vanilla and orange extracts, orange zest, and chopped Craisins until the Craisins are evenly distributed. Don't overmix.

Carefully spoon the batter into an ungreased angel food cake pan. Bake for 30 to 35 minutes until light brown on top.

Cool the cake in the pan by putting it upside down on your counter if your pan has "feet." If not, put the pan upside down around the neck of a bottle or a funnel until the pan cools to room temperature. Run a long, sharp knife blade between the cake and the pan and loosen the cake out onto a plate. Let cool completely. Sprinkle with powdered sugar before cutting into slices with a serrated knife or angel food cake cutter.

italian wedding cookies

The William Henry Miller Inn

MAKES ABOUT 4 DOZEN

3 cups	flour
½ teaspoon	salt
½ cup	sugar
3 teaspoons	baking powder
3 tablespoons	butter
3	eggs
½ cup	milk
1 teaspoon	lemon extract

Preheat the oven to 375 degrees.

Mix the dry ingredients. Add the rest of the ingredients and mix well.

When the dough is smooth, take small amounts and roll into balls (flour your hands first as the dough is very sticky).

Place the balls on a parchment paper-lined cookie sheet and bake for 12 to 15 minutes. Cool the cookies before glazing.

for the glaze

1 cup	confectioners' sugar
2 tablespoons	half-and-half
1 teaspoon	fresh lemon juice

Combine and drizzle over the cookies.

key lime pie

Birchwood Inn

SERVES 7

4	egg yolks
5 teaspoons	grated lime zest, divided
1 (14-ounce) can	sweetened condensed milk
½ cup	fresh lime juice (3 to 4 limes or 15 key limes)
1¼ cups	graham cracker crumbs
3 tablespoons	sugar
5 tablespoons	unsalted butter, melted

for the filling

Beat the egg yolks and 4 teaspoons of the lime zest together for about 2 to 3 minutes, until the mixture is slightly green. Beat in the sweetened condensed milk and lime juice.

Set the filling aside at room temperature until it thickens, for about 10 minutes.

for the pie crust

Preheat the oven to 325 degrees.

In a separate bowl, mix the graham cracker crumbs and sugar together. Add the melted butter and mix, using a fork, until well blended.

Grease a 9-inch pie plate with cooking spray. Spoon the graham mixture into the pie plate. Spread evenly in the bottom and up the sides. Press the mixture down firmly, using your fingers, the back of a large spoon, or the bottom of a glass.

Bake for 15 to 20 minutes, until the crust is golden brown. Remove the pie plate from the oven and let cool to room temperature.

to make the pie

Spoon the thickened filling into the pie crust. Bake for 15 to 20 minutes, until the filling is set but still jiggles in the center.

Remove the pie from the oven and let cool to room temperature on a wire rack. Refrigerate until the pie is well chilled, for about 3 hours.

Serve as is, sprinkling the remaining zest on the top, or top with whipped cream, sprinkled with the zest.

kristie's chocolate chip oatmeal cookies

Lookout Point Lakeside Inn

SERVES 12 (OR LESS, DEPENDING ON HOW MANY COOKIE
MONSTERS ARE IN THE HOUSE)

1 cup	butter
1 cup	brown sugar, lightly packed
1 cup	sugar
2	large eggs
1 teaspoon	vanilla
2 cups	flour
1 teaspoon	baking powder
½ teaspoon	baking soda
1 teaspoon	salt (I prefer kosher salt for baking)
2½ cups	oatmeal
1 cup	chocolate chips
½ cup	pecans, chopped

Preheat the oven to 375 degrees.

Cream the butter and sugars together. Add the eggs and vanilla.

In a separate bowl, whisk the flour, baking powder, baking soda, and salt.
Add to the butter mixture and beat until mixed. Add the oatmeal. Stir in
the chocolate chips and pecans.

Drop by spoonfuls onto a parchment paper-lined baking sheet. Bake for 10
to 12 minutes—don't overbake.

Note: This recipe makes a great cookie cake! Simply spread all of the batter
onto a greased rimmed pizza pan and bake for approximately 18 minutes
or until lightly golden brown.

lemon butter cookies

The William Henry Miller Inn

MAKES 3 TO 4 DOZEN

This dough freezes well, then can be thawed for later use.

½ cup	granulated sugar, plus more for shaping cookies
½ cup	powdered sugar
¾ cup	butter, softened
¼ cup	oil
1 tablespoon	lemon zest
1 tablespoon	lemon juice
1	egg
2½ cups	flour
½ teaspoon	cream of tartar
½ teaspoon	baking soda
¼ teaspoon	salt

In a large bowl, beat the sugars, butter, and oil until light and fluffy.

Add the lemon zest, lemon juice, and egg. Stir in the remaining ingredients, mixing well.

Cover with plastic wrap and refrigerate for 1 hour for easier handling.

Preheat the oven to 350 degrees.

Make the dough into 1-inch balls. Roll in the additional granulated sugar. Place 2 inches apart on ungreased cookie sheets. Bake for 7 to 12 minutes until set.

Immediately remove the cookies from the cookie sheet.

lemon pound cake

The William Henry Miller Inn

SERVES 16

for the cake

2½ cups	all-purpose flour
1½ cups	sugar
3 teaspoons	baking powder
½ teaspoon	salt
¾ cup	apricot nectar or orange juice
¾ cup	oil
2 teaspoons	lemon extract
4	eggs

for the glaze

1½ cups	powdered sugar
½ cup	lemon juice

Preheat the oven to 325 degrees.

Generously grease and flour a 12-cup Bundt pan.

In a large bowl, combine all of the cake ingredients. Blend at low speed until moistened. Beat for 3 minutes at medium speed. Pour the batter into the greased and floured pan.

Bake for 40 to 50 minutes or until tester comes out clean.

Remove the cake from the oven. With a long-tined fork, poke deep holes in the cake every inch.

In a small bowl, blend the glaze ingredients until smooth. Spoon half of the glaze over the hot cake in the pan.

Let the cake stand upright in pan for 10 minutes. Invert the cake onto a serving plate. Spoon the remaining glaze over the cake. Allow to cool completely.

macarthur park's
san francisco bay mud pie

Birchwood Inn

SERVES 8

½ pound	chocolate chip cookies, homemade if possible
5 tablespoons	unsalted butter, softened
1½ pints	premium dark chocolate ice cream
1½ pints	premium coffee ice cream
2 tablespoons	liquid espresso coffee, very black and very strong
¼ cup	coffee liqueur (Kahlua)
2 ounces	unsweetened baking chocolate, grated
1 tablespoon	unsalted butter
½ cup	boiling water
1 cup	granulated sugar
⅛ cup	corn syrup
1 teaspoon	pure vanilla extract
	sweetened whipped cream, for garnish

for the pie crust

Cool a 10-inch pie plate in the freezer.

Break the cookies into coarse chunks and place them in a food processor. Add the softened butter. Use the "pulse" option in one-second bursts, checking between each burst until the cookies and butter have formed a coarse and crumbly paste (not smooth), for about 10 to 15 seconds.

Remove the pie plate from the freezer and line it with the butter-cookie mixture using your fingers to pat it down evenly. Return the pie plate to the freezer.

for the filling

Soften both ice creams at room temperature until soft enough to handle.

Spoon the ice cream into a bowl for an electric mixer. Run the mixer at low speed, gradually increasing the speed to medium, and continue mixing until the ice creams are well melted, thoroughly mixed, and creamy/frothy. Stop the mixer and add the liquid espresso and the coffee liqueur.

Run the mixer again long enough to completely mix in the new ingredients.

Immediately spoon the filling into the ice-cold pie shell, filling the shell to the brim.

for the filling (con't)

Cover the pie loosely with aluminum foil and return the pie to the freezer, making sure that it is absolutely level.

Freeze the pie long enough to freeze, not necessarily rock-hard, but firm enough so that it can be cut into wedges without melting—usually for 2 to 3 hours.

for the fudge topping

You can use any fudge topping, but if you have time, this is the ultimate.

Set up a double boiler with the water gently bubbling and actually touching the bottom of the top saucepan.

Melt the grated baking chocolate with the butter in the top saucepan, stirring continuously.

At the same time, in a separate pan or kettle, heat the water to boiling.

As soon as the chocolate is melted, add the boiling water, sugar, and corn syrup, vigorously working them together.

Lift the pan out of the double boiler, quickly dry its bottom, and place it on direct heat, gently bringing the contents up to the boiling point, still stirring continuously. Let the fudge sauce gently bubble, still stirring it fairly often, uncovered for 6 minutes.

Take the saucepan off the heat and let the fudge sauce cool for 5 minutes. Stir in the vanilla extract.

The fudge sauce at this point should be fairly thick but still thin enough to be spreadable with a lightly buttered rubber spatula. If it is too thick, you can thin it with a dash or two more of corn syrup. Hold the fudge sauce, covered, in the saucepan to be reheated later.

for serving

Put the serving plates in the freezer for 10 minutes until they are ice-cold.

Gently reheat the fudge sauce in the double boiler.

When the fudge sauce is quite hot and thin enough to be spoonable, this is the time to serve your pie.

Cut the pie into wedges. Place each wedge on an ice-cold plate. Spoon a generous amount of the hot fudge sauce on top of each wedge. Garnish with whipped cream.

pastry dough

Birchwood Inn

MAKES 2 PIE CRUSTS

2 cups	all-purpose flour, preferably chilled, plus more for the rolling process
⅔ teaspoon	salt
½ pound	unsalted butter, very cold and cut into large cubes
2	egg yolks, cold
	ice water

Add the flour and salt to a food processor fitted with a steel blade. Process for a second or two to mix.

Drop the cold butter into the food processor and process until the butter is incorporated (for about 15 seconds) and the mixture resembles coarse meal.

In a 1-cup liquid measuring cup, lightly beat the egg yolks with a fork. Add enough ice water to the egg yolks to yield ½ cup of liquid.

Start the food processor and pour the egg/water mixture into the processor in a steady stream.

When the dough just begins to form a ball (you may need to add a few more drops of ice water), in about 6 seconds, stop the processor.

Transfer the dough onto a lightly floured pastry board, or even better, a marble board.

Knead the dough for a couple of minutes; cut in half, making 2 balls.

Wrap each ball of dough in wax paper covered with plastic wrap, and refrigerate or freeze (in a freezer bag) until ready to use.

peach clafouti

The Beechmont Inn Bed and Breakfast

SERVES 8

A clafouti is a traditional French dessert often made with cherries. Blueberries, apples, pears, and peaches are also great in this dish.

2	large peaches, peeled and sliced
½ teaspoon	ginger
½ teaspoon	cinnamon
¾ cup	heavy cream
¾ cup	half-and-half
1 teaspoon	vanilla extract
4	large eggs
½ cup	sugar
½ cup	flour, sifted

Preheat the oven to 375 degrees. Butter or spray a tart pan or 10-inch pie plate. Place the peaches on the bottom of the baking dish.

Sprinkle ginger and cinnamon over the peaches. If you use fruit other than peaches, adjust the seasonings, using nutmeg and cinnamon with apples, for example.

Combine the heavy cream and half-and-half in saucepan. Heat over medium setting until the mixture almost boils. Remove from the heat. Stir in the vanilla. Let the cream mixture cool.

In medium-size bowl, lightly beat the eggs. Gradually add the sugar until blended. Add the flour a little at a time until thoroughly incorporated.

Add the cream mixture to the eggs and sugar. Whisk constantly, as you slowly add the cream.

Pour the custard over the peaches and place the dish in the oven. Bake for 30 to 40 minutes (time will vary depending upon how shallow the baking dish is) or until the custard is set. The custard will puff up and then settle, which is normal. Let it cool for at least 15 to 20 minutes and then serve.

pecan pie

Lookout Point Lakeside Inn

MAKES 1 PIE

1	unbaked pie shell
1 cup	pecans, whole or broken
3	eggs, lightly beaten
⅔ cup	sugar
⅓ teaspoon	salt
⅓ cup	butter, melted
½ cup	dark corn syrup
½ cup	light corn syrup
1 teaspoon	vanilla

Preheat the oven to 450 degrees.

Place the nuts in the unbaked pie shell. Whisk together the remaining ingredients and pour over the pecans. The nuts will float to the top. (Whole pecans make a prettier pie while using broken pecan pieces saves money and makes the pie easier to cut.)

Bake at 450 degrees for 10 minutes. Reduce the heat to 300 degrees and bake for an additional 35 minutes. Bake until set; a knife inserted into the pie will come out clean when done.

pennsylvania dutch soft sugar cake cookies

The Beechmont Inn Bed and Breakfast

MAKES 2 TO 3 DOZEN

3½ cups	flour
1 teaspoon	baking soda
1 teaspoon	baking powder
1 teaspoon	salt
2 cups	sugar, plus additional sugar for sprinkling
1 cup	butter
2	eggs
1 tablespoon	vanilla
1 cup	buttermilk

Preheat the oven to 375 degrees.

Sift together the flour, baking soda, baking powder, and salt. Set aside.

Cream together the sugar and butter. Add the eggs one at a time and beat. Add the vanilla and beat.

Stir the flour mixture into the sugar mixture, alternating with the buttermilk. Stir until smooth.

Drop by tablespoonfuls (or use a small ice cream scoop) onto a greased cookie sheet (or for best results, use cookie sheet lined with parchment paper). Sprinkle the tops with sugar. Bake for 7 to 10 minutes.

Remove the cookies from cookie sheet and cool on rack. Store in airtight container.

pound cake

Brampton Bed and Breakfast Inn

SERVES 16 TO 20 (2 LOAF CAKES)

This is a quintessential pound cake. We bake it in loaf pans, topping the slices with fresh strawberries, peaches, or any fresh fruit in season. Leftover slices are frozen and used at a later date for trifles.

4 cups	unbleached flour
1 teaspoon	baking powder
1 teaspoon	salt
1 pound	unsalted butter, at room temperature (4 sticks)
2 cups	white sugar
8	large eggs, at room temperature
1 tablespoon	pure vanilla extract
	juice and finely grated zest of 1 lemon

Preheat the oven to 325 degrees.

Coat 2 (4 x 12 x 3-inch) baking pans with cooking spray.

Sift together the flour, baking powder, and salt in a large bowl. Set aside.

In the bowl of an electric mixer, beat the butter and sugar until light and fluffy (for about 6 minutes).

Add the eggs one at a time, beating well after each addition.

Mix in the vanilla, lemon juice, and lemon zest.

Gradually add the flour mixture, mixing gently until totally incorporated.

Distribute the batter evenly between the 2 pans and bake in the preheated oven for 60 to 70 minutes, until an inserted tester comes out clean. Don't overbake.

Cool for 10 minutes. Turn the cakes out onto a wire rack. Cool completely.

prize-winning apple cake

Birchwood Inn

SERVES 12

for the cake

½ cup	unsalted butter, melted
1 cup	sugar
2	eggs
1 teaspoon	vanilla extract
2 cups	all-purpose flour
2 teaspoons	baking powder
¼ teaspoon	baking soda
¼ teaspoon	salt
½ cup	sour cream
4 to 6	large baking apples, peeled
	cinnamon, to taste

for the topping

½ cup	butter
1 cup	sugar
2	eggs

You will need to use a springform pan with a removable tube in the center. Finding the right pan is the trickiest part of the recipe. Grease the pan well.

Preheat the oven to 350 degrees.

In an electric mixer, combine the melted butter, sugar, and eggs. Add the vanilla and combine.

Combine the dry ingredients and add to the batter. Add the sour cream and mix well. The batter will be somewhat stiff. Transfer the batter to the well-greased pan. Level the batter off.

Cut each apple into 8 equal-size slices.

Insert the apples into the batter, cored side down and as close together as possible, making a ring of apples in the batter. Push the apples gently into the batter. Sprinkle liberally with cinnamon. Bake for 35 minutes. Note: The cake will not be done.

While the cake is baking, combine the topping ingredients.

After the first 35 minutes of baking, pour the topping over the hot cake, and bake for an additional 25 to 30 minutes, until the topping is golden and crunchy.

Cool the cake on a rack for 5 to 10 minutes. Carefully run a knife around the rim and remove the side of the pan.

Invert the cake onto a plate and carefully remove the bottom of the pan.

Flip the cake onto the serving plate.

Cool.

Sprinkle with powdered sugar before serving.

raspberry kiwi trifle

Brampton Bed and Breakfast Inn

SERVES 12

During the month of December, we offer a "Holiday High Tea." This is the showstopper dessert!

1	pound cake (see recipe on page 179)
4	large ripe kiwi, sliced into ¼-inch slices (save 3 slices to decorate)
¼ cup	simple syrup (see recipe on page 145)
¼ cup	Grand Marnier or any other orange liqueur
4 half-pints	fresh raspberries, divided (save 3 to 5 raspberries to decorate)
1½ cups	vanilla custard (see recipe on page 186)
½ cup	cold heavy cream
1 teaspoon	sugar
¼ teaspoon	pure vanilla extract

Cut the pound cake into 12 (¾-inch) slices. Remove the crust. Set aside.

Peel and slice kiwi. Set aside.

In a 1-cup measure, mix the simple syrup and Grand Marnier (if desired). Divide into 3 portions. Set aside. If you prefer to make a trifle without alcohol, use ½ cup of simple syrup flavored with orange zest.

Place a layer of cake in the bottom of a 2½ to 3-quart glass trifle bowl, cutting the pieces to fit. Sprinkle with ⅓ of the simple syrup mixture.

Arrange a layer of raspberries and gently spoon ½ cup of vanilla custard over the berries. Don't go too close to the edge of the bowl as you want the fruit to be visible from the outside.

Repeat a layer of cake and simple syrup mixture. Top with kiwi slices, overlapping, if necessary, and a layer of custard. Once again, don't go too close to the edge.

Add the third layer of cake, simple syrup, raspberries, and custard. Refrigerate for 1 hour.

Whip the cream in the bowl of an electric mixer fitted with the whisk attachment. When it starts to thicken, add the sugar and vanilla and continue to whip it until stiff peaks have formed.

Decorate the trifle with whipped cream and the reserved kiwi slices and raspberries.

rhubarb crisp

Swiss Woods Bed & Breakfast Inn

SERVES 6

Prepare this in spring when rhubarb is plentiful. If you like a sweeter crisp, replace some of the rhubarb with washed, stemmed strawberries.

1½ pounds	red rhubarb stems (about 6 cups)
	zest and juice of 1 large orange
1 cup	sugar, divided
½ cup	flour, divided
3 tablespoons	cornstarch
1½ cups	rolled oats
½ cup	almonds, chopped
1 teaspoon	cinnamon
½ teaspoon	salt
½ cup	cold butter, cut into 8 pieces

Preheat the oven to 375 degrees.

Using a small sharp knife, strip the rhubarb stems of the stringy skin, being careful not to take off too much. Slice into ½-inch slices. Add the orange juice.

In a large bowl, mix the rhubarb, ¾ cup sugar, 3 tablespoons flour, cornstarch, and orange zest.

Grease and flour a 9 x 13-inch baking pan. Pour the rhubarb mix into the pan.

In a separate bowl, mix the topping: oats, remaining flour, almonds, cinnamon, and salt. Add the butter and work it with your fingers until the mixture is crumbly.

Distribute evenly over top of the rhubarb mixture.

Bake for 25 to 30 minutes, or until bubbly around the edges and the top is lightly browned.

strawberry/raspberry streusel bars

Lookout Point Lakeside Inn

SERVES 20

1 cup	butter, softened
1 cup	sugar
2 cups	all-purpose unbleached flour
1	egg
¾ cup	pecans, coarsely chopped
1 (10-ounce) jar	strawberry or raspberry preserves, jam, or spread

Preheat the oven to 350 degrees.

Combine the butter and sugar in large mixing bowl. Beat at low speed, scraping bowl often until well blended. Add the flour and egg. Beat until mixture is crumbly, for 2 to 3 minutes. Stir in the pecans.

Reserve 1 cup of the crumb mixture. Press remaining crumb mixture onto bottom of a greased 8 or 9-inch square baking pan.

Spread the preserves to within ½-inch of the edge of crust. Sprinkle the reserved crumb mixture over the preserves.

Bake for 40 to 50 minutes or until lightly browned. Cool completely before cutting into bars.

Try your favorite jam in this recipe. One of our favorites in Arkansas is huckleberry, but it's not readily available.

turtle squares

Lookout Point Lakeside Inn

MAKES 24

2 cups	flour
1 cup	brown sugar, packed
½ cup	butter, softened
1 cup	pecans
1⅓ cups	butter (not margarine)
1⅓ cups	brown sugar, packed
1 cup	chocolate chips

Preheat the oven to 350 degrees.

Combine the flour, 1 cup brown sugar, and ½ cup butter to make fine crumbs. Press firmly into a greased 9 x 13-inch pan. Sprinkle with pecans.

In a small saucepan over medium heat, cook 1⅓ cups butter and 1⅓ cups brown sugar, stirring constantly, until the entire surface boils. Boil for 1 minute and pour over the crust.

Bake for 18 to 22 minutes until surface is bubbly. Remove from the oven and immediately sprinkle with the chocolate chips. Allow the chips to melt for a moment, then swirl and spread over the entire base.

vanilla or maple custard

Brampton Bed and Breakfast Inn

MAKES 1½ CUPS

Either one is delicious. This is the custard we pour over the "brown betty" and use to make our "trifles."

4	large egg yolks
¼ cup	granulated sugar or maple syrup
¼ teaspoon	sea salt
1 cup	half-and-half
½ tablespoon	vanilla extract

Can be stored in refrigerator for up to 3 days.

Fill a large bowl with ice. The bowl should be large enough to hold the top of the double boiler.

Add a quart of water to the bottom part of double boiler, making sure it will not reach the bottom of the top pan.

Whisk together the egg yolks, sugar or maple syrup, and sea salt in the top of the double boiler until very well blended.

In a small saucepan, bring the half-and-half to a boil. Remove from the heat and let cool slightly.

Very slowly, pour the hot half-and-half over the yolks, whisking vigorously. You want to be careful or the yolks will curdle.

Place the top of double boiler over hot water and whisk constantly until temperature reaches 165 degrees.

Immediately remove from stove, add the vanilla extract, and set the pan over bowl with ice.

Keep whisking until the custard cools down. Strain the custard through a fine meshed sieve into a container with a lid. Before closing lid, press a piece of plastic wrap on top of the custard to prevent a skin from forming. Close the lid and refrigerate until ready to use.

white chocolate brownies

The William Henry Miller Inn

MAKES 9 LARGE OR 19 BITE-SIZE SERVINGS

½ cup	unsalted butter
8 ounces	white chocolate chips, divided
2	eggs
	pinch of salt
½ cup	sugar
½ teaspoon	vanilla extract
½ teaspoon	salt
1 cup	flour
1¼ cups	semisweet chocolate chips

Preheat the oven to 350 degrees. Lightly grease an 8-inch baking dish.

Melt the butter in a small saucepan over low heat. Remove the pan from the heat and add 4 ounces of the white chocolate chips. Do not stir.

In an electric mixer, beat the eggs and a pinch of salt until frothy. Gradually add the sugar and beat until pale yellow and a slowly-dissolving ribbon forms when the beater is lifted.

Add the white chocolate mixture, vanilla, ½ teaspoon salt, and flour, mixing until just combined. Stir in the semisweet chocolate chips and remaining white chocolate chips.

Bake for 30 minutes. Cool before cutting.

about the authors

Kathryn White–The Beechmont Inn Bed and Breakfast

The Beechmont Inn Bed and Breakfast
www.thebeechmont.com / 717-632-3013
Hanover, Pennsylvania

Experience the history of the Civil War and the hospitality of the Pennsylvania Dutch Country in our award-winning B&B.

Kathryn is the person friends relied upon in snow storms to have a full pantry from which great meals could be prepared.

Ellen Gutman Chenaux–Birchwood Inn

Birchwood Inn
www.birchwood-inn.com / 413-637-2600
Lenox, Massachusetts

A comfortably elegant and romantic 1766 inn, which is the setting for award-winning breakfasts in the heart of the Berkshires.

Ellen's passion for food inspires her to create imaginative breakfasts as well as to encourage others to follow their culinary muses.

about the authors

Danielle Hanscom–Brampton Bed and Breakfast Inn

Danielle believes that every meal is worth a celebration.

Brampton Bed and Breakfast Inn
www.bramptoninn.com / 410-778-1860
Chestertown, Maryland

A romantic oasis on Maryland's Eastern Shore.

Joyce Schulte–Chambered Nautilus Bed and Breakfast Inn

The only thing Joyce loves better than eating great food is preparing great food and sharing it at a bountiful table with good friends.

Chambered Nautilus Bed and Breakfast Inn
www.chamberednautilus.com / 206-522-2536
Seattle, Washington

A comfortable and elegant "urban oasis" by the University of Washington, in the very heart of Seattle.

about the authors

Kristie Rosset–Lookout Point Lakeside Inn

Kristie shares love and hospitality through tasty and pretty food sprinkled with joy.

Lookout Point Lakeside Inn
www.lookoutpointinn.com / 501-525-6155
Hot Springs, Arkansas

A sanctuary of peace and tranquility, comprehensive pampering, and comfortable luxury on Lake Hamilton in Hot Springs, Arkansas.

Debbie Mosimann–Swiss Woods Bed & Breakfast Inn

Swiss Woods Bed & Breakfast Inn
www.swisswoods.com / 717-627-3358
Lititz, Pennsylvania

Acres of bliss in Lititz, the heart of Lancaster County, Pennsylvania.

Debbie loves to teach the nuances of great breakfast preparation almost as much as she enjoys breakfast.

about the authors

Yvonne Martin–The White Oak Inn

The White Oak Inn
www.whiteoakinn.com / 740-599-6107
Danville, Ohio

Your perfect getaway starts here, on a quiet back road in Ohio's Amish Country.

While some people are born with a silver spoon in their mouth, Yvonne was born with a wooden spoon in her hand and she loves to put it to good use.

Lynnette Scofield–The William Henry Miller Inn

The William Henry Miller Inn
www.millerinn.com / 607-256-4553
Ithaca, New York

In the heart of the Finger Lakes ... warm hospitality in downtown Ithaca.

There is nothing that brings a smile to Lynnette more than a table of happy, well-fed guests.

SILVER EDITION
Teacher's Edition with Tests

Interactions 2

LISTENING/SPEAKING

Judith Tanka
Lida R. Baker
Teacher's Edition by Ingrid Wisniewska

McGraw Hill

Interactions 2 Listening/Speaking Teacher's Edition with Tests, Silver Edition

ISBN 13: 978-0-07-329422-3 (Teacher's Edition)
ISBN 10: 0-07-329422-5 (Teacher's Edition)
6 7 8 9 10 QDB 14 13 12

Editorial director: Erik Gundersen
Series editor: Valerie Kelemen
Developmental editor: Terre Passero
Production manager: Juanita Thompson
Production coordinator: Vanessa Nuttry
Cover designer: Robin Locke Monda
Interior designer: Nesbitt Graphics, Inc.

Cover photo: Bob Krist/CORBIS

www.esl-elt.mcgraw-hill.com

The *McGraw·Hill* Companies

Table of Contents

Introduction

Student Book Teaching Notes and Answer Keys

Welcome to the Teacher's Edition

The Teacher's Edition of *Interactions/Mosaic* Silver Edition provides support and flexibility to teachers using the *Interactions/Mosaic* Silver Edition 18-book academic skills series. The Teacher's Edition provides step-by-step guidance for implementing each activity in the Student Book. The Teacher's Edition also provides expansion activities with photocopiable masters of select expansion activities, identification of activities that support a Best Practice, valuable notes on content, answer keys, audioscripts, end-of-chapter tests, and placement tests. Each chapter in the Teacher's Edition begins with an overview of the content, vocabulary, and teaching goals in that chapter. Each chapter in the Student Book begins with an engaging photo and related discussion questions that strengthen the educational experience and connect students to the topic.

▦ Procedural Notes

The procedural notes are useful for both experienced and new teachers. Experienced teachers can use the bulleted, step-by step procedural notes as a quick guide and refresher before class, while newer or substitute teachers can use the notes as a more extensive guide to assist them in the classroom. The procedural notes guide teachers through each strategy and activity; describe what materials teachers might need for an activity; and help teachers provide context for the activities.

▦ Answer Keys

Answer keys are provided for all activities that have definite answers. For items that have multiple correct answers, various possible answers are provided. The answer key follows the procedural note for the relevant activity. Answer keys are also provided for the Chapter Tests and the Placement Tests.

▦ Expansion Activities

A number of expansion activities with procedural notes are included in each chapter. These activities offer teachers creative ideas for reinforcing the chapter content while appealing to different learning styles. Activities include games, conversation practice, presentations, and projects. These expansion activities often allow students to practice integrated language skills, not just the skills that the student book focuses on. Some of the expansion activities include photocopiable black line masters included in the back of the book.

▦ Content Notes

Where appropriate, content notes are included in the Teacher's Edition. These are notes that might illuminate or enhance a learning point in the activity and might help teachers answer student questions about the content. These notes are provided at the logical point of use, but teachers can decide if and when to use the information in class.

▦ Chapter Tests

Each chapter includes a chapter test that was designed to test the vocabulary, reading, writing, grammar, and/or listening strategies taught in the chapter, depending on the language skill strand being used. Teachers can simply copy and distribute the tests, then use the answer keys found in the Teacher's Edition. The purpose of the chapter tests is not only to assess students' understanding of material covered in the chapter but also to give students an idea of how they are doing and what they need to work on. Each chapter test has four parts with items totaling 100 points. Item types include multiple choice, fill-in-the blank, and true/false. Audioscripts are provided when used.

▦ Black Line Masters (Photocopiable Masters)

Each chapter includes a number of expansion activities with black line masters, or master worksheets, that teachers can copy and distribute. These activities and black line masters are optional. They can help reinforce and expand on chapter material in an engaging way. Activities include games;

conversation practice; working with manipulatives such as sentence strips; projects; and presentations. Procedural notes and answer keys (when applicable) are provided in the Teacher's Edition.

▨ Placement Tests

Each of the four language skill strands has a placement test designed to help assess in which level the student belongs. Each test has been constructed to be given in under an hour. Be sure to go over the directions and answer any questions before the test begins. Students are instructed not to ask questions once the test begins. Following each placement test, you'll find a scoring placement key that suggests the appropriate book to be used based on the number of items answered correctly. Teachers should use judgment in placing students and selecting texts.

The Interactions/Mosaic Silver Edition Program

Interactions/Mosaic Silver Edition is a fully-integrated, 18-book academic skills series. Language proficiencies are articulated from the beginning through advance levels <u>within</u> each of the four language skill strands. Chapter themes articulate <u>across</u> the four skill strands to systematically recycle content, vocabulary, and grammar.

▨ Reading Strand

Reading skills and strategies are strategically presented and practiced through a variety of themes and reading genres in the five Reading books. Pre-reading, reading, and post-reading activities include strategies and activities that aid comprehension, build vocabulary, and prepare students for academic success. Each chapter includes at least two readings that center around the same theme, allowing students to deepen their understanding of a topic and command of vocabulary related to that topic. Readings include magazine articles, textbook passages, essays, letters, and website articles. They explore, and guide the student to explore, stimulating topics. Vocabulary is presented before each reading and is built on throughout the chapter. High-frequency words and words from the Academic Word List are focused on and pointed out with asterisks (*) in each chapter's Self-Assessment Log.

▨ Listening/Speaking Strand

A variety of listening input, including lectures, academic discussions, and conversations help students explore stimulating topics in the five Listening/Speaking books. Activities associated with the listening input, such as pre-listening tasks, systematically guide students through strategies and critical thinking skills that help prepare them for academic achievement. In the Interactions books, the activities are coupled with instructional photos featuring a cast of engaging, multi-ethnic students participating in North American college life. Across the strand, lectures and dialogues are broken down into manageable parts giving students an opportunity to predict, identify main ideas, and effectively manage lengthy input. Questions, guided discussion activities, and structured pair and group work stimulate interest and interaction among students, often culminating in organizing their information and ideas in a graphic organizer, writing, and/or making a presentation to the class. Pronunciation is highlighted in every chapter, an aid to improving both listening comprehension and speaking fluency. Enhanced focus on vocabulary building is developed throughout and a list of target words for each chapter is provided so students can interact meaningfully with the material. Finally, Online Learning Center features MP3 files from the Student Book audio program for students to download onto portable digital audio players.

▨ Writing Strand

Activities in each of the four Writing books are systematically structured to culminate in a *Writing Product* task. Activities build on key elements of writing from sentence development to writing single paragraphs, articles, narratives, and essays of multiple lengths and genres. Connections between writing and grammar tie the writing skill in focus with the grammar structures needed to develop each writing skill. Academic themes, activities, writing topics, vocabulary development, and critical thinking strategies prepare students for university life. Instructional photos are used to strengthen engagement and the educational experience. Explicit pre-writing questions and discussions activate prior knowledge, help organize ideas and information, and create a foundation for the writing product. Each chapter includes a self-evaluation rubric which supports the learner as he or she builds confidence and autonomy in academic writing. Finally, the Writing Articulation Chart helps teachers see the progression of writing strategies both in terms of mechanics and writing genres.

Grammar Strand

Questions and topical quotes in the four Grammar books, coupled with instructional photos stimulate interest, activate prior knowledge, and launch the topic of each chapter. Engaging academic topics provide context for the grammar and stimulate interest in content as well as grammar. A variety of activity types, including individual, pair, and group work, allow students to build grammar skills and use the grammar they are learning in activities that cultivate critical thinking skills. Students can refer to grammar charts to review or learn the form and function of each grammar point. These charts are numbered sequentially, formatted consistently, and indexed systematically, providing lifelong reference value for students.

Focus on Testing for the TOEFL® iBT

The all-new TOEFL® iBT *Focus on Testing* sections prepare students for success on the TOEFL® iBT by presenting and practicing specific strategies for each language skill area. The Focus on Testing sections are introduced in Interactions 1 and are included in all subsequent levels of the Reading, Listening/Speaking, and Writing strands. These strategies focus on what The Educational Testing Service (ETS) has identified as the target skills in each language skill area. For example, "reading for basic comprehension" (identifying the main idea, understanding pronoun reference) is a target reading skill and is presented and practiced in one or more *Focus on Testing* sections. In addition, this and other target skills are presented and practiced in chapter components outside the *Focus on Testing* sections and have special relevance to the TOEFL® iBT. For example, note-taking is an important test-taking strategy, particularly in the listening section of the TOEFL® iBT, and is included in activities within each of the Listening/Speaking books. All but two of the *Interactions/Mosaic* titles have a *Focus on Testing* section. Although *Interactions Access Reading* and *Interaction Access Listening/Speaking* don't include these sections because of their level, they do present and develop skills that will prepare students for the TOEFL® iBT.

Best Practices

In each chapter of this Teacher's Edition, you'll find Best Practices boxes that highlight a particular activity and show how this activity is tied to a particular Best Practice. The Interactions/Mosaic Silver Edition team of writers, editors, and teacher consultants has identified the following six interconnected Best Practices.

---

* TOEFL is a registered trademark of Educational Testing Services (ETS). This publication is not endorsed or approved by ETS.

Best Practices

Each chapter identifies at least six different activities that support six Best Practices, principles that contribute to excellent language teaching and learning. Identifying Best Practices helps teachers to see, and make explicit for students, how a particular activity will aid the learning process.

Making Use of Academic Content

Materials and tasks based on academic content and experiences give learning real purpose. Students explore real world issues, discuss academic topics, and study content-based and thematic materials.

Organizing Information

Students learn to organize thoughts and notes through a variety of graphic organizers that accommodate diverse learning and thinking styles.

Scaffolding Instruction

A scaffold is a physical structure that facilitates construction of a building. Similarly, scaffolding instruction is a tool used to facilitate language learning in the form of predictable and flexible tasks. Some examples include oral or written modeling by the teacher or students, placing information in a larger framework, and reinterpretation.

Activating Prior Knowledge

Students can better understand new spoken or written material when they connect to the content. Activating prior knowledge allows students to tap into what they already know, building on this knowledge, and stirring a curiosity for more knowledge.

Interacting with Others

Activities that promote human interaction in pair work, small group work, and whole class activities present opportunities for real world contact and real world use of language.

Cultivating Critical Thinking

Strategies for critical thinking are taught explicitly. Students learn tools that promote critical thinking skills crucial to success in the academic world.

Education and Student Life

In this chapter, students will read about different aspects of education and student life, such as starting conversations with strangers, the university system, accepting and refusing invitations, and finding your way on campus. In Part 1, they will learn to recognize stressed and reduced forms and practice ways of showing interest. In Part 2, they will listen to a lecture about the university system in North America. They will also discuss the issue of plagiarism. In Part 3, they will practice getting meaning from context by listening to a variety of college campus conversations. In Part 4, they will learn how to describe and understand locations. The topics in this chapter will encourage students to discuss various aspects of their student life.

Chapter Opener

❑ Have students look at the photo of college students in their dormitory room. Ask them the questions from the Connecting to the Topic section. Have students discuss as a class.

❑ Read and discuss the quotation. What is an *empty* mind? What is an *open* mind? What view of education is proposed in this statement? (A possible interpretation is that education is meant to expose people to a variety of ideas and perspectives.) What other views are there?

❝ Education's purpose is to replace an empty mind with an open one. ❞

—Malcolm Forbes
American art collector, author, and publisher, 1919–1990

Chapter Overview

Listening Skills and Strategies

Listening for main ideas

Listening for details

Making inferences

Getting meaning from intonation

Recognizing compass directions

Understanding expressions and statements of location

Using the prepositions *in, on, at* in addresses and locations

Speaking Skills and Strategies

Showing interest

Comparing university systems in different countries

Talking about cheating

Making, accepting, and refusing invitations

Using expressions of location

Describing map locations

Critical Thinking Skills

Interpreting a photo

Getting meaning from context

Speculating about hypothetical situations

Using a lecture introduction to predict content

Writing effective lecture notes

Using a Venn diagram to compare and contrast

Vocabulary Building

Terms for academic life

Terms for showing interest

Terms used at an academic orientation

Expressions for making, accepting, and refusing invitations

Compass directions

Expressions of location

In, on, and *at* in addresses and locations

Pronunciation

Identifying and practicing stressed words

Identifying and practicing reduced pronunciation

Language Skills

Using context clues to guess locations

Vocabulary

Nouns		Verbs
career	quiz	attend
cheating	requirement	be into
discussion section	teaching assistant	fail a course
experiment	term paper	get ahead
laboratory ("lab")		get kicked out
lecture		major in
midterm exam		sign up
plagiarism		take notes

Can You Guess?

■ Ask students to discuss the questions below in groups and compare their answers with the correct answers.

■ Discuss the issues raised by these questions: Do people think that an old university is better than a new one? Is this belief justified? What factors affect the numbers of international students? What factors affect the numbers of male and female graduates?

1. What is the oldest university in the world? A. *Al Azhar University in Cairo, Egypt, may be the oldest university in the world. It was founded in A.D. 969. Europe's oldest university was founded in the northern Italian city of Bologna in 1088.*

2. What is the percentage of international students at U.S. universities? A. *International students make up about 5 percent of the total student enrollment at U.S. universities. The University of Southern California has the largest number of international students (6,647 in 2003–04).*

3. Are more U.S. university graduates men or women? A. *In 2002 women in the United States received 57 percent of all bachelor's degrees, 59 percent of all master's degrees, and 46 percent of all doctorates.*

Footnotes:
* Source: http://ask.yahoo.com/ask/20020501.html
** Source: http://opendoors.iienetword.org/?p=49931
† Source: http://ww.money.cnn.com/2004/04/23/pf/women_occupations

Before You Listen

Best Practice

Activating Prior Knowledge

The prelistening questions activate students' prior knowledge. This type of activity will help students relate their own experience of starting conversations with strangers to the new language in this chapter. When students activate their prior knowledge before learning new material, they are better able to map new language onto existing concepts, which aids understanding and retention.

1   **Prelistening Questions**

❑ Have students work in groups to describe the people and the location shown in the picture. Ask them to guess what these people are talking about.

❑ Have the students read the questions and discuss them in groups.

❑ Compare answers as a whole class.

❑ As a whole class, make a list of ways to start a conversation with a stranger. Organize the list under topic headings such as verbal, nonverbal, weather, sports, asking for help or information.

2   **Previewing Vocabulary**

❑ Play the recording and ask students to listen to the underlined words.

❑ Have students complete the vocabulary preview individually.

❑ Compare their answers as a whole class and write the correct answers on the board.

❑ Ask students for paraphrases (or examples) for each item, e.g., 1. enroll 2. specialize 3. be crazy about 4. be successful 5. collocations with career: career prospects, career advice, career counseling/counselor.

❑ Practice the pronunciation of new words or phrases by repeating after the audio.

ANSWER KEY

1. d 2. c 3. b 4. a 5. e

Listen

3 **Comprehension Questions**

(The audioscript follows Activity 4 in this Teacher's Edition.)

- ❏ Explain that these questions will help students focus on the main ideas in the listening. They do not need to understand every word to answer the questions.

- ❏ You may want to write the questions on the board.

- ❏ Read the questions aloud.

- ❏ Play the recording.

- ❏ After listening, have students compare their answers in pairs.

- ❏ Check the answers as a class.

ANSWER KEY

1. They are going to Campbell Hall to take a placement test. 2. Nancy is an English teacher. 3. Mari is a student. She comes from Japan. 4. When Mari was little, her family used to come to the U.S. every summer to visit her grandmother. 5. She needs to improve her writing skills. 6. She wants to major in international business.

Content Notes

- ▣ Check comprehension of the different terms: *school*, *college*, and *university*.

- ▣ It may be of interest to students to discuss the university system in the U.S. and in other countries. For example, entry requirements, length and dates of semesters, credits, exams, fees, and funding.

- ▣ Note that this is the topic of the lecture in Part 2. Students will discuss and compare university systems in different countries in Part 2 in Activity 8.

STRESS

- ▣ Read aloud the instruction note and practice the example sentence.

- ▣ Play the recording and ask students to listen and repeat the sentence they hear.

- ▣ Write these sentences on the board and ask students to identify the stressed words.

    What's your ***name***? / ***Where*** are you ***from***? / ***I'm*** a ***student***. / ***Nice*** to ***meet*** you.

4 **Listening for Stressed Words**

- ❏ Listen to the recording again, this time with books open.

- ❏ Pauses on the recording will allow time for students to repeat and write the missing words.

- ❏ After listening, have students check their answers with the audioscript in their books.

- ❏ Have students read the conversation with a partner, paying attention to stressed words in their pronunciation.

- ❏ After listening, have students check their answers with the audioscript in their books.

- ❏ Have students read the conversation with a partner, paying attention to stressed words in their pronunciation.

AUDIOSCRIPT and ANSWER KEY

Mari: *Excuse* me. Could you *tell* me where Kimbell Hall is?

Nancy: Oh, you mean *Campbell* Hall?

Mari: Oh yeah, *right*.

Nancy: Do you see that *brown* building over there?

Mari: Uh, behind the *fountain*?

Nancy: Yeah, that's it. Come on, *I'm* going there too. Are you here for the English *placement* test?

Mari: Yes, I *am*. How about *you*?

Nancy: Actually, I'm one of the *English* teachers here.

Mari: Oh really? Maybe I'll be in your *class*!

Nancy: It's *possible*. What's your *name*?

Mari: *Mariko Honda*, but *most* people call me Mari. And you?

Nancy: I'm Nancy Anderson. So, where are you *from*?

Mari: Japan.

Nancy: Aha. And, uh, how long have you *been* here?

Mari: Just *three weeks*.

Nancy: Really? But your English sounds *great*!

Mari: Thanks. That's because my *family* used to come here every summer to visit my grandmother when I was *little*. I can *speak* pretty well.

Nancy: Mmm - hmmm.

Mari: . . . but now I want to go to *college* here, so I need to improve my skills, especially *writing*. Yeah, so, uh, that's why I signed up for this *English* program.

Nancy: I see. Uh, what do you want to *major* in?

Mari: International *business*. My father has an *import*-export company, and he does a *lot* of business here in the States.

Nancy: Oh, I see.

Mari: And I *also* want to take *art* classes, because I'm *really* into art.

Nancy: Art and business. Wow. That's an interesting combination. But, *can't* you study those things in *Japan*?

Mari: Well, sure, but you have to speak good *English* these days to get ahead in *business*. It's *better* for my career if I go to college *here*.

Nancy: Well, here's Campbell Hall. Good *luck* on the *placement* exam. It was nice *meeting* you, Mari.

Mari: Thanks. You too.

Nancy: See you later.

Mari: Bye-bye.

 EXPANSION ACTIVITY

▪ The purpose of this activity is for students to get to know each other, to establish shared goals for the class, and to practice starting conversations and ways of showing interest.

▪ Please see Black Line Master "Class Survey" on page BLM 1 of this Teacher's Edition. Photocopy and cut it into strips.

▪ Give one strip to each student. There are ten different questions. If you have more than ten students, have students work in pairs or threes.

▪ Ask two or three students the first question, *Excuse me. Why do you want to study English?* and model taking notes of the answers.

- Explain that the aim is for each student to ask everyone in the class.

- Have students walk around the room (with their notebooks and pens with them) and ask other students their question, taking notes about the answers.

- At the end of the activity, they will report to the class on the information they have collected. For example, *I found that most students want to . . .*

REDUCTIONS

- Read aloud the instruction note.

- Play the recording and ask students to repeat the reduced forms.

Content Note

Some students may think of reduced forms as incorrect. Emphasize that these forms are commonly used in spoken English and it is important to be able to understand them. It is not essential for communication to use them, but if they do not use reduced forms, their English may sound too formal.

5 Comparing Unreduced and Reduced Pronunciation

- Play the recording and have students listen and read the sentences.

- Play the recording again and have students repeat the sentences.

- Listen carefully and correct pronunciation as a group.

- You can also have students volunteer to repeat the sentences individually.

6 Listening for Reductions

- Have students read through the conversation and try to guess the missing words.

- Play the recording and have students write their answers.

- After listening, have students check their answers with the audioscript in their books. Check the answers as a whole class.

- Have students practice the conversation in pairs, paying attention to reduced forms in their pronunciation.

ANSWER KEY

A: Could you help me, please? My name is Ali Hashmati. I *used to* be a student in this school.

B: Oh yeah, I remember you. How are you?

A: Fine, thanks.

B: Can I help you with something?

A: Yes, I *want to* get an application for the TOEFL® test.

B: *You mean* the international TOEFL® iBT? Let's see. They *used to* be here on this shelf. It looks like they're all gone. I'm sorry, you'll *have to* wait until they come in next week.

A: *How about* sending me one when they come in?

B: No problem. *What's your* name and address?

After You Listen

7 Reviewing Vocabulary

- Have students ask and answer the questions in pairs.

- Ask pairs to report to the class on their partner's answers.

Using Language Functions

SHOWING INTEREST

- ■ Read the instruction note.
- ■ Mime the meaning of these phrases: *making eye contact, nodding your head.*

> ### Content Note
>
> Non-verbal language for showing interest may be different in other cultures. Making eye contact may be impolite, for example, and nodding may show impatience. Explain that non-verbal language, like verbal language, has to be learned and used appropriately in different cultures.

> **Best Practice**
>
> #### Interacting with Others
>
> This type of activity is an example of collaborative learning to encourage fluency and confidence. In this activity, designed to practice verbal and non verbal ways of showing interest, communication is more important than grammar. Students can practice these strategies in pairs and then improve their performance by switching roles or partners. By providing feedback to each other, they learn skills of self-evaluation.

8 Showing Interest

- ❑ Read through the list of topics and ask students for possible suggestions for each topic in the list.

- ❑ Divide students into groups of three or four. In each group, one student will talk about the topic for two minutes, while the second student shows interest. The other students will give feedback on the use of verbal and nonverbal expressions of interest. Then rotate roles using a different topic.

- ❑ You may wish to set a time limit for each topic.

- ❑ Make sure students understand the task and their roles by asking one or two students to repeat the instructions back to you.

- ❑ Set a time limit of 20 minutes.

- ❑ Monitor the groups as they are doing the activity and make notes of errors.

- ❑ At the end of the activity, ask a representative from each group to report back on ways of showing interest. Which ones were easy or difficult? Which ones were used the most?

Before You Listen

- ❏ Read aloud the information above the photo.

- ❏ Ask for some suggestions about what kind of information would be given at an orientation meeting. For example: directions to places on campus, college facilities, library and office hours, places to meet, study, eat, get advice.

- ❏ Ask students to look at the photo and describe what this person is doing. How are lectures and classes in the U.S. different from those in other countries?

- ❏ Read aloud the information in the Culture Note.

Best Practice

Making Use of Academic Content

The prelistening quiz helps students to evaluate their existing knowledge on the topic of universities in North America. This type of activity mirrors the type of preparation they might do before listening to a lecture. Evaluating what they already know, or don't know, will help students relate their existing knowledge of education in North America to the new information in this chapter.

1   Prelistening Quiz

- ❏ Read through the list of questions and check comprehension of any new words.

- ❏ Have students answer the questions individually and compare their answers in pairs.

- ❏ Review the responses as a class.

ANSWER KEY

1.T 2.F 3.F 4.F 5.F 6.F 7.F 8.T

2   Previewing Vocabulary

- ❏ Play the recording and ask students to listen to the words.

- ❏ Have students check the words they know.

Then compare answers with a partner. Explain that they will work out the meaning of the new words by listening to the lecture and doing the activities that follow.

Listen

3   Note-Taking Pretest

- ❏ Explain that students will listen to a lecture and practice listening and taking notes. The lecture has an introduction followed by two parts.

- ❏ Ask students to close their books, listen to the lecture, and take notes in any way they like.

- ❏ After playing the first part of the recording, ask students to open their books and use their notes to answer the questions.

- ❏ Go over the answers.

- ❏ Ask students to compare their notes with one or more classmates. Have them discuss the four questions.

ANSWER KEY

1.a 2.c 3.a and d

AUDIOSCRIPT

(Introduction)

Good morning, everyone. My name is Richard Baldwin, and I am the academic advisor here at the English Language Center. If you have any questions about applying to a university, or if you need help with your application, you can come see me in my office.

So . . . uh, this . . . this morning I want to give you a general introduction to the university system in the United States and Canada. First, I'm going to tell you about three types of university courses. And then my second main topic is course requirements . . . uh, course requirements, which means what you have to *do* in order to pass the course. OK? So I'll talk about those two topics, and then you'll have time to ask questions before we take a break. OK?

(Part 1)

All right, now as I said, first I want to tell you about three types of university courses. And I should explain that I'm talking about undergraduate courses now, because the system is different at the graduate level. All right. The most common type of undergraduate course is called a lecture course. Got that? A lecture course. Now basically, in a lecture course, the professor talks and the students sit and take notes. This is very important—taking notes, I mean . . . because most of the time the information in a lecture is not the same as the information in your books, and you can expect to have questions on your exams that are based on the lectures. So you see, it isn't enough to just read your textbooks, like it is in some countries; in the U.S. and Canada the system is that you have to attend lectures. And during the lecture, you can't just sit there and listen, you have to take notes. Then later you use the notes to study for your exams. I hope that's clear.

Now, as an undergraduate in almost any major, you'll probably spend four to six hours a week attending lectures. But that's four to six hours for <u>each</u> lecture course. Do you understand? And students normally take three or four lecture courses per semester, so figure it out . . . you're going to spend a lot of hours each week listening to lectures. And the last thing about lecture courses is that they're often held in very large rooms because undergraduate courses like Introduction to Psychology can have two or three hundred students in them, especially at large universities.

And so . . . Well, what if you have a question or need help? There's no w—there's no way that one professor can meet with 300 students, right? That's why, each week, all the students in a lecture course are divided into groups for a special kind of class called a discussion section, which meets for two or three hours a week, and

it's smaller, maybe 20 or 30 students. Your discussion section is the place where you can ask questions about the lectures and the readings and go over homework. But this class isn't taught by your professors. At large universities, it's taught by graduate students called teaching assistants, or TAs.

Let's see. So far, I've told you about lecture courses and discussion sections. The third kind of class I want to mention is especially important for science majors, and that's the lab class. *Lab* is short for "laboratory." If your major is chemistry or physics or any other kind of science, you'll have to spend several hours a week in the lab. This is where you do your experiments.

Using the Introduction to Predict Lecture Content

- Read the information in the Strategy box.
- Answer any questions. Tell students that they will practice this in the next activity.

4 Taking Notes on the Introduction

- ❑ Play the introduction to the lecture again.
- ❑ Give students time to write the answers.

ANSWER KEY

Topic of the lecture: University system in the U.S. and Canada

Main ideas: 1. types of courses 2. requirements

AUDIOSCRIPT

Good morning, everyone. My name is Richard Baldwin, and I am the academic advisor here at the English Language Center. If you have any questions about applying to a university, or if you need help with your application, you can come see me in my office.

So . . . uh, this . . . this morning I want to give you a general introduction to the university system in the United States and Canada. First, I'm going to tell you about three types of university courses. And then my second main topic is course requirements . . . uh, course requirements, which means what you have to *do* in order to pass the course. O.K.? So I'll talk about those two topics, and then you'll have time to ask questions before we take a break. O.K.?

Strategy

Three Keys to Writing Effective Lecture Notes

- Read the information in the Strategy box.

- Give examples for each point (see below).

- Ask students to explain each key in their own words.

Indentation (example):

    University system in the U.S. and Canada

        1. types of courses

        2. requirements

Key words (example):

    courses, requirements

Abbreviations and symbols (example):

    & = and; @ = at (for other abbreviations, see page XX in the Student Book.)

5 **Identifying the Three Keys to Writing Effective Lecture Notes**

- ❑ Go over the outline for the lecture.

- ❑ Play the recording again.

- ❑ Pause the recording after each main point and notice the use of indentation, key words, abbreviations, and symbols.

6 **Indenting**

- ❑ Explain that these notes are indented incorrectly. Students will have to revise the outline, using the correct indentation.

- ❑ Play the second part of the recording.

- ❑ Have one or two students write their ideas on the board.

- ❑ Have all students copy the correct outline into their notebooks.

ANSWER KEY

Course Requirements

1. Tests or exams
    a. midterm
    b. final
    c. quizzes
2. Term paper
  Steps
    a. choose a topic
    b. do research
    c. use notes to write the paper
    d. 5–25 pages long
3. plagiarism
  plag. = cheating
    a. def.: copying
    b. punishment
    c. fail a course
    d. get kicked out of university

AUDIOSCRIPT

(Part 2)

Let's move on now to the second major topic I mentioned, which is course requirements. As I told you, *course requirements* means the things you have to do in order to pass a course. First of all, nearly every class you take will have one or more tests, or exams. Most university courses have at least two big exams: one in the middle of the course, called a midterm, and another big one at the end, called the final exam. You might also have smaller tests from time to time. A small test is called a quiz.

Also, in many courses you might also have to do something called a term paper or research paper, so let me tell you a little about that. A term paper is a large written report that has several steps. First, you choose a topic related to the course. Then you do research on this topic, either in a library or on the Internet. *Do research* means that you read and take notes on the topic. And finally, you use your notes to write a paper in your own words. A research paper can be anywhere from five pages to 25 pages long.

Now, this is a good place for me to introduce you to something called plagiarism. That's spelled P-L-A-G-I-A-R-I-S-M. Plagiarism is a kind of cheating, and it's a serious problem at American universities. Do you remember I just said that when you write a term paper, it has to be in your own words? That means you can't copy your paper or even small parts of your paper from another student or a book or the Internet. If you do, I mean if you copy, that's plagiarism. If you plagiarize and you get caught, the punishment can be very serious. You can fail the course or even get kicked out of the university. So as I said, this is a very serious thing, and you need to be very careful about it.

OK; does anyone have questions at this point about types of university courses, about course requirements, or about plagiarism? No? Then let's stop here and take a break.

After You Listen

7 Reviewing New Vocabulary

❑ Look back at the vocabulary list in the Student Book, Activity 2 on page 11.

❑ Have students work in small groups to ask each other questions about the new vocabulary.

Example:

Student A: What is a lecture?

Student B: The professor talks and the students sit and take notes.

Best Practice

Organizing Information

Activities such as the next one will teach students to organize information using a graphic organizer called a Venn diagram. This allows students to better assimilate and recall information at a later date, a valuable study tool. In this case, students categorize similarities and differences between university systems. Other types of graphic organizers are used throughout this book.

Strategy

Graphic Organizer: Venn Diagram

▪ Read the information in the Strategy box about Venn diagrams.

▪ You may want to draw an example on the board, using a different topic such as subjects studied at school and university.

8 Discussing the Lecture

❑ Give students five minutes to complete the diagram with notes on differences between the American school or university system and that of a different country.

❑ They can use the list of topics as a guide.

❑ Move around the room to monitor their work.

❑ Then ask students to explain their diagrams to a partner.

On the Spot!

❑ Explain to the students that when you're "on the spot," you have to make a difficult decision. In the On the Spot! activities in this book, students will work with classmates to solve difficult problems or discuss difficult situations.

Best Practice

Cultivating Critical Thinking

This is an example of a collaborative team activity. This type of activity requires students to process the information they have learned and apply it to a situation that could happen in real life. It involves reinterpretation, synthesis, and application of concepts. The process of comparing different viewpoints on the topic of plagiarism, trying to reach agreement, and listing alternative courses of action will help develop critical thinking skills.

9 What Would You Do?

- ❑ Read the situation with the class, or ask students to read it silently.

- ❑ Give students ten minutes to read the questions in groups and discuss their answers.

- ❑ Groups can decide who will report on each of the questions. (Try to make sure every student gets a chance to speak.)

- ❑ Brainstorm a list of different possible reactions to this situation and write them on the board.

- ❑ Discuss the issue of plagiarism, and refer students to school regulations on plagiarism if appropriate.

Content Note

The definition of plagiarism varies in different cultures. Students may understand this concept differently, or the issue may have different ethical implications for them. It is important not to assume that all plagiarism is intentional. On the other hand, students should be aware that plagiarism in homework or on tests is treated very seriously at North American colleges and can have serious consequences.

EXPANSION ACTIVITY

REPRODUCIBLE

- ▦ The aim of this activity is to help students understand the concept and definition of plagiarism within a North American cultural context and its possible consequences.

- ▦ Please see Black Line Master "What is Plagiarism?" on page BLM 2 of this Teacher's Edition. Photocopy and distribute one to each student.

- ▦ Divide the students into groups of four and have each person in the group choose one question.

- ▦ Students can use a search engine typing in keywords like *plagiarism* or *what is plagiarism*? or use the websites below. Please check these websites before giving them to students.

  http://owl.english.purdue.edu/handouts/research/r_plagiar.html

  http://gervaseprograms.georgetown.edu/hc/index.htm

  http://sja.ucdaves.edu/avoid.htm

- ▦ Students will individually research their chosen question on the web. This can be done in a computer lab class or assigned for homework.

- ▦ Then re-form their groups to complete the worksheet.

- ▦ Finally, ask for volunteers to share the information from part 2 with the class.

Getting Meaning from Context

Focus on Testing

- ▨   Read the information in the box.
- ▨   Give examples for each point (see below).

  - ▪   words = What are the key words that help identify the main idea?

  - ▪   synonyms and paraphrases = Are any unfamiliar words explained by using different words with the same meaning?

  - ▪   transitions = Are there any signpost words, e.g., *on the other hand, 'finally*?

  - ▪   stressed words = Which words are louder, and clearer?

  - ▪   intonation = Which words are higher?

  - ▪   a speaker's tone of voice = Is the message friendly? helpful? angry?

  - ▪   your knowledge of the culture, speakers, or situation = What type of communication usually takes place in this type of context?

Using Context Clues

- ▨   This recording has four sections. There is a question at the end of each section. Play each section of the recording.

- ▨   Pause after the question to allow students to fill in their answers and write the clues.

- ▨   Then play the final sentence which gives the correct answer.

ANSWER KEY

Answers	Clues
1. b. in a library	*term paper, books, checked out*
2. d. a T.A.	*confused, lab, leave early, missed demonstration*
3. c. German	*language lab*

4. c. plagiarized a term paper	*research paper, same, another student*

AUDIOSCRIPT

Conversation 1

A: What's wrong?

B: Well, I've got a term paper due in a week, and all the books I need are checked out!

A: I know what you mean. There are a million books in this place, and I can never find what I need.

Question 1: Where are the speakers?

B: Maybe I'll try the other library.

Conversation 2

A: Can I come see you tomorrow?

B: Sure, what's the problem?

A: I am totally confused about this week's chemistry experiment.

B: Didn't you come to the lab yesterday?

A: Yeah, but I had to leave early and I missed part of your demonstration.

Question 2: Who is the student probably talking to?

B: OK, can you come to the T.A.'s office tomorrow at noon?

Conversation 3

A: What are the requirements for the course?

B: There'll be a quiz every Monday and a final exam. Also, you're required to go to the language lab two hours ever week. And, of course, your attendance and class participation are very important.

Question 3: What class is this?

B: And one more thing. Each student is required to give a short speech in German.

Conversation 4

A: You asked to see me, Professor Jansen?

B: Yes, Sheila. Would you like to explain what happened on this research paper?

A: What do you mean, sir?

B: It is almost exactly the same as a paper I received from another student two years ago.

Question 4: The student probably ...

B: I'm going to let you rewrite your paper this time. But if you ever plagiarize again, you will fail the course. Is that clear?

Focused Listening

GETTING MEANING FROM INTONATION

- Read the Instruction note about getting meaning from intonation.

- Play the recording and check the answers.

ANSWER KEY

1.b 2.c 3.a

1 **Listening for Intonation Clues**

❑ This recording has four sections. There is a question at the end of each section. Play each section of the recording.

❑ Pause after the question to allow students to circle their answers.

❑ Then play the final sentence, which gives the correct answer.

ANSWER KEY

1A. a 1B. b 2A. b 2B. a

AUDIOSCRIPT

Conversation 1A

Kathy: Hello?

Ron: Kathy? Uh, this is Ron, you know, from your history class?

Kathy: Oh, hi!

Ron: Listen, I was wondering . . . um, were you planning to go to Ali's party Saturday?

Kathy: Hmm. I haven't really thought about it yet.

Ron: Well, would you like to go?

Kathy: You mean, with you?

Ron: Yeah.

Question 1: How does the woman feel about the invitation?

Kathy: Well sure, Ron, I'd love to go.

Conversation 1B

Kathy: Hello?

Ron: Kathy? Uh, this is Ron, you know, from your history class?

Kathy: Oh, hi.

Ron: Listen, I was wondering . . . um, were you planning to go to Ali's party Saturday?

Kathy: Hmm. I haven't really thought about it yet.

Ron: Well, would you like to go?

Kathy: You mean, with you?

Ron: Yeah.

Question 2: How does the woman feel about the invitation?

Kathy: Well thanks, Ron, but I just remembered that I'm busy that night.

Conversation 2A

A: Did you hear the news? Professor Bradley had to go out of town suddenly. All his classes are cancelled this week.

B: Cancelled? Oh, wow.

Question 3: How do the students feel about the situation?

A: I'm really worried about my score on the last test. Now I'll have to wait until next week to find out.

Conversation 2B

A: Did you hear the news? Professor Bradley had to go out of town suddenly. All his classes are cancelled this week!

B: Cancelled? Oh, wow!

Question 4: How do the students feel about the situation?

A: I'm so happy! Now I'll have an extra week to work on my term paper.

2   Using Intonation to Express Feelings

❑   Read the steps of the activity.

❑   Model one example for part 2.

❑   You can set a time limit of five minutes for students to practice in pairs.

❑   Ask for volunteers to give examples of their own sentences. The rest of the class will guess the answers.

Using Language Functions

MAKING, ACCEPTING, AND REFUSING INVITATIONS

▪   Read the instruction note.

▪   Ask for volunteers to read the conversation (with the appropriate intonation).

▪   Check comprehension of the terms: *invite, accept, and refuse*.

3   Making, Accepting, and Refusing
Invitations

❑   Have students work individually or in pairs to complete the chart.

❑   Go over the answers as a class.

ANSWER KEY

Inviting	Accepting	Refusing (with an excuse)
I was wondering . . .	Well, sure!	Thanks, but I just remembered that I'm busy that night.
Were you planning to …?	I'd love to go.	Thanks for the invitation, but I have to study for a test.
Would you like to …?	That sounds like fun!	Sorry, I've already got plans. Maybe another time.
How about going to…?	Great!	I'd love to, but I'm going out of town.
Let's go to …	Good idea!	I'd like to go, but my parents are staying with me this weekend.

4 Role-Play: Making, Accepting, and
Refusing Invitations

❑ Read through the situations.

❑ Have students work in pairs and choose one situation.

❑ Set a time limit of ten minutes for students to write and practice their conversations.

❑ Invite volunteers to perform their conversation for the class.

 EXPANSION ACTIVITY

▦ The aim of this activity is to practice the language functions of making, accepting, and refusing invitations.

▦ Please see Black Line Master "Would You Like to . . .?" on page BLM 3 of this Teacher's Edition. Photocopy and distribute one to each student.

▦ Explain that they will choose four activities for their calendar.

▦ Select one student and ask: *Would you like to go to a film on Thursday at 4:00?* Mime *yes* by nodding so that the student will accept. Then write their name in your calendar, and gesture that they should do the same.

▦ Ask another student to invite you to go to a party on Thursday. Say, *Thanks, but I'm going to a film with (name of first student).*

▦ Explain that students will walk around the room and invite other students. They can only invite each student to one thing.

▦ When students have filled their calendars, they can sit down.

Before You Listen

1 Reviewing Compass Points

❑ If possible, bring a compass to class and pass it around the room.

❑ Have students look at the compass in the book, or draw the points of the compass on the board.

❑ Practice the pronunciation of each direction.

❑ Establish the direction of north in the classroom.

❑ Call out one direction and have students stand and face the correct direction.

❑ Have students take turns calling out directions.

Listen

2 Expressions of Location

❑ Have students read through the list of expressions.

❑ Play the recording and ask students to repeat each expression.

❑ Have students work individually to write the numbers from the map next to the correct expression.

❑ Play the recording again. Check the answers as a whole class.

ANSWER KEY

a. 8 b. 2 c. 4 d. 1 e. 5 f. 6 g. 9 h. 10 i. 7 j. 3 k. 11

Language Tip

▪ Read aloud the information about prepositions.

▪ Have students read the sentences aloud.

▪ Ask for volunteers to give personal information about their street, address, city, and state using the prepositions *in*, *on*, and *at*.

3 Expressions of Location in Context

❑ Give students one or two minutes to study the map of the college campus.

❑ Play the recording and give students time to write their answers.

❑ Check the answers as a class.

ANSWER KEY

1.F (Strictly speaking, because we're looking at a map, the answer is false. However, in everyday language, we can say that the Math Building is down the street from Memorial Cafeteria.); 2.T 3.T 4.F 5.F 6.T 7.T (Clearly, on the north side of College Boulevard, this is true, but south of College Boulevard this is false.); 8.T (This may also be interpreted as *across from*, *behind* (if the doors to the Science Hall are on the west side), or *next to*.)

AUDIOSCRIPT

1. The Math Building is down the street from Memorial Cafeteria.

2. The Computer Science building is across the street from the theater.

3. The Business Hall is at the intersection of Campus Road and Jones Street.

4. Memorial Cafeteria is in the middle of the block on Bridge Road.

5. There is a park beside the Math Building.

6. The boathouse is between Lakeshore Drive and College Lake.

7. There are buildings on both sides of Bradford Avenue.

8. Smith Library is opposite the Science Hall.

After You Listen

4 **Using Expressions of Location**

- ❏ Give students time to write their own sentences.

- ❏ Ask for volunteers to read their sentences to the whole class.

5 **Describing Map Locations**

- ❏ Have students work in pairs. Student A should look at the map on page 244. Student B should look at the map on page 252.

- ❏ Remind students not to show their page to their partner.

- ❏ Ask for two volunteers to read the example conversation.

- ❏ Set a time limit of ten minutes.

- ❏ Move around the room to monitor use of expressions of location and take notes of errors.

EXPANSION ACTIVITY

- ▪ The aim of this activity is to practice language for describing locations and apply it to real contexts.

- ▪ Have students work in pairs to create a map of your college campus or of the local neighborhood. The maps should show the locations of eight to ten buildings.

- ▪ Buildings can be shown as squares and numbered.

- ▪ Below the map, students should list descriptions of the locations of each building.

- ▪ Pairs will then exchange maps and identify the buildings and their numbers.

- ▪ At the end of the activity, you may want to collect the maps for display in the classroom.

Best Practice

Scaffolding Instruction

This learning log develops skills of evaluating one's own progress in learning. By completing the log at the end of each chapter, learners will review what they have learned, identify the language functions and study skills they have practiced, and evaluate how well they have understood the chapter.

Self-Assessment Log

- ❏ The Self-Assessment Log at the end of each chapter helps students track their own strengths and weaknesses and also encourages them to take ownership of their own learning.

- ❏ Explain to students that thinking about their learning can help them decide what to focus on in their lessons and homework and help them chart their progress.

- ❏ Read the directions aloud and have students check vocabulary they learned in the chapter and are prepared to use. Have students check the strategies practiced in the chapter (or the degree to which they learned them).

- ❏ Put students in small groups. Ask students to find the information or an activity related to each strategy in the chapter.

- ❏ Tell students to find definitions in the chapter for any words they did not check.

- ❏ If possible, meet privately with each student on a regular basis and review his or her assessment log. This provides an opportunity for the student to ask key questions and for you to see where additional help may be needed and to offer one-on-one encouragement.

City Life

In this chapter, students will read about different aspects of city life, such as looking for accommodations, neighborhood crime prevention, housing repairs, and giving directions. In Part 1, they will learn to recognize stressed and reduced forms and practice ways to open and close a phone conversation. In Part 2, they will listen to a talk about the neighborhood watch. They will also discuss the issue of gun safety. In Part 3, they will practice different forms of address between people. In Part 4, they will learn how to request and give directions using a map.

Chapter Opener

❑ Have students look at the photo of landmark homes called "Painted Ladies" in San Francisco. Ask them to discuss the questions from the Connecting to the Topic section. Have students discuss as a class.

❑ Read and discuss the quote. What is a neighborhood? What kind of neighborhood do you think the writer lives in? Is it like your neighborhood? What kind of "identity" does your neighborhood have?

❑ Brainstorm adjectives to describe life in a city and life in the country or in the suburbs, for example, *safe/dangerous, expensive/cheap, stressful/relaxing, noisy/peaceful.*

❝ I love cities. I love neighborhoods and the ways in which they interact with each other . . . I love the long gradual shifts in culture they contain. I love the fact that they work at all. ❞

—Jason Sutter
U.S. blogger (1976–)

Chapter Overview

Listening Skills and Strategies

Listening for main ideas

Listening for details

Making inferences

Listening for clues to relationships between people

Following directions

Speaking Skills and Strategies

Using the phrase *by the way*

Opening and closing phone conversations

Talking about crime

Expressing frustration

Learning names of professions

Requesting and giving directions

Saying you don't understand

Critical Thinking Skills

Predicting questions speakers will ask

Getting meaning from context

Speculating about hypothetical situations

Taking notes on statistics

Using transitions as cues for note-taking

Taking notes on an informal talk

Vocabulary Building

Expressions for opening and closing conversations

Terms for expressing frustration

Expressions for requesting and giving directions

Names of professions

Terms for expressing lack of understanding

Using the phrase *by the way*

Pronunciation

Identifying and practicing stressed words

Identifying and practicing reduced pronunciation

Language Skills

Using context clues to identify a speaker

Using context clues to guess a person's job

Vocabulary

Nouns	Verbs	Adjective	Expressions
alarm	break into	violent	can't miss
break-in	bug		get into the habit
deadbolt	come by		make it
decal	prevent		never lift a finger
device			
front/back (of)			
license			
right			
slob			
(car) theft			
timer			
valuables			

Can You Guess?

- Ask students to discuss the questions below in groups and compare their answers with the correct answers.

- Discuss the issues raised by these questions: Why is it difficult to determine the answers to these questions? Why is it difficult to measure the population of a city? What factors are measured to determine safety? What are the different ways of measuring the size of a department store? What are the differences between living in an old city and a newly built city?

1. Which three world cities have the largest populations? A. *Tokyo, Japan; Mexico City, Mexico; and Seoul, Korea.*

2. What is the world's safest city?
A. *"Luxembourg ranks as the world's top city for personal safety and security, according to a quality of life survey by Mercer Human Resource Consulting."*

3. What and where is the world's largest department store? A. *Macy's in New York City covers an area of 2.15 million square feet (198,500 square meters).*

4. What is the world's oldest continuously inhabited capital city? A. *Damascus, Syria.*

Before You Listen

1   Prelistening Questions

- Have the students look at the photo on page 28, read the questions on page 29, and discuss them in pairs.

- Compare answers as a whole class.

- As a whole class, make a list of questions a roommate might ask Mari and write them on the board.

2   Previewing Vocabulary

- Play the recording and have students listen to the underlined words.

- Have students complete the vocabulary preview individually.

- Compare their answers as a whole class and write the correct answers on the board.

- Practice the pronunciation of new words or phrases.

ANSWER KEY

1. b   2. e   3. d   4. f   5. a   6. c

Listen

3   Comprehension Questions

(The audioscript follows Activity 4.)

- Explain that these questions will help students focus on the main ideas in the listening. They do not need to understand every word to answer the questions.

- You may want to write the questions on the board.

- Read the questions aloud.

- Play the recording.

- After listening, have students compare their answers in pairs.

- Check the answers as a class.

ANSWER KEY

1. Nancy and Mari.

2. Mari is calling about a room for rent.

3. Mari is living in a house with some other students, but it's really noisy, and it's not very clean.

4. The other people in the house are Nancy's husband, Andrew, and her cousin, Jeff.

5. The neighborhood is safe, and she can walk to school.

6. Mari will come by to see the house at 5:00 P.M.

4 **Listening for Stressed Words**

❑ Review the meaning of stressed words from the previous unit.

❑ Listen to the recording again, this time with books open.

❑ The recording has pauses to allow time for students to repeat and write the missing words.

❑ After listening, have students check their answers with a partner, looking at the audioscript in their books.

❑ Have students read the conversation with a partner, paying attention to stressed words in their pronunciation and intonation.

AUDIOSCRIPT and ANSWER KEY

Nancy: Hello?

Mari: May I speak to Nancy, please?

Nancy: _Speaking_.

Mari: Uh hi, uh, my name is Mari, and I'm calling about the _room_ for rent. I saw your _ad_ at the campus _housing_ office.

Nancy: Oh, right. OK, uh, are you a _student_?

Mari: Well, right now, I'm just studying _English_, but I'm planning to start _college_ full-time in _March_.

Nancy: I see. _Where_ are you living _now_?

Mari: I've been living in a _house_ with some other students, but I _don't like_ it there.

Nancy: Why? What's the _problem_?

Mari: Well, _first_ of all, it's really _noisy_, and it's not very clean. The other people in the house are real _slobs_. I mean they never lift a _finger_ to clean _up_ after themselves. It really _bugs_ me! I need a place that's cleaner and more _private_.

Nancy: Well, it's really _quiet_ here. We're not _home_ very much.

Mari: What do you _do_?

Nancy: I teach _English_ at the college.

Mari: _Wait_ a minute! Didn't we meet yesterday at the _placement_ exam?

Nancy: Oh . . . _you're_ the girl from _Japan_! What was your name again?

Mari: Mari.

Nancy: Right. What a _small world_!

Mari: It really is. By the way, who _else_ lives in the house? The ad said there are _three_ people.

Nancy: Well besides me there's my _husband_, Andrew, and my _cousin_, Jeff. He's a musician and a part-time _student_. Uh, are you OK with having _male_ roommates?

Mari: Sure, as long as they're clean and not too _noisy_.

Nancy: _Don't_ worry. They're both _easy_ to live with.

Mari: OK. Um, is the _neighborhood_ safe?

Nancy: Oh sure. We haven't had _any_ problems, and you can _walk_ to school from here.

Mari: Well, it sounds really _nice_. When can I come by and _see_ it?

Nancy: Can you make it this _evening_ around _five_? Then you can meet the _guys_, too.

Mari: Yeah, five o'clock is _good_. What's the _address_?

Nancy: It's 3475 Hayworth Avenue. Do you know where _that_ is?

Mari: No, I don't.

Nancy: OK. From University Village you go seven blocks _east_ on Olympic Avenue. At the intersection of Olympic and Alfred there's a _stoplight_. Turn _left_, and go _up_ one and a half blocks. Our house is in the _middle_ of the block on the _left_.

Mari: That sounds _easy_.

Nancy: Yeah, you _can't miss_ it. Listen, I've got to go. Someone's at the door. See you this _evening_.

Mari: OK, see you _later_. Bye.

Nancy: Bye-bye.

Language Tip

- Point out that _by the way_ is not used to introduce a main or an important idea.

- Read aloud the information in the box.

- Ask two students to read the short conversation.

 EXPANSION ACTIVITY

- The purpose of this activity is to practice opening and closing phone conversations on the topic of looking for housing.

- Please see Black Line Master "Looking for a Place to Live" on page BLM 4 of this Teacher's Edition. Photocopy and cut it into strips.

- Give one strip to each student. There are ten different strips. If you have more than ten students, have students work in pairs or threes.

- Explain that some people are looking for accommodations, and some are offering accommodations.

- Students walk around the room and try to find their partner. Ask them not to show their paper to the other students. They must "phone" each person they meet until they find a partner.

- When they have found a partner, they can sit down and practice their conversation again.

Reductions

5 **Comparing Unreduced and Reduced Pronunciation**

- ❑ Read the directions aloud.

- ❑ Play the recording and have students listen and read the sentences.

- ❑ Play the recording again. This time, pause the audio to allow time for students to repeat.

6 **Listening for Reductions**

- ❑ Before listening to the conversation, you can first have students read through the conversation and try to guess the missing words.

- ❑ Play the recording, pausing after each conversation to allow time for students to write their answers.

- ❑ After listening, have students check their answers with the audioscript in their books.

- ❑ Have students practice the conversation in pairs, paying attention to reduced forms in their pronunciation.

AUDIOSCRIPT

Conversation 1

Mari: Hey Jeff, *where are you* going?

Jeff: I *want to* get a present for Nancy. It's her birthday, *you* know.

Mari: Yeah, I know. *What do you* think I should get her?

Jeff: Well, she likes music. *How about* a CD?

Conversation 2

Nancy: *How do you* like my new haircut, Mari?

Mari: It's great! Who's your hairstylist?

Nancy: His name's José.

Mari: *Can you* give me his phone number?

Nancy: Sure, but he's always very busy. *You can* try calling him, but he might not be able *to* see *you* until next month.

Conversation 3

Andrew: *What do you want to* do tonight, Nancy?

Nancy: Nothing special. I've *got to* stay home *and* correct my students' compositions.

After You Listen

7 Reviewing Vocabulary

- ❑ Review the vocabulary items in the box.
- ❑ Model the conversation with a student.
- ❑ Ask students to suggest one or two ways of continuing the conversation.
- ❑ Have students practice the conversation in pairs. Remind them to include vocabulary from the box.
- ❑ Ask for volunteers to perform the conversation for the class.

Using Language Functions

OPENING A PHONE CONVERSATION

- ▪ Read the instruction note.
- ▪ Ask students to repeat the expressions using their own or imaginary names.

CLOSING A PHONE CONVERSATION

- ▪ Read the instruction note.
- ▪ Have students reread the conversation between Mari and Nancy to see a typical closing of a phone conversation.

Best Practice

Interacting with Others

This type of activity is an example of collaborative learning to encourage fluency and confidence. This is an information gap activity designed to practice ways of opening and closing phone conversations. It is similar to real-life situations because students have to share information to complete the task. In this activity, communication is more important than grammar. Students can practice phone strategies in pairs and then improve their performance by switching roles or partners. By providing feedback to each other, they learn skills of self-evaluation.

---

8 Role-Play

- ❑ Have students work in pairs. Student A should look at page 245. Student B should look at page 253.
- ❑ Remind students not to show their page to their partner.
- ❑ Ask for two volunteers to read the example conversation.
- ❑ Set a time limit of ten minutes.

❏ Move around the room to monitor use of appropriate phone language and take notes of errors.

❏ Ask for volunteers to perform conversations for the class.

Best Practice

Scaffolding Instruction

This type of activity mirrors the authentic experience of using language on the telephone. By practicing fixed phrases that can be used in many different situations, students will learn to predict the kinds of language they will come across in telephone conversations. They will later learn to vary these phrases more freely according to their own individual needs.

9 **Telephone Game**

❏ This game is homework for students to practice their phone language using real phones.

❏ Before the class, make a numbered list of "secret" messages to give to various groups in your class. You will need one message for each group. The messages may be complex, but in simple language.

Examples:

The concert will begin at 8:00 on Friday night, but I can't go because it is my sister's birthday and we're having a party.

The time of the reading exam tomorrow has been changed from 9:30 A.M. to 10:30 A.M.

❏ Read the instructions for the game.

❏ Help students form groups and exchange phone numbers.

❏ Make sure they each know who will call first in the group.

❏ At the beginning of the next class, ask the first person and the last person in each group to read out their messages to see if they are the same.

❏ **Note:** If you do not want to ask students to exchange phone numbers because of privacy issues, have students role-play this activity in class using made-up phone numbers.

Before You Listen

- ❑ Read the information that introduces the next listening.

- ❑ Look at the signs about Neighborhood Crime Watch. These will be discussed in the next activity.

- ❑ Read the *Culture Note*. Explain that a Neighborhood Watch is a type of citizens' organization (not police) that tries to prevent crime and vandalism in its neighborhood by watching out for suspicious activity.

1 Prelistening Discussion

- ❑ Read through the list of questions.

- ❑ Have students work in groups to answer the questions.

- ❑ Review the responses as a class.

2 Previewing Vocabulary

- ❑ Play the recording and ask students to listen to the words.

- ❑ Have students check the words they know. Then discuss their meanings with a partner.

- ❑ Explain that they will work out the meaning of the new words by listening to the talk. As they learn new words, they should come back to this list and check them.

Listen

Strategy

Taking Notes on Statistics

- ▪ Read the information in the Strategy box.

- ▪ Tell the students that they will fill in the blanks when they do the next activity.

3 Abbreviating Statistics

- ❑ Review the meaning of *abbreviation*, and give some examples.

- ❑ Have students work individually to write the abbreviations for the terms in the box.

- ❑ Check the answers as a class.

- ❑ Emphasize that students may use their own symbols as long as they are clear and easy to read.

ANSWER KEY

Nouns:

% percent

\# number

½ half

⅓ third

¼ quarter

Verbs:

↑ increase, go up, rise

↓ decrease, decline, go down

X2 double

Other phrases:

< less than

> more than

= equal to or the same as

4 Taking Notes on Statistics

- ❑ Explain that students will hear three sentences.

- ❑ They will take notes using their abbreviations from Activity 3.

- ❑ Have students work in pairs to recreate the sentences.

- ❑ Invite volunteers to write the sentences on the board.

ANSWER KEY

1. last yr 48 burglaries ↑ 60 this yr

2. # car thefts x2

3. ½ (50%) burglaries unlocked doors & windows

AUDIOSCRIPT

1. A year ago, there were 48 burglaries in your area; this year it's gone up to 60 so far.

2. The number of car thefts has almost doubled.

3. Did you know that in half of all burglaries, 50 percent, the burglars enter through unlocked doors or windows?

Strategy

Transitions (Connecting Words)

Read the information in the Strategy box. Ask if students can think of any other examples, e.g., *first, the main thing, finally.*

Best Practice

Scaffolding Instruction

The transition outline helps students to organize the lecture into main and secondary ideas. By providing students with the transitions as a support, they can see how the transitions help the listener to structure the content of the talk. This guided activity prepares them for the skill of identifying main and secondary ideas without the help of an outline.

5 **Listening for Transitions**

❑ Read the directions and then give students a couple of minutes to read the transition word outline.

❑ Play the recording. The recording is in two sections. You may want to pause between the two sections to check answers.

❑ Have students write their answers individually and then compare their answers in pairs.

❑ Read the questions in part 2.

❑ Play the recording again.

❑ Compare answers as a class.

❑ Note that students will be introduced to numbering conventions used in outlines in the next chapter. At this stage, they should focus only on transitions.

❑ Next, have students answer the three questions on page 40 of the Student Book.

ANSWER KEY

PART 1

First of all, *outside lights*

Next, *lights inside the house*

All right then. The next topic I want to discuss is *locks.*

First of all, *cheap locks are not safe.*

Also, *there are special locks for windows.*

PART 2

OK, now let's move on and talk about *how to prevent car theft*.

First, *put car in garage*.

The most important thing is *put valuables in the trunk*.

Now my last point is *neighbors can help each other.*

The main thing is *when you go on vacation, ask someone to watch your house.*

Also, *if you see something unusual, call the police.*

And one more thing: *put Neighborhood Watch decal in window.*

ANSWER KEY

1. Four main ideas
   Transitions: First of all; The next topic; Now let's move on; Now, my last point is
2. They are subheadings under the main heading.
3. No, they don't contain essential information.

AUDIOSCRIPT

Part 1

Police Officer: Good evening. My name is Officer Jenkins. Thanks for inviting me tonight. OK, so, as you know, there have been a number of break-ins recently in your neighborhood, and even though it's true that there's been very little *violent* crime, um, especially compared to other parts of the city, burglary and car theft are both up in this area. Let me give you some statistics. OK, a year ago there were . . . 48 burglaries in your area; this year, it's gone up to 60 so far, and the number of car thefts has almost doubled, too. Now, I'm not here to try to scare you. What I want to do tonight is to give you some simple suggestions that will make your homes and automobiles safer. OK?

So, first of all, let's talk about lights outside the house. If you live in a house, you need to have lights both in the front of your house and in the back, and be sure to turn on those lights at night. In my opinion, this is the most important thing you can do to prevent burglaries.

Next, let's talk about lights inside the house. It's . . .

Woman in Audience: Excuse me, what about apartments? I mean, I live in an apartment building . . .

Police Officer: Yeah, good question. If you live in an apartment building, you want to have good, bright lighting in the garage, the hallways, and by the door to your apartment. If a light is broken, don't ignore it. Report it to your manager immediately. And whether you live in a house or an apartment, it's a good idea to put automatic timers on your lights. You know what a timer is, right? It's like a lock that turns on your lights automatically, so it looks like someone is home even if you're out. Are you with me on that?

All right, then . . . the next topic I want to discuss is locks. First of all, forget cheap locks 'cause they're not safe. Every door in your place should have a deadbolt . . . um, a deadbolt at least one inch thick. Also, there are special locks you can buy for your windows. By the way, did you know that in half of all burglaries, 50 percent, the burglars enter through unlocked doors or windows? I'm telling you, even in a peaceful neighborhood like this, where you know all your neighbors, you have to get into the habit of keeping your windows and doors locked.

Part 2

OK, now let's move on and talk about how you can prevent car theft. First, if you have a garage, use it for your car, not for your ping-pong table! [Laughter] But seriously, the most important thing is—and I hope this is obvious—if you've got valuables in the car, hide them in the trunk. Don't leave them out on the seat, not even for five minutes! Last week, we got a report from a guy who left his laptop on the car seat while he ran in to buy a cup of coffee. When he came back, it was gone. The thief just broke the car window and reached in and took it. And also . . .

Man in Audience: What about a car alarm?

Police Officer: Well, most research shows that noisy alarms don't do anything to prevent car theft. It's better to have the kind of device thieves can see, like a lock on your steering wheel. But the best thing of all is just to lock your car and keep valuables out of sight.

All right. Now my last point is what you, as neighbors, can do to help each other. The main thing is that when you go on vacation, ask someone to watch your house for you, to collect your mail, take in your newspaper, stuff like that. Also, If you see something unusual, like a strange van or truck in your neighbor's driveway, or people carrying furniture out, *don't* go out there and try to stop it. Just call the police! And one more thing. Each of you should put this Neighborhood Watch decal

—this picture right here of the man in a coat looking over his shoulder—in your front window. This tells criminals that this area has a Neighborhood Watch and that someone might be watching them. OK, are there any questions?

Man in Audience: Yeah, there's something I want to know . . . Do you think it's a good idea to keep a gun in the house?

Police Officer: Well now, that is a very complicated question. I think that it's a bad idea to have a gun in your house, especially if you have kids. Thousands of people die in gun accidents each year in this country. So, in my opinion, it's just not safe to have a gun in your house. But of course it *is* legal to have a gun, if that's what you want. Just make sure you get the proper license and that you take a course in gun safety, OK? All right. Anything else?

Best Practice

Organizing Information

This type of activity uses an outline to categorize information. Using an outline encourages students to process and organize information while they are listening and also provides a record for them to refer to when reviewing their notes. This type of graphic organizer emphasizes listing and categorizing skills. It also helps them practice using abbreviations and symbols to take notes. Other types of graphic organizers are used throughout this book.

6 Taking Notes

(See audioscript in the previous activity.)

❏ Point out the use of underlining, indenting, and numbering in the outline.

- Ask students to identify which type of words are underlined, indented, and numbered.

- Have students complete the outline, using their notes from Activities 4 and 5. Remind them to use abbreviations.

- Play the recording again so they can check their answers.

ANSWER KEY

Date:

Ways to Prevent Crime

PART 1

Intro:

Very little violent crime in neighbor-hd. But:

Burglaries ↑:

— Last yr: _48_

— This yr: _60_

Car theft ↑ _2x_

How to keep home & auto safe:

1. House lights
   - need lights in front and _back_
2. _Lights inside the house_
   - bright lights in garage, hallway, apt. door
   - fix broken lights
   - house or apt: use automatic _timers_
3. _Locks_
   - _Cheap locks are_ not safe
   - every door needs _a deadbolt_
   - get special locks for _windows_
     — 50% _enter through unlocked doors and windows_

PART 2

4. _How to prevent car theft_
   - use _your garage_
   - put _valuables in the trunk_
   - alarms don't _work_
   - better to have _a steering wheel lock_

5. _Neighbors can help each other_
   - Go on vacation, _ask someone to watch your house_
   - See something (st) unusual, _call the police_
   - Put _Neighborhood Watch decal in window_

After You Listen

Best Practice

Activating Prior Knowledge

This is an example of an activity that encourages students to make text-to-self connections. The discussion questions ask students to relate the content of the lecture on crime prevention to their own lives. This aids understanding and retention of new material.

7 **Discussing the Lecture**

- Have students discuss the questions in groups.

- Encourage students to use the new vocabulary in their discussion.

- Ask for representatives from each group to report back on the discussion.

8 **Reviewing Vocabulary**

- Look back at the vocabulary list in Activity 2 on page 37 in the Student Book.

- Have students work in small groups to ask each other questions about the new vocabulary.

On the Spot!

Best Practice

Making Use of Academic Content

This is an example of a group discussion on a real-world issue. This type of activity requires students to agree and disagree and give reasons for their opinions. They will also have to utilize skills for interrupting, holding the floor, and taking their turn in the discussion. Active participation in discussion is a course requirement in many academic courses.

9 What Would You Do?

❑ Read the situation with the class, or ask students to read it silently.

❑ Give students 10 –15 minutes to read the questions in groups and discuss their answers.

❑ Choose one person from each group to report to the class.

❑ Write a list of arguments for and against owning guns on the board.

Content Note

This topic is one that may be very sensitive for students who have been victims of violence. You may wish to advise students to maintain a balanced discussion on general issues of crime prevention and the law and avoid discussing personal experiences.

REPRODUCIBLE EXPANSION ACTIVITY

■ The purpose of this activity is to help students be aware of safety issues and develop skills for using the Internet to get advice.

■ Students can use a search engine typing in keywords such as *campus safety* or *campus crime prevention*.

■ The research part of this activity can be done in a computer lab class or assigned for homework.

■ Please see Black Line Master "Safety on Campus" on page BLM 5 of this Teacher's Edition. Photocopy and distribute one to each student.

■ Divide the students into groups of four and have each person in the group choose one issue.

■ Students will research their chosen issue on the web and write the safety tips in the appropriate circle in the mind map, a type of graphic organizer.

■ Then re-form their groups to complete the worksheet. As students listen to their group members' reports, have them write the information they hear in the mind map.

■ Display the worksheets on the classroom wall.

5. c. He's annoyed with Donna.	annoyed tone of voice

Getting Meaning from Context

Focus on Testing

Using Context Clues

- Remind students of strategies for using context clues. (See Chapter 1, Part 3, page 17.)

- Read the instructions.

- This recording has five sections. There is a question at the end of each section. Play each section of the recording.

- Pause after the question to allow students to circle their answers and write the clues.

- Then play the final part of each section which gives the correct answer.

ANSWER KEY

Answers	Clues
Questions 1 through 3 are based on a conversation between a man and a woman.	
1. b. the apartment manager	check for you, fifth of the month, Mr. Bradley
2. c. an exterminator	cockroaches, spray, kill those bugs
3. c. It's too expensive.	said you'd fix, hole in the …, still haven't done that
Questions 4 and 5 are based on a conversation between two neighbors.	
4. d. He is happy to help Donna.	pleasant tone of voice

AUDIOSCRIPT

Conversation 1

Manager: Yes? Who is it?

Tenant: It's Donna from 206. I've got a check for you.

Manager: Oh, it's you. Do you know it's the fifth of the month?

Tenant: Yes, Mr. Bradley. I'm sorry. I know it was due on the first, but my grandma got sick, and I had to go out of town suddenly.

Question 1: Who is the man?

Manager: Look, my job as manager here is to collect the rent on the first. If you're late again next month, you'll have to look for another place to live.

Conversation 2

Tenant: OK, Mr. Bradley. But look, while I'm here, I need to talk to you about a couple of things.

Manager: Yeah?

Tenant: First, about the cockroaches. They're all over the kitchen again. I'm sick of them!

Manager: Have you used the spray I gave you?

Tenant: It's no good. I need something stronger to kill those horrible bugs once and for all.

Question 2: Who will the manager probably need to call?

Manager: OK, I'll call the exterminator next week.

Conversation 3

Tenant: Next week?! Last week you said you'd fix the hole in the ceiling, and you still haven't done that! I'm fed up waiting for you to fix things around here!

Question 3: What can you guess about Donna's apartment?

Tenant: Why should I pay so much rent for a place in such bad condition?

Manager: Well, you're not the only tenant in this building. If you don't like it, why don't you move out?

Conversation 4

John: Hi, Donna. What do you need this time?

Donna: Hello, John. A couple of eggs. Do you mind?

John: No, come on in.

Question 4: How does John feel about Donna's request?

Donna: Thanks so much, John!

John: You're welcome!

Conversation 5

John: Hi, Donna. What do you need this time?

Donna: Hello, John. A couple of eggs. Do you mind?

John: No, come on in.

Question 5: How does John feel about Donna's request?

Donna: Thanks, John.

John: OK, but next time go ask somebody else, all right?

Focused Listening

GUESSING RELATIONSHIPS BETWEEN PEOPLE

- Read the information note about guessing relationships between people.

- Ask students for examples of how they address people they know.

1 **Listening for Clues to Relationships Between People**

- ❑ Have students read the directions for Activity 1.

- ❑ Have them work in groups of four, divided into two pairs. One person will look at page 245. The other person will look at page 253.

- ❑ Set a time limit of ten minutes for this activity.

- ❑ Invite volunteers to perform the conversations for the class.

> ## Content Note
> Formality and politeness vary in different cultures. In some cultures, it is impolite to be too informal with one's teacher. Therefore, it may be difficult for some students to address the teacher by his or her first name.

Using Language Functions

EXPRESSING FRUSTRATION

- Read the instruction note.

- Review use of intonation to express feelings.

- Ask them to give some situations that make people frustrated.

2 **Role-Play**

- ❑ Have students work in pairs. One student will look at page 246. The other student will look at page 254.

- ❑ Set a time limit of ten minutes for students to practice their conversations.

- ❑ Monitor the groups as they are doing the activity and make notes of errors.

- ❑ Invite volunteers to perform their conversation for the class.

3 **Follow-up Discussion**

- ❑ Review the vocabulary in the chart and practice the pronunciation as needed.

❏ Have students work in groups to discuss the questions.

❏ Ask representatives from each group to report to the class.

EXPANSION ACTIVITY
REPRODUCIBLE

▪ The aim of this activity is to practice language of building repairs and repair workers.

▪ Have students work in small groups.

▪ Please see Black Line Master "Can You Fix It?" on page BLM 6 of this Teacher's Edition. Photocopy and distribute one to each group of students.

▪ Explain that they will discuss the problems with their group and write the problems in the correct places on the chart.

▪ Check the answers as a class.

▪ Students who finish early can go on to part 2.

▪ Invite representatives from one or two groups to perform their conversations for the class.

ANSWER KEY

Answers for this Expansion Activity will vary depending on the skills in the group. Mice and cockroaches, for example, could be dealt with by buying commercial products from a hardware store.

Possible answers:

Plumber	Electrician
Dripping faucet	Microwave doesn't work
Broken toilet	
Leaking water pipe	Lights don't work
Shower doesn't work	No electricity
	Refrigerator doesn't work

Carpenter	Exterminator
Broken window	Mice
Broken front door	Cockroaches
Broken closet door	
Fix it yourself	
Broken shower curtain	
Bugs in the food	

Before You Listen

1 Prelistening Questions

❑ Ask students to make a list of all the expressions they know for requesting and giving directions.

❑ Practice requesting and giving directions using the map.

❑ Then read the information in the box about language for requesting and giving directions.

ANSWER KEY

Answers will vary. Possible answers:

1. How do I get to the Chinese restaurant? / Could you tell me how to get to the Chinese restaurant?

2. Go straight for two blocks. Turn right on Main Street. Walk for two blocks. It's on your right.

Listen

REQUESTING AND GIVING DIRECTIONS

▪ Review expressions for giving directions from Chapter 1, Part 4, pages 21 and 22 of the Student Book.

▪ Read the information in the *Requesting and Giving Directions* note.

▪ Practice the expressions using places that are well known to the students.

2 Following Directions

❑ Give students some time to study the map.

❑ Check comprehension of any new vocabulary.

❑ The recording has four sections. Each section will be heard twice. There is a question at the end of each section.

❑ Play each section of the recording.

❑ Pause after the question to allow students to write their answers.

❑ Play the recording again. Check the answers as a whole class.

ANSWER KEY

1. department store 2. public library
3. supermarket 4. bookstore

AUDIOSCRIPT

1. You are at the X. Go two blocks west on 2nd Avenue. Turn left and go down one block. What's on your left?

2. You are at the intersection of Main Street and 3rd Avenue. Go one block south on Main. Turn left. Go straight for half a block. What's on your left?

3. You have just eaten dinner at the French restaurant at the intersection of 4th and Pine. Go south on Pine Street to 2nd Avenue. Turn right. Go one block west on 2nd. Turn left. Go down Main Street for half a block. What's on your right?

4. You work in the office building at the intersection of 3rd and Main. After work you decide to go shopping. Go one block east on 3rd. Turn left and go one block up Pine Street. Turn right. Go one block east until you reach Oak Street. What's on your right?

After You Listen

SAYING YOU DON'T UNDERSTAND

▪ Read the instruction note about language for saying you don't understand.

▪ Have students practice saying these expressions with the correct pronunciation and intonation.

Best Practice

Cultivating Critical Thinking

This is an example of a problem-solving activity where students have to share information. In this activity, students first have to read and interpret maps. Then they have to give and understand directions in order to complete the task. This requires applying language to new contexts, checking understanding, and synthesizing written and verbal information.

3 Requesting and Giving Directions

❑ Have students work in pairs. One student will look at the map on page 246. The other student will look at the map on page 254.

❑ Set a time limit of ten minutes for students to practice their conversations.

❑ Monitor the groups as they are doing the activity and make notes of errors.

❑ Invite volunteers to perform their conversation for the class.

EXPANSION ACTIVITY

▪ The aim of this activity is to practice language for requesting and giving directions using real locations.

▪ Have students work in pairs and write questions asking for directions to a place somewhere near your school.

▪ Have pairs of students exchange questions and write the answers.

▪ (If students finish early, have them exchange with another pair.)

▪ Move around the room and monitor their work, taking notes of any errors.

▪ Have students read out their directions. The other students in the class will try to guess where they are going.

Self-Assessment Log

❑ The purpose of the log is to help the students reflect on their learning.

❑ Read the directions aloud and have students check vocabulary that they learned in the chapter and are prepared to use.

❑ Have students check the strategies they understand.

❑ Put students in small groups. Ask students to find the information or an activity related to each strategy in the chapter.

❑ Tell students to find definitions in the chapter for any words they did not check, or they can look in their dictionaries.

3

Business and Money

In this chapter, students will read about different aspects of business and money, such as borrowing money, how to start a business, how to use banking services, and finally, how to balance a checkbook. In Part 1, they will learn to recognize stressed and reduced forms and practice ways of requesting and giving advice. In Part 2, they will listen to a lecture about the process of starting your own company. In Part 3, they will listen to advertisements for different banking services. At the end of the chapter, they will learn about how to balance a checkbook. These topics will encourage students to think about ways of spending and saving money and the function of money in our economy.

Chapter Opener

❑ Have students look at the photo of a young woman with a check written out to her for $58,900,000. She bought a winning lottery ticket in Georgia, U.S.A. Ask them the questions from the Connecting to the Topic section. Have students discuss as a class.

❑ Read and discuss the quote. Discuss the meaning of *you'll never make it* (meaning *you'll never be successful*) and *always put the customer first* (meaning *always consider, or think about, what the customer wants*). What values are represented by the quote? Are these values typical of businesses today?

❑ Brainstorm different ways to save and invest money. Write a list of useful words on the board, e.g., *bonds, stocks, pensions, investment account, savings account*.

❝ If you work just for money, you'll never make it, but if you love what you're doing and you always put the customer first, success will be yours. ❞

—Ray Kroc
American businessman, founder of McDonald's Corp., 1902–1984

Chapter Overview

Listening Skills and Strategies

Listening for main ideas

Listening for details

Making inferences

Distinguishing between *can* and *can't*

Distinguishing between teens and tens

Recognizing expressions of advice

Speaking Skills and Strategies

Talking about managing money

Talking about entrepreneurs

Talking about abilities

Using the words *borrow* and *lend*

Asking for, giving, and refusing advice

Critical Thinking Skills

Outlining a lecture

Getting meaning from context

Taking notes on a process

Vocabulary Building

Terms for talking about money

Borrow vs. *lend*

Expressions for asking for, giving, accepting, and rejecting advice

Terms for talking about entrepreneurs and the entrepreneurial process

Terms related to banking

Pronunciation

Identifying and practicing stressed words

Identifying and practicing reduced pronunciation

Pronouncing *can* and *can't*

Pronouncing teens and tens

Language Skills

Using context clues to identify banking services

Vocabulary

Nouns	Verbs	Adjective	Expressions
balance	balance a checkbook	broke	an arm and a leg
brilliant idea	earn		make ends meet
budget	enter		
income	found		
interest	have (something) in common		
quality	hire		
solution	identify		
team	pay off		
tightwad	raise capital		
vision	solve		
	surf the Internet		
	take risks		

Can You Guess?

- Ask students to discuss the questions below in groups and compare their answers with the correct answers.

- Brainstorm different types of taxes, e.g., federal, state, income, sales, property, etc. How are they collected? What are they used for?

1. What is the average yearly salary in the United States? A. *About $36,000.*

2. Which of the following countries have no income tax: Sweden, Kuwait, Switzerland, the Bahamas, Venezuela, Taiwan? A. *Kuwait and Bahamas.*

3. In which of the following countries do people save the largest percentage of their salaries: Switzerland, Korea, Sweden, Argentina, China, Germany, Japan? A. *China: 30 percent; Taiwan: 20 percent; Germany: 11 percent; Korea: 10 percent; Japan: 5 percent; United States: 1 percent.*

Before You Listen

Best Practice

Activating Prior Knowledge

The prelistening questions activate students' prior knowledge. This type of activity will help students relate their own experience of saving and spending money to the new language in this chapter. When students activate their prior knowledge before learning new material, they are better able to map new language onto existing concepts, which aids understanding and retention.

1 **Prelistening Questions**

- ❑ Have the students look at the photos and try to guess what the people are talking about.

- ❑ Have the students read the questions and discuss them in small groups.

- ❑ Compare answers as a whole class.

- ❑ As a whole class, make a list of ways to borrow money or tips for managing your budget.

2 **Previewing Vocabulary**

- ❑ Play the recording and have students listen to the underlined words.

- ❑ Have students complete the vocabulary preview individually.

- ❑ Compare their answers as a whole class and write the correct answers on the board.

- ❑ Ask students for additional paraphrases (or examples) for each item, e.g., 1. very expensive, 2. spends more than she earns, 3. stingy, 4. short of money, 5. carefully planned amount of spending money, 6. earnings / salary, 7. make money.

- ❑ Practice the pronunciation of new words and phrases.

ANSWER KEY

1. a 2. d 3. c 4. b 5. f 6. e

Content Note

In some cultures, it is not acceptable to discuss one's financial situation. In the U.S., students would normally feel comfortable telling who was paying for their college education and how much an item of clothing costs. However, other financial information, such as how much a person makes is considered personal information.

Listen

3 **Comprehension Questions**

(The audioscript follows Activity 4.)

❑ Explain that these questions will help students focus on the main ideas in the listening. They do not need to understand every word to answer the questions.

❑ You may want to write the questions on the board.

❑ Read the questions aloud.

❑ Play the recording.

❑ After listening, have students compare their answers in pairs.

ANSWER KEY

1. He's broke. 2. Make a budget; Don't spend more than you earn; Work more hours at the computer store. 3. He won't have time to study if he works any more hours. 4. He's angry.

4 Listening for Stressed Words

❑ Listen to the recording again.

❑ There will be a pause on the recording at the end of each sentence to allow time for students to repeat and write the missing words.

❑ After listening, have students check their answers with the audioscript in their books.

❑ Have students read the conversation with a partner, paying attention to stressed words in their pronunciation and intonation.

AUDIOSCRIPT and ANSWER KEY

Dad: Hello?

Jeff: Hi, Dad.

Dad: Jeff! How _are_ you?

Jeff: I'm fine Dad. How's Mom? Did she get over her _cold_?

Dad: Yes, she's _fine_ now. She went back to _work_ yesterday.

Jeff: That's good. Um, Dad, I need to _ask_ you something.

Dad: Sure, son, what _is_ it?

Jeff: Well, uh, the truth is, I'm _broke_ again. Could you _lend_ me $200 just till the end of the month?

Dad: Broke again? Jeff, when you moved _in_ with Nancy and Andrew, you said you could _make_ ends _meet_. But this is the _third_ time you've asked me for help!

Jeff: I know, I know, I'm sorry. But, see, my old guitar broke, and I had to buy a _new_ one. I _can't play_ on a broken guitar, right?

Dad: Look Jeff, if you want to play in a _band_, that's OK with me. But you _can't_ keep asking _me_ to pay for it!

Jeff: OK, OK, you're right. But what do you think I ought to _do_? Everything costs an _arm_ and a _leg_ around here.

Dad: Well, first of all, I think you'd better go on a _budget_. Make a list of all your _income_ and all your expenses. And then it's simple. Don't _spend_ more than you _earn_.

Jeff: But that's _exactly_ the problem! My expenses are _always_ larger than my income. That's why I need to borrow money from _you_.

Dad: Then maybe you should work more hours at the _computer_ store.

Jeff: Dad! I _already_ work 15 hours a week! How can I _study_ and _work_ and find time to play with my band?

Dad: Come _on_, Jeff, when _I_ was your age . . .

Jeff: I know, I know. When _you_ were my age you were already _married_ and working and going to school . . .

Dad: That's right. And if I could do it, why can't _you_?

Jeff: Because _I'm_ not _you_, Dad, that's why!

Dad: All right, Jeff, calm down. I don't _expect_ you to be like me. But I _can't lend_ you any more money. Your mother and I are on a budget _too_, you know.

Jeff: Maybe I should just drop *out* of school, *work* full-time, and play in the band in the evenings. I can go back to school *later*.

Dad: I wouldn't do that if I were you . . .

Jeff: Yeah, but you're *not* me, remember? It's my life!

Dad: All right, Jeff. Let's not *argue*. Why don't you *think* about this very carefully and call me *back* in a few days. And in the meantime, you'd *better* find a way to *pay* for that new guitar.

Jeff: Yes, Dad.

Dad: All right. Good-bye, son.

Jeff: Bye.

Language Tip

- The difference between *lend* and *borrow* can be confusing because some languages use the same word for both actions. The action is the same, but it is seen from two different points of view: *borrow* is from the point of view of the person receiving the money; *lend* is from the point of view of the person giving the money. You may find this easier to illustrate by drawing a diagram.

- Check comprehension by saying, for example, "*I'm* going to *give you* $10. I'm going to _____ you $10." (class should respond *lend*) or "*You're* going to *give me* $10. I'm going to _____ $10." (class should respond *borrow*). Practice with individual students, or have students practice in pairs.

REPRODUCIBLE EXPANSION ACTIVITY

- Please see Black Line Master "Lend or Borrow?" on page BLM 7 of this Teacher's Edition. Photocopy and distribute one copy to each student.

- Model the activity. Choose a student who doesn't have a cell phone and say: *I really need to phone my sister. Can you lend me your cell phone?* The student should answer *I'm sorry, I don't have a cell phone.* Then choose a student who has a cell phone and say: *I really need to phone my sister. Can you lend me your cell phone?* The student should answer *Yes, of course. Here you are.* Write the student's name on your list.

- Divide the class in half. One half is part of group A. They will look at Table A and ask to borrow things. The other half is part of group B. They will look at Table B. They have things to lend.

- Have students walk around the room and ask each other questions until they write someone's name next to each item. Point out that they can use a classmate's name only once. They can start with any item on the list. (The items to be lent or borrowed are imaginary. They do not have to physically lend or borrow these items.)

- When students have completed the worksheet, they can sit down.

- Then have them switch roles.

Reductions

5 Comparing Unreduced and Reduced Pronunciation

- ❑ Play the recording and have students listen and read the sentences.

- ❑ Play the recording again. This time, ask students to repeat.

6 Listening for Reductions

- ❑ If you wish, and if you have time, have students read through the text first and try to guess the missing words.

- ❑ Play the recording and have students write their answers.

❏ After listening, have students check their answers with the audioscript in their books. You can check answers in the audioscript on the next page.

❏ Have students practice the conversation in pairs, paying attention to reduced forms in their pronunciation and intonation.

AUDIOSCRIPT

Customer: Hi, my name is Chang Lee.

Teller: How _can_ I help you?

Customer: I _want to_ check my balance.

Teller: OK. _Can_ I have your account number, please?

Customer: 381335.

Teller: Your balance is $201.

Customer: OK. _And_ I _asked_ my father _to_ wire me some money. I'd like _to_ know if it's arrived.

Teller: I'm sorry, your account doesn't show any deposits.

Customer: Oh, no. I need _to_ pay my rent tomorrow. _What do you_ think I _ought to_ do?

Teller: Well, we're having some computer problems today. So, uh, why _don't you call_ us later to check again? Or _you can_ come back. We're open till 5:00.

Customer: OK, thanks.

Teller: You're welcome.

After You Listen

7 Using Vocabulary

❏ Review the vocabulary items in this activity. Check that students know which ones are verbs and nouns.

❏ Brainstorm a few example questions with the class. Remind students they should not ask personal questions.

Example questions:

When did you last borrow something? (What did you borrow?)

When did you last lend something to somebody? (What did you lend?)

How much does a (name of a job) or (name of a movie / sports star) earn in a year?

What percentage of your income do you save (or would you like to save) every month?

How much do you spend on gas every month?

❏ After they write their questions, have students work in pairs. Student A will look at page 247 in the Student Book. Student B will look at page 255.

❏ Explain that they have different sets of sentences that they will have to read and answer appropriately. They should not show each other their books.

❏ Have students read their sections and ask if there are any questions.

❏ Model the pair work activity with one pair of students.

❏ Set a time limit of five minutes.

❏ Check the answers as a class.

❏ If there is time, have students choose one pair of sentences and continue the conversation.

ANSWER KEY

1. **A:** You look worried. What's wrong?
   B: I'm broke again. I can't pay my rent.

2. **A:** I can't make ends meet on $600 a month. I need more money!
   B: Maybe you should get a part-time job.

3. **A:** My father won't give me any more money this month.
   B: My dad is a tightwad too.

4. **A:** What's the secret to living on a budget?
   B: Don't spend more than you earn.

5. **A:** Why didn't you go to the concert?
    B: Because the tickets cost an arm and a leg.

Pronunciation

CAN VERSUS *CAN'T*

- Read the instruction note and practice the examples.

> ### Pronunciation Note
>
> - Students sometimes have difficulty distinguishing *can* from *can't* because they listen for the final *t* in *can't* which often disappears in rapid speech, especially if the following word starts with a *t* or a *d e.g.*, *I can't dance.*
> - The main differences are in the sound of the vowel / ʌ / in *can* and / æ / in *can't* and in the stress pattern. *Can* is usually unstressed (unless indicating emphasis or contrast). *Can't* is usually stressed.

8 **Pronouncing *Can* and *Can't***

- Read the directions for the activity.
- Play the recording. There will be a pause after each sentence to allow time for students to repeat and write an accent mark over the stressed words.

ANSWER KEY

Affirmative	Negative
1. Jeff **can pláy** on a broken guitar.	1. Jeff **cán't pláy** on a broken guitar.
2. Jeff's father **can páy** for his new guitar.	2. Jeff's father **cán't páy** for his new guitar.
3. Jeff **can wórk** more hours at the computer store.	3. Jeff **cán't wórk** more hours at the computer store.

4. I **can lénd** you more money.	4. I **cán't lénd** you more money.
5. Jeff **can gó** back to school later.	5. Jeff **cán't gó** back to school later.

9 **Distinguishing Between *Can* and *Can't***

- Play the recording and have students circle the correct answers.
- Have students compare answers in pairs. Then play the recording again.
- Write (or ask a student to write) the correct answers on the board.

ANSWER KEY

1. can 2. can't 3. can't 4. can 5. can't 6. can't
7. can 8. can't 9. can 10. can

AUDIOSCRIPT

  1. Sue can pay her bills by herself.
  2. Jeff can't work and study at the same time.
  3. I can't find my wallet.
  4. You can pay with a credit card here.
  5. You can't open an account without identification.
  6. Anna can't work in the United States.
  7. I can lend you five dollars.
  8. We can't make ends meet.
  9. You can apply for a loan at the bank across the street.
10. Jeff can play the guitar very well.

10 **Talking About Abilities**

- Read the directions and model the example. Add a further example with *can't*.

❏ Go through the list, saying what you can and can't do, and have students raise their hands to identify *can* or *can't* (left hand for *can*, right hand for *can't*).

❏ Check comprehension of any new vocabulary.

❏ Divide students into pairs and have them complete the activity, telling their partners what they can and can't do. Monitor pronunciation of *can* and *can't* while walking around the classroom.

❏ When all or most students have completed the activity, have students tell the class three things that their partner can and can't do.

Using Language Functions

11 Recognizing Expressions of Advice

❏ Explain that you are looking for different expressions for asking for and giving advice. Ask students to come up with their own ideas orally.

❏ Direct students to pages 270–271 in the Student Book to look at the audioscript and fill out the chart.

ANSWER KEY

Asking for advice	Giving advice
Jeff: What do you think I should do?	Jeff's father: 1. You'd better go on a budget. 2. Don't spend more than you earn. 3. Maybe you should work more hours at the computer store. 4. I wouldn't do that if I were you. 5. Why don't you think about this very carefully and call me back in a few days?

12 Role-Play

❏ Read through the expressions in the chart. Model some short dialogs with two or three students by asking for advice. Respond using expressions from the chart.

> Example problems: I don't have enough money for a new car; My credit card payments are very high; I lost my ATM card; I want to save more money every month; I think there's a mistake on my pay check.

❏ Read through the four situations with the class. Ask each pair to choose a situation that interests them. Have students practice in pairs, switching roles and partners if there is time. Remind them to use expressions from the chart.

❏ Ask volunteers to perform one of their role-plays for the class. Make notes of significant errors.

❏ After everyone has finished, comment on general errors without mentioning students by name.

Before You Listen

- ❑ Read the information that introduces the next listening.

1 Prelistening Discussion

Question 1

- ❑ Have students answer these questions in small groups.

- ❑ You may want to write the word *entrepreneur* on the board. Ask students what they know about the word: its meaning, the contexts in which it is used, its grammatical form.

Question 2

- ❑ Brainstorm qualities that make a businessperson successful and write them on the board. Examples: creativity / creative, imagination / imaginative, confidence / confident, determination / determined, adventurous, brave, ruthless, tenacious, risk-taking.

  Alternatively, write a list of adjectives on the board and have students rank them in order of importance.

Question 3

- ❑ Invite students to talk about friends or family who have started their own businesses. Relate their stories to the vocabulary in part 2.

Question 4

- ❑ Encourage students to think about their own strengths and skills in relation to this topic.

2 Previewing Vocabulary

- ❑ Play the recording and have students listen to the words.

- ❑ Have students check the words they know. Then compare answers with a partner. Explain that they will work out the meaning of the new words by listening to the lecture and doing activities that follow the lecture.

Listen

3 Taking Notes

(The audioscript follows Activity 4.)

- ❑ Explain that students will listen to a lecture and practice listening and taking notes. The lecture is in two parts and they will hear each part twice. The first time, they should try to answer the main idea questions and take notes of any other important points. The second time, they will practice outlining.

- ❑ Play part 1 of the recording and check the answers to the questions.

ANSWER KEY

1. An entrepreneur is a person who starts a completely new business or industry.
2. Characteristics of successful entrepreneurs are: They have vision; They are not afraid to take risks.

Strategy

Outlining

- Go over the outline pattern in the Strategy box. Point out the use of Roman numerals and the visual and spatial relationship between the three sets of letters and numbers and the different columns.

- Have students look at the photos. Ask them what they know about each person and each company.

4 **Outlining the Lecture**

- ❑ Go over the sample outline for the lecture. Have students use their notes to fill in the information. Check the answers and write them (or have a student write them) on the board.

Content Note

- Amazon.com is an online bookstore where you can search for and order from a choice of millions of new and used books, which are mailed directly to your home. It now also sells CDs, video games, electronics, and clothing.

- FedEx (Federal Express) is the name of a company that transports packages and mail by air and ground using a system of planes and trucks that operate across the United States. You can send mail with guaranteed overnight delivery.

- Anita Roddick is the founder of The Body Shop, a chain of stores selling cosmetics made from natural ingredients not tested on animals. The chain has associated its name with environmental issues. Customers can return product containers to the store to be refilled for a 15 percent discount.

ANSWER KEY

Topic: Entrepreneurs

I. Intro
- A. Example: Jeff Bezos
- B. Def. of entrep: starts new business / industry

II. Characteristics
- A. vision—see opportunities
  - 1. Ex. Jeff Bezos' idea to sell products on the Internet
- B. risk takers
  - 1. Ex. Frederick Smith / FedEx

III. Diffs. in background
- A. well educated / not well educated
  - 1. Ex. Jeff Bezos graduated Princeton
  - 2. Ex. Bill Gates didn't graduate college
- B. rich and poor
  - 1. Ex. Frederick Smith (founder of FedEx) from wealthy family
- C. immigrants
  - 1. Ex. Jerry Yang from Taiwan, founder of Yahoo!
- D. young and age 40 or older
- E. men and women
  - 1. Ex. Anita Roddick of The Body Shop

AUDIOSCRIPT

Part 1

How many of you know the name Jeff Bezos? OK, how about Amazon.com? Have you heard of that? Well, Amazon is the world's first and largest Internet bookstore. And Jeff Bezos is the man who started Amazon back in 1995. Five years later, Amazon was serving millions of customers in 120 different countries. Amazing, right? And this is the reason why, in 1999, Jeff Bezos was selected as *Time* Magazine's Person of the Year, a very great honor.

Now, Jeff Bezos is actually not the topic of my lecture today, but he is a perfect example of my topic, which is entrepreneurs. That's *entrepreneurs*, spelled E-N-T-R-E-P-R-E-N-E-U-R-S. *Entrepreneur* is a French word meaning a person who starts a completely new business or industry; um, someone who does something no one else has done before; or who does it in a completely new way, like Jeff Bezos. Entrepreneurs like Jeff Bezos are very highly respected in American society and, I think, in many other countries too. So, in today's lecture I want to talk about three things. First, the characteristics of entrepreneurs—I mean, what kind of people they are. Second, the kind of background they come from. And third, the entrepreneurial process, that is, the steps entrepreneurs follow when they create a new business.

OK, let's begin by looking at the characteristics or, um, the qualities, of entrepreneurs. There are two qualities that I think all entrepreneurs have in common. First, entrepreneurs have vision. I mean that they have the ability to see opportunities that other people simply do not see. Let's look again at the example of Jeff Bezos. One day in 1994, he was surfing the Internet when suddenly he had a brilliant idea: why not use the Internet to sell products? Remember, at that time, no one was using the Internet in that way. After doing some research, Bezos decided that the product he wanted to sell was books. That's how Amazon got its start.

The other quality that I think all entrepreneurs have is that they're not afraid to take risks. I mean they're not afraid to fail. As an example, let me tell you about Frederick Smith. He founded FedEx, the company that delivers packages overnight. Smith first suggested the idea for his company in a college term paper. Do you know what grade he got on it? A C! Clearly, his professor didn't like the idea, but this didn't stop him. Today FedEx is worth more than 20 billion dollars and employs more than 130,000 people.

OK, we've just seen that all entrepreneurs have at least two important qualities in common. But now let's take a look at some differences. We'll see that their backgrounds can be very different. First of all, some entrepreneurs are well educated, like Jeff Bezos, who graduated from Princeton University. But others, like Bill Gates, the founder of Microsoft, never even finished college. Next, some entrepreneurs come from rich families, like Frederick Smith, the founder of FedEx. In contrast, other entrepreneurs come from poor families, and many are immigrants or the children of immigrants. A great example is Jerry Yang, one of the men who started Yahoo.com. He was born in Taiwan and came to America as a young boy in the 1970s.

OK, the third difference is that although many entrepreneurs start their businesses at a young age, lots of others don't start until age 40 or later. And finally, I think it's important to remind you that entrepreneurs are not always men. A famous woman entrepreneur, for example, is Anita Roddick. She founded The Body Shop. You can find her natural cosmetics shops all over the world. So, to conclude this section, you can see that entrepreneurs come from many different backgrounds.

5   **Taking Notes on a Process**

❑   Explain that students will listen to the second part of the lecture on the steps in the entrepreneurial process. They will listen and try to fill in the outline.

❑   Play the recording of part 2 of the lecture.

ANSWER KEY

IV. Entrepreneurial Process

    A. Identify problem

    B. Think of solution

    C. Prepare business plan

    D. Hire team (finding the right people to work in the new business)

E. Test market

F. Raise capital (money)

AUDIOSCRIPT

Part 2

I want to move on now and take a look at the entrepreneurial process. There are six basic steps that most entrepreneurs follow when they start their businesses. In the first step, they identify a problem; in other words, they see a need or a problem that no one else sees. Then in the second step, they think of a solution, what needs to be done to solve the problem or meet the need. I think we've already seen several examples today of people who saw a need or an opportunity and then came up with a creative solution.

Step three is to prepare a business plan. This means looking at things like equipment, location, financing, marketing, and so on. There are thousands of details to think about when you start a new business; as a result, this stage can take months or even years.

The next step, the fourth step, is putting together a team—in other words, hiring the right people to work with the entrepreneur in the new business. After that, the fifth step is something called *test marketing*. That's test marketing. This involves making and selling a small amount of the product or service just to try it out and see if customers like it. And if they do, then, finally, entrepreneurs go to the sixth step, which is raising capital. *Capital* is another word for "money." The entrepreneur has to raise a lot of money, you know, from the bank, or friends, or family, in order to produce and sell the product or service in large quantities.

I want to say, in conclusion, that entrepreneurs like Jeff Bezos are among the most respected people in the United States. They are cultural heroes, like movie stars or sports heroes. Why? Because, starting with a dream and working very hard, these people created companies that

solved serious, important problems. They provided jobs for millions of people, and in general, their companies made life easier and more pleasant for all of us. If you ever order a book from Amazon, or use natural make-up from the Body Shop, say thanks to the remarkable people who created these companies.

After You Listen

6 **Discussing the Lecture**

❑ Have students work in pairs to complete and discuss questions 1–6 of this activity.

❑ Compare answers as a class.

ANSWER KEY

1. 1. e 2. a 3. d 4. c 5. b

2. They have vision and they take risks.

3. They can be well educated or not; they can be rich or poor; they can be immigrants; they can be men or women.

4. The six steps are: a. Identify a problem b. Think of a solution c. Prepare a business plan d. Hire a team e. Test the market f. Raise capital (money)

5. Entrepreneurs are cultural heroes because they started with a dream and worked very hard to create companies that make our lives better and provide jobs for millions of people.

6. Answers will vary.

7 **Reviewing Vocabulary**

❑ Refer students to Activity 2 on page 61 of the Student Book. Review any new items and have students check the meaning in a dictionary if necessary.

Talk It Over

Best Practice

Cultivating Critical Thinking

This is an example of a collaborative team activity resulting in a final product. This type of activity requires students to process the information they have learned and apply it to a new situation. This involves reinterpretation, synthesis, and application of concepts. The process of manipulating language and concepts in this way will create deeper processing of new material, which will allow students to evaluate whether they have understood the new material and help them remember it better.

8 Become an Entrepreneur!

❏ Read the instructions with the class.

❏ Brainstorm possible ideas for new products and services and write them on the board.

❏ Divide the class into groups and have each group develop an idea by following steps 1 and 2. (They can choose one from the list, provided another group has not chosen it, or they can come up with their own idea.)

❏ Set a time limit of 15 minutes for groups to follow the steps in part 3.

❏ If there is time in class, have students present their business plan to the class. Or you may assign preparation for this as homework and ask students for their presentation in the next class.

REPRODUCIBLE EXPANSION ACTIVITY

▪ The aim of this activity is for students to use the Internet as a resource to obtain information about famous entrepreneurs. They will then process the information by discussing and making notes about it in their groups.

▪ Students can use a search engine entering *entrepreneurs* or the name of the websites below. Check these websites before passing them on to students.
www.entrepreneurs.about.com/od/famousentrepreneurs/
www.financial-inspiration.com/famous-entrepreneurs.html/

▪ The research part of this activity can be done in a computer lab class or assigned for homework.

▪ Please see Black Line Master "Famous Entrepreneurs" on page BLM 8 of this Teacher's Edition. Photocopy and distribute one to each group.

▪ Divide the students into small groups and have each person in the group choose one famous entrepreneur from the list.

▪ Students will research their chosen entrepreneur on the web. Then re-form their groups to complete the worksheet.

▪ If students need more room to write, they can write on the back of the page, making 4 new boxes.

▪ Note that if there is an entrepreneur you would like to include, or who is famous in your area, feel free to include that person (or those persons) in the list of options.

▪ Finally, ask for volunteers to share the information from part 2 with the class.

Getting Meaning from Context

1 Prelistening Questions

- ❑ Point to the picture and ask students to describe it. Where is it? What are these people doing? Why are they waiting? Answers: They are standing in line for an ATM (automated teller machine). They might be waiting to get cash, make a deposit, or check their balance.

- ❑ Question 1 can be approached by either first looking at the lettered list of banking services in Activity 2 or by first brainstorming a list of services offered by banks in the U.S. and comparing it with the list in Activity 2. Check that students understand all these items.

- ❑ Discuss Questions 2 and 3 as a class.

Best Practice

Scaffolding Instruction

This is an example of an activity that raises metacognitive awareness of learning strategies. In real life, we use surrounding context clues to work out the meanings of unfamiliar words. This activity asks students to use the surrounding verbal clues in each advertisement to work out the main topic. By writing the clues, students are guided through the steps of developing this skill.

Focus on Testing

Using Context Clues

- ▦ This recording has four advertisements. Play each advertisement, pausing after the question at the end of the advertisement to allow students to circle their answers and write the clues.

- ▦ Then play the final part of each section, which gives the correct answer.

ANSWER KEY

Topic	Clues (These answers may vary.)
1. a. a safety-deposit box	valuable possessions, protect, safe place, lock up
2. c. a home improvement loan	lend you money, remodeling, old house, new one, heating, roof, bank, finance
3. d. an automated banking machine (an ATM machine)	Insta (like *instant*), bank, money, easy, get cash, bank is closed
4. b. a savings account	earn interest, money, deposit, investor

Content Note

In the U.S., Europe, and many other countries, you can pay for store-bought items with a credit card or with a debit card. If you use a credit card, it means that you borrow money and may have to pay interest. If you use a debit card, it means that the money is taken directly from your account, so there is no interest, although there is sometimes a small store fee.

AUDIOSCRIPT

Advertisement 1

Every person has valuable possessions that are difficult or impossible to replace, for example, family photographs, jewelry, a passport, old coins, or insurance policies. You should protect these priceless valuables by putting them in a safe place. Lock up your treasures in International Bank, and you'll never have to worry about losing your valuables again.

Question 1: The speaker is talking about . . .

The International Bank Safe-Deposit Box—safety and protection the easy way!

Advertisement 2

Right now International Bank can lend you money for dozens of projects. For instance, remodeling a kitchen or a bathroom can change an old house into an exciting new one. Thinking about solar heating? Need a new roof? International Bank can help you finance them.

Question 2: The speaker is talking about . . .

For any home improvement loan, talk to International Bank first.

Advertisement 3

With an Insta-Teller Card from International Bank, you're close to your money night or day. The Insta-Tellers operate 24 hours a day, seven days a week, 365 days a year. It's an easy way to get cash, pay your bills, make a deposit, or check your balance even when your bank is closed.

Question 3: The speaker is talking about . . .

Insta-Teller automated banking machines—any transaction, any time.

Advertisement 4

How would you like to earn 4.5 percent interest and still be able to take out money any time you need it? You can do both! Just deposit $5,000 and keep a minimum average balance of $500. Come in and ask about our investor's plan.

Question 4: The speaker is talking about . . .

International Bank Investor's Plan—a savings account and more!

Pronunciation

TEENS AND TENS

- Read the information about the pronunciation of *teens* and *tens*.

- Model some examples of each number. Have students raise their hands to identify if it is a *teen* or a *ten* (left hand for *teen* and right hand for *ten*).

2 **Pronouncing *Teens* and *Tens***

- ❑ Read the directions for Activity 2.

- ❑ There will be a pause on the recording after each pair of words to allow time for students to repeat.

3 **Distinguishing Between *Teens* and *Tens***

- ❑ Play the recording.

- ❑ Have students compare answers in pairs.

- ❑ Play the recording again and check the answers as a class.

ANSWER KEY

1. $40.10
2. $16.99
3. 18
4. 90
5. 230
6. 260
7. 14.5
8. $2,215
9. 1764
10. 1890

AUDIOSCRIPT

1. He paid $40.10 for the bottle of wine.

2. *Woman*: How much does this dictionary cost?
   Man: $16.99.

3. Most credit card companies charge 18 percent interest per month on your outstanding balance.

4. We drove at a speed of 90 miles per hour.

5. I bought my coat in Paris for 230 euros.

6. The plane from Buenos Aires carried 260 passengers.

7. My dog weighs 14 and a half kilos.

8. The rent on this apartment is $2,215 a month.

9. My aunt lives at 1764 Wilson Avenue.

10. International Bank is located at 1890 West Second Street.

4 Pair Practice with *Teens* and *Tens*

❏ Have students work in pairs. Student A will look at page 247 in the Student Book. Student B will look at page 255.

❏ Students will take turns reading the sentences and circling the numbers they hear.

❏ Monitor the activity while walking around the classroom.

❏ Select a few students to model the pronunciation for the whole class.

On the Spot!

5 What Would You Do?

❏ Read the directions and the four situations.

❏ Ask students to decide what they would do in each situation and to write their answers.

6 Discussing the Situations

❏ Divide students into small groups of three or four. Give them five minutes to discuss questions 1–3.

❏ Ask a leader from each group to report the results of their discussion to the class.

EXPANSION ACTIVITY

- The aim of this activity is to practice vocabulary connected with the theme of banking services and to encourage students to express personal opinions about why they do or not use each of these services.

- Please see Black Line Master "Group Survey" on page BLM 9 of this Teacher's Edition.

- Photocopy and cut the page into strips. You will need one strip for each student in your class. If there are more than ten students in your class, photocopy more than one page. (This activity can be done as a whole class walk-around activity, which will take longer, or in smaller groups.)

- Distribute strips to the students.

- Explain that they will have to ask a *yes/no* question based on their sentence in order to find out whether their sentence is true or false *about their class or group*.

- Model the activity with one student. Select one student and ask: *Do you have a credit card?* If they say *yes* mark one check in the *Yes* section.

- Remind students they should keep a note of which students they have asked, so as not to ask the same student twice!

- At the end of the activity, have students report their findings to the class. Tell whether their statement is true or false, based on the number of *yes/no* answers.

  For example, Student A might say: *My sentence was* Everyone in this group has a credit card. *I found that my sentence is true because I asked everyone in this class, and they all have a credit card. It's the most convenient way to pay for things in the store.*

Before You Listen

- ❑ Have students read the information about a checking account. Answer any questions they might have.

- ❑ Explain (or ask students to explain) the difference between checking and savings accounts.

- ❑ If possible, bring in examples of bank brochures for different types of accounts (in English or in the students' own languages) and an example of a checkbook record.

1   Prelisting Questions

- ❑ Put the students in small groups.

- ❑ Have them read and discuss questions 1–4.

2   Previewing Vocabulary

- ❑ Play the recording and have students listen to the words and phrases.

- ❑ Explain that the words in the left-hand column will appear in the recording.

- ❑ Have students work individually to match each phrase with a definition from the right-hand column. Then compare answers as a class.

ANSWER KEY

1.c 2.e 3.d 4.a 5.b

Listen

3   Balancing a Checkbook

- ❑ Ask students to look at the checkbook record. Check comprehension by asking questions. For example:

  What's the account number? (132-98804)

  What's in the first column? (check number)

  When did they pay the Electric Company? (October 27)

  How much did they pay to Compu-Tech on November 1? ($125)

  How much was in their account on November 8? ($525.18)

- ❑ Read the directions.

- ❑ Check that students understand which items are missing. (11 items)

- ❑ Play the recording.

- ❑ Have students compare their answers in pairs. Encourage them to use math to check the amounts.

- ❑ Play the recording again.

- ❑ Check the answers as a whole class.

ANSWER KEY

No.	Date	Description	Payment	Deposit	Balance
200	10/25	**ABC market**	30.21		490.31
201	10/27	Electric company	57.82		**432.49**
202	10/27	Time magazine	**35**		**397.49**
203	10/30	**Birthday present**	70		327.49
204	11/1	Compu-Tech	125.00		202.49
205	**11/1**	Dr. Painless	40		162.49
	11/1	Deposit		1234.69	**1397.18**
206	11/2	**House payment**	412		985.18

207	11/4	Visa payment	155.00		830.18
208	11/8	**Auto insurance**	305.00		525.18
209	11/10	Traffic ticket	**68**		**457.18**

Content Note

It used to be traditional in the United States for married couples to have a joint checking account. It is now more common for husbands and wives to have separate checking accounts and sometimes a joint account for household expenses.

AUDIOSCRIPT

George: Let's see here. Check number 200. October 25th. Did you write this check?

Martha: $30.21. Oh, yes. That was last Thursday. ABC Market.

George: OK, so that leaves a balance of $490.31. Next: number 201. Electric bill. $57.82. So now we have $432.49. Next: October 27th. *Time* magazine. I forgot to enter the amount.

Martha: I remember that. It was $35.00.

George: OK. So that leaves $397.49. Now what's this $70?

Martha: That was for your sister's birthday present.

George: Oh, yes. OK . . . And here's check 205. When did we pay the dentist?

Martha: The same day I deposited my paycheck. November first.

George: Fine. So after the deposit, the balance was $1,397.18. And then I made the house payment, check number 206. That's $412, and the VISA payment—that's $155, so now our balance is $830.18.

Martha: You know, George, we should really pay off our credit card balance. The interest is 18 percent a year.

George: You're right. But we can't afford it right now. Look at this car insurance bill! $305 to Auto Insurance of America. And that's just for four months. And here's another traffic ticket!

Martha: Last month it was you, this month it was me.

George: Oh, man . . . How much was it this time?

Martha: $68. What's the balance now?

George: $457.18. I guess we're OK for the rest of the month as long as we don't get any more traffic tickets.

After You Listen

4 Discussion

❑ Have students form small groups to discuss Questions 1–3.

❑ Set a time limit of five minutes.

❑ Ask group leaders to report to the class on the results of the discussion.

5 Find Someone Who...

❑ Read the instructions with the class.

❑ Explain that students must turn each statement into a question, e.g., *Are you carrying any money today? Do you or have you ever worked in a bank?*

❑ Model example dialogs with two or three students. Use the question openers from the *Language Tip* box on page 71 of the Student Book.

❑ Set a time limit of ten minutes. Have students walk around the class to complete the activity.

❑ Monitor the activity by walking around the classroom.

❑ At the end of ten minutes, have students sit down and compare how many names they collected.

Talk it Over

6 **Interview**

❑ Assign this task for homework. Suggest that students interview someone who is not from their own cultural background. Remind them to use the question openers from the *Language Tip* box on page 71 of the Student Book.

❑ During the next class, have students share their information in groups.

❑ Have group leaders present a summary to the class at the end.

 EXPANSION ACTIVITY

▨ The aim of this activity is to practice the math and language skills associated with balancing a checkbook. It also reviews pronunciation of *teens* and *tens*.

▨ Have students work in pairs.

▨ Please see Black Line Master "Balancing Your Checkbook" on page BLM 10 of this Teacher's Edition.

▨ Photocopy the Black Line Master, one copy for each pair of students. Cut each page in half, one half for each student in a pair.

▨ Remind students they must not look at their partner's paper.

▨ Explain that they will have to ask questions to complete the missing information in their "checkbook." Their partner has the answers.

▨ Model the activity with one student. Select a Student A and ask: *How much was the auto payment on May 23?* Student A will answer: *$160.00.*

▨ At the end of the activity, have students check their answers by comparing papers.

ANSWER KEY

No.	Date	Description	Payment	Deposit	Balance
					598.12
150	5/21	(B) Phone	(A) 118.06		480.06
151	5/21	(A) Gas	60.17		(B) 419.89
152	5/23	Auto payment	(B) 160.00		(A) 259.89
153	5/26	(B) Groceries	(A) 180.14		79.75
	5/30	Deposit		(B) 625.00	(B) 704.75
154	6/02	(A) House insurance	(B) 219.45		(A) 485.30
155	6/03	(B) Credit card payment	(A) 415.00		(B) 70.30
	6/05	Deposit		(A) 316.00	386.30
156	6/08	Groceries	(A) 150.17		236.13
157	6/09	(A) Doctor	(B) 15.00		(A/B) 221.13

Self-Assessment Log

❑ The purpose of the log is to help the students reflect on their learning.

❑ Read the directions aloud and have students check vocabulary that they learned in the chapter and are prepared to use.

❑ Have students check the strategies they understand.

❑ Put students in small groups. Ask students to find the information or an activity related to each strategy in the chapter.

❑ Tell students to find definitions in the chapter for any words they did not check, or they can look in their dictionaries.

4

Jobs and Professions

In this chapter, students will read about various topics related to jobs and professions, such as looking for a job, interviewing, and comparing jobs. In Part 1, they will learn to recognize stressed and reduced forms and practice ways to apologize and reconcile. In Part 2, they will listen to a talk about changes in the U.S. job market. They will also practice a job interview. In Part 3, they will practice listening to conversations and guessing people's jobs. In Part 4, they will practice sequencing events in the typical day of a househusband.

Chapter Opener

❏ Have students look at the photo of a veterinarian listening to a cat's heartbeat with a stethescope. Ask them the questions from the Connecting to the Topic section. Have students discuss as a class.

❏ Read and discuss the quote. What makes work seem like play? When do you enjoy working? What aspects of your job do you (or would you) enjoy most?

❝ Work and play are words used to describe the same thing under differing conditions. **❞**

—Mark Twain
American author and humorist, 1835–1910

Chapter Overview

Listening Skills and Strategies

Listening for main ideas

Listening for details

Making inferences

Recognizing the intonation of tag questions

Recognizing a sequence of events

Taking notes on causes and effects

Creating abbreviations

Taking notes on statistics

Speaking Skills and Strategies

Talking about jobs and careers

Apologizing and reconciling

Role playing a job interview

Learning idioms related to housework

Talking about "men's" and "women's" jobs

Interviewing a person about his/her job

Giving a short oral report

Critical Thinking Skills

Interpreting information in a table

Getting meaning from context

Speculating about hypothetical situations

Taking notes on a lecture

Predicting the order of a set of pictures

Using a matrix diagram to organize ideas

Vocabulary Building

Terms related to jobs and careers

Expressions for apologizing and reconciling

Idioms related to housework

Terms signaling cause and effect

Pronunciation

Identifying and practicing stressed words

Identifying and practicing reduced pronunciation

Asking and answering negative tag questions

Language Skills

Using context clues to guess people's jobs

Vocabulary

Nouns		Verbs	Expressions
automation	job market	complain	in the mood
bottom line	labor costs	grow by X%	the worst
categories	manufacturing	spend time	
competition	rank	support	
economy	salary		
health care	service		
illnesses	trend		

Can You Guess?

- Ask students to discuss the questions below in groups and compare their answers with the correct answers.

- Discuss the issues raised by these questions: Why do people decide to change jobs? What factors make a person want to stay in hi or her job? What makes a job stressful? What kinds of jobs have disappeared? What new jobs are becoming popular?

1. How many times does the average American change jobs in his or her lifetime? A. *U.S. Department of Labor Statistics shows that the average person makes four to six career changes and 12 to 15 job changes in his or her lifetime.*

2. Which of the following jobs is the most stressful, according to research? Why?
   A. Computer programmer. B. Mail carrier.
   C. Teacher. D. Veterinarian. E. Carpenter.
   A. *Teacher. According to research done in Great Britain, the most stressful jobs involve direct contact with the public in emotionally intense situations. Such jobs included teachers, paramedics, police officers, and social workers.*

3. Name three occupations that will be in high demand in the United States between now and the year 2012. A. *The following occupations will be in the highest demand in the United States through 2012:*
   1. *Teachers (K-12)*
   2. *Registered nurses*
   3. *College instructors*
   4. *Customer service representatives*
   5. *Computer support staff*

Before You Listen

- ❑ Read the text that introduces the next listening. Students will discuss the photo in the next activity.

1 Prelistening Questions

- ❑ Have the students read the questions and discuss them in pairs.

- ❑ Compare answers as a whole class.

- ❑ As a whole class, make a list of places you could go to find a job. These might include: Classified ads in the newspaper, employment websites or company websites on the Internet, job center, employment agency, community notice board.

2 Previewing Vocabulary

- ❑ Play the recording and have students listen to the underlined words and phrases.

- ❑ Have students complete the vocabulary preview individually.

- ❑ Compare their answers as a whole class and write the correct answers on the board.

ANSWER KEY

1. d 2. c 3. e 4. b 5. a

Listen

3 Comprehension Questions

(The audioscript follows Activity 4.)

- ❑ Explain that these questions will help students focus on the main ideas in the listening. They do not need to understand every word to answer the questions.

- ❑ You may want to write the questions on the board.

- ❑ Read the questions aloud.

- ❑ Play the recording.

- ❑ After listening, have students discuss their answers in pairs.

- ❑ Check the answers as a class.

ANSWER KEY

1. He wants a full-time job; 2. In a record store;
3. In a fast-food restaurant; 4. It was boring;
5. It's very tiring, and the classes are too large;
6. Because she is an international student (which means that she probably doesn't have a work permit); 7. that they all go out for dinner

Stress

4 Listening for Stressed Words

❑ Play the recording again, this time with books open.

❑ There will be a pause at the end of each sentence to allow time for students to repeat and write the missing words.

❑ After listening, have students check their answers with the audioscript in their books.

❑ Have students read the conversation with a partner, paying attention to stressed words in their pronunciation.

AUDIOSCRIPT and ANSWER KEY

Mari: Hey, Jeff, what's going _on_?

Jeff: Oh, I'm looking at the _classified_ ads. It looks like I have to get a _job_.

Mari: I thought you _had_ a job, at a computer store or something?

Jeff: Yeah, but that's _part_-time. I need something _full_-time.

Mari: Really? But what about _school_? What about your _band_? How can you work full-time?

Jeff: Well, to tell you the _truth_, I'm probably going to drop _out_ of school for a while. I'm just not in the _mood_ for _studying_ these days. I'd rather spend my time _playing_ with my band. But my father won't _support_ me if I'm not in school.

Mari: I see . . . Well, what kind of job do you want to _get_?

Jeff: Well ideally, something involving _music_, like in a record store. But if _that's_ not possible… I don't know, but whatever I do, it'll be better than my _first_ job.

Mari: Oh yeah? What was _that_?

Jeff: Believe it or not, the summer after I finished _high_ school I worked at Burger Ranch.

Mari: You? In a _fast_-food place? What did you _do_ there?

Jeff: I was a _burger_ flipper. You know, I made hamburgers all day long.

Mari: That sounds like a pretty _boring_ job!

Jeff: It was the _worst_. And I haven't gone inside a Burger Ranch since I _quit_ that job.

Nancy: Hi, what's so _funny_?

Jeff: Do you remember my _job_ at the Burger Ranch?

Nancy: Oh yeah. That was pretty _awful_. But actually, it doesn't sound so bad to me right now.

Mari: Why, Nancy? What's _wrong_?

Nancy: Oh, I'm just really, really _tired_. I'm teaching four different _classes_ this term, and _two_ of them are really _large_. Sometimes I think I've been _teaching_ too long.

Mari: How long have you been _teaching_?

Nancy: Twelve years. Maybe it's time to try something _else_.

Mari: Like _what_?

Nancy: Well, I've always wanted to be a _writer_. I could work at home . . .

Jeff: Oh, _don't_ listen to her, Mari. She _always_ talks this way when she's had a bad day at school. At least you _have_ a good _job_, Nancy. Look at me: I'm _broke_, and Dad won't _lend_ me any more money . . .

Nancy: Oh, stop _complaining_. if you're so poor, why don't you go _back_ to the Burger Ranch?

Mari: Listen you two, stop _arguing_. Look at me! I _can't_ work at _all_ because I'm an international student.

Jeff: OK, OK I'm _sorry_, Nancy. Tell you what. Let's go out to _dinner_. _I'll_ pay.

Nancy: But you're _broke_!

Jeff: All right, _you_ pay!

Reductions

5 **Comparing Unreduced and Reduced Pronunciation**

❑ Review the meaning of reduced forms.

❑ Play the recording and have students listen and read the sentences.

❑ Play the recording again. This time, ask students to repeat.

6 **Listening for Reductions**

❑ Explain that students will hear a conversation between a manager and a job applicant.

❑ You may want to have students read through the conversation and try to guess the missing words.

❑ There will be a pause on the recording after each conversation turn to allow students time to write their answers. (Students should write the long forms.)

❑ Check the answers to Activity 6 with the audioscript.

❑ Have students practice the conversation in pairs, paying attention to reduced forms in their pronunciation. You may want to try asking students to read the line silently, then look up and say the line to their partner. This will help them to focus on pronunciation, not reading.

❑ Move around the room to monitor pronunciation and provide help if needed.

AUDIOSCRIPT

Manager: I'm _going to_ ask you some questions, O.K.? What _kind of_ jobs have you had?

Applicant: Mostly factory jobs. The last five years I worked in a plastics factory.

Manager: _What_ _did_ _you_ do there?

Applicant: I _used to_ cut sheets of plastic.

Manager: _What do you want to_ do here?

Applicant: I _don't know_. I'll do anything. I'm good with my hands, and I'm a hard worker.

Manager: Why _don't you_ fill out an application in the office. It looks like we're _going to_ have an opening next week. I'll call you.

Applicant: Thanks.

After You Listen

7 **Reviewing Vocabulary**

❑ Have students work in pairs. One student will look at page 248 in the Student Book. The other student will look at page 256.

❑ Have students read their section and ask if there are any questions.

❑ Set a time limit of five minutes.

❑ Check the answers as a class.

❑ If there is time, have students choose one pair of sentences and continue the conversation.

ANSWER KEY

1. A: How was your trip to New York last summer?

   B: It was the worst. It snowed for five days straight.

2. A: What on earth happened to your arm?

   B: I fell down the stairs and broke it.

3. A: Do you want to go to the beach this afternoon?

   B: No, thanks. I'm not in the mood.

4. A: I heard your mother got a full-time job.

   B: Yeah. She's supporting me while I finish my B.A.

5. A: What's your brother doing these days?

   B: He spends all his time studying. I almost never see him.

Using Language Functions

APOLOGIZING AND RECONCILING

- Read the information note.

- Ask two students to read the dialog using the appropriate intonation.

- Read the information in the *Content Note*. Ask students for more examples of each one, for example, invite someone for dinner, buy some flowers, next time I'll be more careful.

Best Practice

Interacting with Others

This type of activity is an example of collaborative learning to encourage fluency and confidence. In this activity, communication is more important than grammar. Students can practice apologizing and reconciling in pairs. They can improve their confidence by switching roles or partners and practicing the same situations again. By providing feedback to each other, they learn skills of self-evaluation.

8 Role-Play

- [ ] Read the situations and check comprehension of any new vocabulary.

- [ ] Have students work in pairs to practice the role-plays.

- [ ] Set a time limit of five minutes.

- [ ] Move around the room to monitor and provide feedback. Take notes of errors.

- [ ] Comment on common errors, without mentioning who made them.

- [ ] Ask for volunteers to perform conversations for the class.

9 Discussion

- [ ] Ask students to read through the situations and questions silently and ask about any unfamiliar vocabulary.

- [ ] Have students work in groups of three or four to discuss the questions.

- [ ] Set a time limit of ten minutes.

- [ ] Move around the room to monitor and provide feedback.

- [ ] At the end, ask for volunteers to summarize their group's discussion.

EXPANSION ACTIVITY

- The purpose of this activity is to practice appropriate responses to situations where you need to apologize.

- Put the students in small groups of three or four.

- Please see Black Line Master "Saying You're Sorry" on page BLM 11 of this Teacher's Edition. Photocopy one copy for each group.

- Cut each copy into strips and distribute one set of strips to each group of students.

- Students will place the strips face down in the center of the group.

- Each student in turn will pick up a strip, read the situation, and apologize.

- The other students in the group will advise the student on an appropriate way to reconcile (each suggestion must be different).

- The person with the best suggestion gets a point (chosen by the person who picked and read the situation).

- Demonstrate the activity with one group.

- Set a time limit of ten minutes.

- Monitor groups and provide feedback.

- At the end of the activity, ask for examples of the most interesting or most creative ways of reconciling.

Before You Listen

- ❑ Read the text that introduces the next listening.

1   Prelistening Discussion

- ❑ Have students look at the table.

- ❑ Ask students to explain the title in their own words.

- ❑ Before reading, ask students to try and predict what kinds of occupations they think will be the "fastest growing."

- ❑ Read the list of occupations and check comprehension of any new words.

- ❑ Have students work in pairs to answer the questions below the table.

- ❑ Review the responses as a class.

ANSWER KEY

1. Information about which professions are increasing most rapidly.

2. The table covers the years 2002–2012.

3. The four columns give information about
   a) The types of jobs that will grow fastest
   b) The percentage increase in the number of people in these jobs c) The salary for that job in relation to other jobs.

4. Answers will vary.

5. All jobs require a college education except numbers 1, 4, 7, 10, and 12.

6. The jobs with the highest salaries in this table are mainly computer- or health-related, and all require a college degree.

2   Previewing Vocabulary 🎧

- ❑ Play the recording and have students listen to the words.

- ❑ Have students check the words they know and then compare answers with a partner.

- ❑ Explain that they will work out the meaning of the new words by listening to the lecture.

Listen

Strategy

Taking Notes on Cause-and-Effect Statements

- ▪ Read the information in the *Strategy* box.

- ▪ Review the difference in meaning between *cause* and *effect*.

- ▪ Point out the use of punctuation with these different expressions.

3   Taking Notes on Cause-and-Effect Statements

- ❑ Read the directions and have students work individually to take notes from the sentences in the box.

- ❑ Remind them to write key words, use abbreviations, and use symbols for cause and effect. (= or ❑ or ↓)

ANSWER KEY

Note: In this answer key, the cause is followed by the effect to avoid confusion.

1. robots → factory jobs ↓

2. robots less $ than humans → factory robots ↑

3. humans ≠ 24 hrs → robots ↑

4. labor cost in Asia less $ → U.S. factories to Asia

5. robots → no fact. jobs ↓

6. robots less $ → robots ↑, humans ↓

7. automation → 1st cause of unempl.

4   Creating Abbreviations

- ❑ Have students read the words in the table.

- ❑ Use dictionaries to check the meanings if necessary.

❏ For each word, students should come up with a symbol or abbreviation that they will find easy to remember and use.

ANSWER KEY
Possible answers:

Words	Abbreviations
economy	econ.
manufacturing	manf.
service	svce
technology	tech.
approximately	approx.
number	#
million	m.
medical	med.
computer	comp.
percent	%
Bachelor of Arts	BA

5 **Listening and Taking Notes on Causes and Effects**

❏ Play the recording and have students take notes using their symbols.

❏ Have students listen to each statement twice before taking notes. Otherwise, they won't benefit from the repetition because they'll be starting to write already.

ANSWER KEY
1. tech → manf w/ machine, not people
2. tech → ↓ manf jobs
3. people live longer → ↑ med services
4. med tech → people live longer
5. working wmn → growth

AUDIOSCRIPT

1. Because of technology, we're able to manufacture goods by using machines instead of human workers.

2. As a result, thousands of manufacturing jobs don't exist anymore.

3. We're going to need more medical services because people are living longer and longer.

4. Also, because of developments in medical technology, people with serious illnesses are able to live much longer than they could in the past.

5. The main reason for the huge growth in this category is that most married women now work outside the home.

6 **Taking Notes on Statistics**

❏ Review the box on page 38 in the Student Book about taking notes on statistics.

❏ Play the recording and have students take notes using their symbols.

❏ They will hear each statement twice.

❏ Have students compare notes with a partner and try to reconstruct the sentences on the recording.

❏ Compare answers as a class. Write the sentences on the board.

ANSWER KEY
1. 2.5m manf. jobs ↓ since 2001
2. svce jobs ↑ 20m nxt 10 yrs
3. ½ jobs in hlth
4. hlth jobs ↑ 3m nxt 10 yrs
5. # comp. jobs ↑ 30% nxt 10 yrs

AUDIOSCRIPT

1. According to the United States government, approximately 2.5 million manufacturing jobs have disappeared just since the year 2001.

2. At the same time that the number of manufacturing jobs is decreasing, the number of service jobs is probably going to grow more than 20 million just in the next ten years!

3. Almost half of the jobs on the list are in the field of health care.

4. According to the United States Department of Labor, the number of health care jobs will increase by almost three million in the next ten years.

5. The number of jobs in the computer industry is expected to grow by almost 30 percent in the next ten years.

7 Taking Notes

(The audioscript follows Activity 8.)

❑ Read the questions and have students focus on them as they listen and take notes the first time.

❑ Play the recording.

❑ Check the answers as a class.

ANSWER KEY

Part 1

1. from a manufacturing economy to a service economy
2. because of technology and foreign competition

Part 2

3. health care, computers, and personal care and services
4. get a degree

8 Outlining the Lecture

❑ Ask student to use their notes to complete the outline.

❑ Play the recording again.

❑ Have students fill in any missing information.

❑ Check the answers as a class.

ANSWER KEY

The Changing U.S. Job Market

Part 1

I. 2 questions this lec. will answer:
  A. *best jobs?*
  B. *how to prepare?*

II. History: Last 100 yrs., change in U.S. labor market: from *manuf*. to *service* economy
  A. Definitions
    1. *manuf. = make things*
      e.g.: *cars, furniture, clothes*
    2. *service = do things*
      e.g.: *cut hair, fix shoes, sell computers*

III. Reasons for ↓ in manuf. jobs
  A. *techn*.
  B. *for. comp.*
    1. stat: *2.5m.* ↓ since 2001
    2. *trend to continue in 21st cent.*

IV. ↑ *in service jobs*
  A. stat: ↑ *20m nxt 10 yrs.*

Part 2

V. Fastest growing service jobs

    A. *health care*

        1. e.g.: *medical assts, phys therapy, dent hygienists*

        2. Reasons

            -we live longer

            -techn ↓ ill people live longer

    B. computers

        1. e.g.: *engineers, database admin.*

        2. Stat: ↑ *30% next 10 yrs*

    C. *personal care services*

        1. e.g.: *caterers, home health workers, and day care providers*

        2. Reason: ↑ *women workers*

VI. Educ. requirement for good jobs: *college degree*

AUDIOSCRIPT

Part 1

Lecturer: If you'll be graduating from high school or college in the next year or two, then I'm sure you're very concerned about finding a job. There are two questions that young people like you always ask me. First, what are the best jobs going to be? And second, how can I prepare myself to get one of those good jobs? Well in the next few minutes, I want to try to answer these questions for you, and I hope this information will help you make the right choices about your future career.

Let's start with a little history. In the last 100 years, there's been a big change in the U.S. job market, from a manufacturing economy to a service economy. What does that mean? Well, in a manufacturing economy people <u>make</u> things, like cars or furniture or clothes. In a service economy, people <u>do</u> things. Uh, they cut your hair, they fix your shoes, they sell you a computer. Uh, airline pilots, doctors, restaurant workers—all of these are examples of service workers. OK? So again, my point is that the number of manufacturing jobs has been going down for quite a long time. Now why do you think that is? What's the cause?

Student 1: I think automation, you know, robots, computers . . .

Lecturer: That's one reason, yes. Because of technology, we're able to manufacture goods by using machines instead of human workers. As a result, thousands of manufacturing jobs don't exist anymore. OK, can you think of another reason?

Student 2: Foreign competition. I mean . . . most manufacturing is done outside of the U.S. now, in countries where the labor costs are cheaper.

Lecturer: Yes, that's right. According to the U.S. government, approximately 2.5 million manufacturing jobs have disappeared just since 2001. And that trend is definitely going to continue as we move further into the 21st century.

But now let's talk about service jobs. Here the trend is exactly the opposite. At the same time that the number of manufacturing jobs is decreasing, the number of service jobs is probably going to grow by more than 20 million just in the next ten years! Now, would everybody please look at the handout I gave you, which shows a list of the occupations that will grow the fastest between the years 2002 and 2012. If you study the list carefully, you'll see that most of the jobs on the list are in three categories: health care, computers, and personal care and services. Let me say a few words about each of these categories

Part 2

First, health care. Almost half of the jobs on the list are in the field of health care. Uh, medical assistants, physician assistants, physical therapy aides, dental hygienists—these are just a few examples. According to the U.S. Department of Labor, the number of health care jobs will increase by almost three million in the next ten years. And why is that? Simple. We're going to need more medical services because people are living longer and longer. Also, because of developments in medical technology, people with serious illnesses are able to live much longer than they could in the past. And many of them need a lot of special care and medical help.

All right, now, getting back to the list, you can see that there will be many new jobs related to computers. We're going to need people who can design and build computers, like engineers, but in addition, there will be lots of jobs for people who manage and operate computers, like database administrations. As you know, computers are used in everything

these days from rockets to coffee machines, so it's no surprise that the number of jobs in the computer industry is expected to grow by almost 30 percent in the next ten years.

Now let me explain the third category, personal-care services. Some examples of jobs in this group are caterers, home-health workers, and day care providers. One reason for the huge growth in this category is that most women now work outside the home. So a lot of the work that women used to do in the home, like cooking and taking care of small children, is now done by service workers.

OK, now while we're looking at the list, there's one more thing I'd like you to notice. Look at all the jobs that have a salary rank of 1. OK? And what do you notice about the educational requirements for those jobs? That's right. They all require at least a Bachelor of Arts degree.

So in conclusion, let me go back to the two questions I mentioned at the beginning of this talk. First, where will the good jobs be?

We've seen today that the areas of greatest growth will be in the fields of computers, health care, and personal services. If you still haven't decided which career you want to follow, you should think about getting a job in one of these fields. However, it's important to remember that many service jobs don't pay very well. The best jobs all require a college education. So the answer to the second question—how you can prepare yourself to get a good job—the answer is simple. Go to college and get a degree. That's the bottom line.

After You Listen

Best Practice

Activating Prior Knowledge

This is an example of an activity that encourages students to make text-to-self connections. The discussion questions ask students to relate the content of the lecture on changes in the job market to their own lives. This aids understanding and retention of new material.

9 Discussing the Lecture

- ❏ Have students discuss the questions in groups.
- ❏ Encourage students to use the new vocabulary in their discussions.
- ❏ Ask for representatives from each group to report back on the discussions.

10 Reviewing Vocabulary

- ❏ Ask students to complete this activity individually.
- ❏ Review the answers together in class.

ANSWER KEY

1. manufacturing; 2. service; 3. trend;
4. economy; 5. automation; 6. competition;
7. labor costs; 8. categories; 9. health care;
10. salary; 11. bottom line

On the Spot!

Best Practice

Making Use of Academic Content

This is an example of collaborative problem-solving. Interviewing skills are important at many different stages of students' academic experience. This type of activity requires students to process information and practice their interviewing skills. They will also practice self-evaluating and evaluating each other.

11 What Would You Do?

- ❏ Read the situation with the class, or ask students to read it silently.
- ❏ Give students time to read the instructions.
- ❏ You can ask students to explain the instructions in their own words.
- ❏ Help students to form groups. Include one interviewer and three applicants in each group.
- ❏ Note on page 260 that there are four positions available. For each position, there are descriptions of three applicants. Assign the four interviewers the positions they'll be interviewing for—manager, checker, stock clerk or butcher.
- ❏ Assign each interviewee the role of one of the applicants.
- ❏ As a group member is being interviewed, have the others in that group go somewhere so they don't hear their group members' interviews.
- ❏ Set a time limit of 20 minutes.
- ❏ Move around the room to provide encouragement and feedback.
- ❏ At the end, invite a representative from each group to report on their decision.

Content Note

In some cultures, it is not advisable to praise oneself and one's abilities at a job interview. Modesty and politeness are more important than showing confidence. You may want to mention some of the cultural assumptions involved in job interviews in the U.S. Identify some of the qualities, such as confidence or initiative, that are considered positive.

▦ Display the worksheets on the classroom wall.

You may wish to suggest some of the following websites, but please check them before doing this activity.

www.careers.org

www.quintcareers.com

www.nycareerzone.org

EXPANSION ACTIVITY

▦ The purpose of this activity is to help students become aware of the kind of information on the Internet that can help them when choosing a career.

▦ Students can use a search engine, typing in keywords like *jobs* or *careers* and the name of their chosen job.

▦ The research part of this activity can be done in a computer lab class or assigned for homework.

▦ Please see Black Line Master "Researching Your Career" on page BLM 12 of this Teacher's Edition. Photocopy and distribute one copy to each student.

▦ Divide the students into groups of four and have each person in the group choose one job (preferably jobs that they are interested in).

▦ Students will research their chosen job on the web. Then re-form their groups to report what they found and have students complete the worksheet. Remind them to write on the back of their piece of paper if they need more room.

Getting Meaning from Context

1 **Prelistening Questions**

❑ Ask students to look at the photos on page 90 and answer the questions on page 91.

❑ Discuss the answers as a class. If any students have had experience with these jobs, have them share their experiences with the class.

Focus on Testing

Using Context Clues

◾ There are five conversations on this recording. There is a question at the end of each one.

◾ Play each section of the recording.

◾ There will be a pause after the question to allow students to write their answers.

◾ Then play the final sentence, which gives the correct answer.

ANSWER KEY

Questions	Clues
_f_ 1. What's the woman's job?	driver's license, ran a red light
_h_ 2. What's the woman's job?	check-up, insurance, dentist
_d_ 3. What's the man's job?	reservation, inside or out, coffee
_a_ 4. What's the woman's job?	taxes, lost money, inherited, professional
_i_ 5. What's the man's job?	sleeves, longer, how much

AUDIOSCRIPT

Conversation 1

Woman:	May I see your driver's license, please?
Man:	What did I do?
Woman:	You ran a red light.
Man:	But I'm sure it was yellow.
Question 1:	What's the woman's job?
Woman:	Are you trying to argue with a police officer?

Conversation 2

Woman:	Is this your first visit?
Man:	No, I come in every six months for a check-up.
Woman:	Oh, I see. Did you bring your insurance form with you?
Man:	Here it is.
Woman:	OK. Take a seat, and the dentist will be with you shortly.
Question 2:	What is the woman's job?
Man:	You're new here, aren't you? What happened to the other receptionist?

Conversation 3

Man:	Do you have a reservation?
Woman:	Yes, Jackson, party of four.
Man:	Inside or out on the patio?
Woman:	Outside. And could you bring us some coffee right away?
Question 3:	What's the man's job?
Man:	I'm the host. I'll ask the waiter to bring you some coffee right away.

Conversation 4

A:	Hi, Jim. It's Carl. It looks like I'm going to need your professional services this year.
B:	I thought you always did your taxes by yourself.

A:	Yeah, but this year things are too complicated. I lost money in the stock market, and then I inherited my uncle's house, remember?
B:	Hmm. You need professional help, for sure.
Question 4:	What is Jim's job?
B:	But you know, it's not a good idea to use your best friend as your accountant. I think you should find someone else.

Conversation 5

Man:	May I help you?
Woman:	The sleeves on this jacket are too short. How much will it cost for you to make them longer?
Man:	Let me look at it . . . I can do it for 30 dollars.
Woman:	That much?
Question 5:	What's the man's job?
Man:	Well, that's what any tailor would charge.

2 Game: Twenty Questions

- ❑ Read the instructions and model an example with one or two students.
- ❑ Have students work in groups to play the game.
- ❑ Set a time limit of ten minutes.

UNDERSTANDING THE INTONATION OF TAG QUESTIONS

- ▪ Read the instruction note.
- ▪ Review the formation of tag questions (see the Expansion Activity on page 74 of this Teacher's Edition for extra practice).
- ▪ Read the examples in the box and ask students to identify the intonation.

3 Recognizing the Intonation of Tag Questions

- ❑ Have the students read the directions.
- ❑ Play the recording.
- ❑ There will be a pause after each item to allow students to write their answers.
- ❑ Check the answers as a class.

ANSWER KEY

Real questions: 1, 4, 5, 7, 10
Expecting agreement: 2, 3, 6, 8, 9

AUDIOSCRIPT

1. We're having a staff meeting tomorrow, aren't we? [rising]
2. You're the programmer from Turkey, aren't you? [falling]
3. This exercise is easy, isn't it? [falling]
4. The supervisor is married, isn't she? [rising]
5. Smoking is forbidden here, isn't it? [rising]
6. That test was really hard, wasn't it? [falling]
7. The secretary speaks Arabic, doesn't he? [rising]
8. That training video was really boring, wasn't it? [falling]
9. The marketing director speaks beautiful Japanese, doesn't she? [falling]
10. We need to sign our names on these reports, don't we? [rising]

Using Language Functions

ANSWERING NEGATIVE TAG QUESTIONS

- ▪ Read aloud the instruction note.
- ▪ Have students practice the three dialogues.

- Tag questions are sometimes difficult to answer. Does the answer agree with the verb in the tag, or not? The answer is that both are possible. Sometimes negative tags get negative answers and sometimes they get positive answers. The answer will be negative or positive depending on the fact given in the answer. For example, *You're 21, aren't you?* can be answered *Yes, I am* (if you are 21) or *No, I'm not* (if you aren't 21). You might also answer with a question, *Am I?*

- A possible student error is to say *yes* when agreeing with the speaker, and *no* when disagreeing with the speaker, for example, *No, I am* or *Yes, I'm not*.

4 Asking and Answering Negative Tag Questions

- ❏ Have students work in pairs. One student will look at page 248 in the Student Book. The other student will look at page 256.

- ❏ Students will take turns asking each other questions.

- ❏ Set a time limit of five minutes.

- ❏ Move around the room to provide feedback on intonation and grammar as needed. Take notes of errors.

- ❏ Invite volunteers to demonstrate their conversations to the class.

REPRODUCIBLE EXPANSION ACTIVITY

- The aim of this activity is to practice the language of negative tag questions.

- Please see Black Line Master "Tag Questions" on page BLM 13 of this Teacher's Edition. Photocopy and distribute one copy to each student.

- Explain that they will first complete the questions with the appropriate tag.

- Then they will go over their answers with a partner.

- Have each pair choose one question and make up a dialog using that question.

- Set a time limit of five minutes.

- Walk around the room to monitor and provide feedback.

- Invite students to perform their dialogs for the class. Check for appropriate intonation.

ANSWER KEY

1. isnt' it; 2. aren't they; 3. aren't we; 4. don't you; 5. doesn't he; 6. weren't you; 7. didn't she (or he); 8. didn't she; 9. won't you; 10. won't we; 11. didn't I; 12. don't you; 13. don't they; 14. aren't you; 15. isn't he (or she); 16. don't you; 17. doesn't she; 18. don't we

Before You Listen

1   **Prelistening Discussion**

❑   Read the questions with the class.

❑   Ask students to suggest answers for each question.

❑   Write the answers to Question 3 on the board.

2   **Previewing Vocabulary**

❑   Play the recording and have students listen to the idioms.

❑   Ask students to complete the chart individually. They may use dictionaries to check the meanings.

❑   Review the answers all together.

ANSWER KEY

Possible answers:

Cook food; wash dishes; prepare the beds for sleeping; keep a record of family income or expenses; wash the clothes; put water on the grass; buy food for the family

3   **Predicting**

❑   Have students work in pairs to describe each picture using idioms from Activity 2.

❑   Then ask them to discuss the probable order of the pictures. They will check their answers when they listen to the recording.

Listen

4   **Sequencing Events**

❑   Play the recording.

❑   Have students number the pictures in the correct order and compare answers with a partner.

❑   Play the recording again if necessary.

❑   Review the answers as a class.

ANSWER KEY

3, 7, 4, 1, 8, 6, 5, 2, 10, 9

AUDIOSCRIPT

Do you want to know what I do on a typical day? Well, I'll tell you what I did yesterday as an example. I woke up before my wife and son, and the first thing I did was to come into the kitchen and make the coffee. Then I made my son's lunch, you know, to take to school, and after that I started cooking breakfast. I made eggs, oatmeal, and toast because I always want my family to start the day with a full stomach. Then my wife and son came into the kitchen and sat down to eat. While they were eating, I threw a basket of laundry into the washing machine, and then I also sat down to eat.

After breakfast, I walked my son to the bus stop, and I waited with him until the bus came. I kissed him good-bye and walked home. As soon as I entered the house, the phone rang. It was my mother-in-law. She wanted to know if my wife was still there, but I told her she had just left. So I talked with her for a few more minutes, about the weather and her garden, and then I got off the phone. After that, uh, let's see, I spent three hours cleaning the house, and after lunch, I went shopping for groceries. By then it was three o'clock, and it was already time to pick up my son at the bus stop. I helped him with his homework, and then my wife came home. Normally she gets home at about 6:00 P.M., but yesterday she was a few minutes early. I was so busy all day that I hadn't had time to water the garden, so I did it while my wife made dinner. Finally, after dinner, I washed the dishes while my wife put our son to bed. And then both of us just collapsed in front of the TV.

And that was my day. Nothing glamorous—just really busy!

After You Listen

5 **Discussion**

- ❑ Have students work in small groups to discuss the questions.
- ❑ Set a time limit of five minutes.
- ❑ Compare answers as a class.

Best Practice

Organizing Information

Activities such as this will teach students to organize information using a graphic organizer called a matrix diagram. This allows students to better assimilate and recall information at a later date, a valuable study tool. In this case, students use the diagram to identify differences between their own opinions and traditional opinions in their culture.

Best Practice

Cultivating Critical Thinking

In this activity, students are asked to examine their own preconceptions about "men's" and "women's" jobs and reflect on them from a critical perspective. They are asked to take a critical stance toward traditional assumptions in their culture and to distinguish this from their own personal opinion. This means that they will have to reinterpret and synthesize their existing mental frameworks in the light of discussion and reflection.

Content Note

Notions of '"traditional" jobs for men and women vary across cultures and may also be closely tied to religious beliefs. In the U.S., it is seen as a sign of progress that *traditional* views of men's and women's jobs are changing, and the word *traditional* has a somewhat negative connotation, but this is not the case in all other cultures. It may be difficult or impossible for some students to separate their own beliefs from those that are widely held in their culture. In such cases, you may wish to ask students to reflect on changing attitudes to men's and women's jobs in the U.S.

Strategy

Graphic Organizer: Matrix Diagram

- ◼ Read the information about a graphic organizer called a matrix diagram.
- ◼ Point out that they can see (and will use) the matrix diagram at the bottom of Student Book page 96.

6 **Talking About "Men's" and "Women's" Jobs**

- ❑ Have students complete the chart individually.
- ❑ Then have students form groups to discuss the questions under the chart.
- ❑ Set a time limit of ten minutes.

7 **Interview**

- ❑ Ask students to complete this activity for homework.
- ❑ Invite students to suggest some additional questions.
- ❑ Encourage them to interview a native speaker of English if possible.
- ❑ Have the students prepare a short oral report. Read the sample report, which students can use as a model.

REPRODUCIBLE EXPANSION ACTIVITY

- The aim of this activity is to practice language for talking about jobs and to practice making a matrix diagram.

- Have students work in pairs to choose a job that they are familiar with.

- Have students draw a matrix diagram similar to the one in Activity 6 on page 96 of the Student Book.

- Make a list of activities involved in carrying out this job.

- For each activity, students should mark if it is interesting, difficult, or both.

- Give an example using the job of teacher.

Job: Teacher	Interesting	Difficult	Both
meet people	✓		
give grades		✓	
every lesson/class is different			✓

- Have students complete the charts in pairs.

- Invite volunteers to read out some of their activities. Other students will try to guess what job it is.

Self-Assessment Log

- ❏ The purpose of the log is to help the students reflect on their learning.

- ❏ Read the directions aloud and have students check vocabulary that they learned in the chapter and are prepared to use.

- ❏ Have students check the strategies they understand.

- ❏ Put students in small groups. Ask students to find the information or an activity related to each strategy in the chapter.

- ❏ Tell students to find definitions in the chapter for any words they did not check, or they can look in their dictionaries.

5

Lifestyles Around the World

In this chapter, students will read about different lifestyle issues in the U.S., such as single parents, working mothers, looking after children, and caring for older people. In Part 1, they will learn to recognize stressed and reduced forms and practice ways of asking for favors. In Part 2, they will listen to a lecture about changes in American families. In Part 3, they will listen to conversations people talking about aspects of their home and family life. At the end of the chapter, they will learn about how to record and interpret statistics using charts and line graphs.

Chapter Opener

- ❑ Have students look at the photo of a father looking at his son playing with a toy truck. Ask the students the three questions in the Connecting to the Topic section.

- ❑ Brainstorm different definitions of the word *lifestyle*. These may include: types of family and work, food, housing, ways of spending money, and ways of spending free time. Have students make a list of the most important things in their lives.

- ❑ Read and discuss the quote.

❝ It takes a village to raise a child. ❞

—African proverb

Chapter Overview

Listening Skills and Strategies

Listening for main ideas

Listening for details

Making inferences

Recognizing stress in two- and three-word verbs

Speaking Skills and Strategies

Talking about single parents

Talking about changes in the American family

Asking for help and favors

Talking about numbers and percentages

Comparing lifestyles in different countries

Critical Thinking Skills

Interpreting information in a line graph

Taking notes on a lecture

Getting meaning from context

Vocabulary Building

Two- and three-word verbs used in a conversation between neighbors

Expressions used to ask for help or a favor

Terms used to talk about changes in the American family

Expressions used to signal examples

Terms used for discussing lifestyles

Pronunciation

Identifying and practicing stressed words

Identifying and practicing the dropped *h* in unstressed words

Pronouncing linked phrases

Language Skills

Using context clues to guess people's lifestyles

Vocabulary

Nouns	Verbs	Adjectives
cost of living	benefit	flexible
day care center	can/can't afford	old-fashioned
flexibility	check up on	
homemaker	look into	
maternity leave	run out	
opportunity	take off	
policy	transfer	
	volunteer	

Can You Guess?

- Ask students to discuss the questions in groups and compare their answers with the correct answers.

- Brainstorm reasons for and against getting married earlier or later; reasons why mothers decide to work or stay at home; reasons for and against paying mothers and homemakers for the work they do.

1. At what age does the average American get married? A. *Men: 27 Women: 25*
   Some other countries:
   Japan: Men: 28 Women: 27
   Korea: Men: 30 Women: 27
   Canada: Men: 28 Women: 26
   England: Men: 29 Women: 27
   France: Men: 29 Women: 27

2. What percentage of single Americans in their mid-20s live with their parents? A. *Twenty percent in the United States.*

3. Which country requires husbands to pay their wives for the housework they do? A. *Taiwan. The law, passed in June, 2003, says that a working spouse must pay a sum to a home-maker for the housework he or she does, the sum to be agreed on between the two spouses.*

Before You Listen

Content Note

In some cultures, it is not acceptable to have children outside of marriage. This topic may be distressing for students who have experienced discrimination because of this issue. There are many cultures where it is unusual for children to be raised by a single parent. If this does happen, it is usually the result of a divorce or the death of one partner. In such cases, relatives in the extended family may step in to help take care of children.

□ Read the text that introduces the next listening.

1 Prelistening Questions

□ Have students look at the photos and try to guess what they're talking about.

□ Have the students read the questions and discuss them in pairs.

□ Compare answers as a whole class.

2 Previewing Vocabulary

□ Play the recording and have students listen to the underlined phrases.

□ Have students complete the vocabulary preview individually.

□ Compare their answers as a whole class and write the correct answers on the board.

□ Ask students for additional synonyms (or examples) for each item, e.g., 1. investigate 2. go/set off/depart 3. traditional 4. getting shorter/not enough 5. make sure

□ Practice the pronunciation of new words or phrases.

ANSWER KEY

1.c 2.e 3.b 4.d 5.a

Listen

3 Comprehension Questions

□ Explain that these questions will help students focus on the main ideas in the listening. They do not need to understand every word to answer the questions.

□ You may want to write the questions on the board.

□ Read the questions aloud.

□ Play the recording.

□ After listening, have students compare their answers in pairs.

ANSWER KEY

1. She wants him to babysit Joey; 2. She has a baby, but never got married; 3. She thought about having a baby before she got married; 4. It's very difficult for a single parent to raise a child.

AUDIOSCRIPT

Jeff: Who's there?

Sharon: It's Sharon and Joey!

Jeff: Hi! Come on in. What's happening?

Sharon: Jeff, can you do me a big favor? I just got a call from the office. They want me to look into a computer problem right away. Would you mind watching Joey until I get back?

Jeff: Sure, no problem. Is he asleep?

Sharon: Yeah, he just fell asleep ten minutes ago. He usually sleeps for a couple of hours at this time of day. But if he wakes up, just give him a bottle.

Mari: Ooh, what a cute baby! He's so little!

Jeff: Mari, this is our neighbor, Sharon, and her son, Joey. Sharon, this is our new roommate, Mari.

Mari: Nice to meet you.

Sharon: You too. Listen, I've got to take off. Thanks so much, Jeff, for helping me out.

Jeff/Mari: Bye!

Mari: Hey, Jeff, I didn't know you liked babies.

Jeff: Well, Joey is special. I take care of him from time to time when Sharon's busy. And then she does

favors for me in return. Like last week she lent me her car.

Mari: And her husband? Is he…

Jeff: She's not married. I don't think she ever was, actually.

Mari: Never?

Jeff: No, never. I think she's happy being a single mother.

Mari: Is that pretty common in America?

Jeff: Well, it's certainly becoming more and more common. Even Nancy talked about it. You know, before she got married.

Nancy: Hi, guys.

Mari/Jeff: Hi.

Nancy: Uh, what were you saying about me?

Jeff: That you used to talk about having a baby by yourself. Before you met Andrew.

Nancy: Oh yeah, I worried that time was running out. You know, like, what if I never got married?

Mari: Maybe I'm old-fashioned, but I could never bring up a baby by myself. I think it would be so difficult . . .

Nancy: Yeah, raising a child is tough. I'm really lucky I met Andrew.

Mari: And, if you have a baby, you'll have Jeff here to help you with babysitting.

Jeff: We'll see. Speaking of babysitting, I'd better check up on Joey.

Stress

TWO- AND THREE-WORD VERBS

- Have students read the instruction note.

- Have them read the three sentences aloud.

- Explain that these two- or three-part verbs (known as *phrasal verbs*) are very common in informal English. Sometimes the meaning is easy to guess from the individual parts of the verb (e.g., *take off* your coat), but sometimes the meaning is quite different (e.g., the plane *took off*). It is best to learn these verbs as separate vocabulary items.

---

4 Listening for Stressed Words (Part I)

- ❏ Listen to the recording of selected sentences from the conversation.

- ❏ There will be a pause at the end of each sentence to allow time for students to repeat and write the missing words.

- ❏ After listening, have students check their answers with a partner.

- ❏ Have students read the sentences with their partner, paying attention to stressed words in their pronunciation and intonation.

ANSWER KEY

1. Come on *in*.
2. They want me to look *into* a computer problem right away.
3. If he wakes *up*, just give him a bottle.
4. Listen, I've got to take *off*.
5. Thanks so much, Jeff, for helping me *out*.
6. I take *care* of him from time to time when Sharon's busy.
7. I worried that time was running *out*.
8. I could never bring *up* a baby by myself.
9. I'd better check *up* on Joey.

5 Listening for Stressed Words (Part II)

- ❏ Play the recording, which is part of the conversation from Activity 3.

- ❏ Have students write the missing words.

- ❏ After listening, have students check their answers.

- ❏ Have students read the conversation with a partner, paying attention to stressed words in their pronunciation and intonation.

AUDIOSCRIPT and ANSWER KEY

Mari: Hey, Jeff, I didn't know you liked *babies*.

Jeff: Well, Joey is *special*. I take care of him from time to time when Sharon's *busy*. And then *she* does favors for *me* in return. Like last week she lent me her *car*.

Mari: And her *husband*? Is he…

Jeff: She's not *married*. I don't think she *ever* was, actually.

Mari: Never?

Jeff: *No*, *never*. I think she's *happy* being a *single* mother.

Mari: Is that pretty *common* in America?

Jeff: Well, it's *certainly* becoming more and more common. Even *Nancy* talked about it. You know, before she got *married*.

Nancy: Hi, guys.

Mari/Jeff: Hi.

Nancy: Uh, *what* were you saying about me?

Jeff: That you *used* to talk about having a *baby* by yourself before you *met* Andrew.

Nancy: Oh yeah, I *worried* that *time* was running out. You know, like, what if I *never* got married?

Mari: Maybe I'm *old-fashioned*, but I could *never* bring up a baby by *myself*. I think it would be so difficult . . .

Nancy: Yeah, raising a *child* is tough. I'm really *lucky* I met Andrew.

| Mari: | And, if you have a baby, you'll have _Jeff_ here to help you with _babysitting_. |
| Jeff: | We'll see. Speaking of babysitting, I'd _better_ check up on Joey. |

 EXPANSION ACTIVITY

▪ The aim of this activity is to practice language for asking for and refusing favors.

▪ Please see Black Line Master "Can You Do Me a Favor?" on page BLM 14 of this Teacher's Edition. Photocopy and distribute one copy to each student.

▪ Model the example dialog with a student. Model writing the student's name and excuse on your chart. Encourage them to think of creative excuses.

▪ Have students walk around the room and ask each other favors so they can fill in the chart. Point out that they can use a classmate's name only once.

▪ When students have completed the worksheet, they can sit down and discuss part 2.

REDUCTIONS

▪ Read aloud the instruction note about reductions.

▪ Read aloud each of the unreduced and reduced forms in sentences. Have students read them aloud.

6 Listening for Reductions

❑ Read the directions.

❑ Play the recording.

❑ There will be a pause after each sentence to allow students time to write their answers and repeat.

❑ After listening, have students check their answers with a partner.

ANSWER KEY

1. he, him 2. — 3. him 4. her 5. — 6. have, here

After You Listen

7 Using Vocabulary

1

❑ Have students work in pairs. Student A will look at page 248 in the Student Book. Student B will look at page 257.

❑ Have students read their section, and ask if there are any questions.

❑ Set a time limit of five minutes.

❑ Check the answers as a class.

❑ If there is time, have students choose one pair of sentences and continue the conversation.

2

❑ Have students discuss the questions in pairs.

❑ Invite volunteers to summarize their opinions for the class.

ANSWER KEY

A: It's three o'clock in the morning. Why aren't you sleeping?

B: I have to finish this paper by 10:00 A.M. Time is running out.

A: Are you leaving?

B: Yes, it's getting dark. I'd better take off.

A: Wake up, Sally. It's 10:00 A.M.

B: I'm tired! I don't want to go to school today!

A: Hello? Is anybody home?

B: Yeah. Come on in.

A: Who takes care of your kids while you're working?

B: My mother.

A: What's wrong with this light? It's not working properly.

B: I know. I told the manager, and he's going to look into it.

A: How's the baby doing?

B: I just checked up on her. She's sleeping.

A: Why did George quit his job?

B: He decided to stay home for a couple of years and bring up his kids.

ASKING FOR HELP OR A FAVOR

- Read the instruction note.

- Ask volunteers to model some of the expressions using a variety of "favors" (see examples below).

  - Lend me your cell phone.

  - Help me with my homework.

  - Show me how to use the computer.

  - Move your papers and books to another office.

---

8 Asking for a Favor

- ❑ Have students work in pairs. One student will look at page 249 in the Student Book. The other student will look at page 257.

- ❑ Set a time limit of five minutes for students to practice their conversations.

- ❑ Monitor the groups as they are doing the activity and make notes of errors.

- ❑ Invite volunteers to perform their conversation for the class.

Interacting with Others

This type of activity is an example of collaborative learning to encourage fluency and confidence. In these role-plays, based around the topic of asking for and offering favors, communication is more important than grammar. Students can practice the role-plays in pairs and then improve their performance by switching roles or partners. By the time they perform the role-play for the class, they should feel more confident in the use of the new language.

9 Role-Play

- ❑ Have students work in pairs and read the seven situations.

- ❑ Check comprehension of any new vocabulary.

- ❑ Set a time limit of ten minutes for students to practice their conversations.

- ❑ Monitor the groups as they are doing the activity and make notes of errors. Tell the students the global errors at the end of the ten minutes. Do not focus on any student in particular, just note that the errors were heard and are things to be careful about.

- ❑ Invite volunteers to perform one of their conversations for the class.

- ❑ Next, have students work in groups to discuss the situations.

  - Which favors would they feel uncomfortable with and why?

  - What language would they use for each request?

- ❑ Rate the requests on a scale of 1 to 10, from *easy to ask* to *difficult or unlikely*.

Before You Listen

Best Practice

Activating Prior Knowledge

The prelistening discussion is an example of personalization. This type of activity encourages students to relate the topic to their own experience. Asking students to predict what kind of differences they think there are between families in the 1950s and now will make it easier for them to assimilate the new information in the lecture.

1   **Prelistening Discussion**

❑   Have the students work in small groups and discuss each question. You can help students discuss each question by looking at the suggestions below.

    1. Brainstorm adjectives to describe each picture. How do you feel about the people in these pictures? Are they similar or different to your family?

    2. Make a chart outlining differences between American families in the 1950s and now.

Families in the 1950s	Families now
Father works	Mother and father both work
Mother does housework	Mother and father share housework

3. Make a list of changes in families in the students' communities.

    ❑   Encourage students to explore various possible reasons for these changes.

2   **Previewing Vocabulary**

❑   Play the recording and have students listen to the words and phrases.

❑   Have students check the words they know and then compare answers with a partner. Explain that they will work out the meaning of the new words by listening to the lecture.

Listen

Strategy

Taking Notes on Examples

▪   Read the information in the *Strategy* box.

▪   Make some general statements and ask students to come up with examples. See below:

    ■   There are many changes in family life since the 50s. For example…

    ■   There are many difficulties in bringing up a child by yourself. To give one example …

    ■   Single parents might face problems at work. For instance….

3   **Taking Notes on Examples**

❑   Explain that students will listen to statements followed by examples and will take notes on the examples.

❑   Remind them to use key words, abbreviations, symbols, and indentation.

❑   Play the recording. Each sentence will be heard twice.

❑   Have students exchange notes with a partner, and using those notes, restate the items. Note that the important thing is not that they understand their partner's notes, but that they see some differences in note-taking. People develop their individual abbreviations and symbols for personal note-taking.

ANSWER KEY

1.↑ 1/2 students in Am. med. school = women childcare? Shopping, cooking, cleaning? school volunteer jobs?

Canada–yes, U.S.–no

AUDIOSCRIPT

1. Women today are working in professions that were not as open to them 30 or 40 years ago. To give just one example, today more than half the students in American medical schools are women.

2. Most American homes don't have a full-time homemaker anymore. And that creates new problems for families; problems like who takes care of babies and old people; who shops, cooks, and cleans; who volunteers at the children's school; and so on.

3. In some countries, companies are required by law to give new parents a paid vacation when they have a new baby. Canada, for instance, has a law like that, but the United States does not.

4 Taking Notes (Part I)

❑ Read the questions or write them on the board.

❑ Have students close their books and take notes as they listen.

❑ Play the first part of the recording.

5 Outlining the Lecture

❑ Have students use their notes from Activities 3 and 4 to complete the outline.

❑ Play the recording again if needed.

ANSWER KEY

Topic: Changes in the American Family

I. "Typical" Am. fam

    A. 1950s: *father works, mother home, 2–3 children*

    B. Changes today:

        1. *families are smaller*

        2. *more single-parent families*

        3. *role of married mothers*
        Stats: *1950s 11% mothers worked, 2002 70%*

        Reasons:
        need money
        more opportunities available

        New problems:
        takes care of babies and grandparents?
        shops, cooks, and cleans?
        volunteers at school?

AUDIOSCRIPT

Have you ever seen the television show *Father Knows Best*? You probably haven't because it was a popular comedy show in the 1950s—way before you were born. It was about a family: a father, who went to work every day; a mother, who stayed home and took care of the house; and the children—two or three, I can't remember. Anyway, in those days that was considered to be a typical American family.

But today, the American family is very different. First, families are smaller today than before. I mean, people are having fewer children. Second, more and more children are growing up in single-parent families—families with only a mother or only a father. I'm not going to go into the reasons for that here because I want to focus on the third and biggest change in the American family: the role of married mothers and the effects of this new role. Consider these statistics: In the 1950s, only 11 percent of married mothers worked outside the home. In 2002, about 70 percent of mothers were employed.

Why is that? Well, there are two important reasons. The first one, very simply, is that they need the money. These days, the cost of living is so high that most families need two salaries in order to make ends meet.

The other reason why married mothers are working in larger and larger numbers is that they have more opportunities than they did 30 or 40 years ago. There are laws in the United States that give women the same opportunity as men to go to college and get jobs. As a result, women today are working in professions that were not as open to them 30 or 40 years ago. To give just one example, today more than half of the students in American medical schools are women.

So, to summarize so far, we've seen that the American family has changed dramatically since the days of those old television shows. In the typical two-parent family today, both the father and the mother have jobs. This means that most American homes don't have a full-time homemaker anymore. And that creates new problems for families: problems like who takes care of babies and grandparents; who shops, cooks, and cleans; who volunteers at the children's school; and so on.

6 Taking Notes (Part II)

- ❑ Have students close their books and take notes as they listen.
- ❑ Play the second part of the recording.
- ❑ Have students use their notes to complete the outline.
- ❑ Play the recording again if needed.

ANSWER KEY

II. Company policies/programs:

    A. *paid maternity leave*

    B. If co. transfers worker, co. finds job for husb./wife

    C. *flextime = 9-5 or 7-3 or 10-6. work 8 hrs, choose start / finish time*

    D. *telecommuting / teleworking = working from home*
       15% of U.S. workers ↑ good for parents / childcare

    E. *day care at office, children can go to work and go home w. parents*

Concl: *very few cos can afford these progs, - gov shd help more*

AUDIOSCRIPT

To help families with working parents deal with these new problems, some American businesses have introduced new programs and policies to make it easier to work and raise children at the same time. Let me give you five examples of these policies and programs.

The first policy is paid maternity leave. What we're talking about is a woman taking time off from work when she has a baby. American law requires companies to give a woman up to 12 weeks of leave when she has a baby. But the problem is that the companies aren't required to pay for those 12 weeks. As a result, many women are forced to go back to work much sooner than they want to. Recently some companies, at least the big ones, have started to offer paid maternity leave. But it's still kind of rare. By the way, a small percentage of companies now also offer *paternity* leave—that means that fathers can take time off for a new baby. I would like to see a law that requires all companies to give paid leave to both mothers and fathers for a new baby. Canada, for instance, already has a law like that.

OK, moving along, here's another example of a policy that helps working families. As you know, big companies like IBM or General Motors often transfer their employees to other cities, right? Well, if a company transfers the husband, for instance, this might create a problem for the wife because now she has to find a new job, too. So now there are companies that will help the husband or wife of the transferred worker find a new job.

A third policy that many companies now offer is called *flextime*. Here's what that means. In the United States, a normal workday is from 9:00 A.M. until 5:00 P.M.—eight hours. With flextime, workers can choose the hour that they start work in the morning and can go home after eight hours. So, for instance, a worker who comes in at 7:00 can leave at 3:00. Or a worker can come in at 10:00 and leave at 6:00. You can imagine how useful this flexibility is for people who have children.

The fourth change I want to describe is *telecommuting*. Or sometimes we say *teleworking*. With telecommuting, people work at home and use the computer or phone to communicate with their workplace. It's estimated that about 15 percent of the U.S. workforce telecommutes now. But the percentage is growing all the time because it saves people time and money. And if parents are allowed to work at home, their children might not have to spend as much time in child care.

And speaking of child care, the fifth program offered by many of the best companies is day care; that is, some companies have day care centers at the office where trained people take care of the employees' children. This means workers come to work with their young children, leave them at the center, and can visit them during lunch or whatever. Then the parents and kids drive home together at the end of the day. With day care at work, parents don't need to worry about their kids because they're right there.

OK, let me review what I've been talking about. I've given you five examples of company policies and programs that make life a little easier for working mothers and fathers. But it's important for me to tell you that only some large companies can afford these kinds of programs. For most people, trying to work and take care of a family at the same time is still very, very difficult. In my opinion, our government and our society need to do a lot more to help working parents and their children.

After You Listen

7 **Discussing the Lecture**

❑ Have students work in groups of three or four to discuss questions 1–5.

❑ Encourage students to use the new vocabulary in their discussion.

❑ Compare answers as a class.

ANSWER KEY

1. Why are more and more mothers in two-parent American families working these days?

   Families need money because the cost of living is high.

   There are more opportunities for work and education today than 30–40 year ago.

2. Challenges about who takes care of babies and grandparents; who shops, cooks, and cleans; who volunteers at the children's school

3. The five programs are:

   1. Paid maternity care (advantage to workers: can afford to take time off to care for young baby; advantage to companies: encourages working mothers to stay in their jobs; disadvantage to workers: usually only get half their salary; disadvantage to companies: expensive, workers may quit after maternity leave)

   2. Help the husband or wife of the transferred worker find a new job (advantage to workers: can transfer to higher paid jobs; advantage to companies: workers are more mobile; disadvantage to companies: expensive)

   3. Flextime (advantage to workers: can choose working hours; advantage to companies: no extra labor costs; disadvantage to companies: office hours may not coincide with busiest times)

   4. Telecommuting (advantage to workers: no commuting, can take care of children at home; disadvantage to workers: initial costs in setting up home office equipment; advantage to companies: lower costs; disadvantage to companies: possible communication problems)

   5. Day care at the workplace (advantage to workers: can visit child at lunch break, can be close if there is an emergency; advantages to companies: encourages working parents to stay in their jobs, fewer

parents forced to take sick leave when child is sick; disadvantage to companies: expensive)

4. Smaller companies cannot afford these programs.

5. Answers will vary.

8 Reviewing Vocabulary

❏ Refer students to Activity 2 on page 109 of the Student Book. Review any new items and have students check the meaning in a dictionary if necessary.

❏ Take a vote on the five most difficult words and have students give example sentences of how they are used.

On the Spot!

Best Practice

Cultivating Critical Thinking

This is an example of a collaborative team activity. This type of activity requires students to process the information from a reading and respond to it critically by generating different alternative solutions. This involves reinterpretation, synthesis, and application of concepts. The process of manipulating language and concepts in this way will create deeper processing of new material and allow students to develop and express their opinions on the topic of lifestyles.

9 What Would You Do?

❏ Have students read the first part of the article individually.

❏ Ask a student to summarize it for the class.

❏ Brainstorm possible predictions for the judge's response and write them on the board.

❏ Check the judge's response on page 261.

❏ Have students work in groups to discuss the second part of the article and part 2 of the activity.

❏ Set a time limit of five minutes.

❏ Ask representatives from each group to summarize their discussion for the class.

❏ Invite the whole class to discuss the third question together.

EXPANSION ACTIVITY

REPRODUCIBLE

▪ The aim of this activity is for students to use the Internet to develop skills using research to support their opinions and arguments.

▪ Please see Black Line Master "Starting a Workplace Day Care Center" on page BLM 15 of this Teacher's Edition. Photocopy and distribute one copy to each student.

▪ In this activity, students may access the same sites to get information, but they will have to adapt the information according to the point of view required by their role.

▪ Students can use a search engine, entering keywords like *workplace child care,* or use the websites below. Please check the websites before giving the assignment to students.

www.workfamily.com/Open/FAQ_Childcare.asp

www.galtglobalreview.com/business/workplace_childcare.html

www.childcareaware.org/en/dailyparent/v18/

▪ The research part of this activity can be done in a computer lab class or assigned for homework.

▪ Divide the students into small groups and have each person in the group choose one role.

▪ Students will research the topic on the web. Then re-form their groups to complete the worksheet. Encourage students to maintain their roles as they complete part 2.

▪ Finally, ask for volunteers to share the information from part 2 with the class.

Focused Listening

LINKING

- Read the instruction note.
- Practice the examples.

1 **Pronouncing Linked Phrases**

- ❏ The recording has three sections. Each section practices a different rule for linking.
- ❏ Play the recording. There will be a pause after each section. Explain, or ask a student to explain, the rule.
- ❏ Have students listen and repeat each phrase.

2 **Pronouncing Sentences**

- ❏ Before listening, have students read the sentences and mark which words they think are linked.
- ❏ Play the recording and have students listen carefully to the linked words.
- ❏ Play the recording again and ask students to repeat. They can also mark the linked words.
- ❏ Have students read the sentences in pairs.
- ❏ Move around the room and give feedback on pronunciation.

Getting Meaning from Context

Best Practice

Scaffolding Instruction

This is an example of an activity that raises metacognitive awareness of learning strategies. In real life, we use surrounding context clues to work out the meanings of unfamiliar words. This activity asks students to use the surrounding verbal clues in each conversation to work out the context. Asking students to write the clues will guide them through the steps of developing this important skill.

Focus on Testing

Using Context Clues

- Read through the chart and check comprehension of any new items.
- Review the purpose of using clues to get meaning.
- This recording has five sections. Play each section of the recording. The recording will pause at the end of the conversation to allow time for students to circle their answers and write the clues.
- Then play the final part of each section, which gives the correct answer.

ANSWER KEY

Answers	Clues
1. b. a retired person	pension, social security
2. d. her parents	come home, baby
3. c. is divorced	ex-wife, kids
4. a. with his parents	lost job, ran out of money, back home
5. a. a retirement home	privacy, friends my own age

AUDIOSCRIPT

Conversation 1

Senior Citizen Man: Well, I tell you, things get pretty tough by the end of the month. I don't have any pension—just Social Security—and that's only $800 a month. Sometimes the check is late, and the rent is due on the first of the month. Do you think the landlord cares?

Question 1: The speaker is . . .

Senior Citizen Man: Sometimes I think no one cares about retired people in this country.

Conversation 2

17-Year-Old Girl: Sometimes I feel like I'm in a prison. "Come home by ten." "Don't go there." "Don't do that." "Turn down the music." They treat me like a baby. They have no respect for my privacy.

Question 2: The speaker is talking about . . .

Girl: My parents forget that I'm 17 years old. I'm not a child anymore.

Conversation 3

Man: My ex-wife and I agreed that the kids would live with me. At first it was hard with all the work and no help. But it's exciting to watch my kids grow up.

Question 3: This man . . .

Man: And fortunately, there are organizations to help divorced fathers like me.

Conversation 4

Young Man: I lived with my parents until I was 18, then I left home to go to college and lived with roommates in an apartment near the campus. When I graduated, I got a job with an engineering firm and got my own place. But last year, I lost my job and ran out of money. So what could I do? I came back home.

Question 4: This person probably lives . . .

Young Man: Boy, it's not easy living with your parents again after all these years.

Conversation 5

Senior Citizen Woman: After I broke my hip, it was too hard to go on living by myself. So I tried living with my son and his family for a while, but their house is small and noisy, and I want my privacy, too. So I came here. And it really isn't bad. I have my own doctor, good food, and plenty of friends my own age.

Question 5: This woman is living in . . .

Senior Citizen Woman: This retirement home is really the best place for me.

---

3 Discussing Lifestyles

❑ Read the descriptions of the five people on the recording.

❑ Have students answer the first question. You may want to ask students to choose which ones they find most interesting to talk about.

❑ Have students discuss Questions 2 and 3 in groups then report back on their discussion to the class.

❑ If there is time, you may want to have a debate on the third question, with each side of the class presenting arguments for and against.

EXPANSION ACTIVITY

- The aim of this activity is to practice expressing opinions about lifestyle issues raised in this chapter.

- Please see Black Line Master "Questionnaire" on page BLM 16 of this Teacher's Edition. Photocopy and distribute one copy to each student.

- Explain that they will first read the statements silently and write their own opinions checking whether they agree or disagree.

- Divide students into groups. They will compare their opinions with their group and try to reach agreement. Have them make a note of the more difficult decisions or of the conditions that might have to exist in order for them to agree or disagree with the statement.

- Set a time limit of 15 minutes.

- At the end of the discussion, have representatives of each group report back on the most controversial issues.

Before You Listen

NUMBERS AND PERCENTAGES

- Read the instruction note about numbers and percentages, focusing on prepositions.

1   Prelistening Discussion

- ❏ Read and discuss the questions with the whole class.

- ❏ If there is time, discuss information about several different communities.

Listen

Strategy

Graphic Organizer: Line Graph

- Read the information in the Strategy box.

- Point out the line graph on page 118 of the Student Book. They will complete this graph in the next activity.

Best Practice

Organizing Information

Activities such as this will teach students to organize information using a graphic organizer called a line graph. This allows students to understand and process information using statistics. In this case, students record statistics about the numbers of women who work, couples who divorce, and elderly people who live alone. Other types of graphic organizers are used throughout this book.

2   Completing Line Graphs

- ❏ Discuss each graph individually, helping students understand what the numbers at the left and across the bottom of each graph mean.

- ❏ Read the captions and ask students to explain them in their own words to show that they understand what each graph is measuring.

- ❏ Play the recording and have students write their answers on the graphs.

- ❏ Point out that the third graph will have two kinds of marks, circles for women and Xs for men.

ANSWER KEY

Graph 1: 1960=37.8, 1980=51.1, 1990=57.5, 2003=61

Graph 2: 1960=2.2, 1970=3.5, 1980=5.2, 1990=4.7, 2003=3.8

Graph 3: 1970: women=35.9 men=10.8, 1980: women=31.9 men=8.1, 1990: women=51.8 men=21.5, 2000:women=40 men=17

AUDIOSCRIPT

Graph 1

Graph 1 gives statistics on American women in the U.S. labor force. In 1960, 37.8 percent of American women had jobs. By 1980, it had jumped to 51.1 percent. In 1990, it was 57.5 percent. And in 2003, 61 percent of American women were working.

Graph 2

Graph 2 shows the divorce rate in the United States. In 1960, the divorce rate was just 2.2 per 1,000 people. In 1970, it rose to 3.5, and in 1980, it jumped to 5.2. However, it declined in 1990 to 4.7, and in 2003 declined even more, to 3.8 per 1,000 people.

Graph 3

Graph 3 presents information on people over age 65 who lived alone from 1970 to 2000. You need to make two sets of points here. Use an *O* for men and an *X* for women.

In 1970, 35.9 percent of elderly women lived alone, compared to 10.8 percent of elderly men. In 1980, the percentage was 31.9 for women and 8.1 for men. In 1990, 51.8 percent of women lived alone, compared to 21.5 percent for men.

And finally, in 2000, 40 percent of women and 17 percent of men were living by themselves.

After You Listen

3 **Talking About Statistics**

- ❑ Have students read the directions and write their five true or false statements.

- ❑ Then ask them to work in pairs. Ask one pair of students to read the example aloud.

- ❑ Set a time limit of five minutes for students to read their statements to each other and respond.

- ❑ When they finish, they can go on to discuss the questions in part 2.

- ❑ Ask the class to come up with a variety of different explanations for the statistics in each graph.

Best Practice

Making Use of Academic Content

This is an example of collaborative problem-solving. Interpreting information from charts and graphs is an important academic skill. This type of activity requires students to work collaboratively to process information in order to complete the charts. They then have to synthesize and reach conclusions based on the data in order to answer the questions.

4 **Comparing Lifestyles in Different Countries**

- ❑ Read the instructions.

- ❑ Have students work in groups of three.

- ❑ Ask one graph of students to read the example.

- ❑ Explain that the three charts are the same except that some information is missing from each one.

- ❑ Each person will choose one chart and ask the others for the missing information.

ANSWER KEY

Charts A, B and C are combined below. The missing answers are boldfaced, and the chart letter that the answer is missing from is in parentheses in front of each answer.

Country	# Children per Woman	Life Expectancy	TV Sets per Person	Per Capita GDP
Korea	1.5	75.5	.4	**(B)** **$17,800**
United States	2.07	**(B) 77.43**	**(A) 1.00**	37,800
Argentina	2.24	75.7	.3	**(C)** **11,200**
France	1.84	79.44	.6	27,600
Senegal	**(A) 4.84**	**(B) 56.56**	.08	1,600
Thailand	1.89	**(C) 71.41**	.5	7,400
Mexico	2.49	74.94	.3	9,000
Italy	1.27	79.54	.5	**(C)** **26,700**
Saudi Arabia	4.11	75.23	.3	11,800
China (PRC)	**(B) 1.69**	71.96	.3	5,000
Egypt	**(C) 2.95**	70.71	.2	4,000
Iran	1.93	69.66	**(B) .1**	7,000
Russia	**(A) 1.26**	66.39	**(C) .5**	8,900
Japan	1.38	**(A) 81.04**	.8	28,200
Turkey	1.98	72.08	.4	**(A)** **6,700**

5 **Discussion**

❏ When students have completed their charts, have them discuss the questions and write sentences as in the example.

ANSWER KEY

1. United States, Japan, France, Italy, Saudi Arabia
2. Senegal, Egypt, China, Iran, Thailand
3. Answers will vary.

EXPANSION ACTIVITY

▨ The aim of this activity is to practice the skills needed for making a line graph like the ones on pages 118-119 of this chapter and to practice research skills on the Internet or in the library. The research part of this activity can be given as homework.

▨ Brainstorm with your students possible topics for a line graph. The topics should relate to some development that takes place over a period of time. Here are some examples:

The average retirement age over the last 50 years

The number of university students over the last 20 years

The number of women at university over the last 20 years

The average age of getting married over the last 50 years

▨ Have students work in groups to design their line graph and plan their strategy for collecting this information. (It is important to draw out the graph at this stage so that students can plan the time scale of the graph and divide up the research.)

▨ Make sure all students know what data they need to research for the next class.

▨ In the next class, have students re-form their groups and transfer their information to the graph.

▨ Display the graphs on the wall of the classroom.

▨ Ask groups to tell the class what was most surprising or unusual and what possible theories might explain the patterns in the data.

Self-Assessment Log

❏ The purpose of the log is to help the students reflect on their learning.

❏ Read the directions aloud and have students check vocabulary that they learned in the chapter and are prepared to use.

❏ Have students check the strategies they understand.

❏ Put students in small groups. Ask students to find the information or an activity related to each strategy in the chapter.

❏ Tell students to find definitions in the chapter for any words they did not check, or they can look in their dictionaries.

Global Connections

In this chapter, students will read about various topics related to international communication. In Part 1, they will talk about communication technology and learn to interrupt politely. In Part 2, they will listen to a lecture about cultural differences. In Part 3, they will practice listening to information about different cultural customs. In Part 4, they will practice writing and taking a general knowledge quiz.

Chapter Opener

- ❑ Have students look at the photo of a farmer in China using a laptop computer in the field. Ask them the questions from the Connecting to the Topic section. Have students discuss as a class.

- ❑ Read and discuss the quote. How can the word *culture* be defined? How do cultures influence each other? Ask students for some examples from the past or the present.

❝ No culture can live if it attempts to be exclusive. **❞**

—Mahatma Gandhi
Indian nationalist and spiritual leader
1869–1948

Chapter Overview

Listening Skills and Strategies

Listening for main ideas

Listening for details

Making inferences

Identifying blended consonants

Taking a trivia quiz

Taking notes on similarities and differences

Speaking Skills and Strategies

Learning computer terms

Practicing intonation of questions

Interrupting politely

Talking about ways to stay in touch

Talking about customs

Generalizing

Talking about a dream vacation

Discussing a reading

Critical Thinking Skills

Getting meaning from context

Speculating about hypothetical situations

Guessing locations of photos

Using a T-chart to compare advantages and disadvantages

Vocabulary Building

Computer terms

Expressions for interrupting

Expressions signaling similarity and difference

Adverbs used for generalizing

Correct use of "trip" vs. "travel"

Pronunciation

Identifying and practicing stressed words

Identifying Intonation patterns

Saying names and sentences with blended consonants

Language Skills

Using context clues to guess about customs and body language

Vocabulary

Nouns	Verbs	Adjectives	Expression
blog	bow	appropriate	No sweat.
charge	catch up on	embarrassing	
chopsticks	download	insulted	
comment	illustrate		
headset	install (software)		
hug	post (a message or comment)		
misunderstanding	stay in touch		
sound card			
title (of a person)			

Can You Guess?

■ Read the six statements below. Have students listen and write true or false for each statement. Go over the correct answers.

■ What possible definitions of *culture* are suggested by these facts? What kinds of miscommunication can occur when people don't understand each other's cultures?

True or False?

1. In Japan, many people use their cell phones to send and receive e-mail. A. *True* **2.** In the U.S., workers often call their bosses by their first names. A. *True* **3.** In Egypt, it is polite to eat all the food on your plate. A. *False* **4.** You should not give people from Iran yellow flowers. A. *True. In many cultures including Iran, Peru, and Mexico, the color yellow has a negative meaning.* **5.** In some countries, bribery is a normal part of doing business. A. *True* **6.** The country with the largest number of newspapers is India. A. *False; it's Japan*.

Before You Listen

❏ Read aloud the text that introduces the next conversation.

1   **Prelistening Questions**

❏ Play the recording and have students listen to the computer terms and the underlined words and expressions.

❏ Have the students read the questions and discuss them in pairs.

❏ Compare answers as a whole class.

❏ As a whole class, make a list of ways of communicating using technology. These might include: landline phone, cell phone, Internet, email, text messaging, fax.

2   **Previewing Vocabulary**

❏ Play the recording and have students listen to the computer terms and the underlined words and expressions.

❏ Have students complete the activity individually.

❏ Compare their answers as a whole class and write the correct answers on the board.

ANSWER KEY

1.

blog – (web log) a website where people can post comments regularly, usually based around a specific theme

headset – (headphones) ear pieces used for listening to audio files on a computer or music player

sound card – computer card that can store sound in digital form

download – transfer electronic files form the Internet to your computer

install (software) – add software to your computer

post (a message or comment) – put a message onto a website

2.
1. b   2. a   3. e   4. c   5. d

Listen

3   **Comprehension Questions**

❏ Explain that these questions will help students focus on the main ideas in the listening. They do not need to understand every word to answer the questions.

❏ Read the questions.

❏ Play the recording.

❏ After listening, have students compare their answers in pairs.

❏ Check the answers as a class.

ANSWER KEY

1. at Jeff's computer at home 2. He is posting messages on a blog about hip hop. 3. He is a blogger in Turkey. 4. Her cell phone bill was $160. 5. She wants to know how to call overseas using the Internet. 6. She will need a sound card, a microphone, and a headset 7. It's free.

Stress

4 **Listening for Stressed Words**

❑ Play the recording again.

❑ Allow time for students to repeat and write the missing words.

❑ After listening, have students check their answers with the audioscript in their books.

❑ Have students read the conversation with a partner, paying attention to stressed words in their pronunciation.

AUDIOSCRIPT and ANSWER KEY

Jeff: Come in!

Mari: Am I _interrupting_?

Jeff: It's OK, I was just catching up on my _blog_.

Mari: Oh yeah? What's it _about_?

Jeff: Mostly it's about _hip-hop_. Like here's a _comment_ from a guy named Hasan talking about, let's see… hip-hop in Istanbul.

Mari: In Turkey? _Turkish_ hip-hop?

Jeff: Sure. And _here's_ one from my friend Hiroshi, the _drummer_ in Tokyo.

Mari: Hmm. Maybe _I_ should start a blog about learning _English_.

Jeff: Well, it's a great way to meet _new_ people, that's for sure. And all you need is an _Internet_ connection.

Mari: Well, _speaking_ of the Internet, I wanted to ask your _advice_ about something.

Jeff: OK. What's up?

Mari: Well, I just got my _cell_ phone bill for last month, and it was $160!

Jeff: Ouch.

Mari: Yeah, I can't _believe_ it. Cell phone calls are so _expensive_ here.

Jeff: Are they _cheaper_ in Japan?

Mari: _Much_ cheaper. And we use our cell phones for _email_, too. A lot of people don't even _own_ a computer.

Jeff: It's _amazing_ what you can do with cell phones these days. Talk, take _pictures_, send email . . .

Mari: Yeah. But _anyway_ Jeff, I need to find a cheaper way to stay in _touch_ with my parents and my friends in Japan. And I _heard_ there's a way you can call overseas for _free_ using your computer. Do you know anything about that?

Jeff: Of course, it's a _technology_ called Voice over Internet. I use it all the _time_.

Mari: How does it _work_?

Jeff: Well, you need a computer with a _sound_ card, if you've got that.

Mari: Yeah, I do…

Jeff: And you also need a microphone and a _headset_.

Mari: Hmm. I don't have those.

Jeff: No sweat, you can buy them at any _electronics_ store.

Mari: OK. What else?

Jeff: Well, then you'll need to _download_ the software, which is _free_, and then if the person you're calling installs the _same_ software, there's no _cost_ for calling.

Mari: But what if they _don't_? Can I call from my _computer_ to someone's

Jeff: Yes. There's a _charge_ for that, but it's a lot cheaper than using your _cell phone_, believe me.

Mari: Could you show me how it works on _your_ computer?

Jeff:	Right now?
Mari:	No, it's *nighttime* in Japan now. Can we do it in about three *hours*?
Jeff:	No problem. I'll be here.
Mari:	Great. See you later.

Intonation

INTONATION IN QUESTIONS AND REQUESTS

- Read the instruction note.

- Model the intonation of the examples in the box. (You may want to emphasize the intonation by replacing the words with 'dah.')

5 Practicing Intonation of Questions

- ❑ Play the recording and have students listen and read the sentences.

- ❑ Play the recording again. This time, have students repeat the questions.

6 Identifying Intonation Patterns

- ❑ Explain that students will hear six different questions. They will have to identify whether the intonation is rising or falling.

- ❑ Play the recording and have students write their answers.

- ❑ After listening, check the answers as a class.

ANSWER KEY

1. Are you working on the computer right now? (rising)
2. Can you help me? (falling)
3. Where do you want me to put this paper? (falling)
4. Could you please repeat that? (rising)
5. What kind of computer do you have? (falling)
6. Did you check your email today? (rising)

After You Listen

7 Reviewing Vocabulary

- ❑ Have students work in pairs and take turns asking and answering the questions.

- ❑ Review the answers as a class.

Using Language Functions

INTERRUPTING POLITELY

- Read the instruction note.

- Ask students to read the examples, using appropriate questions to complete the sentences.

Content Note

In some cultures, it is considered extremely rude to interrupt anyone, particularly an older person in a position of responsibility, such as a teacher. In the United States, however, it is common for students to politely interrupt a teacher if they don't understand something. Most teachers consider that an important part of the learning process is having students let them know when something is not clear.

Best Practice

Interacting with Others

This type of activity is an example of collaborative learning to encourage fluency and confidence. In this activity, communication is more important than grammar. Students practice interrupting politely in groups of three. They can then improve their confidence by switching roles or partners and practicing the same situations again. By providing feedback to each other, they learn skills of self-evaluation.

8 **Role-Play**

- ❑ Read the situations and check comprehension of any new vocabulary.

- ❑ Have students work in groups of three to practice the role-plays.

- ❑ Set a time limit of five minutes.

- ❑ Move around the room to monitor and provide feedback. Take notes of errors.

- ❑ Ask for volunteers to perform conversations for the class.

9 **The Interrupting Game**

- ❑ Prepare a list (or ask students for ideas) of popular conversational topics, e.g., baseball, TV, music, computers.

- ❑ Have students work in groups of four to five students. Each person in the group should think of a story about one of the topics.

- ❑ Have students read the example.

- ❑ Set a time limit of ten minutes.

- ❑ Move around the room to monitor and provide feedback.

10 **Survey: Find Someone Who . . .**

- ❑ Remind students of the rules of this activity, or ask a student to explain it to the class.

- ❑ Read through the list and check comprehension of any new vocabulary.

- ❑ Set a time limit of 15 minutes.

- ❑ Move around the room to monitor and provide feedback.

- ❑ Ask for volunteers to summarize what they found out.

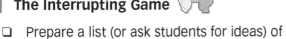 **EXPANSION ACTIVITY**

- ▪ The purpose of this activity is to practice strategies for interrupting politely and using new vocabulary on the topic of communication technology.

- ▪ Please see Black Line Master "Interrupting Politely" on page BLM 17 of this Teacher's Edition. Photocopy one page for each group of four students.

- ▪ Cut each copy into squares and distribute one set of squares to each group of students.

- ▪ Students will place the squares face down in the center of the group.

- ▪ Each student in turn will pick up a square and answer the question.

- ▪ The other students will try to prevent the first student from finishing the sentence by interrupting (politely!).

- ▪ Students gain one point for every successful and polite interruption and one point for answering the question.

Before You Listen

☐ Read the text that introduces the next lecture.

1 **Prelistening Discussion**

☐ Have students describe the pictures.

☐ Have students work in pairs to answer the questions, or give one question to each group of students.

☐ Review the responses as a class and compare some of their experiences.

2 **Previewing Vocabulary**

☐ Play the recording and have students listen to the words.

☐ Have students check the words they know and then compare answers with a partner.

☐ Ask for explanations or paraphrases of each word.

Listen

Strategy

Taking Notes on Similarities and Differences

■ Read the information in the Strategy box.

■ Ask students for additional examples of similarities or differences.

■ Write some of these examples on the board, using the expressions in the box.

3 **Taking Notes on Similarities and Differences**

☐ Have students read the directions.

☐ Play the recording and have students write the notes for each item.

☐ In pairs, have students try to recreate the original sentences from their notes.

☐ Invite volunteers to write their notes on the board.

ANSWER KEY

1. *Ams = comf. using 1st names / <u>others last names</u>*

2. *Egypt: leave food on plate / <u>Bolivia eat all</u>*

3. *Bolivia: eat everyth. on plate / <u>US same</u>*

4. *Many Jap. bow when they greet / <u>Thailand prayer hands</u>*

5. *U.S. + West. countries: <u>touch, e.g., handshake, hug, kiss</u>*

AUDIOSCRIPT

1. Maybe you've noticed that many Americans use people's first names very freely, even if they've just met someone. Some people even call their bosses by their first names. In contrast, people in most other cultures are more formal . . .

2. In Egypt, you should leave some food on your plate at the end of a meal. However, Bolivians expect visitors to eat everything on their plates.

3. Bolivians expect visitors to eat everything on their plate, and Americans also think that a clean plate means you were satisfied with the food.

4. Many Japanese people bow when they greet each other, while people from Thailand prefer to hold their hands in a prayer position.

5. In the United States, greetings often involve some sort of touching, such as a handshake, a hug, or a kiss if the people know each other very well. And most Western countries are similar to the United States in this way.

4 **Taking Notes (Part I)**

(The audioscript follows Activity 5.)

☐ Remind students of the keys to good note-taking (see Student Book Chapter 1, pages 12 and 13.)

❑ Tell students they are going to take notes on part of a lecture about cultural differences and similarities.

❑ Play the recording and have students take notes in any way they choose in their notebook or a separate piece of paper.

5 **Outlining the Lecture**

❑ Ask students to use their notes to complete the outline.

❑ Play the recording again.

❑ Have students fill in any missing information.

❑ Check the answers as a class.

ANSWER KEY

Part 1

Topic: *Similarities/Differences Among Cultures*

Intro: *Mex. girl red envelope from Chin. boss = confusion*

I. Greetings

A. N. America + West. countries: *touch, e.g., handshake, hug, kiss*

B. France: *kiss*

C. Asia: *don't touch*

   1. *Japan / bow*

   2. *Thailand prayer hands*

II. *Names & titles*

A. Americans: *first names*

B. *others = title*

  ex: Mr. Ms.

C. Korea: *title + family name e.g. Teacher Park*

AUDIOSCRIPT

Lecturer: Good afternoon, class. I want to start today by telling you a little story.

Once there was a young woman from Mexico named Consuela who came to New York to work. And she got a job at a factory owned by a man from Taiwan. One day, when Consuela came to work, her Taiwanese boss handed her a red envelope. She looked inside and saw 50 dollars. And what do you think she did? She became very upset and threw the envelope back at him! Of course her boss was totally shocked. Can you guess why? Well, he had given her the red envelope and the money because it was the Chinese New Year. And on the Chinese New Year, it's traditional to give money to young, single people for good luck. But Consuela didn't know about this Chinese custom. She thought her boss was asking her for sex. Naturally, she was very insulted and refused to take the money.

Now, what does this story show us? What's the point? Yes?

Student: It shows that an action can have totally opposite meanings in different cultures. Like in this case, the boss thought he was being generous, but Consuela was insulted.

Lecturer: Exactly. Every culture has its own rules for appropriate and inappropriate behavior. And serious misunderstandings, like the one with Consuela and her boss, can occur if we don't know other people's cultural "rules." Um, to illustrate this point, I'd like to offer some examples from four areas. First, the way people greet each other in different cultures. OK . . .

Second, the way they use names and titles. Third, the way people eat. And finally, the way they exchange gifts. All right?

So, let's start with greeting customs—I mean, how people behave when they say hello. First of all, I'm sure you know that in the United States, greetings often involve some sort of touching, such as a handshake, a hug, or a kiss if the people know each other very well. And most Western countries are similar to the United States in this way. Also, did you know that people from France kiss almost everyone on the cheek, even strangers? On the other hand, people from most Asian countries don't usually feel as comfortable touching in public. I mean, it's normal for businessmen to shake hands; that's true. But many traditional Japanese prefer a bow, while people from Thailand, for example, normally hold their hands together in a kind of prayer position, like this, you see. So imagine what would happen if an American was invited to someone's home in Japan or Thailand and he or she tried to hug the host! It would be very embarrassing, right? And yet that behavior would be perfectly acceptable in the United States or Latin America.

OK, now, another behavior that differs from culture to culture is the use of names. Maybe you've noticed that many Americans use people's first names very freely, even if they've just met someone. Some people even call their bosses by their first names.

In contrast, people in most other cultures are more formal and prefer to use family names to address people, like "Mr. Martinez" or "Ms. Schultz." In some countries, like Korea for example, it's polite to use a person's title or position with their family names. So you'd say, for example, Teacher Park or Manager Kim.

6 Taking Notes (Part II)

❑ Play the second part of the recording. Have students take notes in their own way on paper or in their notebooks.

❑ Have students use their notes to complete the outline.

❑ Play the recording again if necessary.

❑ Check the answers as a class.

ANSWER KEY

III. *Eating customs*
    A. Utensils
        1. *Asia = chopsticks*
        2. *West= fork / knife / spoon*
        3. *India / Arab = fingers*
    B. Clean plate
        1. Egypt: *leave food = polite*
        2. Bolivia & U.S.: *eat all = polite*
        3. Americans = clean plate = polite
IV. *Gifts*
    A. *U.S.*
        1. for dinner: bring flowers, wine, small gift from your country
        2. business: *no gifts*
    B. Jap. + other Asians: frequent gifts, thank doctor, teacher, strict rules
    C. some gifts are impolite, e.g., yellow flowers / Iran
V. *we should learn about cult. diffs.*

AUDIOSCRIPT

Now moving on, the third area I want to look at is eating customs. I don't mean the foods that people like to eat in different countries but rather some of the behaviors that are connected with eating. Um, one of these is the use of utensils. You probably know that people in many Asian cultures use chopsticks while in the West they usually use forks, knives, and spoons. Or for example, in parts of India, and in traditional Arab families, too, it's customary to eat with your fingers or to use a piece of bread to scoop up food. Another example is that in some cultures eating everything on your plate is impolite. In Egypt, for example, you should leave some food in your dish at the end of the meal in order to show that your hosts were generous and gave you more than enough to eat. However, people from Bolivia, in South America, expect visitors to eat everything on their plates, and Americans also think a clean plate means you were satisfied with the food.

Finally, the last area of behavior that I want to mention today is gift giving. The rules of gift giving can be very complicated, and it can be embarrassing if you don't know them. For example, in the United States, if you're invited to someone's home for dinner, you can bring wine or flowers or a small gift from your country, but Americans generally don't give gifts in business situations. On the other hand, the Japanese, like many other people in Asia, give gifts often, especially if they want to thank someone like a teacher or a doctor for their kindness. In Japan, the tradition of gift giving is very ancient, and there are detailed rules for everything from the color of the wrapping paper to the time of the gift presentation. Another interesting fact about gift giving is that many cultures have strict rules about gifts you should *not* give. For example, never give yellow flowers to people from Iran, or they'll think you hate them!

So to conclude, I hope all these examples will help you to understand my main point today, which is that each culture has its own unique rules for social behavior. We should never assume that our way of doing things is the only way or the best way. Learning about other people's customs is part of being good international citizens.

After You Listen

Best Practice

Activating Prior Knowledge

This is an example of an activity that encourages students to make text-to-self connections. The discussion questions ask students to relate the content of the lecture on cultural differences and similarities to their own lives. This aids understanding and retention of new material.

7 Discussing the Lecture

❏ Have students discuss the questions in groups.

❏ Encourage students to use the new vocabulary in their discussion.

❏ Ask for representatives from each group to report to the class.

8 Reviewing Vocabulary

❏ Ask students to test each other in pairs.

❏ Invite volunteers to give example sentences using the new vocabulary in Activity 2 on page 134 of the Student Book.

On the Spot!

Strategy

Graphic Organizer: T-chart

- Have students read the information in the Strategy box.

- As an example, you can make a T-chart about something that would interest your class, e.g., advantages and disadvantages to studying English online.

Best Practice

Cultivating Critical Thinking

This is an example of a collaborative team activity resulting in a final product. This type of activity requires students to process the information they have learned and apply it to a new situation. This involves reinterpretation, synthesis, and application of concepts. The process of manipulating language and concepts in this way will create deeper processing of new material which will allow students to evaluate whether they have understood the new material and help them remember it better.

Best Practice

Organizing Information

Activities such as this will teach students to organize information using a graphic organizer called a T-chart. This allows students to better assimilate and recall information at a later date, a valuable study tool. In this case, students use the diagram to identify differences and similarities between cultures.

9 What Would You Do?

- Read the situation with the class, or ask students to read it silently.

- Give students time to read the instructions.

- Ask one student to explain the instructions in his or her own words.

- Help students to form groups.

- Set a time limit of 20 minutes for students to discuss the questions and complete the T-chart.

- Move around the room to provide encouragement and feedback.

- Invite a representative from each group to report on their decision.

 EXPANSION ACTIVITY

- The purpose of this activity is to practice using the Internet for research and to gain an understanding of naming practices in different countries.

- Students can use a search engine, typing in keywords such as *naming practices* and the name of their chosen country.

- The research part of this activity can be done in a computer lab class or assigned for homework.

- Please see Black Line Master "Naming Practices" on page BLM 18 of this Teacher's Edition. Photocopy and distribute one copy to each student.

- Divide the students into groups of four and have each person in the group choose one country (they can choose alternative countries if they wish).

- Students will research their chosen topic on the web. Then they will re-form their groups to report what they found and complete the worksheet.

- Ask a representative from each group to summarize the differences and similarities in naming practices.

Focused Listening

BLENDING CONSONANTS

- Review the meaning of *vowel* and *consonant*.

- Read the instruction note and practice the examples.

1 Pronouncing Names with Blended Consonants

- ❏ Have students read the directions. Then have them read silently the 12 names.

- ❏ Play the recording and have students repeat each example.

2 Listening for Blended Consonants

- ❏ Read the examples and have students try to identify the blended consonants before listening.

- ❏ Play the recording and have students mark their answers.

- ❏ Play the recording again and ask students to repeat the examples.

- ❏ Review the answers as a class.

ANSWER KEY

1. Yesterday Yolanda had a really bad day.
2. June ninth is the date of Valerie's last test.
3. Let's save money to buy a car radio.
4. Ron needs a tall ladder to reach that high window.
5. Please bring me some hot tea.
6. Camille lives in a dangerous city.
7. Malik called his mother eight times.

3 Pronouncing Sentences

- ❏ Review the meaning of blended consonants, linked sounds, stressed and reduced sounds, and intonation.

- ❏ Read the examples and have students try to identify the blended consonants before listening.

- ❏ Play the recording and have students mark their answers.

- ❏ Play the recording again and ask students to repeat the examples.

- ❏ Review the answers as a class.

ANSWER KEY

1. We need to cancel our dinner reservations.
2. I live with three roommates.
3. Have a good day.
4. I don't know her phone number. ("w" and "h" in "know" and "her" could be linked if "h" is reduced.)
5. This song is so sad.
6. We're ready to take a walk.
7. Did he put his black coat away? ("d" and "h" in "Did" and "he," and "t" and "h" in "put" and "his" could be linked if "h" is reduced.)
8. She bought an expensive vase.

Getting Meaning from Context

Focus on Testing

Using Context Clues

- There are five sections on this recording. There is a question at the end of each one.

- Play each section of the recording.

- Have students write their answers.

ANSWER KEY

Answers	Clues
1. c. Koreans and Americans have different ideas about arriving on time.	American, Korean, 4:00 P.M., 3:45 P.M., surprised
2. b. Keep your feet on the floor.	rude to point or show bottoms of shoes
3. c. A smile can have different meanings in different cultures	American friendly, Japan sad or apologetic, Korean foolish, Puerto Rico you're welcome
4. a. an old tradition	old shoes, married couple, some people believe
5. d. You could be arrested.	illegal

AUDIOSCRIPT

Conversation 1

Harold O'Connor, a professor of English at an American university, invites his students to his home at the end of the semester. He asks them to come at 4:00 P.M. for coffee and cake. At 3:45 the doorbell rings. He opens the door and is surprised to see several of his Korean students standing there. He feels embarrassed.

Question 1: Why did the students arrive at 3:45?

Conversation 2

The feet are the lowest part of the body. For that reason, many people from the Middle East believe it is rude to point your feet at someone or to show them the bottoms of your shoes. Some people also think it is impolite to step over someone, for example, at a theater or sports event.

Question 2: Which of the following is probably a good idea if you are a visitor in a Middle Eastern home?

Conversation 3

Americans smile mainly to show friendliness or happiness. In Japan, people smile when they are sad, happy, apologetic, angry, or confused. In traditional Korean culture, smiling meant that a person was foolish or thoughtless. On the island of Puerto Rico, a smile can have many positive meanings, including *please*, *thank you*, and *you're welcome*.

Question 3: What can we conclude from these examples?

Conversation 4

In the United States, you can sometimes see old shoes attached to a newly married couple's car. What's the origin of this custom? Some people believe that old shoes can help a couple to have many children. Some people even put old shoes in trees that don't give enough fruit!

Question 4: What is this passage mainly about?

Conversation 5

A bribe is an amount of money that someone offers a public official, such as a police officer, to get some kind of special favor or treatment. In some countries, bribes are a normal part of doing business. However, in the United States, bribery is illegal.

Question 5: What could happen if you try to bribe a police officer in the United States?

Using Language Functions

GENERALIZING

- Read the instruction note.

- Have students make a list of things they do every day. For example: get up, have breakfast, read the newspaper and so on.

- Have students make sentences about themselves using the expressions in the box.

Best Practice

Making Use of Academic Content

This is an example of an activity that encourages students to use reading as a model for a short presentation. After discussing the content and structure of the reading, they can use this as a model for presenting information about their own lives.

4 Discussing a Reading

❑   Give students time to read the text silently.

❑   Check comprehension of any new vocabulary.

❑   Ask for volunteers to answer the questions.

❑   Have students prepare a short presentation about their typical day as an international citizen.

❑   Move around the room to give feedback and help.

EXPANSION ACTIVITY

▦   The aim of this activity is to practice the language of making general statements with appropriate adverbs.

▦   Have students work in groups to make a list of everyday habits that are common in the United States or in their country.

▦   Each person in the group will make a suggestion. For example, *People in the United States usually eat cereal for breakfast*. The rest of the class (or group) will agree or disagree with their statement.

▦   For each statement, the first student should state whether they conform to this general habit or not, and why. For example: *I generally eat cereal because it is fast and easy to prepare.*

▦   This activity can be done as whole class or in group work.

❑ Have students read the text above the photo on page 144 about a popular game in the U.S.

❑ Go over the term *trivia*.

Before You Listen

1 **Prelistening Discussion**

❑ Discuss the idea of quiz games and the game Trivial Pursuit.

❑ If possible, bring in a game of Trivial Pursuit to show students.

❑ Discuss each of the questions with the students.

Listen

2 **Taking a Trivia Quiz**

❑ Explain that students will hear a conversation between two people talking about a quiz.

❑ Play the recording.

❑ Compare answers and scores as a class.

ANSWER KEY

1. c 2. a 3. b 4. b 5. c 6. a 7. d 8. d

AUDIOSCRIPT

Kevin: Hey, Joyce, what are you doing?

Joyce: I was just reading the paper. Oh, here's another one of those trivia quizzes that you love to take, Kevin.

Kevin: What's it about?

Joyce: The title is "Global Connections." It's about transportation and communication around the world. Want to try it?

Kevin: Sure, why don't you read it to me while I make a salad for dinner?

Joyce: OK, first question. Which country has the largest number of time zones: The United States, Canada, Russia, or China?

Kevin: That's easy. Russia.

Joyce: Right. OK, second question: which which country is the most popular tourist destination in the world? Is it France, the United States, Italy, or China?

Kevin: France.

Joyce: Right again. Go Kevin! OK, next. Oh, the third one's hard: This region has 12.5 percent of the world's population and 29 percent of the world's Internet users. Is it North America, Europe, Latin America, or the Middle East?

Kevin: Hmm. Let me think. OK, I guess the Middle East.

Joyce: Wrong. It's Europe.

Kevin: Europe, huh? I guess that makes sense. OK, keep going.

Joyce: All right, number 4. Looks like another computer question. Which of the following countries has the largest actual number of Internet users? And the choices are China, the U.S., Russia, or Canada.

Kevin: Well, not Canada. Canada has a small population, compared to its size. I'll say . . . the United States.

Joyce: Right. Good job.

Kevin: Thanks. I hope the next question is easier.

Joyce: Let's see. Number 5. How many hours does it take to fly from New York to Cairo: 5 hours, 8 hours, 11 hours, or 15 hours?

Kevin: Wow. I have no idea. I think it's about six hours to London, so it's more than that. How about . . . eight hours?

Joyce: No. Eleven.

Kevin: OK, what's next?

Joyce: Which of the following countries has the largest number of daily newspapers: Mexico, Russia, England, or Greece?

Kevin: I'm sure it's England.

Joyce: Wrong! It's Mexico!

Kevin: No kidding! I wonder why . . . OK, next.

Joyce: Number 7 . . . The most frequently used language on the Internet is English. Which language is second: German, Spanish, Japanese, or Chinese?

Kevin: Wow. That's a tricky question. I am going say . . . Chinese.

Joyce: Yeah.

Kevin: Actually, I wasn't sure if it was Chinese or Japanese.

Joyce: Well, you got it right. Do you want to keep going?

Kevin: Yeah, one more. Then we can eat.

Joyce: OK, question 8. Which city has the longest subway system? Moscow, New York, Tokyo, or London?

Kevin: London. For sure.

Joyce: You're right.

Kevin: Yeah, I studied in London last summer, and I took the underground everywhere. So what's my score?

Joyce: Five right and three wrong. Not too bad.

Kevin: Yeah, but not great, either! All right. Let's eat. I'm starving!

After You Listen

3 Designing a Trivia Game

❑ Have students write five trivia questions and answers about their community.

❑ Collect the questions and answers. Choose those you'd like to use in class.

❑ Divide the class into teams.

❑ Have one student come to the board to keep the score.

❑ Read the questions and have teams write down their answers. Then have each team tell their answer to the class. Each team who answers correctly gets a point.

❑ Alternatively, you can read the questions and give a point to the team who first gives the correct answers.

Talk It Over

4 Choosing Your Dream Vacation

❑ Have students work in groups to discuss the photos and questions.

❑ Compare answers as a class.

❑ Make a list on the board of the most important features of a dream vacation.

❑ Have students work in pairs or groups to plan their dream vacation.

❑ Set a time limit of ten minutes.

❑ Invite volunteers to report to the class.

Self-Assessment Log

❑ The purpose of the log is to help the students reflect on their learning.

❑ Read the directions aloud and have students check vocabulary that they learned in the chapter and are prepared to use.

❑ Have students check the strategies they understand.

❑ Put students in small groups. Ask students to find the information or an activity related to each strategy in the chapter.

❑ Tell students to find definitions in the chapter for any words they did not check, or they can look in their dictionaries.

7

Language and Communication

In this chapter, students will read about various topics related to language and communication. In Part 1, they will talk about cultural stereotypes and learn to contradict politely. In Part 2, they will listen to a lecture about differences between American and British English. In Part 3, they will practice listening to conversations and learn to understand the meaning of interjections. In Part 4, they will practice spelling.

Chapter Opener

❑ Have students look at the photo of a couple in a restaurant having a discussion, or possibly an argument. Ask them the questions in the Connecting to the Topic section. Discuss the answers as a class.

❑ Read and discuss the quote. What knowledge do you gain by learning another language? Do people think differently in different languages?

ff To have another language is to possess a second soul. **JJ**

—Charlemagne
King of the Franks, Emperor of the West, (742?–814)

Chapter Overview

Listening Skills and Strategies

Listening for main ideas

Listening for details

Making inferences

Understanding statements with rising intonation

Identifying correct spellings in a spelling bee

Speaking Skills and Strategies

Discussing the meaning of friendship

Comparing American and British English

Contradicting politely

Talking about stereotypes

Using interjections

Using expressions for guessing

Critical Thinking Skills

Getting meaning from context

Taking notes on classifications

Vocabulary Building

Terms used to talk about friendship vs. friendliness

Terms used for talking about languages and dialects

Examples of vocabulary differences between American and British English

Interjections

Expressions for guessing

Slang expressions

Pronunciation

Identifying and practicing stressed words

Language Skills

Using context clues to guess about language and communication

Vocabulary

Nouns	Verbs	Adjectives	Adverbs	Expressions
category	catch on	identical	whereas	Have a seat.
dialect	make friends	in the dark	while	It's hard to say.
friendliness		noticeable		
friendship		two-faced		
majority		unique		
sample				
standard				

Can You Guess?

- ■ Ask students to discuss the questions in groups and compare their answers with the correct answers.

- ■ Discuss the issues raised by these questions: Why do we have so many languages in the world? What would happen if we all spoke the same language?

1. How many languages are spoken in the world? A. *More than 2,700 languages.*

2. Can you name one language that is not related to any other language in the world? A. *The best known language "isolate" is Basque, spoken in north-western Spain and south-western France. Others are Ainu, spoken in Japan, Burushaski (northern Pakistan), and Korean.*

3. What are the world's top five languages, based on number of native speakers?
   A. *1. Mandarin Chinese*   *6. Portuguese*
      2. English   *7. Bengali*
      3. Spanish   *8. Russian*
      4. Hindi   *9. Japanese*
      5. Arabic   *10. German*

Before You Listen

- ❑ Read the text aloud that introduces the next conversation.

1 Prelistening Questions

- ❑ Have the students read the questions and discuss them in pairs.

- ❑ Compare answers as a whole class.

- ❑ As a whole class, make a list of different ways of showing friendliness in different cultures.

2 Previewing Vocabulary

- ❑ Play the recording and have students listen to the underlined words and expressions.

- ❑ Have students complete the activity individually.

- ❑ Compare their answers as a class and write the correct answers on the board.

ANSWER KEY

1. b 2. h 3. f 4. a 5. g 6. d 7. c 8. e

Listen

3 Comprehension Questions

- ❑ Read the questions aloud.

- ❑ Play the recording and have students write their answers.

- ❑ After listening, have students compare their answers in pairs.

- ❑ Check the answers as a class.

ANSWER KEY

1. They are acquaintances but not friends. 2. Mari is confused because Katrina seems friendly but never has time to meet. 3. People are friendly, but that doesn't mean they want to be friends. 4. No. 5. *How are you?* means "Hello."

AUDIOSCRIPT

Mari:	Yolanda! Hi!
Yolanda:	Hi, Mari, how are you?
Mari:	Fine, thanks. Um, is anyone sitting here?
Yolanda:	No, have a seat.
Mari:	Thanks. So how have you been?
Yolanda:	Oh, you know, busy. I've got school, and work, and I'm getting ready for my brother's wedding next month.
Mari:	Oh, yeah.

Yolanda: Anyway, it's going to be a huge wedding and . . .

Mari: Oh, excuse me, uh . . . Nancy! Over here!

Nancy: Hi!

Mari: Nancy, this is Yolanda. She works in the library. Yolanda, this is my housemate, Nancy. She teaches English here.

Nancy: Nice to meet you, Yolanda.

Yolanda: You too. Well, listen, actually, I've got to go. I have to be at work in ten minutes. I'll see you soon, Mari. We'll go to a movie or something.

Mari: Sure. How about Thursday night?

Yolanda: Uh, I have to check my calendar. I'll call you, OK?

Mari: OK, see you.

Mari: I don't understand Americans.

Nancy: Huh?

Mari: Did you hear what she said? "We'll go to a movie. I'll call you." But every time I try to pick a specific day or time, she says she's busy, she has to check her calendar. And then she doesn't call.

Nancy: Mm hmm . . .

Mari: Why do Americans say things they don't mean? They act so nice, like they always say, "How are you," but then they keep on walking and don't even wait for your answer. They're so . . . how do you say it . . . two-faced?

Nancy: I know it seems that way sometimes, Mari. But it's not true. It's just that for Americans, friendliness and friendship aren't always the same thing.

Mari: What do you mean?

Nancy: Well, you know how Americans can be very open and friendly. Like, they invite you to sit down, they ask you questions, they tell all about their families. So naturally you think they're trying to make friends with you. But actually, friendship, real friendship, doesn't happen so quickly.

Mari: So, when people say "How are you," they're just being polite? They don't really care?

Nancy: Not exactly. The thing you have to understand is that "how are you" isn't a real question. It's more like a way of saying hello.

Mari: Aha, I get it! And "Have a nice day" is just a friendly way to say good-bye?

Nancy: Exactly. Now you're catching on.

Mari: But I'm still in the dark about Yolanda. Does she want to be my friend or not?

Nancy: It's hard to say. Maybe she's just too busy these days. I guess you'll just have to be patient.

Mari: Hmm. That's good advice, I guess. Thanks.

Stress

4 Listening for Stressed Words

❏ Play the recording again.

❏ Have students write the missing words.

❏ After listening, have students check their answers with the audioscript in their books.

❏ Have students read the conversation with a partner, paying attention to stressed words in their pronunciation.

ANSWER KEY

Mari: I don't understand Americans.

Nancy: Huh?

Mari: Did you _hear_ what she said? "We'll go to a _movie_. I'll call you." But every time I try to pick a _specific_ day or time, she says she's _busy_, she has to check her _calendar_. And then she _doesn't_ call.

Nancy: Mm hmm . . .

Mari: Why do Americans say things they don't _mean_? They _act_ so nice, like they _always_ say "How are you," but then they keep on _walking_ and don't even wait for your _answer_. They're so . . . how do you say it . . . _two_-faced?

Nancy: I know it _seems_ that way sometimes, Mari. But it's _not true_. It's just that for Americans, friendliness and friendship _aren't_ always the same thing.

Mari: What do you _mean_?

Nancy: Well, you know how Americans can be very _open_ and friendly. Like, they _invite_ you to sit down, they _ask_ you questions, they _tell_ you all about their families. So naturally you think they're trying to make _friends_ with you. But actually, friendship, _real_ friendship, doesn't happen so _quickly_.

Mari: So, when people say, "How are you," they're just being _polite_? They don't really _care_?

Nancy: Not exactly. The thing you have to _understand_ is that "how are you" isn't a _real_ question. It's more like a _way_ of saying hello.

Mari: Aha, I _get_ it! And "Have a nice day" is just a _friendly_ way to say good-bye?

Nancy: Exactly. _Now_ you're catching on.

Mari: But I'm _still_ in the dark about Katrina. Does she _want_ to be my friend or _not_?

Nancy: It's _hard_ to say. Maybe she's just too _busy_ these days. I guess you'll just have to be _patient_.

Mari: Hmm. That's good _advice_, I guess. Thanks.

Intonation

STATEMENTS WITH RISING INTONATION

- Read the instruction note.
- Model the intonation of the examples. You may want to emphasize the intonation by replacing the words with _dah_.

5 Understanding Statements with Rising Intonation

❑ Read the directions for the activity.

❑ Play the recording while students listen and write questions.

ANSWER KEY

1. Are you going?
2. Do you remember my friend Alicia?
3. Hasn't he done his homework yet?
4. Is it at the intersection of First and Main?
5. Is Jack Rose's brother?

AUDIOSCRIPT

1. You're going?

2. You remember my friend Yolanda?

3. He hasn't done his homework yet?

4. It's at the intersection of First and Main?

5. Jack is Rose's brother?

8. A: Why is it so hard to make friends with Americans?

B: You have to be patient. Friendships don't happen overnight.

After You Listen

6 **Using Vocabulary**

❑ Have students work in pairs. Student A should look at page 249 in the Student Book. Student B should look at page 258.

❑ Set a time limit of five minutes.

❑ Review the answers as a class.

ANSWER KEY

1. A: Do you understand tonight's homework assignment?

B: No, I'm in the dark, too.

2. A: You look really stressed out.

B: I am. It's really hard to study and have a job at the same time.

3. A: I have an appointment with Dr. Brown at 3:00 P.M.

B: Please have a seat. The doctor is with another patient right now.

4. A: Jerry is a two-faced liar. He told my girlfriend I was seeing another woman!

B: He did? I thought he was your best friend.

5. A: I like Claudette. She's very friendly.

B: I agree. She's very nice.

6. A: I've known my best friend since we were three years old.

B: Really? You're lucky to have such a close friendship.

7. A: I've told John six times that I don't want to go out with him, but he keeps asking me.

B: It sounds like he's a little slow to catch on.

Using Language Functions

CONTRADICTING POLITELY

▨ Read the instruction note.

▨ Ask students to read the examples.

▨ Give some additional statements (see examples below) and ask students to contradict you using the expressions from the box.

Examples:
Video games are too violent.
Fast food is bad for you.
It's easier to learn a language when you are young.
People with college degrees earn more money.

Best Practice

Interacting with Others

This type of activity is an example of collaborative learning to encourage fluency and confidence. In this activity, communication is more important than grammar. Students can improve their confidence to contradict politely by switching roles or partners and practicing the same situations again. By providing feedback to each other, they learn skills of self-evaluation.

7 **Contradicting Stereotypes**

❑ Read the directions and have students read the Language Tip. Clarify any questions.

❑ Have students work in pairs to discuss the questions.

❑ Compare answers as a class.

Talk It Over

Best Practice

Cultivating Critical Thinking

This is an example of an activity that encourages students to examine their own cultural assumptions. By trying to define their personal and social concepts of friendship, and comparing them with others, they can develop a more critical awareness of the cultural relativity of these kinds of concepts.

8 **What Is Friendship?**

❑ Read the list of situations and check comprehension of any new vocabulary.

❑ Have students work in groups to discuss the questions.

❑ You can set a time limit of 10 to 15 minutes.

❑ Invite volunteers to summarize their discussion.

REPRODUCIBLE EXPANSION ACTIVITY

■ The purpose of this activity is to practice strategies for contradicting politely and expressing opinions on the topic of language and communication.

■ Please see Black Line Master "Do You Agree?" on page BLM 19 of this Teacher's Edition. Photocopy and distribute one copy to each student.

■ Have students complete the sentences individually. Have them choose either the positive or negative phrase in sentences 1, 5, 6, 7, and 8, depending on their opinions.

■ Have students work in groups to read their sentences using contradicting strategies to disagree with each other.

■ Set a time limit of 10 to 15 minutes.

■ Move around the room to monitor and provide feedback.

■ Invite volunteers to read out the most controversial statements.

Before You Listen

- ❏ Have students describe the pictures. What sort of misunderstanding is being illustrated? Can they think of any other similar examples?

- ❏ The first caption illustrates American English; the second illustrates British English.

1   Prelistening Discussion

- ❏ Have students work in groups to answer the questions.

- ❏ Review the responses as a class and compare some of their experiences.

- ❏ Ask for some examples of British, Australian, or Canadian English (vocabulary, grammar, or pronunciation).

2   Previewing Vocabulary

- ❏ Play the recording and have students listen to the words.

- ❏ Have students check the words they know.

- ❏ Ask students to compare answers with a partner. They will find out the meanings of these words by listening to the lecture.

Listen

Best Practice

Organizing Information

This is an example of a graphic organizer. In this exercise it is used to classify lecture organization. This type of study tool helps students to organize new information so that it is easier to recall. It will also help them when they want to review their notes. There are many types of graphic organizers used in this book.

Strategy

Classifying and Taking Notes on Classification

- ▪ Read the information in the Strategy box.

- ▪ Introduce the graphic organizer.

3   Classifying Lecture Organization

- ❏ Ask for some suggestions for sub topics for each of the main topics.

- ❏ Play the recording and have students write key words.

- ❏ Compare answers as a class and write the answers on the board.

Best Practice

Scaffolding Instruction

This is an example of an activity that raises awareness of learning strategies. In real life, we use a combination of different strategies to identify and interpret information. In this exercise, students focus on one strategy for identifying and classifying lecture organization. These short guided tasks will help students to use this strategy independently in the context of a lecture.

ANSWER KEY

1. Computers: at home, in business, in education

2. U.S. population: growth and characteristics

3. Differences between BE and AE: pronunciation, vocabulary, grammar

AUDIOSCRIPT

Lecture 1

Personal computers have revolutionized the way people work and communicate. I could talk for hours about the wide use of personal computers, but today we only have time to introduce three major uses of computers: at home, in business, and in education.

Lecture 2

In today's lecture, I will provide the most recent information concerning the growth and characteristics of the U.S. population.

Lecture 3

You may have guessed by now that my topic for today's lecture is differences between American and British English. In particular, I want to examine three categories of difference. First, and most obvious, is pronunciation; second, vocabulary; and third, grammar.

SOME VOCABULARY DIFFERENCES BETWEEN AMERICAN AND BRITISH ENGLISH

- Compare the words in each of the lists.

- Have students circle the words they've heard.

---

4 Taking Notes (Part I)

(The audioscript follows Activity 5.)

❑ Remind students of the keys to good note-taking. (See Student Book Chapter 1 pages 12 and 13.)

❑ Tell students they are going to hear part of a lecture about differences between British and American English.

❑ Play the recording.

❑ Go over the word lists in the box.

5 Outlining the Lecture

❑ Ask students to use their notes to complete the outline.

❑ Play the recording again.

❑ Have students fill in any missing information.

❑ Check the answers as a class.

ANSWER KEY

Differences between American and British English

I. Pronunciation

Sound	Am.E.	B.E.
1. 'a' e.g. *can't*	/kænt/	/kant/
2. 'r' e.g. *car*	/kar/	/ka/
3. 'd' e.g. *little*	liddle	little
	twenny-one	twenny-one

AUDIOSCRIPT

Part 1

Lecturer: Good afternoon. To introduce my topic today, I'd like you to listen to two speech samples and tell me where the speakers are from. Ready? OK, here's the first one.

Speaker 1: "Today's weather forecast calls for partly cloudy skies in the morning, clearing by mid-afternoon with winds up to 15 miles an hour out of the west. The high temperature will be 80 degrees Fahrenheit, and the low will be 64."

Lecturer: OK. Now, where do you think that speaker was from?

Audience: America . . . the United States . . . Canada.

Lecturer: Yes, most of you got it. That was what we call a standard American accent, which means the accent that is spoken by the majority of people who live in the United States and Canada.

Now, listen to a different speaker reading the same text.

Speaker 2: "Today's weather forecast calls for partly cloudy skies in the morning, clearing by mid-afternoon with winds up to 15 miles an hour out of the west. The high temperature will be 80 degrees Fahrenheit, and the low will be 64."

Lecturer: And where is that speaker from?

Audience: England . . . the United Kingdom . . . Great Britain.

Lecturer: Yes, of course. That was British English. So you may have guessed by now that my topic for today's lecture is differences between standard American and British English. In particular, I want to examine three categories of difference. First, and most obvious, is pronunciation; second, vocabulary; and third, grammar.

So to begin, let's go back to the subject of accent, or pronunciation. You had no trouble identifying the North American and British accents because each of them has a unique sound. What is it? Well, one obvious difference is in the pronunciation of the letter *a*. For example, most Americans say /kænt/, but the British say /kant/. Or Americans say /bæth/ and the British say /bath/. The /æ/ sound is very common in American English, but not very common in British English.

Another noticeable difference between American and British pronunciation is the /r/ sound. In British English, the /r/ sound is very often dropped; it disappears. To give some examples, Americans say /kär/ but the British say /ka/. Americans say /fûrst/ but British say /f^st/. A big American city is *New* /yôrk/ for Americans, but New /yok/ to the British. In the two speech samples you heard at the beginning of this lecture, the American speaker said /forkæst/, but the British said

/fohkast/. In that single word, you can hear the difference both in the *a* vowel and in the pronunciation of /r/. Listen again: /forkaest/, /fohkast/.

A third difference is the pronunciation of the /t/ sound in the middle of words. In British English, it is normally pronounced, but in American English, it changes to a /d/ or disappears. For example: a British person will say "little," but an American says "liddle." You can hear this difference particularly with numbers: Brits say "twenty one, twenty two," and so on, but Americans drop the /t/ and say "twenny one, twenny two," and so on.

So there you have just three of the differences that give American and British pronunciation their unique sounds. There are many more. But now let's go on to talk about vocabulary.

6 **Taking Notes (Part II)**

❑ Play the second part of the recording. Have students take notes in their own way on paper or in their notebooks.

❑ Have students use their notes to complete the outline.

❑ Play the recording again if necessary.

❑ Check the answers as a class.

ANSWER KEY

II. Vocabulary
- *Eng. has over 1 m. words*
- *# of vocab diffs between Am.E. and B.E.: small*

■ *Examples:*

Am.E.	*B.E.*
truck	*lorry*
elevator	*lift*
wash up = *wash hands and face*	*wash up =* *wash dishes*
sausages and mashed *potatoes*	*bangers and mash*

III. Grammar

■ *Am.E. almost = B.E.*

■ *few diffs:*

Grammar	*Am.E.*	*B.E.*
1. Verbs	*gotten*	*got*
2. have	*do you have?*	*have you?*
3. prepositions	*different from*	*different than*

IV. Br. E and Am. E. are 2 varieties of 1
language

AUDIOSCRIPT

Part 2

Some people believe that American-English vocabulary and British-English vocabulary are very different, but actually they are not. The English language has more than one million words. Yet there are only a few hundred words and expressions that are different in American and British English. You can see a few of them in the chart right here. So for instance, Americans say *truck*, but the Brits say *lorry*. Another well-known example is *elevator*, which is used in the United States and *lift*, which is the British term. Now, although the number of vocabulary differences is small, funny misunderstandings can sometimes occur. For instance, if an American says, *I'm going to wash up*, he would go into the bathroom and wash his hands and face. But a British person may be quite surprised to see him go to the bathroom because in England, to *wash up* means to wash the dishes.

Vocabulary differences can also create some

confusing situations in restaurants. If an Englishman traveling in the United States enters a restaurant and orders "bangers and mash," the American waiter would be totally confused. He wouldn't know that the man wanted sausage and mashed potatoes.

Finally, let's talk a bit about grammar. I've left this category for last because in the area of grammar, standard American and British English are nearly identical. One common difference, however, involves the past participle of the verb *get*. For example, an American might ask, "Have you gotten your grade yet?" whereas a Brit would ask, "Have you got your grade yet?" Another difference is in the use of the verb *have*, especially in questions. Americans say, "Do you have any ideas?" but the British might say, "Have you any ideas?" or "Have you got any ideas?" There are also differences in prepositions. So for instance in the United States, it's correct to say that John is different *from* Mary, but the British will say that John is different *than* Mary. But these differences are very small and few in number.

And this brings me to my conclusion, which is this:Standard British and standard American English are so similar that most speakers of these two types will have no trouble understanding one another. American and British English are not two different languages. Rather, they are two dialects, two varieties, of the same language, English.

After You Listen

Best Practice

Activating Prior Knowledge

This is an example of an activity that encourages students to make text-to-self connections. The discussion questions ask students to explore their existing knowledge on the topic of differences between different varieties of English. They can then add the new information to their existing knowledge framework. This aids understanding and retention of new material.

7 Discussing the Lecture

- ❑ Have students discuss the questions in groups.
- ❑ Encourage students to use the new vocabulary in their discussion.
- ❑ Ask for representatives from each group to report to the class on the discussion.

8 Reviewing Vocabulary

- ❑ Ask students to look back at the vocabulary in Activity 2 on page 157 of the Student Book and to test each other in pairs.
- ❑ Invite volunteers to give examples sentences using the new vocabulary.

Talk It Over

9 Comparing American and British English

- ❑ Ask students to complete the activity individually.
- ❑ Have students compare their answers.
- ❑ If the sentence is in British English, how would they change it to American English (and vice versa)?
- ❑ Suggest that students check their answers at home using a dictionary or the Internet.

ANSWER KEY

American	British	
_____	___✓___	1. A lorry hit my car on the motorway.
___✓___	_____	2. Can you help me lift this trash can?
_____	___✓___	3. Hundreds of people queued up at the cinema.
___✓___	_____	4. Please open the trunk so I can put in these suitcases.

_____	___✓___	5. Ask the chemist if this medicine is safe.
_____	___✓___	6. I need a new rucksack, but I'm not sure what color to get.

EXPANSION ACTIVITY
REPRODUCIBLE

- ▪ The purpose of this activity is to practice using the Internet for research and to gain an understanding of different varieties of English spoken around the world.
- ▪ Students can use a search engine to find the vocabulary items or use keywords, for example, *Australian English*.
- ▪ You can also have them use this website: www.wordwebonline.com, but check it first to make sure you want to introduce it to them.
- ▪ The research part of this activity can be done in a computer lab class or assigned for homework.
- ▪ Please see Black Line Master "Varieties of English" on page BLM 20 of this Teacher's Edition. Photocopy and distribute one to each student.
- ▪ Have students work in groups to complete as much as they can. Assign the rest of the worksheet for homework.

Getting Meaning from Context

Focus on Testing

Using Context Clues

- Explain that students will hear three different conversations.

- Play the recording and have students write their answers.

- Check the answers as a class. Note that the answers for the clues will vary.

ANSWER KEY

Answers	Clues
Conversation 1 1. b. a language	language, Where is it spoken? Who speaks this language now? 15 million people speak Esperanto.
2. d. from a magazine article	the article, it says here
3. b. It has no native speakers.	artificial, comes from lots of different languages
Conversation 2 4. b. to kill the bees	beehive under the roof, exterminator, kill
5. d. taste	where, how far away, how much
6. b. the study of insects	learn about bugs
Conversation 3 7. b. to save time	dictation, slow typist
8. a. try Rita's software	Can I try it? I should get one
9. c. It's useful for students and writers.	don't have to type, I have three term papers

AUDIOSCRIPT

Conversation 1

A: Have you ever heard of Esperanto?

B: Huh?

A: Esperanto. It's a language.

B: Really? I've never heard of it. Where is it spoken?

A: Lots of places. According to this article, it's actually an artificial language; it was invented in 1887 by a man from Poland.

B: That's interesting. So who speaks this language now?

A: Well, it says here that there may be as many as 15 million people who speak Esperanto as a second language.

B: What does *Esperanto* mean, anyway? It doesn't sound like Polish.

A: It's not. The vocabulary of Esperanto comes from lots of different languages. *Esperanto* means "hope" in Latin.

B: Well, I hope I never have to learn it. It's hard enough trying to learn English.

Question 1: What is Esperanto?

Question 2: Where did the woman get her information about Esperanto?

Question 3: Which of the following is probably true about Esperanto?

Conversation 2

A: Look, there's a beehive under the roof.

B: I guess we'd better call an exterminator.

A: Yeah, you're right . . . But I really don't want to kill them. Did you know bees can communicate with one another?

B: Really? How?

A: They use body language to show where food is, how far away it is, and how much food is available.

B: No kidding . . .

A: Yeah, see that one there? See how she's going around and around in circles, like she's dancing? That means the food is nearby. If the food is farther away, the bee points to it with her body. And the faster she dances, the more food is available.

B: How do you know so much about bees?

A: I took an entomology class in college. I was a biology major, and I thought it would be interesting to learn something about bugs.

Question 4: Why does the man want to call an exterminator?

Question 5: Which information about food is *not* conveyed by the bee's body language?

Question 6: What is entomology?

Conversation 3

Man: Why are you talking to your computer?

Woman: I'm not talking to it. I'm giving a dictation.

Man: What do you mean?

Woman: It's this great software program. It understands what I'm saying and writes down the words.

Man: Wow. So you don't have to type at all?

Man: No, that's the point. I'm a slow typist,so this program is a lifesaver.

Man: Can I try it?

Woman: Well, first you have to train the computer to recognize your voice.

Man: Oh. Why?

Woman: Because everybody's pronunciation is different. If it doesn't know your voice, it makes mistakes.

Man: I see. I should get one of these for my computer. I have three term papers due this month.

Question 7: Why does the woman use this software program?

Question 8: What will the man probably do next?

Question 9: What is probably true about this computer program?

Focused Listening

INTERJECTIONS

■ Read the instruction note about interjections.

■ Ask if students can think of any other examples or different meanings for the ones given.

1 **Understanding Interjections**

❑ Explain that they will listen to six different conversations and write the meanings of the interjections they hear.

❑ Play the recording while students write their answers.

❑ Review the answers as a class.

ANSWER KEY

1. Yes. 2. That hurts. 3. I dropped something.
4. What? (or What does that mean?) 5. No.
6. I forgot.

AUDIOSCRIPT

Conversation 1

Student: Can we use a dictionary on the test?

Teacher: Uh-huh.

Conversation 2

Mother: Here, let me brush your hair.

Child: Ouch! Not so hard!

Conversation 3

Father: Could you please carry this bag of groceries into the house? Be careful; it's heavy.

Son: Sure . . . oops! Sorry.

Conversation 4

A: The computer is down because of a virus that crashed the hard drive.

B: Huh?

Conversation 5

A: I'm expecting an important letter. Has the mail arrived yet?

B: Uh-uh.

Conversation 6

A: Did you remember to buy stamps when you went to the post office?

B: Uh-oh.

Using Language Functions

GUESSING

- ▧ Read the instruction note about *Guessing*.

- ▧ Read the example aloud. Substitute the expressions in B. For example, "Hmm. I'd say it's something Scandinavian. It could be Swedish, but it might be Danish."

---

2 **Using Interjections**

- ❑ Have students work in pairs.

- ❑ Student A should look at page 250 in the Student Book. Student B should look at page 258.

- ❑ Set a time limit of five minutes.

- ❑ Move around the room to monitor and provide feedback.

- ❑ Review the answers as a class.

3 **Guessing Meanings of Slang Expressions**

- ❑ Review the meaning of the word *slang*. When is slang appropriate or inappropriate?

- ❑ Have students work in pairs to guess the meanings of these slang expressions.

- ❑ When they have finished, they can check their answers on page 261.

Before You Listen

☐ Read the text in the box about spelling bees. This is what the next conversation is about.

1 **Prelistening Questions**

☐ Discuss the idea of a spelling bee and find out if students have ever participated in a spelling competition.

☐ Discuss some of the reasons why English spelling can cause problems (vowels have different sounds, some vowels are silent, some consonants are silent e.g., *r* in *hour*, *l* in *half*).

☐ Discuss the questions in groups or as a class.

Listen

2 **Identifying Spellings**

☐ Explain that students will hear a recording of a spelling bee.

☐ As they listen, they will try to identify the answers given by the participants.

☐ Play the recording.

☐ Compare answers as a class.

ANSWER KEY

1. c right 2. a wrong 3. a right 4. c right
5. b wrong 6. b right 7. b wrong 8. a right
9. a wrong 10. c right

AUDIOSCRIPT

Teacher: Our contestants in today's spelling bee are Jack, Marisa, Yolanda, Evan, and Tony. As you know, I will say the word and then say it in a sentence. Are you ready to begin?

All: Ready. Yes.

Teacher: All right. The first word is for Tony. The word is *tries*. "He always tries to do a good job."

Tony: Tries. OK, T-R-I-E-S.

Teacher: Correct. All right. The next word is for Jack. Your word is *choose*. "Which flavor ice cream will you choose?"

Jack: Choose. C-H-O-S-E.

Teacher: I'm sorry, but that is wrong. The correct spelling of *choose* is C-H-O-O-S-E. Good try, Jack. OK, the next word goes to Marisa. Your word is *effect*. "Jogging has a good effect on our health."

Marisa: Effect. E-F-F-E-C-T.

Teacher: Right! Marisa, you stay in the game. The next word is for Evan. Your word is *quizzes*. "We had two grammar *quizzes* last week."

Evan: OK, quizzes. Uh, Q-U-I-Z-Z-E-S.

Teacher: Yes, that's right. Now, for Yolanda, your word is *succeed*. "You must study hard if you want to succeed."

Yolanda: Hmm. Succeed. S-U-C-C-E-D-[pause]-E.

Teacher: I'm sorry, Yolanda, that's wrong. It's S-U-C-C-E-E-D. Good try. OK, let's see who's still in the game: Marisa, Evan, and Tony. Are you ready for the second round?

All: Yes, yeah, let's go.

Teacher: OK, Tony. Your word is *ninety*. "The shoes cost ninety dollars."

Tony: N-I-N-E-T-Y. Ninety.

Teacher: You're right! Well done. The next word is for Marisa. *Analyze.* "After a test, you should analyze your mistakes."

Marisa: Wow, that's hard. OK: A-N-A-L-I-Z-E. Analyze.

Teacher: Sorry, Marisa. It's A-N-A-L-Y-Z-E. Please sit down. Evan, you're next. Your word is *possibility*. "There is a possibility of snow tonight."

Evan: Possibility. OK. P-O-S-S-I-B-I-L-I-T-Y.

Teacher: Great! OK, it's down to Tony and Evan. First Tony. Your word is *mysterious*. "During the night we heard mysterious noises."

Tony: Um, M-I-S-T-E-R-I-O-U-S. I think.

Teacher: Oh no, that's not correct. It's M-Y-S-T-E-R-I-O-U-S. You almost got it. Well, that leaves Evan. If you spell this word correctly, you'll be the winner today. The last word is *lightning*. "We were scared by the thunder and lightning."

Evan: L-I-G-H-T-N-I-N-G. Lightning.

Teacher: Right! Congratulations, Evan! You're our winner today.

Talk It Over

Best Practice

Making Use of Academic Content

This type of activity is an example of using real-world global content to help students identify English language errors and understand why they might have been made. In academic contexts, students must always analyze their own writing. This activity can help them understand subtleties of language and why certain errors are made, helping them to avoid these errors in their own work.

After You Listen

Content Note

The National Spelling Bee in the U.S. is a competition sponsored by newspapers and educational foundations. The participants are school children and they go through many local and regional rounds before reaching the final round, which is shown on national television. The winner gets a cash prize. The basic rules are that once the contestant has started to spell a word, he or she may start over, but the letter or sequence of letters already spoken may not be changed. If a contestant fails to spell a word correctly, he or she is disqualified. The competition is conducted in rounds until only one contestant remains.

4 Dialogues

❑ Have the students read the directions and look at the photos on pages 169 and 170 of the Student Book. Clarify any questions.

❑ Have students create a dialog for each photo. Encourage them to use as many of the expressions as possible from the box in each dialog.

❑ You can decide if you want students to read their dialogues or perform them (or one of them) with a partner.

3 Class Spelling Bee

❑ Organize the class into teams.

❑ Set a time limit of five minutes for each team to prepare a list of words (you may want to assign certain chapters of the book to each team to avoid overlap).

❑ Have team leaders read out the words and keep score.

REPRODUCIBLE **EXPANSION ACTIVITY**

- The aim of this activity is to practice the spelling of some commonly misspelled words.

- Please see Black Line Master "Spelling Bee" on page BLM 21 of this Teacher's Edition. Photocopy one for each pair. Cut each copy in half.

- One student will be A and the other will be B. Students will take turns reading out a word and asking the other student to spell it. You may ask students to write their partner's spelling next to each word, as a kind of dictation.

- Compare notes as a class. Which words were most commonly misspelled?

- For more commonly misspelled words, you might want to check this website:

www.yourdictionary.com/library/misspelled.html

Self-Assessment Log

- ❑ The purpose of the log is to help the students reflect on their learning.

- ❑ Read the directions aloud, and have students check vocabulary that they learned in the chapter and are prepared to use.

- ❑ Have students check the strategies they understand.

- ❑ Put students in small groups. Ask students to find the information or an activity related to each strategy in the chapter.

- ❑ Tell students to find definitions in the chapter for any words they did not check, or they can look in their dictionaries

8

Tastes and Preferences

In this chapter, students will read about various topics related to tastes and preferences. In Part 1, they will talk about likes and dislikes and practice making an impromptu speech. In Part 2, they will listen to a lecture about changing fads and fashions and learn to recognize paraphrasing. In Part 3, they will practice listening to conversations and learn to express approval and disapproval. In Part 4, they will practice writing a personal ad.

Chapter Opener

❏ Have students look at the photo of the two young women, or teens, listening to music at a record store. Ask the students the three questions in the Connecting to the Topic section. Discuss with the class.

❏ Discuss the quote. What shapes our tastes and preferences? Do our tastes influence fashions, or do fashions influence us?

❝ Markets change, tastes change, so the companies and the individuals who choose to compete in those markets must change. ❞

—Dr. An Wang
Chinese-American inventor, co-founder of Wang Laboratories, 1920–1990

Chapter Overview

Listening Skills and Strategies

Listening for main ideas

Listening for details

Making inferences

Understanding reduced questions

Distinguishing between present and past yes/no questions

Understanding comparisons of people

Recognizing paraphrases

Speaking Skills and Strategies

Talking about likes and dislikes

Giving an impromptu speech

Comparing the characteristics of generations

Talking about fads

Expressing approval and disapproval

Describing your ideal partner

Critical Thinking Skills

Getting meaning from context

Speculating about hypothetical situations

Evaluating people's positive and negative qualities

Interpreting the language of personal ads

Taking notes in columns

Predicting note organization

Vocabulary Building

Expressions for likes and dislikes

Expressions of approval and disapproval

Terms signaling paraphrases

Ways to say that something is popular

Pronunciation

Identifying and practicing stressed words

Language Skills

Using context clues to identify people's tastes and preferences

Using intonation to identify feelings

Vocabulary

Nouns	Verb	Adjectives	Expressions
brand	identify with	Caucasian	can't stand
conflict		confident	don't/doesn't care for
consumer		diverse	have a good time
developed country		hip (informal)	I'm crazy about it!
dish		loyal	see eye to eye
income		optimistic	
phenomenon		significant	
standard of living		tolerant	

Can You Guess?

- Ask students to discuss the questions below in groups and compare their answers with the correct answers.

1. What is the most popular children's educational television program in the world? A. *Sesame Street. It is broadcast to 180 countries.*

2. What is the most popular sport in the world? A. *Soccer.*

3. What is the most-recorded pop song in history? A. *"Yesterday" by John Lennon and Paul McCartney.*

Before You Listen

Best Practice

Activating Prior Knowledge

The prelistening questions activate students' prior knowledge. This activity will help students relate their own likes and dislikes to the new language in this chapter. When students activate their prior knowledge before learning new material, they are better able to map new language onto existing concepts, which aids understanding and retention.

1   Prelistening Questions

- Have the students read the questions and discuss them in pairs.

- Compare answers as a whole class.

- Make a list of ways to ask about people's likes and dislikes. Ask students to classify these according to whether they are slang, informal, or formal.

2   Previewing Vocabulary

- Play the recording and have students listen to the underlined words and phrases.

- Have students complete the exercise individually.

- Compare their answers as a whole class and write the correct answers on the board.

ANSWER KEY

1.c 2.e 3.b 4.f 5.d 6.a

Listen

3   Comprehension Questions

- Explain that these questions will help students focus on the main ideas in the listening. They do not need to understand every word to answer the questions.

- Read the questions aloud.

- Play the recording.

- After listening, have students compare their answers in pairs.

- Check the answers as a class.

ANSWER KEY

1. Mari and Dan disagree on most things.

2. They agree to go to a science fiction movie.

3. (Answers in chart below.)

	Dan likes	Mari likes
Music	rock	jazz
Food	Mexican, American	Japanese, Indian
Art	modern art	19th-century art
Sports	American football	basketball
Movies	science fiction	science fiction

AUDIOSCRIPT

Jeff: Come in!

Dan: Hi.

Jeff: Hey, Dan, how ya doin'?

Dan: Great, thanks. Hey, I burned you some new CDs.

Jeff: Cool.

Dan: Hi. You were at our show last night, right?

Mari: Yeah, I was.

Jeff: Sorry, Mari, this is Dan. Dan, this is Mari.

Mari: It's nice to meet you.

Dan: Nice to meet you too.

Jeff: Oh, let me get that. I'll be right back.

Dan: OK. So Mari, did you have a good time at the club last night?

Mari: Yeah, it was pretty wild.

Dan: What did you think of our band?

Mari: Well, your music is great for dancing, but to tell you the truth, it was kind of loud. I guess I really prefer jazz.

Dan: Do you go to concerts much?

Mari: No, not very often. I can't afford them. They're so expensive!

Dan: Yeah, I know what you mean. Well, what do you like to do for fun?

Mari: I love to eat! I love going to different ethnic restaurants and trying new dishes.

Dan: What's your favorite kind of food?

Mari: Well, Japanese, of course. What about you?

Dan: Well, I'm not crazy about sushi or sashimi. But I really like Mexican food.

Mari: Ooh, I can't stand beans, and I don't like cheese. Uh . . . What about Indian food?

Dan: I don't care for it. Too spicy. Um . . . you like American food? You know, hamburgers, hot dogs, French fries . . .

Mari: Yuck! All that fat and salt and sugar . . . We don't see eye to eye on anything, do we?

Dan: Well, let's see. What's your opinion of modern art? There's a wonderful show at the county museum right now.

Mari: To be honest, I don't get the modern stuff. I prefer 19th-century art, you know, Monet, van Gogh, Renoir.

Dan: Hmm. How do you feel about sports? Are you interested in football?

Mari: American football? I hate it!

Dan: Basketball?

Mari: It's OK.

Dan: How about tall musicians with curly hair?

Mari: It depends.

Dan: OK, I got it. How about tall musicians with curly hair who invite you to a movie?

Mari: Science fiction?

Dan: Sounds great!

Mari: Finally, we agree on something!

Stress

4 Listening for Stressed Words

❑ Play the recording again.

❑ Have students repeat the phrase or sentence and write the missing words.

❑ After listening, have students check their answers with the audioscript in their books.

❑ Have students read the conversation with a partner, paying attention to stressed words in their pronunciation.

❑ Explain that students will hear five short conversations. They will rewrite the sentences as questions.

❑ Play the recording, allowing time for students to write.

❑ Ask volunteers to write their answers on the board and compare answers as a class.

ANSWER KEY

Dan: What did you think of our _band_?

Mari: Well, your music is _great_ for _dancing_, but to tell you the truth, it was kind of _loud_. I guess I really prefer _jazz_.

Dan: Do you go to _concerts_ much?

Mari: No, not very often. I _can't afford_ them. They're _so_ expensive!

Dan: Yeah, I know what you _mean_. Well, what do you like to do for _fun_?

Mari: I _love_ to _eat_! I love going to different _ethnic_ restaurants and trying new _dishes_.

Dan: What's your _favorite_ kind of food?

Mari: Well, _Japanese_, of course. What about you?

Dan: Well.... I'm _not crazy_ about sushi or sashimi. But I really like _Mexican_ food.

Mari: Ooh, I _can't stand_ beans, and I don't like _cheese_. Uh . . . What about _Indian_ food?

Dan: I don't _care_ for it. Too _spicy_. Um... Do you like _American_ food? You know, hamburgers, hot dogs, French fries . . .

Mari: _Yuck_! All that fat and salt and sugar . . . We don't see eye to eye on _anything_, do we?

Dan: Well, let's see. What's your opinion of _modern_ art? There's a _wonderful_ show at the county _museum_ right now.

Mari: To be _honest_, I don't _get_ the modern stuff. I prefer _19th_-century art, you know, Monet, Van Gogh, Renoir.

Dan: Hmm. How do you feel about _sports_? Are you interested in _football_?

Mari: _American_ football? I _hate_ it!

Dan: Basketball?

Mari: It's OK.

Dan: How about tall musicians with _curly_ hair?

Mari: It _depends_.

Dan: OK, I got it. How about _tall_ musicians with _curly_ hair who invite you to a _movie_?

Mari: Science fiction?

Dan: Sounds _great_!

Mari: _Finally_, we agree on _something_!

REDUCTIONS

- Read the instruction note.

- Ask students if they can think of any other examples.

---

5 **Listening for Reductions**

- ❏ Have students read the directions.

- ❏ Play the recording and have students write the full questions for the reduced ones in each of the five dialogues.

ANSWER KEY

1. Do you like Japanese food?
2. Are you tired?
3. Is anybody home?
4. Are you leaving already?
5. Does he have kids?

AUDIOSCRIPT

1. **A:** Do you like Chinese food?
   B: Not really.
   A: Japanese?
2. **A:** Whew! What a day!
   B: Tired?
3. **A:** Anybody home?
   B: I'm here. I'm in the kitchen.
4. **A:** I guess it's time to go.
   B: Leaving already?
5. **A:** Does he have a wife?
   B: Yes.
   A: Kids?

After You Listen

6 Reviewing Vocabulary

- ❑ Have students work in pairs. Student A will look at page 251 in the Student Book. Student B will look at page 259.

- ❑ Set a time limit of five minutes.

- ❑ Review the answers as a class.

ANSWER KEY

1. **A:** What is this delicious dish?

   B: It's humus. It's from the Middle East. I love it, too.

2. **A:** Sally has a new boyfriend. To be honest, I'm not crazy about him.

   B: Really? What's his name?

3. **A:** What do you think of action movies?

   B: I can't stand them. I prefer comedies.

4. **A:** Did you have a good time in San Diego last weekend?

   B: No. It rained all day Saturday and Sunday, so we came home early.

5. **A:** Why did you break up with your girlfriend?

   B: Because we didn't see eye to eye on anything.

6. **A:** I don't care for this new chair you bought. It's not very comfortable.

   B: OK, I'll take it back to the store.

Using Language Functions

TALKING ABOUT LIKES AND DISLIKES

- ▪ Read the instruction note.

- ▪ Ask students to read the examples.

- ▪ Practice pronunciation and intonation by giving topics to which students can respond with one of these expressions, e.g. *Mexican food? Jazz music? Ice hockey?*

7 Asking About Likes and Dislikes

- ❑ Read the directions for the activity.

- ❑ Have students complete the questions individually.

- ❑ Practice the questions and answers in pairs.

- ❑ Remind students to use the expressions from the language box, along with the appropriate intonation, to answer the questions.

ANSWER KEY

1. *What did you think of* our band?
2. *What's your favorite* kind of food?
3. *Do you like* American food?
4. *What's your opinion of* modern art?
5. *How do you feel about* sports?
6. *Are you interested in* football?
7. *How about* tall musicians with curly hair?

Best Practice

Interacting with Others

This type of activity is an example of collaborative learning to encourage fluency and confidence. In this activity, communication is more important than grammar. Students can improve their confidence in talking about likes and dislikes by switching roles or partners and practicing the same situations again.

8 Talking About Likes and Dislikes

- ❑ Have students work in pairs to complete the chart and discuss each topic.

- ❑ Set a time limit of five minutes.

- ❑ Move around the room to provide feedback and encouragement.

- ❑ Ask volunteers to retell their conversation to the class.

Talk It Over

Best Practice

Making Use of Academic Content

This is an example of an activity that encourages students to practice impromptu speaking skills. When participating in debates or discussions in class, they may sometimes be asked to defend their opinions without having a lot of preparation time. This activity provides an opportunity to practice this skill.

9 Giving an Impromptu Speech

❏ Read the instructions and ask one or two students to explain the activity to the rest of the class.

❏ Have students choose a topic from the box and write one question about that topic. Read the example questions to point out the difference between the general and specific questions.

❏ Collect the questions and put them in a box or a bag.

❏ One at a time, have students pick a question from the box and talk about it for one minute.

❏ You may do this activity in groups or as a whole class.

 EXPANSION ACTIVITY

■ The purpose of this activity is to practice asking and answering questions about likes and dislikes.

■ Please see Black Line Master "What Kind of Person Are You?" on page BLM 22.1 and BLM 22.2 of this Teacher's Edition. Photocopy one set for each pair of students.

■ Have students ask their partner questions to fill out the questionnaires.

■ Move around the room to monitor and provide feedback.

■ When they have finished asking the questions, have them add up the points for their partner and read the result to their partner.

Before You Listen

1   Prelisting Discussion

- ❑ Have students describe the pictures and talk about the information.
- ❑ Have students work in pairs to answer the questions.
- ❑ Review the responses as a class and compare some of their experiences.

2   Previewing Vocabulary

- ❑ Play the recording and have students listen to the words.
- ❑ Have students check the words they know.
- ❑ Ask students to compare answers with a partner and define or explain the words they know.

Listen

Strategy

Recognizing Paraphrases

- ▦ Read the information in the *Strategy* box.
- ▦ Review the meaning of paraphrasing and give some examples, using the phrases in the box.

3   Practicing Paraphrase Signals

- ❑ Read the directions for the activity and have students match each sentence with a paraphrase and then write the sentence.

ANSWER KEY

1.b   2.c   3.d   4.e   5.a

4   Predicting Note Organization

- ❑ Explain that students will be listening to an interview rather than a lecture as in previous chapters.

- ❑ Ask for some suggestions about how they will organize their note-taking.

Best Practice

Scaffolding Instruction

This outline helps students to organize their notes into main and secondary ideas. By providing students with the outline as a support, they can see how key words and numbering can be used to structure the content of the interview. This guided activity prepares them for the skill of identifying main and secondary ideas without the help of an outline.

5   Taking Notes (Part I)

(See the audioscript following Activity 6.)

- ❑ Ask students to take notes in their own as they listen.
- ❑ Play the recording.

6   Rewriting Your Notes

- ❑ Ask students to complete the outline using their notes.
- ❑ Play the recording again if necessary.

ANSWER KEY

Generation Y	
Questions/Topics	Answers
Meaning of Gen Y?	1. Young Am. born late 1970s–early 1990s, i.e. 1977–1994
	2. Number = *70 mil.*
B. Number—significant?	Yes. Reason: *now 2nd lgst. by 2020 lgst.*
	⟶ *future mkt*
	⟶ *imp. for marketing*
C. <u>Characteristics</u>	1. ¹/₄ *from single-parent homes*
	2. ³/₄ *have mothers who work*
	3. ¹/₃ *not Caucasian*

D. Tolerant?	_yes_ Also _optimistic, confident, independent, rich_
E. _rich_	Stats: 1. Total income/yr: _$211 bil._ 2. Spend _av. $30 on a trip to the mall_

AUDIOSCRIPT

Host: Dr. Harris, thank you for joining us today.

Dr. Harris: My pleasure.

Host: To begin, could you tell us the meaning of the term _Generation Y?_

Dr. Harris: Sure. Generation Y refers to young Americans who were born between the late 1970s and the early 1990s, uh, that is between 1977 or 1978 and 1993 or 1994. In other words, the youngest ones are still teenagers, and the oldest ones are young adults. And there are more than 70 million of them.

Host: Is that number significant?

Dr. Harris: It is extremely significant. Generation Y is the second-largest generation in U.S. history, and by the year 2020 it will be the largest. So this generation is the future market for almost all consumer brands. Marketers know they have to stay in touch with this generation if they want their products to succeed.

Host: What are some of the most important characteristics of this generation?

Dr. Harris: Well, first let me give you some statistics, OK? One-fourth, that is one in four people in this generation, grew up in single-parent homes. Three-fourths, I mean 75 percent, have mothers who work. And one-third are not Caucasian. To put it another way, this is the most diverse generation in U.S. history.

Host: Would you say they are tolerant?

Dr. Harris: Very tolerant. Also optimistic, confident, independent, and . . . rich!

Host: Rich? Explain that.

Dr. Harris: OK. Here are some more statistics: According to a study by the Harris company, members of Generation Y have total incomes of $211 billion a year. These kids spend an average of $30 on every trip to the mall. And if you have teenagers, you know that this generation practically lives at the mall.

7 **Taking Notes (Part II)**

- ❏ Play the second part of the recording.
- ❏ Have students take notes in their own way as before.
- ❏ Then have students use their notes to complete the outline.
- ❏ Play the recording again if necessary.

ANSWER KEY

F. _spend money on?_	_Fashion, fast food, movies, CDs, electronics, concert tickets._
G. _Preferred brands?_	_Change brands fast, whatever is in fashion_
H. _Internet gen._	1. _grow up w/ media → smart shoppers_ 2. _Don't like trad. advert._

	3. *not loyal to brands*
	4. *love fads*
I. *only U.S.?*	No. Internat'l, but diff. in other countries, e.g.:
	1. *E. Europe 1st gen. w/o communism*
	2. *Korea/Greece hi stand. of living*

AUDIOSCRIPT

Host: Two hundred and eleven billion. That's an incredible amount of money. What do they spend it on?

Dr. Harris: Fashion, fast food, movies, CDs, electronics, concert tickets. Generation Y-ers like to have fun.

Host: Are there special brands that this generation prefers?

Dr. Harris: No, not in the way that their parents preferred Levis jeans or SUVs. Generation Y-ers like anything that's hip or hot at the moment, but that can change very fast.

Host: So what do marketers need to know if they want to sell to this group?

Dr. Harris: I think the main thing to remember is that this is the Internet generation, the generation of instant messaging. They have grown up with the media, so they are very smart shoppers. They don't like traditional advertising techniques. And as I said, they are not loyal to specific brands. And they love fads, like right now graphic T-shirts and flip-flops are totally in.

Host: Is Generation Y found only in the U.S., or is it in other countries as well?

Dr. Harris: Generation Y is actually an international phenomenon, although it has different characteristics in different countries. In Eastern Europe, for example, it's the first generation to grow up without communism. And in other countries like, oh, Korea and Greece, this is the first generation to grow up with a high standard of living. These young people want to be modern. I mean they are not interested in the traditional way of life. Also, they identify more closely with the West, and that can cause conflict between them and the generations that came before them.

Host: Dr. Harris, before we conclude, may I ask you a personal question?

Dr. Harris: Go ahead.

Host: What generation are you?

Dr. Harris: I'm a baby boomer, born in 1960. But my daughter, who was born in 1984, is Generation Y. And believe it or not, she loves listening to my old Beatles records.

Host: No kidding. Dr. Harris, this has been very interesting. Thank you for being with us today.

Dr. Harris: You're welcome.

After You Listen

8 Discussing the Lecture

- ❏ Have students discuss the questions in groups.
- ❏ Encourage students to use the new vocabulary in their discussion.
- ❏ Ask for representatives from each group to report to the class on the discussion.

9 **Reviewing Vocabulary**

❑ Ask students to look back at the vocabulary in Activity 2 and to test each other in pairs.

❑ Invite volunteers to give examples sentences using the new vocabulary.

Talk It Over

Best Practice

Organizing Information

Activities such as this will teach students to organize information by completing a chart. This specific activity allows students to understand and process information by categorizing. Here, students identify and list specific items within broader categories. Seeing information in a chart like this helps students organize the information and see the relationship of the items to each other.

10 **Talking About Fads**

❑ Brainstorm ideas for different types of fads.

❑ Have students read the directions and the questions.

❑ Have them read the FYI note and the Language Tip. Clarify any questions.

❑ Have students work in groups of three or four people.

❑ Have students fill in the charts and answer the questions.

❑ Ask for volunteers to give examples to the class.

❑ Other related questions might be: Who starts fads? Are they started by young people or by companies trying to sell new products? What makes a fad popular?

REPRODUCIBLE **EXPANSION ACTIVITY**

▪ The purpose of this activity is to practice paraphrasing.

▪ Please see Black Line Master "What Do You Mean?" on page BLM 23 of this Teacher's Edition. Photocopy and distribute one to each student.

▪ Have students work in groups or pairs to complete the sentences.

▪ Set a time limit of ten minutes.

▪ Compare answers as a class. The focus should be on accuracy of meaning, rather than grammar.

▪ Take a vote on the best sentence completions and write them on the board.

ANSWER KEY

Answers will vary. Possible answers:

1. don't require computer skills

2. about 66 percent of U.S. teens have cell phones

3. go online and download the latest music

4. go to the cinema to see movies

5. buying big cars because gas is expensive

6. more people are taking sport vacations far away

7. more people are thinking about how much salt and sugar they eat

8. you can save time by shopping online

9. watch movies on TV or listen to music on a stereo

10. wait to read the news in a newspaper

Focused Listening

YES/NO QUESTIONS WITH *DO*, *DOES*, OR *DID*

- Read the instruction note.
- Read aloud the examples.

1 Yes/No Questions with *Do*, *Does*, or *Did*

- ❑ Read the directions for the activity.
- ❑ Play the recording and have students repeat the questions.

2 Distinguishing Among *Do*, *Does*, and *Did*

- ❑ Read the instructions.
- ❑ Play the recording and have students circle their answers.

ANSWER KEY

1.a 2.a 3.b 4.a 5.b 6.b 7.b 8.a

AUDIOSCRIPT

1. Do you have time to eat lunch?
2. Does he play the piano?
3. Did they need help?
4. Do I look like my sister?
5. Did she understand the instructions?
6. Do we need to rewrite the composition?
7. Did they own a house?
8. Did we sound good?

3 *Do*, *Does*, and *Did* in Questions

- ❑ Play the recording.
- ❑ Allow time for students to write the missing words.
- ❑ Compare answers as a class.

ANSWER KEY

1. *Did he* decide to take the job?
2. When *do we* eat?
3. *Do I* have to rewrite this composition?
4. Where *did we* park the car?
5. *Do they* know what to do?
6. *Did she* miss the bus again?
7. *Do you* usually walk to school?
8. *Did you* remember to turn off the light?

Focus on Testing

Using Context Clues

- Review strategies for getting meaning from context.
- Explain that students will hear five different conversations.
- Play the recording and have students write their answers.
- Check the answers as a class.

ANSWER KEY

Answers	Clues
1. b. a painting	look at that; colors and shapes; it's modern
2. b. a tie	don't wear the brown one; suit
3. d. snowboarding	cold and windy; flying down a mountain
4. b. She doesn't like it.	different

| 5. a. She likes it. | (There are no specific words, but the speaker's intonation and tone show excitement and approval.) |

AUDIOSCRIPT

Conversation 1

Woman: Look at that! Isn't it interesting? I love the colors and shapes.

Man: What's it supposed to be?

Woman: It's not supposed to *be* anything. It's modern. Don't try to analyze it.

Man: Well how much does it cost?

Woman: Let's see. Five thousand dollars. What do you think?

Question 1: What are the speakers talking about?

Man: Five thousand dollars? For *that* painting? I don't think so.

Conversation 2

Woman: Don't wear the brown one.

Man: Why not? What's wrong with it?

Woman: Well, it doesn't go with your suit. Brown and black don't look good together.

Man: Well, what if I wear it with my other suit?

Question 2: What are the man and woman talking about?

Woman: No, you should just wear a different tie. I don't really like brown anyway.

Conversation 3

A: Do you want to try it? It's really fun!

B: No thanks. It's too cold and windy. And honestly, I'm not crazy about the idea of flying down a mountain on one thin piece of wood.

A: But that's the fun part!

Question 3: What sport are the people talking about?

B: I'm sorry, snowboarding isn't for me. I'd rather stay inside by the fire.

Conversation 4

Teen Girl: You colored your hair.

Teen Boy: Yeah, I finally did it. Do you like it?

Girl: Uh, you look so . . . different.

Boy: What do you mean, "different"?

Question 4: How does the girl feel about the boy's hair?

Girl: Uh, I'm not crazy about it. Sorry.

Conversation 5

Teen Girl: You colored your hair!

Teen Boy: Yeah, I finally did it. Do you like it?

Girl: You look so different!

Boy: What do you mean, "different"?

Question 5: How does the girl feel about the boy's hair?

Girl: I love it! It's so cool!

Using Language Functions

EXPRESSING APPROVAL AND DISAPPROVAL

- Read the instruction note.

- Review the difference in meaning between *approve/disapprove* and *like/dislike*.

4   Practicing Expressions of Approval and Disapproval

❑ Read the directions for the activity and have students work individually to complete the sentences.

❑ Have students discuss their answers with a partner.

❑ Compare answers as a class.

On the Spot!

5   What Would You Do?

- ❑ Give students time to read the instructions.

- ❑ Ask one student to explain the instructions in their own words.

- ❑ Have students complete the chart individually.

- ❑ Help students to form groups and have them discuss their charts by answering the three questions.

- ❑ Encourage them to use expressions from page 190 of the Student Book.

- ❑ Set a time limit of 20 minutes.

- ❑ Move around the room to provide encouragement and feedback.

- ❑ At the end, invite a representative from each group to report on the most controversial topic in their discussion.

REPRODUCIBLE   EXPANSION ACTIVITY

- ▪ The aim of this activity is to practice the language of expressing approval and disapproval on the topic of fads and fashions.

- ▪ Please see Black Line Master "Fads and Fashions" on page BLM 24 of this Teacher's Edition. Photocopy and distribute one to each student.

- ▪ Have students work in groups to discuss one of the topics in the box. Point out that the topics are written like short advertisements.

- ▪ As a group, they should try to think of reasons why each group of people in the chart might approve or disapprove of this topic.

- ▪ Have students fill out the chart with their ideas.

- ▪ Each group member should then choose one of the roles.

- ▪ The group will then role-play a discussion using the information they have gathered.

- ▪ Set a time limit of 15 minutes.

- ▪ Ask a representative from each group summarize the main points of the discussion.

Before You Listen

1 Describing Your Ideal Partner

- ❑ Set a time limit of three minutes for students to write their lists.
- ❑ Have students compare lists with their partner.
- ❑ Discuss the questions in groups or as a class.

Listen

2 Comparing People's Qualities

- ❑ Look at the photo and brainstorm a list of adjectives about each person.
- ❑ Play the recording and have students complete the chart.
- ❑ Play the recording again if necessary.
- ❑ Ask a volunteer to write the answers on the board.

ANSWER KEY

	Katherine	Jean
Positive qualities	parents like her	smart
	intelligent	loves sports
	interesting to talk with	good sense of humor, tells funny jokes
	loves kids	good at managing money, shares cost of dates
Negative qualities	sensitive, gets offended	quiet
	not good at managing money	not easy to talk with
	has a bad temper, gets angry	not sure about having kids

AUDIOSCRIPT

I don't know what to do. Katherine and Jean are both wonderful women. So how am I supposed to choose between them? Take Katherine. We went to the same high school and college, and my parents are crazy about her. Also, Katherine is very intelligent, and she's interesting to talk with; we spend hours discussing art and politics and books.

Now Jean is also very smart, but she's much quieter than Katherine. It's not as easy to talk to her. But even though she's quiet, she's crazy about sports, just like me, and she has a great sense of humor; I mean, she tells the funniest jokes, and I love the way she laughs. On the other hand, Katherine is sometimes too sensitive; what I mean is, she doesn't understand that I'm just joking, so she gets offended.

And another thing I don't like about Katherine is that she's not good at managing money. She has a very good job and a good salary, but somehow she never seems to have any money! That's not very responsible, is it? But Jean is great with money. She even insists on sharing the cost of our dates.

On the other hand, I want to have children, but Jean says she's not sure. That could be a problem later on. Katherine loves kids, but sometimes she has a bad temper; she gets angry whenever I'm five minutes late!

I'm really confused. Katherine and Jean—they're so different and I really like them both. But you know, I don't know if either one is serious about me anyway. What do you think I should do?

After You Listen

3 Discussion

- ❑ Have students work in pairs to discuss the answers.
- ❑ Compare answers as a class.

Talk It Over

Best Practice

Cultivating Critical Thinking

This is an example of a collaborative team activity resulting in a final product. This type of activity requires students to process the information they have learned and apply it to a new situation. The process of manipulating language and concepts in this way will create deeper processing of new material which will allow students to evaluate whether they have understood the new material and help them remember it better.

4 Reading Personal Ads

❑ Explain the context of personal ads (see the Content Note below).

❑ Read the ads and check comprehension. Have them choose the most interesting ad and explain their choice to a group.

Content Note

Although meeting people through personal ads in the newspapers or online is fairly common in the U.S. and other Western countries, there are still risks associated with it, and many people in the U.S. would disapprove of or be suspicious of meeting people in this way. It is unusual and may be considered unacceptable in other cultures.

5 Writing Personal Ads

❑ Read the information in the boxes. Explain that each student will write a personal ad for him or herself. Set a time limit of ten minutes.

❑ Move around the room to provide feedback.

❑ Collect the ads and pin them to the wall. You may want to give each ad a number.

❑ Have students read all the ads and guess who wrote them.

EXPANSION ACTIVITY

▪ The aim of this activity is to practice vocabulary for describing personal characteristics.

▪ Write the following list of words on the board. Students may use their dictionaries.

adventurous	bad-tempered	confident
considerate	have a sense	independent
optimistic	of humor	sensitive
responsible		

▪ Each pair of students can choose three words. They will prepare a question for each word to find out if their classmates have this characteristic. They must not use the word in their questions.

Example: generous

Question: How much do you usually spend on a birthday present for your best friend?

▪ Set a time limit of five minutes. Move around the room to monitor progress and provide feedback.

▪ At the end of the time limit, ask students to choose someone in the class and read out their questions. The chosen student will try to answer truthfully. The other students will try to guess which characteristic is being described.

Self-Assessment Log

❑ Have students check vocabulary that they learned in the chapter and are prepared to use.

❑ Have them check strategies they understand.

❑ Put students in small groups. Ask students to find the information or an activity related to each strategy in the chapter.

❑ Tell students to find definitions in the chapter for any words they did not check, or they can look in their dictionaries.

New Frontiers

In this chapter, students will read about various topics related to advances in science. In Part 1, they will talk about the issue of cloning and learn to introduce surprising information. They will also practice the pronunciation of voiced and voiceless /*th*/. In Part 2, they will listen to a lecture about the benefits of exploring Mars and learn to distinguish facts from theory. In Part 3, they will discuss inventions and discoveries and learn to express interest or surprise. They will also practice the pronunciation of -*ed* endings. In Part 4, they will listen to a quiz show and practice ordering events in a story.

Chapter Opener

❑ Have students look at the photo of American astronaut David A. Wolf in space. His foot is anchored and that helps him stay in place. Discuss the questions in the Connecting to the Topic section.

❑ Read and discuss the quote. Ask students to think of examples that contradict or support this statement.

66 I never did anything worth doing by accident, nor did any of my inventions come by accident; they came by work. 99

—Thomas Alva Edison
American inventor, 1847–1931

Chapter Overview

Listening Skills and Strategies

Listening for main ideas

Listening for details

Making inferences

Distinguishing between *-ed* endings

Listening to game show questions and answers

Speaking Skills and Strategies

Talking about cloning

Introducing surprising information

Expressing interest and surprise

Talking about Mars

Solving a science problem

Talking about personal discoveries

Critical Thinking Skills

Getting meaning from context

Distinguishing fact from theory in a lecture

Ordering events in a story

Vocabulary Building

Terms for talking about scientific progress

Terms for talking about space exploration

Terms for signaling facts and theories

Terms for solving a science problem

Terms for talking about inventions and discoveries

Expressions for signaling surprise

Pronunciation

Identifying and practicing stressed words

Pronouncing the *th* sound

Pronouncing *-ed* endings

Language Skills

Recognizing signal words to guess the correct answer

Vocabulary

Nouns	Verbs	Adjectives	Expression
disaster	analyze	critical	all for
endangered species	explore	extinct	
evidence	fascinate	fascinating	
planet	scare	weird	
research			
resources			
solar system			
stem cell			
telescope			

Can You Guess?

- Ask students to discuss the questions in groups and compare their answers with the correct answers.

1. Who was the first woman in space and what country did she come from? A. *Valentina Tereshkova, Russian.*

2. What do the following inventions have in common: the yo-yo, Post-it notes, dynamite, and Velcro? A. *They were all accidental inventions.*

3. Where were the following things invented: Piano, chocolate, toothbrush? A. *piano— Italy; chocolate—Central America/Mexico; toothbrush—China*

Content Note

- The piano (originally known as a pianoforte) was developed from an older instrument, the harpsichord, in around 1720 by Bartolomeo Cristofori of Padua, Italy.

- The Olmec Indians of Central America are believed to have grown cocoa beans as early as 1500 B.C. In 600 A.D., Mayans and Aztecs took beans from the "cacao" tree and made a drink they called *xocoatl*.

- Toothbrushes were first invented by the ancient Chinese who made them from pigs hair.

Source
inventors.about.com/od/famousinventions

Before You Listen

Best Practice

Activating Prior Knowledge

The prelistening questions activate students' prior knowledge. This activity will help students relate their own knowledge of medical advances to the new language in this chapter. When students activate their prior knowledge before learning new material, they are better able to map new language onto existing concepts, which aids understanding and retention.

1 **Prelistening Questions**

- ❑ Have the students read the questions and discuss them in pairs.

- ❑ Compare answers as a whole class.

- ❑ As a whole class, try to come up with a definition of *cloning* or discuss the definitions below.

Content Note

- Cloning is the process of making a genetically identical copy of a cell or organism.

- Cloning can refer to the technique of replacing the nucleus of an unfertilized egg with the nucleus of a body cell from the organism. The first adult mammal cloned in this way was Dolly the sheep in 1997.

- Therapeutic cloning is the process of extracting stem cells from the human egg after it has divided. The stem cells can be used to generate virtually any type of specialized cell in the human body. The extraction process destroys the embryo, which raises a variety of ethical concerns. Researchers hope that one day, stem cells can be used to serve as replacement cells to treat heart disease, Alzheimer's, cancer, and other diseases. However, some people oppose this kind of research on ethical grounds.

2 **Previewing Vocabulary**

- ❏ Play the recording and have students listen to the underlined words and phrases.

- ❏ Have students complete the activity individually.

- ❏ Compare their answers as a whole class and write the correct answers on the board.

ANSWER KEY

1.e 2.a 3.d 4.f 5.c 6.b 7.g

Listen

3 **Comprehension Questions**

(The audioscript follows Activity 4.)

- ❏ Explain that these questions will help students focus on the main ideas in the listening. They do not need to understand every word to answer the questions.

- ❏ Read the questions aloud.

- ❏ Play the recording.

- ❏ After listening, have students compare their answers in pairs.

- ❏ Check the answers as a class.

ANSWER KEY

1. sheep, mice, and rabbits 2. human cloning
3. to save endangered species; to solve medical problems 4. $20,000 5. dog 6. similar

Stress

4 **Listening for Stressed Words**

- ❏ Play the recording again.

- ❏ Allow time for students to repeat and write the missing words.

- ❏ After listening, have students check their answers with the audioscript in their books.

- ❏ Have students read the conversation with a partner, paying attention to stressed words in their pronunciation.

AUDIOSCRIPT and ANSWER KEY

Mari: Your dog is so _adorable_, Nancy. How old is he?

Nancy: Eleven.

Mari: Wow, that's pretty _old_.

Nancy: Yeah. I just love him so much. I don't know what I'll do when he's _gone_.

Mari: Well, you can _clone_ him, you know.

Nancy: Clone him? You're _joking_, right?

Mari: Yeah, of course. But actually, it _is_ possible. _Scientists_ in Korea have cloned a dog, you know; I saw a _picture_ of it in _Time_ magazine.

Nancy: Really? I've heard of cloned _sheep_, and mice and rabbits. But not _pets_ like dogs.

Andrew: Oh, yeah. _Believe_ it or not, there is a company in California that _offers_ a pet cloning service. For $15,000, you can have an _exact_ copy of your pet.

Nancy: That's so _weird_. Actually, it kind of scares me. Pretty soon, they'll start cloning _people_ and then...

Andrew: Nah, I don't think that's going to _happen_. I think cloning will be used in _positive_ ways.

Nancy: Like what?

Andrew: Like saving endangered species. For example, scientists could save the giant _panda_ and other animals before they become _extinct_.

Mari: Oh, yeah, and _another_ thing. I heard that scientists will be able to clone _body_ parts. You know, just grow a new heart, or a new _tooth_.

Andrew: Uh-huh. That's what stem cell research is all *about*, which is *similar* to cloning. A lot of medical problems are going to be *solved* with that for sure.

Nancy: Well, I'm all *for* that. Especially if it can help us live *longer*.

Mari: Or if they can help your *dog* live longer, right?

Nancy: Right!

After You Listen

5 Using Vocabulary

- ❑ Read the questions and check comprehension of new vocabulary items.
- ❑ Have students work in pairs to discuss the questions.
- ❑ Set a time limit of five to ten minutes.
- ❑ Move around the room to provide feedback.
- ❑ Invite volunteers to summarize answers for the class.

Pronunciation

PRONOUNCING *TH*

- ▩ Read the instruction note.
- ▩ Practice the pronunciation of /*th*/.

6 Pronouncing Voiced and Voiceless /*th*/

- ❑ Play the recording. Allow time for students to repeat all together.
- ❑ Select students to pronounce the words individually.

7 Distinguishing Between Voiced and Voiceless /*th*/

- ❑ Have students read the sentences silently and try to predict which /*th*/ sounds are voiced or voiceless.

- ❑ Play the recording and have students mark the sentences.
- ❑ Check the answers as a class.
- ❑ Practice saying the sentences.

ANSWER KEY

1. (Th)at's so weird.
2. (Th)ere's no wea(th)er on the moon.
3. I don't think (th)at's going to happen.
4. (Th)ere's another thing to talk about.
5. (Th)ey discovered some(th)ing new.
6. Can (th)ey grow a new too(th) in a laboratory?
7. What's (th)e coldest place on Ear(th)?

Using Language Functions

INTRODUCING SURPRISING INFORMATION

- ▩ Read the instruction note.
- ▩ Brainstorm some ways of completing the sentences.
- ▩ Practice the expressions using the correct intonation.

Best Practice

Making Use of Academic Content

This is an example of an activity that encourages students to practice impromptu speaking skills. When participating in debates or discussions in class, they may sometimes have to come up with ideas without having a lot of preparation time. This activity provides an opportunity to practice this skill.

8 Fact or Fiction Game

- ❑ Read the instructions and ask one or two students to explain the activity to the rest of the class.

❑ Model the activity with two or three students first.

❑ Set a time limit of ten minutes.

EXPANSION ACTIVITY

▨ The purpose of this activity is to practice telling and asking questions about strange stories from the newspaper.

▨ Ask students to find one funny, interesting, or strange story from the newspaper and bring it to the next class.

▨ Have students work in pairs to tell each other their stories using the expressions from the box.

▨ The listener should ask questions about the details of the story to make sure they understand.

▨ Then have students change partners and re-tell their partner's story to their new partner.

▨ Student A tells story to student B. Student B tells A's story to Student C. Student C pairs up with A and tells A's story back to A.

▨ To check comprehension, the new partner should now pair up with the person who told the original story.

▨ Set a time limit of 15 minutes.

▨ Move around the room to monitor and provide feedback.

▨ When they have finished, ask for volunteers to tell the strangest or most unusual story.

Before You Listen

1 Prelistening Discussion

- ❑ Have students describe the photo.
- ❑ Have students work in pairs to answer the questions.
- ❑ Review the responses as a class and compare some of their experiences.
- ❑ Ask a volunteer to write on the board all the facts they know about Mars.

2 Previewing Vocabulary

- ❑ Play the recording and have students listen to the words.
- ❑ Have students check the words they know.
- ❑ Ask students to compare answers with a partner. They will find out the meanings of these words by listening to the lecture.

Listen

Strategy

Recognizing Facts and Theories

- ▪ Read the information in the Strategy box.
- ▪ Ask students to explain why it is important to distinguish facts from theories.
- ▪ Ask for some examples of facts and theories.

3 Listening for Fact and Theory in the Lecture

- ❑ Read aloud the directions.
- ❑ If necessary, have students review the signal words and phrases in the Strategy box.
- ❑ Play the recording and have students check Fact or Theory.

ANSWER KEY

1. fact 2. theory 3. fact 4. theory 5. theory
6. theory

AUDIOSCRIPT

1. It's a well-known fact that Mars, just like Earth, has clouds, winds, roughly a 24-hour day, four seasons, volcanoes, canyons, and other familiar features.

2. It's possible that there was some kind of life there thousands of years ago.

3. Scientists know there was water on Mars from analyzing the surface of the rocks where the Mars rovers landed.

4. There's a chance that some form of life existed and perhaps still does exist on Mars.

5. The ability to live on another planet may become necessary in the future.

6. There are possibly more than eight other planets in our solar system.

Best Practice

Organizing Information

The next two activities, Activities 4 and 5, use a graphic organizer to categorize information. Using an outline encourages students to process and organize information while they are listening and also provides a record for them to refer to when reviewing their notes. This type of graphic organizer emphasizes listing and categorizing skills. Other types of graphic organizers are used throughout this book.

Best Practice

Scaffolding Instruction

The next two activities, Activities 4 and 5, support scaffolding. This outline helps students to organize their notes into main and secondary ideas. By providing students with the outline as a support, they can see how key words and numbering can be used to structure the content of the lecture. This guided activity prepares them for the skill of identifying main and secondary ideas without the help of an outline.

4 Taking Notes and Outlining (Part I)

❑ Ask students to take notes as they listen.

❑ Remind them to use abbreviations and symbols.

❑ Play the recording.

❑ Ask students to complete the outline using their notes.

❑ Play the recording again if necessary.

❑ Check the answers as a class.

ANSWER KEY

PART 1

I. Intro

  A. Mars—popular topic

  B. NASA & ESA : _put humans on Mars by 2030_

  C. Lecture topic: _why is Mars interesting?_

II. Reasons

  A. _2nd closest planet, easy to see_

  B. Similar to Earth (_clouds, winds, 24-hr day, 4 seasons, volcanoes, canyons, etc._)

III. Life on Mars?

  A. Most scientists think _no_

  B. It's possible that _there was life many years ago_

    1. in 2003: _discovered Mars had water in the past, prob. salty water_

    2. If water → _some kind of life_

AUDIOSCRIPT

Part 1

The planet Mars has fascinated people since ancient times, and that fascination has continued to this day. In fact, these days Mars is again receiving a lot of attention. If you watch the news, you probably already know that several countries have announced plans to put humans on Mars. Both the United States Space Agency—NASA—and the European Space Agency—ESA—plan to do this by the year 2030. So what's so fascinating about Mars? Why explore Mars and not other planets? After all, there are eight other planets in our solar system, and possibly more. What makes Mars so attractive to explore? That's what I want to talk about today.

OK. To begin with, Mars is the second closest planet to Earth. It's our closest neighbor after Venus. And for this reason, it's easy to see in the night sky. Second, Mars is similar to Earth in several ways. It's a well-known fact that Mars, just like Earth, has clouds, winds, a roughly 24-hour day, four seasons, volcanoes, canyons, and other familiar features.

Because of these similarities between Earth and Mars, the obvious question, of course, is "Is there life on Mars?" Well, we don't know. Most scientists think there isn't, but—and this is an important _but_—it's possible that there was _some kind_ of life there thousands of years ago. Why do scientists think so? Well, in 2003, a critical discovery was made. Scientists found some very strong evidence that Mars had water, actually a lot of water, some time in the past. They know this from analyzing the surface of the rocks where the Mars rovers landed. And the surface shows that there most probably was a large body of water there, probably salty seawater.

Now this discovery, that there was water on Mars in the past, is critical because without water, life cannot exist. And if there was water on Mars, then there's the possibility of life also. In other words, there's a chance that a long time ago some form of life existed on Mars.

5 Taking Notes and Outlining (Part II)

❑ Play the second part of the recording.

❑ Have students take notes in their own way as before.

❑ Then have students use their notes to complete the outline.

❑ Play the recording again if necessary.

ANSWER KEY

PART 2

IV. *How does life on Mars benefit us?*

   A. Exploring Mars ⑧ *find out things about Earth*

   B. People need to live on M. if

      1. *not enough space and resources on Earth*

      2. *there is a disaster*

      3. *limited resources on Earth*

AUDIOSCRIPT

Part II

Now, while this is an exciting discovery for most of us, some people still ask, "So what? Why should we care? How does this benefit us right here on Earth?" Well, there are lots of ways that we could benefit. First, by exploring Mars, we might be able to find out things about Earth such as why and how life formed here. Second, we might also find that Mars could be a place for people to live in the future. The ability to live on another planet may become necessary in the future—after all, we have limited space, and limited resources here on Earth, right? And finally, we might need someplace else to live in case of a global disaster—you know—a natural disaster or a nuclear war.

So yes, it makes a lot of sense to continue to explore Mars. Not only because human beings have always done that, have always explored new areas, new frontiers of their own knowledge, but also because this specific planet, Mars, seems to be very much like our own Earth and therefore holds so many possibilities for the

future. As I said earlier, Mars is our neighbor, and it's time we go over and say hello.

After You Listen

6   **Discussing the Lecture**

❑ Have students discuss the questions in groups.

❑ Encourage students to use the new vocabulary in their discussion.

❑ Ask for representatives from each group to report to the class on the discussion.

7   **Reviewing Vocabulary**

❑ Ask students to look back at the vocabulary in Activity 2 on page 205 in the Student Book and to test each other in pairs.

❑ Invite volunteers to give example sentences using the new vocabulary.

Talk It Over

Best Practice

Cultivating Critical Thinking

This is an example of a collaborative team activity resulting in a final product. This type of activity requires students to process information about facts and theories in order to complete a task. The process of manipulating language and concepts in this way will create deeper processing of new material which will allow students to evaluate whether they have understood the new material and help them remember it better.

8   **Solving a Science Problem**

❑ Read the instructions for the activity.

❑ Check comprehension by asking one or two students to summarize the instructions to the class in their own words.

❑ Set a time limit of ten minutes.

❑ Move around the room to provide feedback.

❑ Ask a volunteer to combine the scores from the different groups to come up with a class list.

___

ANSWER KEY

1. Two 100 lb. tanks of oxygen—no air on the moon
2. 5 gallons of water—you can't live long without water
3. map—needed for navigation
4. dried food—you can live for some time without food
5. solar powered FM receiver-transmitter —communication
6. 50 feet of nylon rope—for travel over rough terrain
7. first aid kit containing injection needles— kit is useful, but needles are useless
8. parachute silk—carrying
9. life raft—some value for shelter or carrying
10. pistols—some use for propulsion
11. dehydrated milk—useless, needs water to work
12. portable heating unit—useless, the lighted side of the moon is hot
13. magnetic compass—useless, moon's magnetic field is different
14. box of matches—useless, no oxygen

EXPANSION ACTIVITY

▨ The purpose of this activity is to practice using the Internet as a research resource and to explore the differences between facts and theories.

▨ Please see Black Line Master "Fact or Theory?" on page BLM 25 of this Teacher's Edition. Photocopy and distribute one copy to each student.

▨ Go over the example. Tell them that the possible theory stated in the example is actually false. Even though Mercury is closest to the sun, Venus is hotter because gases trap the heat.

▨ Have students work in groups or pairs to complete as much information in the chart as they can.

▨ Set a time limit of ten minutes.

▨ Ask volunteers to read out some of their suggestions.

▨ Each student in the group will choose one planet and check the facts and theories suggested by their group by using the Internet. You may assign this as homework or to be done in the computer lab.

▨ In the next class, have students re-form their groups to share their information and complete their charts.

Getting Meaning from Context

Focus on Testing

Signal Words for Guessing 🎧 the Correct Answer

- Read the information in the box and check comprehension of *infer*, *imply*, and *conclude*.

- Explain that students will hear five different talks about discoveries.

- Play the recording and allow time for students to write their answers.

- Check the answers as a class.

ANSWER KEY

Answers	Clues
1. b. An invention helped Columbus make an important discovery.	Someone invented ships, Columbus used a ship to go to America.
2. b. It is a very old practice.	Greeks, Romans, Native Americans
3. b. It makes adding and subtracting easier.	Roman system had no zero, made adding and subtracting hard
4. c. It was accidental.	Some leaves ...fell, accidentally discovered
5. b. Rubber comes from a tree.	Juice of a tree

AUDIOSCRIPT

Passage 1

What is the difference between a discovery and an invention? Well, we discover things that were always there. For example, you often hear that Columbus discovered America. In contrast,

people invent things that did not exist before. Long ago someone invented ships, for instance. Discovery and invention are often related because many discoveries are made with the help of inventions. As an example, Columbus used ships to sail to America.

Question 1: What can we infer from this passage?

Passage 2

The ancient Greeks used the energy of the sun to heat their homes. Later, the Romans followed this example and used solar power to heat baths, houses, and greenhouses. The Native Americans were also early users of the sun's energy. Nowadays, car manufacturers are developing cars that will run only on solar power.

Question 2: What can we conclude about the use of solar energy?

Passage 3

During the Middle Ages, the people of Europe used the Roman numerals one through ten for basic math such as adding and subtracting. However, the Roman system did not have a number for zero. That made adding and subtracting very hard. Three centuries earlier, Arabic people had invented another kind of numbering system, the one we use today, which had a zero. This system was brought to Europe in the 12th century and quickly became popular. Today, Arabic numbers are used universally in mathematics. In contrast, Roman numerals are used only on clock faces—and in outlines!

Question 3: What can we infer about the invention of the number zero?

Passage 4

Shang Yeng was the emperor of China almost 5,000 years ago. For health reasons, he ordered his people to boil their water before drinking it. One day Shang Yeng himself was boiling water outside when some leaves from a bush fell into the large open pot. Before he could remove the leaves, they began to cook. The mixture smelled so good that Shang Yeng decided to taste it. In this way, tea was accidentally discovered.

Question 4: What can we conclude about the discovery of tea?

Talk 5

Rubber is an old discovery. When Columbus arrived in the New World, he saw boys playing with balls made from the hardened juice of a tree. Later, in 1736, a Frenchman working in Peru noticed people wearing shoes and clothes made from the same material. In 1770, an English scientist used the material to rub out his writing mistakes. He named the material *rubber.*

Question 5: What can we infer from the passage?

1 **Talking About Inventions and Discoveries**

❏ Have students discuss which of the discoveries and inventions play a role in their lives. Which of them are most useful and why?

❏ Discuss which of these are inventions or discoveries.

Focused Listening

PRONUNCIATION OF -*ED* ENDINGS

▪ Read the instruction note about the Pronunciation of -ed Endings.

▪ Have students repeat the examples aloud.

2 **Practicing -*ed* Endings**

❏ Read the directions for the activity and then play the recording.

❏ Have students repeat all together after the recording.

❏ Select individual students to practice selected words.

3 **Distinguishing Among -*ed* Endings**

❏ Read the directions.

❏ Play the recording.

❏ Allow time for students to write their answers.

❏ Select individual students to practice selected words.

ANSWER KEY

1. laughed /t/	9. invented /id/
2. described /d/	10. danced /t/
3. rented /id/	11. realized /d/
4. stopped /t/	12. crowded /id/
5. changed /d/	13. worked /t/
6. ended /id/	14. listened /d/
7. helped /t/	15. answered /d/
8. studied /d/	

4 **Pronouncing -*ed* Endings**

❏ Have students work individually to write their answers.

❏ Compare answers as a class and write the answers on the board.

❏ Have students work in pairs to practice pronouncing these words.

❏ If there is time, have students make up sentences and practice the pronunciation of -*ed* forms in a sentence

ANSWER KEY

1. /id/ pointed	6. /id/ waited
2. /d/ dreamed	7. /d/ explored
3. /d/ traveled	8. /id/ interested
4. /t/ kissed	9. /d/ judged
5. /t/ thanked	10. /d/ moved

Language Functions

EXPRESSING INTEREST OR SURPRISE

- Read the instruction note.

- Practice the expressions using the appropriate intonation.

Best Practice

Making Use of Academic Content

This is an example of an activity that requires students to draw on their own experience to give examples of abstract ideas and concepts. In this activity, they are asked to talk about examples of discoveries they have made in their own lives. This provides each student with an opportunity for authentic individualization, which makes their interaction more meaningful.

5 Talking About Discoveries

- Give students time to read the instructions and the information in the chart.

- Ask students to think quietly for one minute and make a list of discoveries they have made.

- Help students to form groups.

- Set a time limit of ten minutes.

- Move around the room to provide encouragement and feedback.

- At the end, invite volunteers to talk about their discoveries.

EXPANSION ACTIVITY

- The aim of this activity is to practice the language of expressing interest and surprise by using real information.

- Please see Black Line Master "That's Amazing!" on page BLM 26 of this Teacher's Edition. Photocopy and distribute one copy to each group.

- Have students read the directions. Then form groups of three.

- Have students discuss their skills and abilities. If necessary, brainstorm a few examples on the board. For example: baking cakes, telling funny stories, playing the piano.

- Students will fill in the diagram together as a group.

- You can tell students to label A, B, and C in the diagram with each student's name in the group.

- Set a time limit of ten minutes.

- Ask students to share their amazing facts with other groups.

- Encourage students to think of imaginative ideas for their enterprises.

Before You Listen

1 Prelistening Questions

- ❑ Look at the photos and answer the questions together as a class.

- ❑ Check understanding of the words *host* and *contestant*.

- ❑ Discuss the concept of game shows and why they are popular.

Listen

2 Listening to a Game Show

- ❑ Read the instructions and make sure students know they will write two sets of answers: their answers and the contestant's answers.

- ❑ Play the recording and allow time for students to complete the chart.

- ❑ Play the recording again if necessary.

- ❑ Ask a volunteer to write the answers on the board.

ANSWER KEY

Note: Contestant's answer is correct in each case.

1. Apple
2. Everest
3. Italy
4. China
5. penicillin
6. the telephone
7. Nicolaus Copernicus

AUDIOSCRIPT

Host: Good evening and welcome to our show! I'm your host, Ronnie Perez. In this game, members of the audience compete with our contestant to answer questions about explorations, inventions, and discoveries. When you hear a question, select your answer from the choices on your answer ballot. Our contestant will do the same. Then we'll see who has the correct answer!

Now let's meet our contestant. He is Roger Johnson from Ottawa, Canada. Roger, as you know, you may continue to play as long as you give correct answers. One wrong answer, however, and the game is over. Are you ready to play?!

Roger: I'm ready, Ronnie.

Host: Then here's our first question. For $1,000, what is the name of the computer company that created the first personal computer? Was it

a. Apple, b. Microsoft, or c. Intel?

Members of the audience, select your answer. Is it Apple, Microsoft, or Intel? OK, audience?

Audience: Apple!

Host: Roger, do you agree?

Roger: Yes I do, Ronnie. It's Apple.

Host: You are right! Well done! Let's go to question number 2. For $2,000: George Mallory, Sir Edmund Hillary, and Tensing Norgay all reached the top of which famous mountain? Was it

a. Mt. Everest in Nepal,
b. Mt. Fuji in Japan, or
c. Mt. Whitney in the United States?

Members of the audience, select your answer. Audience?

Audience: Everest!

Host: Roger? Your answer?

Roger: Everest. Absolutely.

Host: And that is correct. Good work so far, but as you know, our questions become more difficult as we continue playing. Here's question number 3. Marco Polo, who traveled throughout China at the end of the 13th century, was a native of which country? For $3,000, was it

a. Spain,

b. Portugal, or

c. Italy?

First let's turn to our audience . . .

And what is your answer, audience?

Audience: Spain! Italy!

Host: Roger, is it Spain or Italy? Which did you pick?

Roger: It's Italy, Ronnie.

Host: You sound very confident. Is it Italy? Yes! You're on a roll now, Roger. Ready for the next question?

Roger: Ready, Ronnie.

Host: Here it is. In which country was gunpowder invented? For $4,000, was it

a. Italy, b. Egypt, or c. China?

Choose your answers, please, audience. Gunpowder was invented where?

Audience, what is your answer?

Audience: Egypt! China!

Host: Roger?

Roger: Gosh, this one is difficult. I'm pretty sure it wasn't Italy, but I'm not sure about Egypt or China . . . hmmm . . . OK, I'm going to say China.

Host: Egypt or China? Let's take a look . . . It's China! Well done, Roger! How do you feel now?

Roger: Relieved. I really wasn't sure that time.

Host: Well, let's see if you can do it again, for $5,000 this time. In 1928, Alexander Fleming of England discovered this natural substance, which is still used today to kill bacteria and fight infections. What is the name of the substance? Is it

a. penicillin, b. aspirin, or c. ginseng?

Audience members, please choose your answer.

OK, Members of the audience, what do you say? Is it penicillin, aspirin, or ginseng?

Audience: Penicillin!

Host: Do you agree, Roger?

Roger: I sure do, Ronnie. It's penicillin.

Host: Are you right? . . . Yes! The answer is penicillin. Let's see if we can give you something a little more difficult. Are you ready, Roger?

Roger: Yes, sir.

Host: For $6,000, which of the following was *not* invented by the American inventor Thomas Alva Edison? Was it

a. the motion picture, b. the telephone, or c. the light bulb?

Let's give the audience a moment to decide . . .

And what is your answer?

Audience: Telephone! Motion pictures! Light bulb!

Host: It sounds like the audience is not sure this time. How about you, Roger?

Roger: Oh, I'm very sure. It's the telephone.

Host: Right again! The telephone was invented by Alexander Graham Bell, not Thomas Edison. Now, Roger, so far you have won $21,000, and we've reached the last question of the game. We're going to give you a choice: you can go home right now with $21,000, or you can answer one more question. If you answer it correctly, we'll double your money! Of course if you get it wrong, you go home with nothing. What would you like to do?

Roger: I'll . . . go for the question, Ronnie.

Host: He'll go for the question! Very well. For a chance at taking home $42,000, here it is. Five hundred years ago people believed that the Earth was the center of the universe and that the sun revolved around the Earth. In the year 1543, a Polish astronomer proved that the opposite is true; that the sun is the center of our solar system, and all the planets go around it. For $42,000, Roger, what was the name of that astronomer? Was it

a. Isaac Newton, b. Galileo Galilei, or c. Nicolaus Copernicus?

Members of the audience, what is your answer? Audience?

Audience: Galileo! Copernicus! Newton!

Host: Hmmm, no agreement there. Roger Johnson, did you pick the right answer? Who is it?

Roger: Well, uh, let me see. Um, Galileo was Italian, and I'm pretty sure Newton was English. So that leaves Copernicus.

Host: Is that your final answer?

Roger: Yes, it is.

Host: Is he right? For $42,000, the correct answer is . . . Copernicus! Roger Johnson, you have won it all! Congratulations! And that concludes our show for this evening. Please join us next week . . .

After You Listen

3 Reviewing the Listening

- ❏ Have students check their answers on page 261 of the Student Book.

- ❏ Have students write the original quiz questions.

- ❏ Ask volunteers to write the original quiz questions on the board.

Talk It Over

Best Practice

Interacting with Others

This is an example of a collaborative problem solving activity resulting in a final product. This type of activity requires students to process the information, share it with others in the group, and use the shared information to solve a problem, in this case, ordering the events in a story. The process of manipulating language and information in this way will create deeper processing of the information about Marco Polo and will also help them to understand sequential relationships in a text.

4 Ordering Events in a Story

- ❏ Read the information in the box.

- ❏ Read the instructions with the students.

- ❏ Set a time limit of ten minutes.

- ❏ When everyone has finished, compare answers as a class.

ANSWER KEY

C, G, B, F, A, D, E

EXPANSION ACTIVITY

- The purpose of this activity is to practice talking about inventions and discoveries.

- Please see Black Line Master "Inventions and Discoveries" on page BLM 27 of this Teacher's Edition. Photocopy one for each group of about four people.

- Cut them into squares. Give one set of squares to each group of about four people.

- Put the squares face down in the center of the table.

- Each student in turn will pick up one square. They will make statements about the discovery or invention (without saying its name) and the others will try to guess the discovery or invention that is being described.

- Score one point for each correct guess.

- After using all the squares, students may continue using their own ideas.

- You may assign one student in each group to be a fact checker, that is his or her job will be to query any facts that might be incorrect. These can be checked later for homework.

Self-Assessment Log

- ❑ The purpose of the log is to help the students reflect on their learning.

- ❑ Read the directions aloud and have students check vocabulary that they learned in the chapter and are prepared to use.

- ❑ Have students check the strategies they understand.

- ❑ Put students in small groups. Ask students to find the information or an activity related to each strategy in the chapter.

- ❑ Tell students to find definitions in the chapter for any words they did not check, or they can look in their dictionaries.

- ❑ Set a time limit of ten minutes.

Ceremonies

In this chapter, students will read about various topics related to ceremonies in different cultures. In Part 1, they will talk about a baby shower and learn how to make, accept, and decline offers. They will also practice stress in compound nouns. In Part 2, they will listen to a lecture about the use of water in traditional ceremonies in different parts of the world. They will learn to recognize digressions from the main topic. In Part 3, they will listen to conversations about ceremonies and practice affirmative tag questions. They will also practice offering congratulations and sympathy. In Part 4, they will talk about weddings.

Chapter Opener

❑ Have students look at the photo of a ceremony being conducted by Native American Chippewa Indian Chief, One Bear. He's holding up a peace pipe. Ask them the questions from the Connecting to the Topic section. Have students discuss as a class.

❑ Read and discuss the quote. How can the word *culture* be defined? How do cultures influence each other? Ask students for some examples from the past or the present.

❑ Brainstorm a list of adjectives to describe the picture.

❝ There is nothing like a ritual for making its participants think beyond their own appetites, and for making them feel that they belong to something greater, older and more important than themselves. ❞

—Tom Utley
British journalist (1921–1988)

Chapter Overview

Listening Skills and Strategies

Listening for main ideas

Listening for details

Making inferences

Recognizing the meaning of affirmative tag questions

Taking notes on wedding preferences

Speaking Skills and Strategies

Using expressions to offer, accept, or decline help

Talking about water in ceremonies around the world

Asking and answering affirmative tag questions

Offering congratulations and sympathy

Critical Thinking Skills

Getting meaning from context

Recognizing digressions in a lecture

Comparing celebrations across cultures

Vocabulary Building

Expressions to offer, accept, or decline help

Terms to express congratulations and sympathy

Expressions signaling digressions in a lecture

Terms related to ceremonies

Pronunciation

Identifying and practicing stressed words

Using correct stress in compound phrases

Language Skills

Using context clues to identify ceremonies

Vocabulary

Nouns	Verbs	Adjectives	Expression
mother-to-be	cleanse	allowed	go "ooh and ah"
prayer	focus on	due	
priest	host	fascinating	
ritual	involve	pregnant	
sin	narrow (something) down	pure	
symbol	play a part in	silly	
symbolism	pour		
	pray		
	purify		
	register		
	shower		
	sprinkle		
	symbolize		

Can You Guess?

- Ask students to discuss the questions below in groups and compare their answers with the correct answers.

- Discuss the issues raised by these questions: Why are ceremonies important? What kinds of ceremonies are more important in the U.S. and in other cultures?

1. In which culture are women wedding guests not allowed to wear white or black? A. *China*

2. What are the three most popular honeymoon places for Americans? A. *The Caribbean, Hawaii, and Mexico*

3. What culture celebrates a death with a three-day party of singing and drinking? A. *Irish*

Before You Listen

1   **Prelistening Questions**

- Ask students to describe the photo. Who are these people? What are they doing? What are they talking about? thinking? feeling? What kind of ceremony is it and why is it important?

- Discuss similar ceremonies in other cultures.

2   **Previewing Vocabulary**

- Play the recording and have students listen to the underlined words and expressions.

- Have students complete the exercise individually.

- Compare their answers as a whole class and write the correct answers on the board.

ANSWER KEY

1.d 2.a 3.f 4.g 5.c 6.b 7.h 8.i 9.e

Listen

3   **Comprehension Questions**

- Explain that these questions will help students focus on the main ideas in the listening.

- You may want to write the questions on the board.

- Read the questions aloud.

- Play the recording.

- After listening, have students compare their answers in pairs.

- Check the answers as a class.

ANSWER KEY

1. an invitation to a baby shower; 2. Sharon and Carolyn; 3. Jeff isn't invited because baby showers are usually only for women; 4. at the end of May; 5. give gifts, play silly games, eat cake; 6. In Japan, people don't usually open their gifts in front of the person who gave the gift; 7. online

AUDIOSCRIPT

Mari: Hi Jeff. Hi Sharon. Look what I got in the mail.

Jeff: Hey.

Sharon: Hi, Mari.

Jeff: "Join us for a baby shower honoring Nancy Anderson, April 5th, 11:00 A.M.... hosted by Sharon Smith and Carolyn Freeman..."

Sharon: Oh good, you got the invitation. So can you make it?

Mari: I think so, but, well, what is a baby shower exactly?

Jeff: You know, it's a party for a woman who's going to have a baby. Um, it's like a welcoming ceremony for the new baby.

Mari: It's a party? Then why do you call it a *shower*?

Jeff: Because the custom is to *shower* the woman with gifts for the baby. Get it?

Mari: I see. Are you invited too, Jeff?

Jeff: No way! No men allowed!

Mari: Really?

Sharon: Well, not exactly. Lots of baby showers include men these days, but traditionally showers are hosted by a woman's girlfriends or female relatives, and they're only for women.

Mari: Hmm. But isn't Nancy and Andrew's baby due at the end of May? And this invitation says April 5th.

Sharon: Well, yes. The custom is to have a shower *before* the baby is born, when the woman is seven or eight months pregnant.

Mari: Very interesting. And everybody brings a gift?

Sharon: Right. Something for the baby: you know, toys, or clothes, or something for the baby's room.

Mari: OK. The invitation says it's for lunch, so . . .

Sharon: Yeah, we'll have lunch, and afterwards, we'll play games.

Mari: Games? What kind of games?

Jeff: Girl games...

Sharon: Yeah, silly games, like bingo, or guessing games, or baby trivia games. And the winners get small prizes.

Mari: It sounds like fun.

Sharon: It is. And then, at the end of the party, there's usually a cake with baby decorations, and then the mother-to-be opens her presents.

Mari: While the guests are still there?

Sharon: Sure. That's my favorite part! Everybody gets to see the gifts.

Jeff: and go oooh, aaah . . .

Sharon: And see how happy the woman is.

Mari: Wow. That's so different from our custom. In Japan, we usually don't open a gift in front of guests.

Sharon: Really? That is different.

Mari: Well what kind of gift do you think I should get for her?

Sharon: She's registered online, so you can see what she's already gotten and what she still needs. Would you like me to write down the Internet address for you?

Mari: Sure, that would be great.

Mari: Uh, is there anything I can do to help with the party? Maybe do the flower arrangements or something?

Sharon: Oh, thanks, but it's not necessary. Everything is all taken care of. Just come and have fun.

Stress

4 **Listening for Stressed Words**

☐ Review the meaning of stressed words from the previous unit.

☐ Play the recording again.

☐ Have students write the missing words.

☐ After listening, have students check their answers with the audioscript in their books.

☐ Have students read the conversation with a partner, paying attention to stressed words in their pronunciation.

ANSWER KEY

Mari: Hmm. But isn't Nancy and Andrew's baby due at the end of _May_? And this invitation says April _5_.

Sharon: Well, yes. The custom is to have a shower _before_ the baby is born, when the woman is seven or eight months pregnant.

Mari: Very interesting. And everybody brings a _gift_?

Sharon: Right. Something for the baby: you know, _toys_, or clothes, or something for the baby's _room_.

Mari: OK. The _invitation_ says it's for lunch, so...

Sharon: Yeah, we'll have lunch, and _afterwards_, we'll play _games_.

Mari: Games? What _kind_ of games?

Jeff: _Girl_ games...

Sharon: Yeah, _silly_ games, like bingo, or guessing games, or baby trivia games. And the _winners_ get small prizes.

Mari: It _sounds_ like fun.

Sharon: It is. And then, at the _end_ of the party, there's usually a cake with _baby_ decorations, and then the mother-to-be opens her _presents_.

Mari: While the _guests_ are still there?

Sharon: Sure. That's my _favorite_ part! Everybody gets to see the gifts....

Jeff: and go oooh, aaah...

Sharon: . . . and see how _happy_ the woman is.

Mari: Wow. That's so _different_ from our custom. In Japan, we usually _don't open_ a gift in front of guests.

Sharon: Really? That _is_ different.

Mari: Well, what kind of gift do you think I should _get_ for her?

Sharon: She's registered _online_, so you can see what she's already _gotten_ and what she still needs. Would you like me to write down the _Internet_ address for you?

Mari: Sure, _that_ would be great.

After You Listen

5 Using Vocabulary

- ❏ Have students work in pairs to ask and answer these questions.
- ❏ You may want to set a time limit of ten minutes.
- ❏ Compare answers as a class.

Pronunciation

STRESS IN COMPOUND PHRASES

- ▪ Read the instruction note about noun + noun combinations, and adjective + noun combinations.
- ▪ Review the difference between syllable stress and word stress.

6 Pronouncing Noun + Noun **Combinations**

- ❏ Play the recording and have students repeat each phrase.

7 Pronouncing Adjective **+ Noun Combinations**

- ❏ Read the directions.
- ❏ If necessary, read the information in the box about adjective + noun combinations.
- ❏ Play the recording and have students repeat each phrase.

8 Predicting Stress

- ❏ Read the examples in the list.
- ❏ Have students mark the stress in each phrase before listening.

❑ Play the recording and have students check their answers.

❑ Check the answers as a class.

ANSWER KEY

1. young mother	stepmother
2. coffeepot	large pot
3. nice place	fire place
4. flashlight	green light
5. wedding cake	delicious cake
6. hair dryer	dry hair
7. busboy	tall boy
8. fast reader	mind reader

Using Language Functions

OFFERING TO DO SOMETHING

▪ Read the instruction note.

▪ Practice pronunciation and intonation of the phrases.

▪ Write the following list on the board and nominate students to offer, accept, and decline. Examples:
bring you a cup of coffee
help you with your homework
give you a lift home
help you fix your computer
visit you at home this weekend

Best Practice

Interacting with Others

This type of activity is an example of collaborative learning to encourage fluency and confidence. In this activity, communication is more important than grammar. Students can improve their confidence in offering, accepting, and declining offers by switching roles or partners and practicing the same situations again. By providing feedback to each other, they learn skills of self-evaluation.

---

9 **Role-Play**

❑ Have students work in pairs to discuss the photos and create a conversation about each one.

❑ Make sure they look at and use some of the expressions from page 227.

❑ Set a time limit of five minutes.

❑ Invite volunteers to role-play their conversations for the class.

REPRODUCIBLE EXPANSION ACTIVITY

▪ The purpose of this activity is to practice strategies for making, accepting, and declining offers.

▪ Please see Black Line Master "May I Help You?" on page BLM 28 of this Teacher's Edition. Photocopy enough so you have one strip for each student. (There are 10 strips on the page.)

▪ Cut the copies into strips so that you have one strip for each student.

▪ Have students walk around the room and say their sentence to each person they meet. The other students must respond with an offer. The first student will accept or decline the offer.

▪ Remind students to keep notes of what kinds of offers were made in response to their sentences. (They may summarize them later as a class in order of highest frequency.)

▪ Set a time limit of 10 to 15 minutes.

▪ Move around the room to monitor and provide feedback.

▪ Invite volunteers to summarize the offers that were made in response to their statements.

Before You Listen

- ❑ Read the text that introduces the next listening.
- ❑ Ask the students what they see in the photos.

1 Prelistening Discussion

- ❑ Have students work in small groups to discuss the list of meanings and add their own ideas.
- ❑ Review the responses as a class.

Best Practice

Making Use of Academic Content

This type of activity encourages students to connect personal and abstract knowledge. In academic lectures, content is often unrelated to students' daily lives. Students have to learn to connect the content to their own experiences in order to make it more meaningful and memorable. This exercise helps students to use their real-world knowledge and relate it to abstract concepts.

2 Previewing Vocabulary

- ❑ Play the recording and have students listen to the words and phrases.
- ❑ Have students check the words they know.
- ❑ Ask students to compare answers with a partner.

Listen

Best Practice

Scaffolding Instruction

This is an example of an activity that raises awareness of learning strategies. In real life, we use a combination of different strategies to identify and interpret information. In this exercise, students focus on recognizing digressions. Focusing on one strategy in this short section of the audio will help students to use this strategy independently in the context of the lecture.

Strategy

Digressing from (Going off) and Returning to the Topic

- ▪ Read the information in the box.
- ▪ Read the expressions aloud and ask students to say them aloud.
- ▪ Have them circle the expressions they've heard of. Remind them that they will hear all of them in the next activity.

3 Recognizing Digressions

- ❑ Explain that students will hear part of a lecture where the speaker digresses from the main topic. Their task is to identify the digressions by crossing them out.
- ❑ Play the recording.
- ❑ Have students cross out the appropriate topics.
- ❑ Play the recording again if necessary.
- ❑ Compare answers as a class.

ANSWER KEY

A. Thailand
   Speaker's experience
   — April: hottest time of year
   — ~~Thail. doesn't have four seasons.~~
   — ~~dry season: Nov.–Feb.~~
   — ~~hot season: March–June~~
   — ~~rainy season: July–Oct.~~
   — spkr was walking down street & teens threw water on him
   — reason: April 13th = Songkran
     Songkran = water festival
   — people throw water on each other
   — wash hands of elders w/ scented water
   — belief = water will wash away bad luck

AUDIOSCRIPT

So I thought I'd focus on that today: the role of water in celebrations around the world.

Let's take Thailand as an example. I'll never forget my first time there. It was April, the hottest part of the year. And by the way, Thailand doesn't have four seasons like we do here. Um, depending on which part of the country you're in, there are three seasons, the dry season from November to February, the hot season from March to June, and the rainy season from about July to October. Um, so anyway, back to our topic, I was walking down the street in the small village where I lived and suddenly, two teenagers walked past me and as they did, they threw water on me! I was kind of shocked but didn't really mind because it was so hot. Then I realized that it was the 13th, which is Songkran, the Water Festival in Thailand. On that day, people throw water on each other, and also wash the hands of their elders with scented water. It's a custom based on the belief that water will wash away bad luck.

4 Taking Notes

- ❑ Remind students of the keys to good note-taking. (See Chapter 1 pages 12 and 13.)
- ❑ Tell students they are going to hear a lecture about the use of water in ceremonies around the world.
- ❑ Play the recording.
- ❑ Students can take notes in their own way.

Culture Note

Go over the Culture Note about the Peace Corps. This will help give context for the next lecture.

AUDIOSCRIPT

Host: And now I'd like to introduce our speaker, Josh Harrison. Josh has just returned from his latest overseas assignment as a Peace Corps volunteer. He's served in at least three different countries and has traveled to many more than that; that's why I thought he'd be the perfect speaker for today's topic: ceremonies and celebrations around the world. Welcome, Josh.

Speaker: Thank you, Diane. And thanks for inviting me. Well, I've thought about the topic and I thought, gosh, how am I going to narrow this down? I mean, I have seen and participated in so many fascinating celebrations in many fascinating celebrations in many different cultures. Then I remembered something I noticed just recently: Even though the cultures I experienced were completely different, many of their ceremonies had something interesting in common: the use of water. Yeah, water. Some ceremonies involve drinking the water, some involve pouring it, and some involve dunking or going under water. To me, that was a very interesting discovery.

So I thought I'd focus on that today: the role of water in celebrations around the world.

Let's take Thailand as an example. I'll never forget my first time there. It was April, the hottest part of the year. And by the way, Thailand doesn't have four seasons like we do here. Um, depending on which part of the country you're in, there are three seasons, the dry season from November to February, the hot season from March to June, and the rainy season from about July to October. Um, so anyway, back to our topic, I was walking down the street in the small village where I lived and suddenly, two teenagers walked past me and as they did, they threw water on me! I was kind of shocked but didn'treally mind because it was so hot. Then I realized that it was the 13th, which is Songkran, the Water Festival in Thailand. On that day, people throw water on each other, and also wash the hands of their elders with scented water. It's a custom based on the belief that water will wash away bad luck.

Now, this idea of washing away bad things, of cleansing or purifying, is also found in Islamic cultures. For example, when I lived in Saudi Arabia, I learned that traditional Muslims pray five times a day, and before they do, they always wash their faces, hands, and feet with water. And the water has to be very clean and pure. This ritual washing symbolizes the removal of sin and disease, in other words, the cleansing of both body and soul, before speaking to God.

All right, now, another religion where water plays an important role is Christianity. And one particular ritual that comes to mind is baptism. Baptism is a ceremony that welcomes a new baby into the Christian religion and the community. Now, since there are many branches of Christianity, there are also many different ways that baptism can be performed. When I lived in Latin America, I attended several Catholic baptisms. And what they do is they bring the baby to the church, where a priest pours or sprinkles some water on the baby's head. This water symbolizes the washing away of sin—somewhat similar to the meaning in Islam. And then, while pouring the water, the priest says a prayer and tells the parents to raise the baby as a good Christian.

So as you can see, water has different symbolic meanings in

different cultures. In some cultures, it's believed to keep away bad luck, as in Thailand. In Islamic and Christian cultures, it's used to purify and wash away sin. Water has rich symbolism in nearly all cultures. So now I'd like to know what you think and see if you can share some of your own traditions. How does water play a part in celebrations in *your* culture?

5 **Outlining the Lecture**

❑ Ask students to use their notes to complete the outline.

❑ Play the recording again.

❑ Have students fill in any missing information.

❑ Check the answers as a class.

ANSWER KEY

I. Intro

Speaker: _Josh Harrison, Peace Corps volunteer_

General Topic: _ceremonies and celebrations_
around the world

II. Specific Topic: _the role of water in celebrations_
around the world

A. _Thailand_
April 13th, Songkran, the Water Festival in
Thailand
people throw water on each other
wash hands of elders with scented water
believe that water will wash away bad luck

B. _Islamic cultures, e.g., Saudi Arabia_
Muslims pray 5 x a day
before they pray, wash faces, hands, & feet
with water
water v. clean and pure
symbolizes the removal of sin & disease,
cleansing of body and soul before speaking
to God

C. Christian ceremony: baptism
welcomes new baby into Christian religion and community

e.g., Latin America
bring baby to churchpriest pours water on baby's head
symbolizes washing away sin — similar to Islam
while pouring water, priest says a prayer and tells parents to raise baby as a good Christian

III. Conclusion
water has different symbolic meanings in diff. cultures:
in Thailand: keep away bad luck
in Islamic and Christian cultures: purify and wash away sin

After You Listen

Best Practice

Activating Prior Knowledge

This is an example of an activity that encourages students to make text-to-self connections. The discussion questions ask students to explore their existing knowledge on the use of water in ceremonies. They can then add the new information to their existing knowledge framework. This aids understanding and retention of new material.

6 **Discussing the Lecture**

❑ Have students discuss the questions as a whole class or in groups.

❑ Encourage students to use the new vocabulary in their discussion.

❑ Ask for representatives from each group to report to the class on the discussion.

7 **Reviewing Vocabulary**

❑ Ask students to look back at the vocabulary in Activity 2 on page 230 in the Student Book and to test each other in pairs.

❑ Invite volunteers to give examples sentences using the new vocabulary.

Talk It Over

Best Practice

Organizing Information

This is an example of a graphic organizer called a multi-column chart. This type of study tool helps students to organize new information so that it is easier to recall. It will also help them when they want to review their notes. There are many types of graphic organizers used in this book.

8 Interview

- ❏ Read the information in the *Graphic Organizer: Multi-Column Chart* box.

- ❏ Read the directions in the activity.

- ❏ Read the information in the multi-column chart.

- ❏ Ask for suggestions for completing the final box in the first row.

- ❏ Have students work in pairs to interview each other. If there is time, they can interview two or three students. You may want to assign this as homework.

- ❏ Invite students to present their findings to the class.

REPRODUCIBLE   EXPANSION ACTIVITY

- ▥ The purpose of this activity is to practice using the Internet for research and to gain an understanding of ceremonies in different cultures.

- ▥ Students can use a search engine to find the vocabulary items or use keywords, for example, *birthday traditions*.

- ▥ The research part of this activity can be done in a computer lab class or assigned for homework.

- ▥ Please see Black Line Master "Ceremonies Around the World" on page BLM 29 of this Teacher's Edition. Photocopy and distribute one to each student.

- ▥ Have students work in groups to choose a ceremony (encourage groups to choose ceremonies that are different from each other) and complete as much of the chart as they can.

- ▥ Have students use the Internet to research the rest of the information.

- ▥ Have students re-form their groups and share their information to complete the chart.

- ▥ Invite volunteers to summarize their findings to the class.

Getting Meaning from Context

Focus on Testing

Using Context Clues

- Review strategies for getting meaning from context.

- Explain that students will hear five different conversations about ceremonies.

- Read the list of ceremonies and check comprehension of each one.

- Play the recording, pausing after each one to allow time for students to write their answers.

- Check the answers as a class.

- Ask students to identify context clues in each conversation that helped them identify the topic.

ANSWER KEY

1.f   2.c   3.d   4.a   5.g

1   **Talking About Ceremonies**

- ❏ Have students work in groups to discuss their experiences of these ceremonies.

- ❏ Make a list of other ceremonies that are important in their cultures.

- ❏ As a class, discuss why ceremonies are important in society. What is their function and purpose? Are they becoming more or less important?

AUDIOSCRIPT

Conversation 1

Man 1: And now, on behalf of our entire staff, I'd like to present this gold watch to Mr. Harry Kim and express our appreciation for 35 years of dedicated service to our company. Congratulations, Mr. Kim!

Mr. Kim: Thank you, Mr. President. All I can say is, it's been a pleasure working with you all these years. This company has been like a second family to me.

Man 1: What are you going to do with your time from now on?

Mr. Kim: I'm going to play a lot of golf, work in my garden, and visit my grandchildren.

Conversation 2

Woman: Well, that was a very moving service. And I never saw so many flowers. She sure had a lot of friends.

Man: Yep. And the minister spoke beautifully, didn't he? I'm sure it was a comfort to the family.

Woman: I am really going to miss Myra. She was a good neighbor and a good friend.

Man: I can't imagine what Ralph is going to do without her. They were married, what, 40 years?

Woman: Something like that, yes. Poor Ralph.

Conversation 3

Girl: Here they come! Look Mommy, there's Shawna!

Mother: Where?

Girl: She's walking in behind that really tall guy, see?

Mother: Oh yes, yes, I see her. Doesn't she look elegant in her cap and gown, honey? So grown up . . .

Girl: What's going to happen now?

Father: After everyone sits down there'll be speeches, and then they'll give out the diplomas.

Mother: I can't believe that three months from now our little girl is going to be starting college.

Father: I know. Where did the time go?

Conversation 4

Daughter: And now I'd like to propose a toast. To my parents, Lena and Richard: May your next thirty years together be as happy and prosperous as the first thirty have been. Thanks for being an inspiration to us all. Cheers!

All: Cheers! Congratulations!

Father: Thank you, Betsy, and thank you all for coming out to celebrate with us on this happy occasion. You're the best group of friends anyone ever had and we're very grateful. And now *I'd* like to propose a toast: To my wife Lena, who's as beautiful today as she was on our first date more than 30 years ago. To you, darling!

All: Cheers!

Conversation 5

Mother: How are the plans coming?

Daughter: I met with the caterer yesterday and tomorrow we'll order the flowers. We have the rings, and oh, my dress will be ready next Wednesday.

Mother: What about the band for the reception?

Daughter: We hired them months ago. And we ordered the cake too.

Mother: Speaking of cake . . . You and Robert aren't going to shove cake in each other's faces, are you?

Daughter: No, Mom, don't worry.

Focused Listening

Strategy

Affirmative Tag Questions

Read the instruction note and practice the intonation of the examples.

2 **Recognizing the Meaning of** **Affirmative Tag Questions**

❑ Explain that students will hear eight different questions. They will listen and choose the correct interpretation of each question.

❑ Play the recording while students write their answers.

❑ Review the answers as a class.

ANSWER KEY

1.b 2.a 3.b 4.a 5.b 6.b 7.a 8.b

AUDIOSCRIPT

1. Alia didn't forget to buy flowers again, did she? (rising)

2. That wasn't a very long ceremony, was it? (falling)

3. We don't need to bring a present, do we? (rising)

4. You're not going to wear that shirt to the party, are you? (rising)

5. There aren't many people here, are there? (falling)

6. You're not bringing your dog, are you? (rising)

7. The wedding hasn't started yet, has it? (rising)

8. You didn't like the party, did you? (falling)

ANSWERING AFFIRMATIVE TAG QUESTIONS

- Read the information in the box.

- Read the questions and answers. Then have students practice asking and answering them in pairs.

3 Asking and Answering Affirmative Tag Questions

- ❏ Have students work in pairs.

- ❏ Student A should look at page 251 in the Student Book. Student B should look at page 259.

- ❏ Set a time limit of five minutes.

- ❏ Move around the room to monitor and provide feedback.

- ❏ Review the answers as a class.

ANSWER KEY

Student A:

a) You don't smoke, do you?

b) There's no homework tonight, is there?

c) It isn't raining, is it?

d) You don't have children (grandchildren, sisters, brothers), do you?

Student B:

a) You don't eat meat, do you?

b) There's no test tomorrow, is there?

c) You don't have a computer (cell phone), do you?

d) Milk isn't good for adults, is it?

Using Language Functions

OFFERING CONGRATULATIONS AND SYMPATHY

- Read the information in the *Offering Congratulations and Sympathy* box.

- Practice the expressions using appropriate intonation.

4 Role-Play

- ❏ Read the directions for the activity. Have students work in pairs to role-play each of the situations. When they have finished, they can change partners and practice them again.

- ❏ Ask for volunteers to role-play their conversations for the class.

REPRODUCIBLE **EXPANSION ACTIVITY**

- The aim of this activity is to practice the language of offering and responding to congratulations and sympathy.

- Please see Black Line Master "Congratulations and Sympathy" on page BLM 30 of this Teacher's Edition. Photocopy enough so you have one strip for each student. (There are 15 strips on the page.)

- Cut the copies into strips so that you have one strip for each student.

- Have students walk around the room and say their sentence to each person they meet. The other students must respond with an expression of congratulations or sympathy. The first student will then respond appropriately.

- Set a time limit of ten minutes.

- At the end, select individual students to read out their sentence and choose another student in the class to respond.

❑ Read the information about Katsu and Sandra and look at the pictures. Ask students to predict what kind of wedding these people might want to have.

> ### Culture Note
> Read the information in the Culture Note. Ask students to describe their idea of a typical U.S. wedding. Compare with weddings in other cultures if appropriate.

Before You Listen

1   Comparing Wedding Preferences

❑ Read the chart and check comprehension of any new vocabulary.

❑ Have students complete the chart individually and compare answers in groups.

Listen

> ### Best Practice
>
> #### Cultivating Critical Thinking
> This is an example of an activity that requires students to solve a problem collaboratively. Each group of students has a different set of information. They will need to share their information in order to complete the task. This involves comparing, evaluating, and synthesizing information.

2   Taking Notes on Wedding Preferences

❑ You may want to do this activity in a computer lab, or use two audio players in two separate rooms.

❑ Explain that students will divide into two groups and each group will listen to a different recording.

❑ Nominate one person in each group to be in charge of starting, stopping, and replaying the recording.

❑ Set a time limit of ten minutes.

❑ As they listen, they will try to complete the chart.

❑ Bring the groups back together.

AUDIOSCRIPT
Katsu

Consultant: OK, Katsu, to get started, why don't you look at this list for the wedding ceremony, and let me just ask you first of all if there are any items that you have really strong feelings about, like you absolutely must do this or you absolutely refuse to do that . . .

Katsu: Hmm . . . Well, I really don't want a religious service. I think a big, traditional American service would be very strange for my parents. So I'd prefer to get married outdoors, in a garden or something, and have a justice of the peace perform the service.

Consultant: OK. Have you and Sandra discussed a date?

Katsu: Not an exact date but we agree that we'd like to do it in April or May.

Consultant: Got it. What else?

Katsu: I'd like it small, just our families and close friends. And informal. I don't want to wear a tuxedo, and I don't want bridesmaids and all those extra people. I think it would be nice if each of us walked in with our parents and that's it. I really want to honor my parents at my wedding.

Consultant: OK, Katsu, obviously you know that Sandra's family is Christian and they've been in America for generations. So let me ask you, is there anything from that tradition

	that you really like and would want to include in your ceremony?
Katsu:	Let's see . . . Well I'm sure Sandra will want to wear a white dress and that's fine. And, um, well, I don't like organ music, but maybe we could have a flute and a violin, something soft like that.
Consultant:	And what about Japanese culture? Is there something you'd like to include from that?
Katsu:	Wow. That's a hard question. I've never been to a traditional Japanese wedding. But I know that in Japan purple is, like, the color of love, so maybe Sandra could carry purple flowers.

Sandra

Consultant:	OK, Sandra, to start off, I'm going to ask you the same question I asked Katsu. Look at this list of items in a typical wedding ceremony and tell me if there's anything you feel very strongly about.
Sandra:	Well, I've always dreamed of having a big traditional wedding, you know, in a church, with an organ playing, and bridesmaids and groomsmen, and a beautiful white dress. But that was before I met Katsu. His family isn't Christian, you know, and my family's not super religious either, so maybe we could have a garden wedding instead of a church. But I'd like my family's minister to perform the service, and I definitely want my father to walk me down the aisle, and I want my little cousin to be our flower girl. I guess the most important thing is to be able to include everybody. My family is huge, and I want to invite them all.
Consultant:	So you want to wear a white dress.

Sandra:	Of course.
Consultant:	And what about Katsu?
Sandra:	He hates anything formal. It's fine if he wears a suit.
Consultant:	OK, Sandra. Tell me, do you like the color purple?
Sandra:	Purple? At a wedding?
Consultant:	Katsu suggested you could carry purple flowers. He says that in Japanese culture purple is the color of love.
Sandra:	Hmmm . . . purple. That could work. I love irises, and maybe the bridesmaids' dresses could be violet.
Consultant:	That sounds like a wonderful idea. What about music?
Sandra:	Well, if we're outdoors, then we can't have an organ, can we; so, hmmm, how about something soft like classical guitar or flute?

After You Listen

3 Discussion

❑ Help students find a partner from the other group.

❑ In pairs, students will try to complete the chart by asking their partner for information.

❑ Compare answers as a class.

ANSWER KEY

	Sandra	Katsu
Location	garden	outside, in a garden
Date/time of year	(no exact time is mentioned, but it's probably warm weather because Sandra says "...if we're outdoors then...")	April or May
Type of service/ ceremony (e.g., religious, traditional, modern)	religious, family minister	not religious, justice of the peace
Number of guests (approx.)	all the family	close friends and parents
Attendants (bridesmaids, groomsmen, etc.)	flower girl, bridesmaids	none
Role of parents/ grandparents	walk down aisle with father	walk in with parents
Clothing	Sandra: white dress Katsu: suit bridesmaids: violet dresses	Sandra: white dress and purple flowers Katsu: no tuxedo
Music	classical guitar or flute	flute and violin, soft music
Colors	white, violet	white and purple
Other details	Irises sake-sharing ceremony	-----------------

Talk It Over

4 Role-Play

❑ Have students work in groups to role-play planning a wedding.

❑ Then they will role-play a conversation among Katsu, Sandra, and the wedding planner.

❑ They should come to an agreement about all the details of the wedding ceremony.

EXPANSION ACTIVITY

▨ The aim of this activity is to practice affirmative tag questions and answers.

▨ Have students work individually to write down the details of their ideal birthday party. You may suggest the following categories: People/ Place/ Food/ Music/ Activities.

▨ Then students will work in pairs to plan a birthday party. Have them ask and answer affirmative tag questions.

Example:

Your friends will give you lots of presents, won't they?

▨ After five minutes, invite volunteers to summarize the details of their party to the class.

Self-Assessment Log

❑ The purpose of the log is to help the students reflect on their learning.

❑ Read the directions aloud and have students check vocabulary that they learned in the chapter and are prepared to use.

❑ Have students check the strategies they understand.

❑ Put students in small groups. Ask students to find the information or an activity related to each strategy in the chapter.

❑ Tell students to find definitions in the chapter, or look in their dictionaries.

Chapter 1 Part 1: Class Survey

Why do you want to study English?
What subject do you want to major in or did you major in and why?
What kind of job or career do you have or want in the future?
What do you like to do in your free time?
How do you study English outside of class?
What other courses have you signed up for?
What is the most difficult thing about learning English?
What is the most difficult thing about going to college?
What is the easiest thing about learning English?
What skills do you most need to improve in your English?

Name _____ Date _____

Chapter 1 Part 2: What is Plagiarism?

Part 1: Form groups of four students. Each person in the group will choose one of the questions below. Each person will research information about the question and share it with the group.

1. What is the definition of plagiarism? Give one example of what is plagiarism and one example of what is *not* plagiarism. Why is it important?	**2.** Find three different categories of plagiarism.
3. Find three strategies for avoiding plagiarism.	**4.** Describe three possible consequences of academic plagiarism.

Part 2: In your groups, describe one example of plagiarism (real or imaginary) and discuss how you would respond to it if you were a teacher.

Example of plagiarism: (e.g., copying from a textbook)

_____

Teacher's response:

_____

_____

BLM 3

Name _____ Date _____

Chapter 1 Part 3: Would You Like to . . .?

1. Check the activities below that you like to do. Add three activities.

2. Choose four things you want to do next week and write them in your calendar.

3. Invite other students to go with you and write their names in your calendar.

❑ go to a movie   ❑ go shopping in the mall   ❑ play racquetball

❑ have dinner at my home ❑ go to a music concert   ❑ go roller skating

❑ have lunch at a restaurant ❑ go to a party   ❑ _____

❑ visit a museum   ❑ go dancing   ❑ _____

❑ go to the zoo   ❑ watch a baseball game   ❑ _____

	Morning	**Afternoon**	**Evening**
Monday			
Tuesday			
Wednesday			
Thursday			
Friday			
Saturday			
Sunday			

Chapter 2 Part 1: Looking for a Place to Live

You are looking for a place to live. You want a room in a house that is clean, quiet, and near school.
You are looking for a place to live. You want a large room in a house with a garden because you have a very nice friendly dog.
You are looking for a place to live. You want a place where you can practice guitar and drums because you are in a rock group.
You are looking for a place to live. You want a large room in a house with other students. You need parking for your car.
You are looking for a place to live. You want a room in a house that has a large kitchen because you love cooking and you like to invite your friends for dinner.
You are looking for a roommate. You have a small room in a house near the school. No pets. No noise. No parking.
You are looking for a roommate. You have a large room in a house near the school. Large garden. No parking.
You are looking for a roommate. You have a small room in your house. There are three musicians living there. No parking. No neighbors close by.
You are looking for a roommate. You have a large room in your house. There are three other students. Parking is available.
You are looking for a roommate. You have a small room in a house with a large kitchen. No pets. No parking. No noise after 10 P.M.

Name _____ Date _____

Chapter 2 Part 2: Safety on Campus

Part 1: Form groups of four students and have each student choose one of the issues below. Each member of the group will research safety tips about the issue. Write the information in the mind map below.

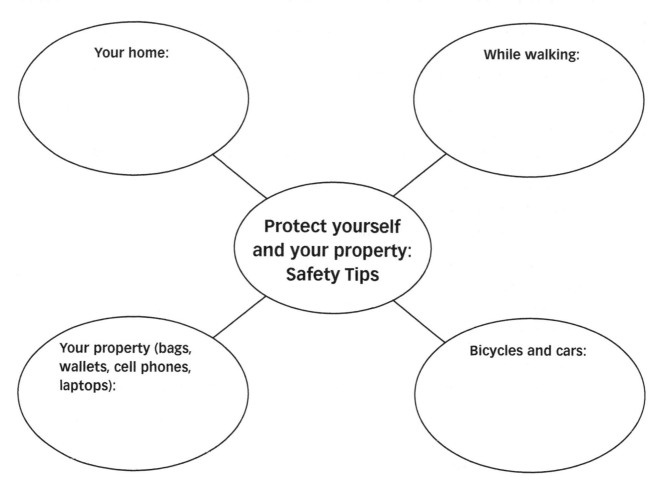

Part 2: Share your information with the group. As you listen to other group members, write the information in the mind map above.

Name _____ Date _____

Chapter 2 Part 3: Can You Fix It?

Part 1: Read the list of problems in the box. Discuss them with your group. Who would you call to fix each problem? Write each problem in a box in the chart.

broken window	broken shower curtain	lights don't work
dripping faucet	broken front door	no electricity
broken toilet	mice	cockroaches
leaking water pipe	bugs in the food	refrigerator doesn't work
microwave doesn't work	broken closet door	shower doesn't work

Plumber	Electrician

Carpenter	Exterminator

Fix it yourself

Part 2: Role-play a conversation with your landlord complaining about one of the problems.

Name _____ Date _____

Chapter 3 Part 1: Lend or Borrow?

Directions: Half of the class will be A and the other half will be B. Take this paper and a pencil. Stand up and move around the classroom. Group A students ask classmates to lend them each of the things in Table A. Group B students are able to lend each of the things in Table B only one time. When you borrow or lend an item write the student's name in the chart. Use *lend* or *borrow* in your requests.

Example: A: Excuse me. Can you do me a favor? Could you lend me your cell phone, please? (or Can I borrow your cell phone, please?)

B. Yes, of course. / No, I'm sorry. I lent it to (student's name).

Table A:

Items you want to borrow	Student's Name
textbook	
watch	
cell phone	
pen	
phone card	
dictionary	

Table B:

Items you can lend	Student's Name
cell phone	
pen	
phone card	
dictionary	
textbook	
watch	

Try to lend and borrow all the items on your lists. Then switch roles—group A will be group B and group B will be group A.

Name _____ Date _____

Chapter 3 Part 2: Famous Entrepreneurs

Part 1: Form groups of four students and choose one of the famous entrepreneurs listed below. Each member of the group will research information about this entrepreneur and then share it with the group.

Michael Dell (computers)   Debbie Fields (cookies)

Sam Walton (supermarkets)   Mary Kay Ash (cosmetics)

1.	**2.**
Name:	Name:
Innovation:	Innovation:
Background:	Background:
Secret of success:	Secret of success:
3.	**4.**
Name:	Name:
Innovation:	Innovation:
Background:	Background:
Secret of success:	Secret of success:

Part 2: In your groups, take a vote on which entrepreneur you admire the most and why. Report the results to the class.

Entrepreneur I admire the most: _____

Reason: _____

Chapter 3 Part 3: Group Survey

Everybody in this group has a bank account.

Number of students: Yes _____ No _____

Most people in this group have a savings account.

Number of students: Yes _____ No _____

Almost everyone in this group has a credit card.

Number of students: Yes _____ No _____

Some people in this group pay their bills online.

Number of students: Yes _____ No _____

No one in this group dislikes using an ATM.

Number of students: Yes _____ No _____

Most people in this group have bought something online.

Number of students: Yes _____ No _____

Most people in this group use a debit card when they go shopping.

Number of students: Yes _____ No _____

Everyone in this group pays their bills by check.

Number of students: Yes _____ No _____

Most people in this group keep a record of their checks each month.

Number of students: Yes _____ No _____

No one in this group has a safety deposit box.

Number of students: Yes _____ No _____

Chapter 3 Part 4: Balancing Your Checkbook

Student A

No.	Date	Description	Payment	Deposit	Balance
					598.12
150	5/21	Phone			480.06
151	5/21		60.17		419.89
152	5/23	Auto payment	160.00		
153	5/26	Groceries			79.75
	5/30	Deposit		625.00	704.75
154	6/02		219.45		
155	6/03	Credit card payment			70.30
	6/05	Deposit			386.30
156	6/08	Groceries			236.13
157	6/09		15.00		221.13

Student B

No.	Date	Description	Payment	Deposit	Balance
					598.12
150	5/21		118.06		480.06
151	5/21	Gas	60.17		
152	5/23	Auto payment			259.89
153	5/26		180.14		79.75
	5/30	Deposit			
154	6/02	House insurance			485.30
155	6/03		415.00		
	6/05	Deposit		316.00	386.30
156	6/08	Groceries	150.17		236.13
157	6/09	Doctor			

Chapter 4 Part 1: Saying You're Sorry

You borrowed your friend's dictionary and left it on the train.
You promised to meet your friend in the library after school yesterday, but you forgot and went home.
You borrowed ten dollars from your friend and said you would pay it back today, but you can't.
You can't go to your friend's birthday party because you have a date with your girlfriend or boyfriend.
Your friend gave you a very nice mug for your birthday, and you broke it.
You promised to take your friend to a baseball game on Saturday, but now you can't go.
You borrowed your friend's cell phone and used up all the free minutes.
You promised to buy your friend some potato chips in the coffee shop, but you forgot.
You borrowed your friend's bicycle and crashed it. It's a little damaged.
You didn't have time to help your friend study for an exam, and she failed.

Name _____ Date _____

Chapter 4 Part 2: Researching Your Career

Part 1: Form groups of four students. Each student will choose a different job and write the job title in the #1 position in the chart below. Use the Internet to complete the information about your job.

Part 2: Go back to your groups and share your information. Listen, ask questions, and take notes on the three other jobs researched by your group.

Job	Training and qualifications needed	Possible places of employment	Websites
#1:			
#2:			
#3:			
#4:			

Part 3: Discuss your opinions about these four jobs. Which job do you think a) needs the most training and qualifications b) is most in demand c) is the most stressful?

Name _____   Date _____

Chapter 4 Part 4: Tag Questions

Directions: Complete the questions with the appropriate tag.

1. This homework is for tomorrow, _____?

2. They are coming to lunch with us, _____?

3. We are going to have a break soon, _____?

4. You live near the school, _____?

5. He has a car, _____?

6. You were absent yesterday, _____?

7. The teacher gave you an *A*, _____?

8. She took her college exam last week, _____?

9. You'll help me with my homework, _____?

10. We'll finish early today, _____?

11. I got the best grade on the quiz, _____?

12. You have to work late tonight, _____?

13. They study very hard, _____?

14. You're worried about the test, _____?

15. Our teacher's very strict, _____?

16. You know how to drive, _____?

17. She takes the bus to school, _____?

18. We have to finish this activity at home, _____?

Name _____   Date _____

Chapter 5 Part 1: Can You Do Me a Favor?

Part 1: Take this paper and a pencil. Walk around the classroom. Ask classmates to do each of these favors for you. Your classmates will refuse with an excuse. (The excuse can be creative or unusual.) Write the student's name and his or her excuse in the chart.

Example

Student A: Can you do me a favor?

Student B: Sure, what do you need?

Student A: Would you mind looking after my cat this weekend?

Student B: Sorry but I'm allergic to cats.

Favor	Student's name	Excuse
1. look after my cat this weekend		
2. help me fix my computer		
3. give me a lift to the airport tomorrow morning		
4. help me take boxes to my car		
5. lend me your phone card		
6. lend me $20		
7. help me with some gardening this weekend		
8. do some shopping for me tonight		
9. get me a sandwich from the coffee shop		
10. lend me your English dictionary		

Part 2: When you have finished, sit down with a partner and compare answers. Who had the most creative excuse?

Name _____ Date _____

Chapter 5 Part 2: Starting a Workplace Day Care Center

Part 1: Form groups of four students and have each student choose one of the roles below. Each member of the group will research information to support the opinions of his or her role.

Role 1: Working mother

You are a working mother. You want to return to work because you are well qualified and you enjoy your job. But childcare is very expensive and unreliable. You want to start a day care center in your company. Research the advantages for the company and present your arguments.

Role 2: Company manager

You are under a lot of pressure from the company director to maintain profits in your company. Research the reasons why it would not be cost-effective to start a day care center in your company and present your arguments.

Role 3: Workplace child care company representative

You have a lot of experience providing day care facilities to companies. Research the kinds of services you could offer and reasons why the company should use your services and present your arguments.

Role 4: Employee representative

Many of your co-workers are against workplace day care because it will cost too much and may reduce other benefits or salaries. Research possible alternatives to providing workplace day care and present your arguments.

Part 2: After researching the information for your role, go back to your group. Role-play a company discussion about starting a workplace day care center. Take notes of the arguments in the chart below.

Arguments in favor	Arguments against

Part 3: Present your final decision to the class and explain the reasons.

BLM 16

Name _____ Date _____

Chapter 5 Part 3: Questionnaire

Directions: Read the sentences and check Agree or Disagree, giving your own opinion. Then work in groups. Try to agree on your responses.

What do you think....?
1. Mothers should stay home to look after their children until they go to school.   My opinion: _____ Agree _____ Disagree   Group opinion: _____ Agree _____ Disagree
2. Fathers should stay home from work to look after their children.   My opinion: _____ Agree _____ Disagree   Group opinion: _____ Agree _____ Disagree
3. All companies should have free child care facilities for their workers.   My opinion: _____ Agree _____ Disagree   Group opinion: _____ Agree _____ Disagree
4. Parents should get paid by the government for looking after their children.   My opinion: _____ Agree _____ Disagree   Group opinion: _____ Agree _____ Disagree
5. Stay-at-home parents should be paid for doing housework.   My opinion: _____ Agree _____ Disagree   Group opinion: _____ Agree _____ Disagree
6. Families should have no more than two children.   My opinion: _____ Agree _____ Disagree   Group opinion: _____ Agree _____ Disagree
7. Elderly parents should be looked after at home by their children.   My opinion: _____ Agree _____ Disagree   Group opinion: _____ Agree _____ Disagree
8. Elderly people should live in retirement homes.   My opinion: _____ Agree _____ Disagree   Group opinion: _____ Agree _____ Disagree

Chapter 6 Part 1: Interrupting Politely

In what way is communicating by email better than by phone?	Why are text messages popular?	What are some dangers of Internet communication for children?	What is most annoying about emails?
How are cell phones different from landline phones?	Why do people like to have blogs?	What are some possible negative effects of email?	What is the best thing about emails?
Why do people write letters less than they did in the past?	Which do you prefer, email or telephone?	How can the Internet help you with your studies?	How can the Internet help you to stay in touch with other people?
What is one way of cutting down on emails?	What is most annoying about cell phones?	What is most useful about cell phones?	What do you think will be the next major development in communication technology?

BLM 18

Name _____ Date _____

Chapter 6 Part 2: Naming Practices

Part 1: Form groups of four students. Each student will choose one of the countries below and write the country in the chart under Country #1. Use the Internet to complete the information about naming practices in that country.

Part 2: Go back to your groups and share your information. Take notes on the other countries researched by your group. Write your notes in the chart.

Part 3: Summarize the differences and similarities in the naming practices of all four countries.

Choose a country:

| Spain | Vietnam | Iceland | Nigeria |

	System for choosing names	Examples of names
Country #1: _____		
Country #2: _____		
Country #3: _____		
Country #4: _____		

Name _____ Date _____

Chapter 7 Part 1: Do You Agree?

Directions: Read and complete each sentence, giving your opinion and a reason for your opinion. Some sentences have phrases in parentheses. Choose the positive or negative in each sentence, depending on your opinion.

1. Languages are (are not) difficult to learn because…
2. It is easier to learn another language if…
3. The best way to learn a language is…
4. Misunderstandings usually happen when…
5. We need (don't need) different languages in the world because…
6. You need (don't need) to know about grammar because…
7. Learning in a group is helpful (unhelpful) because…
8. Children should (should not) learn a second or third language because…
9. American English is…
10. British English is…

Name _____ Date _____

Chapter 7 Part 2: Varieties of English

Part 1: Translate the words and expressions into standard American English.

Part 2: Check your answers by researching them on the Internet.

Part 3: Add some more examples for each category.

Canadian English	Australian English
Vocabulary	**Vocabulary**
chesterfield _____	*barbie* _____
runners _____	*esky* _____
Expressions	**Expressions**
Hang up your skates. _____	*Good day.* _____
Is that skookum? _____	*I'm feeling crook.* _____
Additional examples:	**Additional examples:**
_____	_____
_____	_____
_____	_____

British English	
Vocabulary	
queue _____	
chips _____	
Expressions	
I'm over the moon. _____	
He's at sixes and sevens. _____	
Additional examples:	
_____	
_____	
_____	

Name _____ Date _____

Chapter 7 Part 4: Spelling Bee

Directions: Take turns reading each word aloud to your partner. Your partner will spell the word aloud. Give one point for each correct answer.

Student A

accommodation   _____

independent   _____

separate   _____

disappointed   _____

business   _____

apparent   _____

believe   _____

misspell   _____

license   _____

occasionally   _____

Student B

Directions: Take turns reading each word aloud to your partner. Your partner will spell the word aloud. Give one point for each correct answer.

neighbor   _____

accidentally   _____

changeable   _____

pronunciation   _____

questionnaire   _____

argument   _____

guarantee   _____

height   _____

jewelry   _____

weather   _____

Name _____ Date _____

Chapter 8 Part 1: What Kind of Person Are You?

Student A

Directions: Find out if your partner likes or dislikes the following.

Do you like to . . .	I love it.	It's OK.	I can't stand it.
1. . . . have long conversations on the phone?			
2. . . . talk to other people about your problems?			
3. . . . invite all your friends on your birthday?			
4. . . . go to parties and meet new people?			
5. . . . cook for family and friends?			
6. . . . go out with a group of friends?			
7. . . . be busy all day?			
8. . . . have a job where you can meet lots of people?			
9. . . . meet your friends every lunch break?			
10. . . . go out with your friends every night?			

Scoring system:

I love it. = 3 points

It's OK. = 2 points

I can't stand it. = 1 point

Score:

20–30: You are very sociable and outgoing. You love meeting people and talking.

10–20: You are sometimes sociable, but you like to have your privacy, too.

1–10: You are shy and quiet. You like to have a few close friends who understand you.

Name _____ Date _____

Chapter 8 Part 1: What Kind of Person Are You?

Student B

Directions: Find out if your partner likes or dislikes the following.

Do you like to . . .	I love it.	It's OK.	I can't stand it.
1. . . . read a book when you want to relax?			
2. . . . think quietly on your own when you have a problem?			
3. . . . celebrate your birthday alone?			
4. . . . go to parties where you know everyone?			
5. . . . read a book or a magazine on your lunch break?			
6. . . . go out with just one or two good friends?			
7. . . . be alone for a part of every day?			
8. . . . have a job where you can concentrate and not talk?			
9. . . . have coffee by yourself in a coffee shop?			
10. . . . stay home most nights and go out only once a week?			

Scoring system:

I love it. = 3 points

It's OK. = 2 points

I can't stand it. = 1 point

Score:

20–30: You are very sociable and outgoing. You love meeting people and talking.

10–20: You are sometimes sociable, but you like to have your privacy, too.

1–10: You are shy and quiet. You like to have a few close friends who understand you.

Name _____   Date _____

Chapter 8 Part 2: What Do You Mean?

Directions: Complete the following sentences with appropriate paraphrases:

1. Most jobs nowadays require some computer skills. In other words, there are very few jobs

   that _____.

2. Two-thirds of all teenagers in the U.S. have a cell phone. To put it another way,

   _____.

3. If you want to get the latest music downloads, you have to go online. What I mean is

   _____.

4. More people tend to watch movies at home on video nowadays. That is to say, fewer people

   _____.

5. Higher gas prices mean that people are buying smaller cars. In other words, people aren't

   _____.

6. There has been an increase in demand for sport vacations in distant locations. In other words,

   _____.

7. Consumers are becoming more concerned about the salt and sugar content in their food.

   What I mean is _____.

8. Online shopping is a way for busy people to save time. To put this another way,

   _____.

9. Many people now use their home computer to watch movies and listen to music. That is to

   say, they don't _____.

10. Nowadays you can get news instantly on the Internet, I mean, you don't have to

    _____.

Name _____ Date _____

Chapter 8 Part 4: Fads and Fashions

Directions:

1. Choose one of the topics in the box below. Decide if you approve or disapprove.

2. Work with your group to fill out the chart. Write your reasons why each of the people in the chart might or might not approve of it.

3. Choose one of the roles and discuss your topic.

Topic Choices

New! Cell phones for children aged 5–7!	Home Tattoo Kit. Painless. Easy to use!	Diet foods for teenagers. Delicious and low-calorie!	Car TVs and DVDs. Entertainment for your car!

Group topic: _____

	Reasons for approving	**Reasons for disapproving**
Parents		
Police/Doctors		
Teachers		
Sales representatives		

Copyright © McGraw-Hill

Name _____ Date _____

Chapter 9 Part 2: Fact or Theory?

Directions:

1. Work in groups. Read the information about each planet. Discuss some possible theories based on the facts.

   Example: Mercury is the closest to the sun so it might be the hottest planet.

2. Each person will choose one planet. Use the Internet or a library to check whether the theories suggested by your group are true.

3. Re-form your groups and share your information.

Mercury	Jupiter
Fact: Mercury is closest to the sun.	**Fact:** Jupiter is the largest planet — about 1,000 times the size of Earth.
Theory:	**Theory:**
Mars	**Venus**
Fact: Mars has less gravity than Earth.	**Fact:** Venus is closest to Earth.
Theory:	**Theory:**

BLM 26

Name _____   Date _____

Chapter 9 Part 3: That's Amazing!

Step 1: Work in groups of three students. Fill in the diagram with information about your skills and abilities.

In the space where all three circles overlap, write the skills that all three of you have.

In the space where only two circles overlap, write the skills that two of you have.

In the remaining spaces, write the skills that only one person has.

Step 2: Share your information with other groups and tell them the most amazing, interesting, or surprising things that you found out about your group.

Step 3: Based on the shared abilities in your group, what kind of enterprise or adventure would you be best at? Think of a name for your new enterprise.

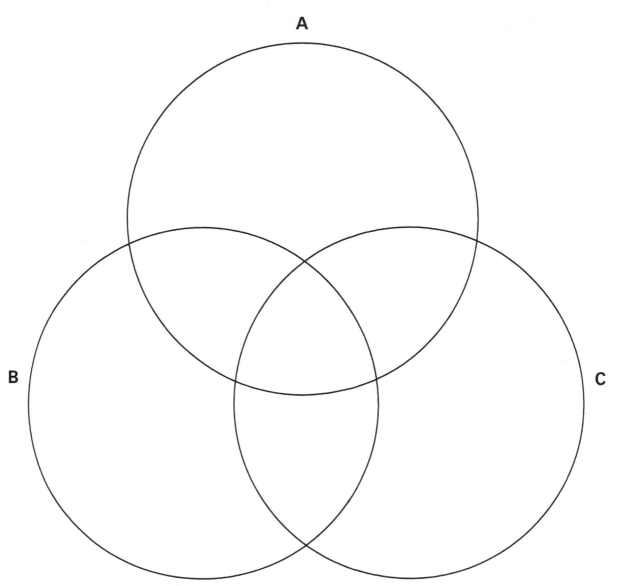

Chapter 9 Part 4: Inventions and Discoveries

penicillin	the Internet	DNA	the theory of gravity
electricity	the home computer	the printing press	the telescope
the telephone	television	the steam engine	Wild card: Choose your own invention or discovery!
gunpowder	chocolate	home video cassette recorder	Wild card: Choose your own invention or discovery!
paper	sewing machine	the automobile	Wild card: Choose your own invention or discovery!

Chapter 10 Part 1: May I Help You?

I'm having a birthday party on Saturday, and my apartment is a mess.
I have a bad backache, and I can't go out.
My parents are coming this weekend, and my car has broken down.
I've invited 20 people to dinner at my house for my sister's birthday.
I have to go away this weekend, and I can't find anyone to look after my cat.
I don't know what to buy for my parents' anniversary.
I have to work overtime this weekend, and I don't have time to shop for groceries.
I can't find anything to wear for my best friend's wedding.
I have to finish my assignment by tomorrow morning, but my computer is broken.
I don't understand my homework assignment.

Name _____ Date _____

Chapter 10, Part 2: Ceremonies Around the World

Part 1: Choose one of the ceremonies from the list below.

Part 2: Choose four countries that have different traditions for this ceremony.

Part 3: Fill out as much of the chart as you can. Use the Internet to research additional information.

Part 4: Share your information with your group.

| birthday | wedding | graduation | coming of age | birth | death |

Name of Ceremony: _____

	Activities	**Clothing (choose one main item)**	**Food (choose one main item)**	**Symbolic meaning of ceremony**
Country 1				
Country 2				
Country 3				
Country 4				

Chapter 10 Part 3: Congratulations and Sympathy

I broke my ankle last weekend when I went skiing.
My cat died yesterday.
I just passed my driver's test.
I won $500 in the lottery.
My uncle's funeral is tomorrow.
I just got a new job.
I passed my college examination.
I won a scholarship for college.
My best friend got injured in a car accident.
I got fired from my job.
I just got promoted.
My bicycle was stolen.
I'm going to graduate tomorrow.
I have just gotten engaged to be married.
I'm getting married on Sunday.

Chapter 1 Test

Section I Listening to a Conversation Listen to the conversation. Then choose the best answer to each question. (4 points each)

1. Where are the two people?
- Ⓐ in a bookstore
- Ⓑ in a library
- Ⓒ on a college campus

2. Which building does the man want to find?
- Ⓐ art museum
- Ⓑ gym
- Ⓒ music building

3. Where is the building?
- Ⓐ at Willow Street and Alumni Street
- Ⓑ at the intersection of Willow Street and College Avenue
- Ⓒ between Willow Street and Alumni Street

4. Which of these is true?
- Ⓐ The woman asks the man to walk with him.
- Ⓑ The woman asks the man if he wants to walk with her.
- Ⓒ The man asks the woman if he can walk with her.

5. When Yumi says, "Oh, really?" what feeling does she express?
- Ⓐ boredom
- Ⓑ interest
- Ⓒ shyness

Section II Listening to a Lecture Listen to the lecture. Then choose the best answer to each question. Listen to the Lecture again. (4 points each)

1. The lecture is about four types of _____.
- Ⓐ colleges
- Ⓑ classes
- Ⓒ subjects

2. What can you practice in the small group classes?
- Ⓐ speaking
- Ⓑ business
- Ⓒ computer skills

3. What do you do in the language lab class?
- Ⓐ work with a teacher
- Ⓑ work in a group
- Ⓒ work individually

4. What is the maximum individual study you can sign up for?

    (A) up to three hours a week

    (B) up to two hours a week

    (C) up to one hour a week

5. What is the most popular type of class?

    (A) small group

    (B) language lab

    (C) individual study

Section III New Words Use the words in the box to complete Activities 1 and 2 below. (4 points each)

attend	career	fail	get ahead	kicked out
major	requirements	sign up	take notes	term paper

1. Fill in the blanks with words from the box.

    1. Midterm exams and term papers are part of the course _____.

    2. It's important to _____ all the classes.

    3. English is important for a _____ in business.

    4. You sometimes have to research and write a _____ in order to get a grade.

    5. You can get _____ of school if you copy someone's work.

2. Find words from the box which have the same meaning.

    6. Yumi wants to *be successful* in college. _____

    7. I am going to *register* for some English courses. _____

    8. Francisco will *not pass* his exam if he doesn't study more. _____

    9. When you listen to a lecture, you *write down the main points*. _____

    10. Joanne wants to *specialize* in computer design. _____

Section IV Using Language Use the five expressions below to complete the dialog.
(4 points each)

I'd love	were you	really
would you	thanks	

Lianne: Hi, Pete. _____ planning to do anything tonight?
                            1

Pete: Well, I wasn't planning to go out.

Lianne: Well, _____ like to go to see a movie?
                         2

Pete: _____, but I have my midterm next week, and I have to study.
                  3

Lianne: _____? You can study tomorrow, can't you?
                  4

Pete: Well, that's true. OK, _____ to go. Thanks for inviting me.
                                         5

TOTAL ____/100 pts.

Chapter 2 Test

Section I Listening to a Conversation Listen to the conversation. Then choose the best answer to each question. (4 points each)

1. Who is Ken talking to?
- Ⓐ a roommate
- Ⓑ a friend
- Ⓒ a house-owner

2. Ken wants to know about _____.
- Ⓐ the rent
- Ⓑ the location
- Ⓒ the rent and the location

3. How many students are living in the house now?
- Ⓐ one student
- Ⓑ two students
- Ⓒ three students

4. Ken is moving because _____.
- Ⓐ he has a cat
- Ⓑ he needs somewhere quieter
- Ⓒ he needs to be alone

5. What does *Do you mind pets?* mean?
- Ⓐ Do you like pets?
- Ⓑ Do you allow pets?
- Ⓒ Do you have pets?

Section II Listening to a Talk Listen to the talk. Then choose the best answer to each question. Listen to the talk again. (4 points each)

1. The talk is about _____ type(s) of security on campus.
- Ⓐ one
- Ⓑ three
- Ⓒ five

2. Which of these should you *not* do?
- Ⓐ loan your key
- Ⓑ lock your door
- Ⓒ leave your room

3. Where should you *not* walk at night?
- Ⓐ in dark areas
- Ⓑ well-lighted areas
- Ⓒ near phones

4. What should you do *before* you go out?
- (A) carry a cell phone
- (B) have your key ready
- (C) tell friends where you are going

5. How can you prevent theft of your property?
- (A) study in the library
- (B) watch your property carefully
- (C) take a self-defense class

Section III New Words Use the words in the box to complete Activities 1 and 2 below. (4 points each)

alarm	break in	can't miss it	come by	device
lifts a finger	prevent	slob	timer	valuables

1. Fill in the blanks with words from the box.

1. A _____ can be used to turn your lights on and off automatically.

2. My roommate never cleans up his room. He's a real _____.

3. If you leave the window of your home open, it's easy for someone to _____.

4. It's a good idea to have a locking _____ on the steering wheel of your car.

5. A car _____ makes a lot of noise, but it does not usually help to prevent car theft.

2. Find words from the box with the same meaning as the words in italics.

6. You should not leave *expensive things* in your car. _____

7. Neighborhood Watch tries to *stop* crime in the neighborhood. _____

8. My house is on the corner. You *will find it easily.* _____

9. My roommate never *helps* with the housework. _____

10. Why don't you *visit* us after school tomorrow? _____

Section IV Using Language Use the five expressions below to complete the dialog.
(4 points each)

> | I'd love | sure | thanks |
> | were you | would you | |

Lianne: Hi, Pete. _____ planning to go to the movies tonight?
  ₁

Pete: I'm not sure…

Lianne: Well, _____ like to go?
  ₂

Pete: _____, but I have my midterm next week, and I have to study…
  ₃

Lianne: You can study tomorrow, can't you?

Pete: Well, that's true. OK, _____ to go. Thanks for inviting me.
  ₄

Lianne: _____ I'm glad you can come.
  ₅

TOTAL ____ /100 pts.

Chapter 3 Test

Section I **Listening to a Conversation** Listen to the conversation. Then choose the best answer to each question. (4 points each)

1. What does the customer want to do?
- (A) apply for a credit card
- (B) borrow some money
- (C) pay back a loan

2. What does the bank clerk advise the customer to do?
- (A) apply for new credit card
- (B) talk to another bank
- (C) speak to a loan specialist

3. The bank clerk suggests that a different type of loan would be _____.
- (A) cheaper
- (B) faster
- (C) easier

4. What is the interest on Elsa's credit card?
- (A) 8%
- (B) 18%
- (C) 80%

5. What kind of loan is Elsa interested in?
- (A) a personal loan
- (B) a car loan
- (C) a home improvement loan

Section II **Listening to a Lecture** Listen to the lecture. Then choose the best answer to each question. Listen to the lecture again. (4 points each)

1. The lecture is about four types of _____.
- (A) products and services
- (B) new inventions
- (C) entrepreneurial ideas

2. The idea of a home computer _____.
- (A) was a new way of doing business
- (B) created a new product
- (C) solved a problem

3. In what way was Anita Roddick's chain of stores a new idea?
- (A) She invented a new type of cosmetic.
- (B) She specialized in natural cosmetics.
- (C) She has 2,000 stores around the world.

4. Henry Ford's idea of the assembly line is an example of _____.

    Ⓐ a new method of production

    Ⓑ a new product or service

    Ⓒ an improvement of an existing product

5. In what way was Jeff Bezos' company a new idea?

    Ⓐ It was a new way of selling books.

    Ⓑ It is a multimillion-dollar business.

    Ⓒ It sells books to customers directly.

Section III New Words Use the words in the box to complete the paragraph below. (4 points each)

balance	borrow	budget	capital	checking
earn	interest	lend	risks	statement

Most people have a _____ account at a bank where they can take

                           1

out money by using a check or a debit card. Whenever you write a check or make a deposit,

you should keep a record of it. Then it will be easier for you to _____

                                      2

your checkbook. The bank usually sends you a _____ at the end of every

                               3

month with details of your account. If you want to make sure that you do not spend more

than you _____, you should try to keep to a _____. It's

              4   5

better not to _____ too much money on your credit card because the rate

                    6

of _____ is usually very high. Banks sometimes _____

      7   8

money to people who want to start their own business, but entrepreneurs also need to raise

_____ by getting other people to invest. They need to be ready to take

      9

_____ because they might make a profit, or they might lose everything.

      10

Section IV Using Language Complete the conversation with the phrases from the box.
(4 points each)

> I suggest that you   you recommend   should I do
>
> can you give me   think about it

Monica: How did it go with your Dad on the phone?

Billy: Oh it's the same story. He says I have to stick to a budget and he won't lend me any money. What

    _____?
       1

Monica: I'm not sure. Have you tried asking your Mom?

Billy: Well, she always agrees with Dad. _____ any other advice? I'm really broke.
                                          2

    What do _____?
             3

Monica: I can lend you some money for this week, but _____ try and get a part-time
                                        4

    job that pays more than that computer store.

Billy: Thanks, I'll _____,
            5

TOTAL ____/100 pts.

Chapter 4 Test

Section I Listening to a Conversation Listen to the conversation. Then choose the best answer to each question. (4 points each)

1. Who is Andrew talking to?
- Ⓐ a friend
- Ⓑ a co-worker
- Ⓒ a manager

2. What kind of job does Andrew want?
- Ⓐ a computer programmer
- Ⓑ a computer analyst
- Ⓒ a computer salesperson

3. How much work experience does Andrew have?
- Ⓐ a lot
- Ⓑ a little
- Ⓒ none

4. What does Andrew do in his spare time?
- Ⓐ He plays on computers.
- Ⓑ He spends money on computers.
- Ⓒ He learns about computers.

5. What did the manager assume about Andrew's education?
- Ⓐ He doesn't have a college degree.
- Ⓑ He already has a college degree.
- Ⓒ He is going to have a college degree.

Section II Listening to a Lecture Listen to the lecture. Then choose the best answer to each question. Listen to the lecture again. (4 points each)

1. What is the main topic of this lecture?
- Ⓐ how technology has changed
- Ⓑ how technology has changed us
- Ⓒ how technology has changed our work

2. One effect has been the trend in people working from home. What does *trend* mean in this sentence?
- Ⓐ ability
- Ⓑ increase
- Ⓒ advantage

3. What is one effect of working from home?
- Ⓐ It's difficult to separate work and home life.
- Ⓑ It's difficult to have time for family life.
- Ⓒ We have to work all the time.

4. Why are workers losing interpersonal skills?
- Ⓐ because they always use email
- Ⓑ because they don't like talking
- Ⓒ because they waste time

5. Why have jobs moved to other countries?
- Ⓐ because people don't have skills in the U.S.
- Ⓑ because there aren't enough workers in the U.S.
- Ⓒ because salaries are lower in other countries

Section III New Words Use the words in the box to complete the sentences below. (4 points each)

automation	competition	complain	labor	manufacturing
market	part-time	salary	service	support

1. Jobs where people make things like cars or clothes are known as _____ jobs.

2. Jobs where people do things like cook food or drive a taxi are known as _____ jobs.

3. If you work for a company and they pay you every month, that is your _____.

4. I was not satisfied with the food in the restaurant, so I called the manager to _____.

5. I work 12 hours a week, so it is only a _____ job.

6. Jon helps _____ his parents so he gives them some money every month.

7. The money employers pay workers is their _____ costs.

8. _____ is causing some companies to cut jobs and increase the number of robots.

9. There are many more computer- and health-related jobs in the job _____ today.

10. It is difficult for U.S. companies to fight _____ from other countries where salaries are lower.

Section IV Using Language Complete the conversation with words from the box. (4 points each)

didn't	aren't	doesn't
haven't	don't	

Peter: You've been working in the library for quite some time, _____ you?
1

Chen: Yes, for about eight years.

Peter: You had some experience before, _____ you?
2

Chen: Yes, I worked in the public library for two years before this.

Peter: And you like this job, _____ you?
3

Chen: It's interesting and I like helping people. Your sister works in a library, _____
4

she?

Peter: Yes, and she loves it.

Chen: I think you're planning to apply for the new librarian's job, _____ you?
5

Peter: How did you guess?

TOTAL ____/100 pts.

Chapter 5 Test

Section I Listening to a Conversation Listen to the conversation. Choose the best answer to each question. (4 points each)

1. Sandra is a _____.
- (A) homemaker
- (B) single mother
- (C) teenager

2. Where is Sandra living now?
- (A) with her parents
- (B) by herself
- (C) with friends

3. What is Sandra looking for?
- (A) a babysitter
- (B) a job
- (C) an apartment

4. Which sentence is true?
- (A) Sandra has a new job.
- (B) Sandra went back to her old job.
- (C) Sandra doesn't have a job.

5. Who is Sandra speaking to?
- (A) a co-worker
- (B) her mother
- (C) a friend

Section II Listening to a Lecture Listen to the lecture. Choose the best answer to each question. Listen to the lecture again. (4 points each)

1. What is the main topic of this lecture?
- (A) people getting older
- (B) workers getting older
- (C) retirement

2. How many babies were born during the baby boom?
- (A) 19 million
- (B) 46 million
- (C) 76 million

3. Who are the baby boomers?
- (A) people born between 1946 and 1964
- (B) people born 19 years ago
- (C) people born in 1978

4. The percentage of workers aged 45 and older will increase _____.

Ⓐ from 25 to 44 percent

Ⓑ from 33 to 40 percent

Ⓒ from 38.7 to 40.7 percent

5. What will happen because of changes in pensions?

Ⓐ Pensions will go up.

Ⓑ People will not be able to retire.

Ⓒ People will retire later.

Section III **New Words** Use the words in the box to complete the paragraph below. (4 points each)

bring up	check up on	cost of living	day care	flexible
homemakers	maternity	old-fashioned	opportunity	run out

Many mothers need to work because the _____ is very high. It is very
                                                      1

difficult for a mother to _____ a child and go out to work at the same time.
                                   2

Companies have to give new mothers 12 weeks of _____ leave. When they
                                 3

_____ of leave, they have to make some difficult decisions. Some companies
                 4

offer _____ centers, where mothers can _____ their children
              5   6

at any time of the day. But most companies prefer to offer more _____ working
                                          7

hours, or the _____ to work from home. Some mothers decide to stay home
                 8

when they have young children. They choose to be _____— doing the shopping,
                                     9

cooking, and housework for the family, but this work is usually unpaid and some people think it

is _____.
   10

Section IV Using Language Complete the conversation with the words and phrases from the box. (4 points each)

would you	let me	do
I'd like	do you need	

Miguel: Cheri, can you _____ me a big favor?

1

Cheri: Yes, of course. What _____?

2

Miguel: _____ mind looking after my little sister while I go to the baseball game on

3
Saturday?

Cheri: Well, _____ to help you, but I'm kind of busy this weekend, you know…

4

Miguel: I don't often ask you for a favor. Please?

Cheri: OK. _____ think about it.

5

Miguel: Thanks.

TOTAL ____/100 pts.

Chapter 6 Test

Section I Listening to a Conversation Listen to the conversation. Choose the best answer to each question. (4 points each)

1. What is Gina's job?
- (A) a student
- (B) a teacher
- (C) a computer programmer

2. What is Gina's problem?
- (A) She doesn't like emails.
- (B) She doesn't have time to answer all her emails.
- (C) She doesn't know how to use email.

3. What advice does Mike give?
- (A) Answer all emails immediately.
- (B) Only answer important emails.
- (C) Answer important emails first.

4. What is Mike's advice about a website?
- (A) Answer emails on a website.
- (B) Write emails to a website.
- (C) Post messages on a website.

5. Which sentence is true?
- (A) Kendra interrupts Gina and Mike because Gina received a phone call.
- (B) Mike interrupts Gina because Gina received a phone call.
- (C) Mike interrupts Gina and Kendra because Kendra received a phone call.

Section II Listening to a Lecture Listen to the lecture. Choose the best answer to each question. Listen to the lecture again. (4 points each)

1. What is the main topic of this lecture?
- (A) rules of politeness in different cultures
- (B) ways of shaking hands
- (C) how to solve misunderstandings

2. What is most important when Americans meet?
- (A) to be friendly
- (B) to offer help
- (C) to use first names

3. What is most important when Japanese meet?
- (A) to make eye contact
- (B) to ask each other for help
- (C) to offer help

4. What message is communicated by avoiding eye contact in American culture?

(A) politeness

(B) insincerity

(C) friendliness

5. What can we learn from this comparison?

(A) that Americans are not polite

(B) that Japanese are more polite

(C) that rules of politeness can cause misunderstandings

Section III New Words Look at the list of words below. Use the words to complete the sentences. (4 points each)

appropriate	bow	catch up on	download	embarrassing
insulted	misunderstandings	post	stay in touch	title

1. Our teacher wants us to _____ messages on our learning blog every week.

2. The same gesture can have different meanings in different cultures, and this can cause

_____.

3. You can _____ the software for this program from the Internet.

4. People use email to _____ with friends.

5. When I am traveling, I always _____ the news by going to the Internet.

6. People in Japan often _____ when they greet each other.

7. If you point your foot at someone in Egypt, a person might feel _____.

8. It is not always _____ to hug someone when you are greeting them.

9. In Korea, it is common to address a teacher or a doctor by his or her _____.

10. If you go to a country and don't learn about cultural customs, you could do something

_____.

Section IV Using Language Match the sentences that have the same meanings. (4 points each)

1. _____ May I interrupt?

2. _____ How does it work?

3. _____ What's up?

4. _____ I want to ask your opinion.

5. _____ What's it about?

a. What's the problem?

b. Could you explain this to me?

c. What's the topic?

d. I'd like to say something.

e. What do you think about it?

TOTAL ____ /100 pts.

Chapter 7 Test

Section I Listening to a Conversation Listen to the conversation. Choose the best answer to each question. (4 points each)

1. What is the main topic of the conversation?
- (A) telephones
- (B) telephone messages
- (C) automated phone systems

2. What doesn't Jenny like?
- (A) phoning
- (B) leaving messages
- (C) waiting

3. Why does Stan disagree with Jenny about the job?
- (A) He thinks it's a boring job.
- (B) He prefers to speak to a real person.
- (C) He thinks it saves time.

4. Which is true at the end of the conversation?
- (A) Jenny contradicts Stan.
- (B) Stan contradicts Jenny.
- (C) Jenny and Stan agree.

5. What does *aha* mean?
- (A) What does that mean?
- (B) I understand.
- (C) I'm not sure. Let me think.

Section II Listening to a Lecture Listen to the lecture. Choose the best answer to each question. Listen to the lecture again. (4 points each)

1. What is the main topic of this lecture?
- (A) mistakes in English
- (B) grammar and vocabulary
- (C) spoken and written English

2. Which three categories are mentioned in the lecture?
- (A) pronunciation, spelling, and grammar
- (B) intonation, vocabulary, and mistakes
- (C) medium of communication, vocabulary, and grammar

3. What can you use to convey mood in written English?
- (A) stress
- (B) punctuation
- (C) intonation

4. Which is not used in formal written English?

    (A) slang

    (B) pronouns

    (C) stress

5. Which sentence is true?

    (A) People often notice mistakes in spoken English.

    (B) People don't often notice mistakes in written English.

    (C) People often make mistakes in spoken English.

Section III New Words Use the words in the box to complete the paragraph. (4 points each)

catch on	dialect	friendliness	friendship	identical
majority	noticeable	two-faced	unique	whereas

When you move to a new culture, it is sometimes difficult to understand differences

in communication. Every culture has its own _____ way of interacting,
₁

and it usually takes a while to _____. In the U.S., for example, people
₂

are often impressed by everyone's _____ when they first meet, but true
₃

_____ takes some time to build up. When someone says *How are you?*, it's just
₄

a greeting like *hello* or *hi*. They do not usually want to know about your health or your mood, but

this does not mean they are _____. Misunderstandings can also arise between
₅

speakers of English because of differences in _____. British and American
₆

English have a few _____ differences in pronunciation and vocabulary. For
₇

example, Americans use the word *elevator* _____ British speakers use the
₈

word *lift*. But the _____ of English speakers have no trouble understanding
₉

each other, and in general, the grammar and vocabulary of these language varieties are almost

_____.
₁₀

Section IV Using Language Match the interjections such as *uh-huh* and *uh-oh* with their meanings.
(4 points each)

1. _____ A: Is this seat free?
B: Uh-huh.

2. _____ A: Be careful with that coffee!
B: Oops!

3. _____ A: Did you remember about the test today?
B: Uh-oh.

4. _____ A: There's a problem with your intermodular
protocol regulator.
B: Huh?

5. _____ A: Do you know where the key to the store room is?
B: Hmm . . .

a. What does that mean?

b. I dropped something.

c. I'm not sure. Let me think.

d. I forgot something.

e. Yes.

TOTAL _____ /100 pts.

Chapter 8 Test

Section I Listening to a Conversation Listen to the conversation. Choose the best answer to each question. (4 points each)

1. What is the conversation is about?
- Ⓐ birthdays
- Ⓑ travel
- Ⓒ food

2. What does Maria think of Mexican food?
- Ⓐ She loves it.
- Ⓑ She doesn't mind it.
- Ⓒ She hates it.

3. What does Joe think of spicy food?
- Ⓐ He likes it.
- Ⓑ He doesn't like it.
- Ⓒ He doesn't hate it.

4. What does Joe think of Indian food?
- Ⓐ He loves it.
- Ⓑ He doesn't mind it.
- Ⓒ He hates it.

5. Which statement is true about Joe?
- Ⓐ He doesn't like to try new food.
- Ⓑ He likes to try new food.
- Ⓒ He is not interested in food.

Section II Listening to an Interview Listen to the interview. Choose the best answer to each question. Listen to the interview again. (4 points each)

1. What is the main topic of this interview?
- Ⓐ food
- Ⓑ fashion
- Ⓒ music

2. What is an example of a natural material?
- Ⓐ wool
- Ⓑ nylon
- Ⓒ polyester

3. What does *spread the message* mean?
- Ⓐ make more money
- Ⓑ make the issue popular
- Ⓒ save the environment

4. What is *vintage clothing*?
- Ⓐ last year's fashion
- Ⓑ environmental fashion
- Ⓒ fashion from the 50s and 60s

5. What does Marietta hope to do by combining old and new?
- Ⓐ make people keep their clothing for longer
- Ⓑ make people buy more clothing
- Ⓒ make people throw their clothing away

Section III New Words Use the words in the box to complete each sentence. (4 points each)

confident	conflict	diverse	income	loyal
optimistic	phenomenon	significant	see eye to eye	tolerant

1. There are more than 70 million people in Generation Y. That is a very _____ number.

2. They come from a variety of ethnic backgrounds. They are _____.

3. They are sure about their ability to succeed. They are _____.

4. They are very positive about the future. They are _____.

5. They accept a wide variety of different opinions. They are _____.

6. They don't stay with one brand or product. They aren't _____ to one type of product.

7. They have different values than their parents. There is sometimes a _____ between their values and those of the older generation.

8. They sometime disagree with their parents. They don't always _____ with their parents.

9. They spend money at the mall. They like to spend a lot of their _____ on fashion, fast food, movies, CDs, electronics, and concert tickets.

10. This generation of young people with these characteristics is found in many countries around the world. It is an international _____.

Section IV Using Language Fill in the blanks with words from the box below. (4 points each)

for	against	in favor
approve	disapprove	

Janet: Are you _____ of laws that forbid smoking?
1

Dan: I _____ of smoking in public spaces or at work, but I think people can do
2

what they like at home. What do you think?

Janet: I'm _____ smoking. It's really bad for your health.
3

Dan: Would you _____ of anti-smoking laws then?
4

Janet: Yes, I'm _____ a total ban.
5

TOTAL ____ /100 pts.

Chapter 9 Test

Section I Listening to a Conversation Listen to the conversation. Choose the best answer to each question. (4 points each)

1. What is the main topic of the conversation?
   (A) heart problems
   (B) medical advances
   (C) new medicines

2. Why did the girl need a second heart operation?
   (A) because her new heart didn't work
   (B) because her old heart didn't work
   (C) because she needed another heart

3. When Jane says *That's so weird.* what does she mean?
   (A) It's good.
   (B) It's not true.
   (C) It's strange.

4. When Jane says, "*Unbelievable!*" What does she mean?
   (A) I don't believe you.
   (B) It's hard to believe.
   (C) It isn't true.

5. Why is the story amazing?
   (A) because the girl's original heart got better
   (B) because the girl was born with two hearts
   (C) because the girl had a new heart

Section II Listening to a Lecture Listen to the lecture. Choose the best answer to each question. Listen to the lecture again. (4 points each)

1. What is the main topic of this lecture?
   (A) theories about life on Mars
   (B) exploration of Mars
   (C) reasons for exploring space

2. According to the lecture, which of these is a fact?
   (A) People want to travel to other planets.
   (B) People want to know if there is life on other planets.
   (C) People have found evidence of life on other planets.

3. Which of these was true in the 19th century?
   (A) They thought there was water on Mars.
   (B) They found evidence of water on Mars.
   (C) They found evidence of life on Mars.

4. Which of these is true about the meteorite from Mars?

    Ⓐ There was evidence of life.

    Ⓑ There was no evidence of life.

    Ⓒ There was disagreement about the evidence of life.

5. How can scientists get more evidence of life on Mars?

    Ⓐ by studying rocks that are similar to the ones they found on Earth

    Ⓑ by getting rocks from Mars where life may have survived the longest

    Ⓒ by collecting older rocks from Mars

Section III New Words Look at the list of words below. Use the words in the box to complete the paragraphs. (4 points each)

all for	analyze	disaster	endangered species	evidence
extinct	planet	resources	solar system	stem cells

[A]   Mars is a _____ that has fascinated humans for hundreds of years.

                                1

Scientists want to _____ rocks from Mars to find out if there is any

                             2

_____ of life. If they find life on Mars, perhaps there will also be life in

                3

other parts of the _____. If Earth is destroyed by a _____,

                       4   5

or if we use up all of the Earth's _____, it may become necessary to live on

                                                6

Mars one day.

[B]   Scientists are studying the possible use of _____ to create clones of

                                                      7

animals. One reason for doing this is to prevent _____ of animals from

                                              8

becoming _____. Although some people are _____

                      9   10

animal cloning, the idea of human cloning can be quite scary.

Section IV Using Language Fill in the blanks with the phrases from the box below. (4 points each)

> believe it or not   all for   I'm shocked
>
> that's an amazing story   I can't believe it

A: I read an amazing story in the paper today.

B: You did? Tell me about it! I'm _____ amazing stories!

                                                1

A: Well, _____ , it was about a woman who left $5 million to her pet cat when she

                         2

died.

B: _____!

                3

A: You are? I was too, but it's true!

B: _____!

                4

A: I couldn't believe it either. But what's more, she said in her will that if the cat dies, she wants them to

make a clone of the cat and the money will go to the clone.

B: Oh, now _____.

                       5

A: Yes, it is, isn't it?

TOTAL ____ /100 pts.

Chapter 10 Test

Section I Listening to a Conversation Listen to the conversation. Choose the best answer to each question. (4 points each)

1. What is this conversation about?
- (A) a wedding
- (B) a baby shower
- (C) a birthday

2. Which sentence is true?
- (A) Mike invites Tina to a party.
- (B) Tina invites Mike to a party.
- (C) Mike and Tina are both hosting a party.

3. Which offer from Mike does Tina decline?
- (A) to bring some food and drinks
- (B) to bring some music
- (C) to bring some ice cream

4. Which offer from Mike does Tina accept?
- (A) to bring some drinks
- (B) to bring some cake
- (C) to bring some ice cream

5. Which sentence is true?
- (A) Mike is Tina's boyfriend.
- (B) Mike is Tina's brother.
- (C) Mike is Tina's friend.

Section II Listening to a Lecture Listen to the lecture. Choose the best answer to each question. Listen to the lecture again. (4 points each)

1. What is the general topic of this talk?
- (A) weddings and divorces
- (B) weddings in the U.S.
- (C) hiring a wedding planner

2. What is the main idea of this talk?
- (A) Large weddings are better than small weddings.
- (B) Couples should hire a wedding consultant.
- (C) Big weddings are important.

3. Which of these is a digression from the main topic?
- (A) Weddings are very popular.
- (B) People who get married again have big weddings.
- (C) The divorce rate for first marriages is 50 percent.

4. Which of these is a digression from the main topic?
- Ⓐ the advantages of a big wedding
- Ⓑ the advantages of having a wedding planner
- Ⓒ the problems of bringing families together

5. What are the disadvantages of a big wedding?
- Ⓐ Families can disagree.
- Ⓑ Families have to cooperate.
- Ⓒ Families can get to know each other.

Section III New Words Use the words from the box to complete the paragraph. (4 points each)

hosted	involve	mother-to-be	pour	pray
priest	purify	shower	sin	symbolize

Many ceremonies around the world _____ the use of water. In Thailand,
                                                    1

the custom is to _____ over other people at the start of the New Year. This
                              2

is meant to _____ washing away of bad luck. In some Islamic countries,
                        3

people wash their faces with water to _____ themselves before they
                                                          4

_____. In the Christian religion, a _____. sprinkles water on
            5   6

the baby's head. This is meant to wash away _____. Another custom connected
                                                                7

with new babies is a baby _____. This has nothing to do with water. It is a
                                          8

kind of party for the _____,which is usually _____ by her
                                    9   10

girlfriends.

Section IV Using Language Complete the tag questions with the correct verbs. (4 points each)

1. You aren't 21 yet, _____ you?

2. You won't forget my birthday, _____ you?

3. You don't want to stay late, _____ you?

4. You didn't phone me yesterday, _____ you?

5. You can't help me with my homework, _____ you?

TOTAL _____ /100 pts.

Chapter 1 Test Answer Key

Section I Listening to a Conversation

1. c 2. a 3. a 4. c 5. b

Section II Listening to a Lecture

1. b 2. a 3. c 4. a 5. c

Section III New Words

1. requirements 2. attend 3. career 4. term paper
5. kicked out 6. get ahead 7. sign up 8. fail 9. take
notes 10. major

Section IV Using Language

1. Were you 2. would you 3. Thanks 4. Really
5. I'd love

Chapter 2 Test Answer Key

Section I Listening to a Conversation

1. c 2. c 3. a 4. b 5. b

Section II Listening to a Talk

1. b 2. a 3. a 4. c 5. b

Section III New Words

1. timer 2. slob 3. break in 4. device 5. alarm
6. valuables 7. prevent 8. can't miss it 9. lifts a finger
10. come by

Section IV Using Language

1. Were you 2. would you 3. Thanks 4. I'd love
5. Sure

Chapter 3 Test Answer Key

Section I Listening to a Conversation

1. b 2. c 3. a 4. b 5. c

Section II Listening to a Lecture

1. c 2. b 3. b 4. a 5. a

Section III New Words

1. checking 2. balance 3. statement 4. earn
5. budget 6. borrow 7. interest 8. lend 9. capital
10. risks

Section IV Using Language

1. should I do 2. Can you give me 3. you recommend
4. I suggest that you 5. think about it

Chapter 4 Test Answer Key

Section I Listening to a Conversation

1. c 2. b 3. c 4. c 5. b

Section II Listening to a Lecture

1. c 2. b 3. a 4. a 5. c

Section III New Words

1. manufacturing 2. service 3. salary 4. complain
5. part-time 6. support 7. labor 8. automation
9. market 10. competition

Section IV Using Language

1. haven't 2. didn't 3. don't 4. doesn't 5. aren't

Chapter 5 Test Answer Key

Section I Listening to a Conversation

1. b 2. a 3. c 4. b 5. a

Section II Listening to a Lecture

1. b 2. c 3. a 4. b 5. c

Section III New Words

1. cost of living 2. bring up 3. maternity 4. run out
5. day-care 6. check up on 7. flexible 8. opportunity
9. homemakers 10. old-fashioned

Section IV Using Language

1. do 2. do you need 3. would you 4. I'd like 5. let me

Chapter 6 Test Answer Key

Section I Listening to a Conversation

1. b 2. b 3. c 4. c 5. a

Section II Listening to a Lecture

1. a 2. a 3. b 4. b 5. c

Section III New Words

1. post 2. misunderstandings 3. download
4. stay in touch 5. catch up on 6. bow 7. insulted
8. appropriate 9. title 10. embarrassing

Section IV Using Language

1. d 2. b 3. a 4. e 5. c

Chapter 7 Test Answer Key

Section I Listening to a Conversation

1. c 2. c 3. a 4. c 5. b

Section II Listening to a Lecture

1. c 2. c 3. b 4. a 5. c

Section III New Words

1. unique 2. catch on 3. friendliness 4. friendship
5. two-faced 6. dialect 7. noticeable 8. whereas
9. majority 10. identical

Section IV Using Language

1. e 2. b 3. d 4. a 5. c

Chapter 8 Test Answer Key

Section I Listening to a Conversation

1. c 2. a 3. b 4. c 5. a

Section II Listening to an Interview

1. b 2. a 3. b 4. c 5. a

Section III New Words

1. significant 2. diverse 3. confident 4. optimistic
5. tolerant 6. loyal 7. conflict 8. see eye to eye
9. income 10. phenomenon

Section IV Using Language

1. in favor 2. disapprove 3. against 4. approve
5. for

Chapter 9 Test Answer Key

Section I Listening to a Conversation

1. b 2. a 3. c 4. b 5. a

Section II Listening to a Lecture

1. a 2. b 3. a 4. c 5. b

Section III New Words

1. planet 2. analyze 3. evidence 4. solar system
5. disaster 6. resources 7. stem cells 8. endangered
species 9. extinct 10. all for

Section IV Using Language

1. all for 2. believe it or not 3. I'm shocked 4. I can't
believe it 5. that's an amazing story

Chapter 10 Test Answer Key

Section I Listening to a Conversation

1. c 2. b 3. a 4. c 5. c

Section II Listening to a Lecture

1. b 2. c 3. c 4. b 5. a

Section III New Words

1. involve 2. pour 3. symbolize 4. purify 5. pray
6. priest 7. sin 8. shower 9. mother-to-be
10. hosted

Section IV Using Language

1. are 2. will 3. do 4. did 5. can

Chapter 1 Test Audioscripts

Section I Listening to a Conversation

Francisco:	Excuse me.
Yumi:	Yes?
Francisco:	Could you tell me where the art museum is?
Yumi:	Yes, of course. It's on Willow Street, across from the gym and next to the music building. It's at the intersection of Willow Street and Alumni Street. I'm walking that way, too.
Francisco:	Could I walk with you?
Yumi:	Yes, of course. Are you an art student?
Francisco:	Yes, I am.
Yumi:	Oh really? I'm majoring in business. It's my second year. How long have you been here?
Francisco:	About two weeks. I'm still finding my way around.
Yumi:	Well, here we are. It was nice to meet you.
Francisco:	Yes, see you again.

Section II Listening to a Lecture

Good morning everyone, my name is Nancy Anderson, and I'm the director of the Study Support Center. OK. This morning I want to give you a general introduction to the kind of study support we offer here. After that, we'll have time for some questions before taking a break for coffee. OK?

First, I want to tell you about the different types of classes we have available here in the Center. There are four main types of classes: small group classes, language lab, computer lab, and individual study.

Small group classes usually have five to eight students. They meet with a teacher once a week to practice speaking and communication skills. Groups are usually divided according to their major: business or law, for example. Language lab classes are for practicing pronunciation and listening skills. You can sign up for language lab classes at any time. There's no teacher, but a teaching assistant will help you find the right program, which you can work through at your own speed. Computer lab classes are in the library. You don't need to sign up. But look at the schedule for times of classes when a teaching assistant can help you with the basics of using computers and the Internet. Finally, you can meet with an individual tutor in our support center to get advice on any problems you're having with your studies. You can meet for one hour up to three times a week. But sign up early, the schedule gets filled up very quickly, especially around exam time!

We hope that you will use our support center, and we'll do our best to help you make the most of your learning experience here with us.

OK, that's it for now. Before we take a break, I'll try to answer some of your questions, and when we come back after the break, we'll talk about some of the course requirements. Now, are there any questions? Yes….

Student: Could you tell me…

Chapter 2 Test Audioscripts

Section I Listening to a Conversation

Ken:	Hello. May I speak to Mrs. Hansen, please?
Mrs. Hansen:	Yes, speaking.
Ken:	Hi Mrs. Hansen. My name is Ken, and I'm calling about the room for rent.
Mrs. Hansen:	Yes, what would you like to know?
Ken:	Could you tell me how much the rent is?
Mrs. Hansen:	It's $400 a month.
Ken:	I see. And how far is it from campus?
Mrs. Hansen:	It's very near, I'd say about ten minutes' walk. Are you a student?
Ken:	Yes, I am. I need somewhere quiet because the dorm is too noisy.
Mrs. Hansen:	We only have one other student here and she's very quiet.
Ken:	And do you mind pets, because I want to bring my cat with me.

Mrs. Hansen: I'm sorry, but we don't allow pets.

Ken: OK. Thanks anyway. Good-bye.

Section II Listening to a Talk

Hello everyone, my name is Pat Sanders, and I'm in charge of college campus security. I'm here to give you a few tips on how to stay safe and how to keep your property safe while you are on campus.

First of all, let's talk about safety in the dormitories. The most important thing is never to loan your keys or ID card to anyone. This is against college regulations. Lock your door when you are sleeping or when you leave the room. If you see anyone suspicious, call campus security.

Next, let's talk about security while you are walking around the campus. Avoid walking alone at night. You should tell other friends where you are going and what time you will be there. Try to walk only in well-lighted areas and know where the emergency telephones are on your route. Have your key ready *before* you get to the door. Take your cell phone and also carry a personal alarm with you. It may be a good idea to take self-defense classes. If someone approaches you, the best defense is to scream, sound an alarm (if you have one), and run to the nearest emergency phone.

OK, now let's move on and talk about how you can prevent theft of your property. By property, I mean your bags, wallets, cell phones, or laptops. You may think you are safe when you're studying in the library or in the cafeteria. But these are all places where thieves look for opportunities to steal. The main thing is never to leave your backpacks or laptops out of your sight. It also helps to label all your valuable items—that includes textbooks—with your name. It is a good idea to keep a list of the make, model, and serial number of valuable property such as laptop computers.

Following these tips will help to make you more safety-aware and will help to protect you and your property. Remember, we're here to help you. So report any crime or any suspicious activity to us immediately. But following these few simple safety procedures could help to save your property and even your life.

Chapter 3 Test Audioscripts

Section I Listening to a Conversation

Bank clerk: Good morning. International Bank. How can I help you?

Elsa: Can you tell me how much I can borrow on my credit card?

Bank clerk: OK, can you give me your name, please?

Elsa: Jansen. J-a-n-s-e-n. My first name is Elsa.

Bank clerk: For security purposes, can you give me the last four digits of your social security number, please?

Elsa: Yes, of course. It's 1234.

Bank clerk: Just a moment, let me look up your records. OK, here we are…yes, you have credit up to $2,000. If you need more than that, you should speak to one of our customer loan specialists.

Elsa: Yes, I think I might need more than that. I want to do some remodeling on my kitchen, and it will cost about $3,000.

Bank clerk: In that case, I advise you to choose one of our other loan options. The interest on your credit card is about 18 percent, but if you take out a personal loan or a home improvement loan, you can borrow the same amount for a much better rate, as low as 8 percent.

Elsa: OK. How do I find out about a home improvement loan?

Bank clerk: Just a moment, I'll put you through to our loan specialist.

Section II Listening to a Lecture

Let's think about a key part of the entrepreneurial process: Coming up with a new idea! It's easy to think of problems in our daily lives. Your car won't start in the morning. Or your alarm clock doesn't wake you up! But have you ever tried to come up with an idea for something completely new and different to try and solve any of these problems? A new idea for a product or a service? It's quite difficult, isn't it?

Well, the good news is that you don't have to come up with a totally new invention in order to be an entrepreneur. Today, I'm going to talk about four different types of entrepreneurial ideas.

First, a small proportion of entrepreneurs actually do come up with ideas for totally new inventions. An example of this is the concept of the home computer, which was chiefly developed in the 70s by entrepreneur Steve Jobs of Apple Computers. This product created a whole new market for something that had not existed before. Now, we can hardly imagine our lives without a home computer.

Many new ideas, however, are actually refinements of existing ideas, or specializations for specific segments of the market. Anita Roddick's chain of cosmetic stores, for example, sells to customers who are interested in environmental issues and want cosmetics made from natural ingredients. Founded in 1976, her company now has almost 2,000 stores around the world.

Another type of innovation is to improve production methods. Henry Ford, for example, invented the assembly line for the production of cars. He didn't invent cars, but he came up with an idea for increasing the speed and decreasing the cost of production, which made cars more affordable for consumers.

And finally, an entrepreneur can develop new ways of doing business to sell existing products. A good example of this is Jeff Bezos of Amazon.com, who was one of the first to use the Internet to sell to customers directly online. Though selling books was not a new idea, selling books via the Internet was a new idea at the time. Nowadays, online selling is a multimillion-dollar business.

Chapter 4 Test Audioscripts

Section I Listening to a Conversation

Manager: Please come in and take a seat.

Applicant: Thank you.

Manager: Now Andrew, what can you tell me about your job experience?

Applicant: Well, I don't have any job experience yet…but I'm very eager to learn.

Manager: OK. So, why are you interested in being a computer analyst?

Applicant: I like solving problems and fixing things. I spend all my spare time learning about computers. I know all about the latest technology.

Manager: Do you think you can work well on a team?

Applicant: Yes, I like working with people.

Manager: And you have a college degree, don't you?

Applicant: Not yet. I hope to graduate this year.

Section II Listening to a Lecture

We all know that we're using more and more technology in our daily lives. Most jobs nowadays require some computer skills and there are many benefits to using technology. Just think of all the jobs that had to be done by hand in the past—processing checks in a bank, for example—and which are now done electronically in a fraction of the time and with fewer mistakes.

The question I want to discuss today is: how have our work lives changed as a result of using more technology?

One effect has been the trend in people working from home. This is an advantage for people who live far away from their office, or who have small children to look after. On the other hand, it is more difficult for them to separate work and home life. Cell phones, pagers, faxes, and email can reach us at any time of the day at home. This can have a negative effect on family and personal relationships. Working from home also means that jobs can be more easily transferred to other parts of the country or to other countries. When you buy insurance, for example, there is no need for the sales representatives to be in your town or city. They can be in Florida, in Texas, or in India. So another effect has been an increase in the number of technology jobs which have moved to countries where salaries are lower.

What about the effects on our job skills? Most people would agree that computers help us to communicate faster and more efficiently. Are there negative effects, too?

Student: We don't talk to each other?

That's right. Because of technology, we don't have to meet our customers or co-workers in person. The downside is that people are losing their face-to-face interpersonal skills. Even in offices, team meetings and informal conversations are often replaced by email messages and conference calls. Some companies even discourage workers from wasting too much time talking!

So, while it is easy to see the benefits of technology, we should not forget there may also be some drawbacks.

Chapter 5 Test Audioscripts

Section I Listening to a Conversation

Sandra: Hi, Jenny.

Jenny: Hey Sandra, how's it going?

Sandra: Fantastic. It's great being back at my old job.

Jenny: It's good to have you back. Did you find an apartment yet?

Sandra: No, I'm still living with my parents…

Jenny: How's that going?

Sandra: It's great because my mother can take care of Timmy during the day. He's still only two years old. On the other hand, it kind of feels like I'm a teenager again.

Jenny: What will you do about Timmy when you find your own place?

Sandra: I guess I'll have to find a babysitter during the day. Too bad our company doesn't offer any workplace child care.

Jenny: Yes, maybe we should try to start one. I'll ask the manager about it at the next meeting.

Section II Listening to a Lecture

Today I'm going to talk to you about the aging labor force in the U.S. and the impact on the U.S. economy. The main reason that a large percentage of the labor force is getting older is because of the large increase in the number of babies born in the U.S. just after the Second World War. This was known as the "baby boom." It began in 1946 and continued through 1964. During those 19 years, 76 million people were born in the U.S. People who were born during the baby boom are all now approaching retirement age . . . all at the same time.

In 1978, when baby-boomers were aged 15 to 32, they made up approximately 45 percent of the labor force. Now, as baby-boomers are starting to age, the percentage of workers aged 45 and older is starting to increase. In 1998, it was 33 percent of the labor force and in 2008, it will be up to 40 percent. At the same time, workers aged 25 to 44 will decrease from 51 percent to 44 percent. As a result, the average age of the labor force will rise from 38.7 years old in 1998 to 40.7 years old in 2008.

What does this mean in terms of impact on the economy? Naturally, if all the baby-boomers suddenly retired at the same time, there would be a problem. Who would pay their retirement or social security? Who would take over their jobs? Well, that's not going to happen. First, the retirement age is going to go up. Over the last 20 years, the age of retirement has remained fairly stable. But—for a number of different reasons—the retirement age will start to increase. Between 2000 and 2022, the normal retirement age will rise from 65 to 67. A second factor is that company pensions no longer provide the same type of benefits for retirement. Workers nowadays have to work longer to get a pension they can live on. These are just two factors which will result in workers staying in the workforce longer.

Chapter 6 Test Audioscripts

Section I Listening to a Conversation

Mike: How many emails do you typically get in a day, Gina?

Gina: Well . . . that's hard to say . . . maybe 20 or 25?

Mike: And do you answer them all?

Gina: I answer the urgent ones, like the ones from students who don't understand their assignments, but I don't manage to answer them all, and I generally have to catch up on the weekend. Do you have any tips?

Mike: What you're doing is a good idea. Choose the most important ones and answer those first.

Gina: OK.

Mike: But it's also a good idea not to answer emails immediately, because very often people come up with the solution by themselves, or they send a second email soon after the first one with a different question. Or another idea is to post general messages on your website, then instead of writing emails, you can just send the website link....

Gina: That's true, I had several emails the....

Kendra: Excuse me for interrupting you Gina, there's a student on the phone who urgently needs to speak with you.

Gina: Thanks, Kendra. I'll come right over. Uh-oh it's probably someone who sent me an email, and I haven't answered it yet! See you later, Mike!

Section II Listening to a Lecture

Today I'm going to talk about greetings in different cultures. And in particular about greetings in more formal work and business settings. Now of course, we all know some of the basic differences in greetings customs, for example, that handshakes are more common in North American and European contexts, while bowing is more common in some Asian cultures, particularly in Japan. But there are also some other differences in rules of politeness that can cause misunderstandings.

In North America, it is usual to shake hands when you first meet someone. When you shake hands, it should be accompanied by eye contact, a smile, and a friendly greeting such as *How are you?* or *I'm glad to meet you*. In this situation, it is polite to ask someone to call you by your first name. The aim is to look and sound sincere and friendly, and to try to decrease social distance by establishing an equal relationship.

In Japan, it is common to bow when first meeting someone. It is polite to avoid eye contact by looking down. The greeting is usually accompanied by a phrase asking for the other person's help, for example, by using the phrase, *doozo yoroshiku o negai shimasu* which may be translated as "I hope you will be able to help me." The appropriate response is "I ask for your help, too." The aim is to establish a relationship of mutual dependence where everyone helps each other.

Now if a Japanese person were to shake hands with an American and tried to translate his or her cultural 'rules' what would happen?

First of all, avoiding eye contact would not show politeness, as intended, it would show distance and perhaps insincerity. Secondly, asking for someone's help when first meeting him or her would sound like you were asking for a favor, which is a little strange when you don't know the person. The American might think he or she was really being asked for help, which could be difficult.

On the other hand, what if an American person were to shake hands with a Japanese person and tried to translate his or her own cultural rules? What would happen? By trying to decrease social distance by eye contact, first names, or a friendly informal tone, that person would seem less polite. Second, when he or she hears someone asking for help, the American person may respond by offering help, which could also sound impolite.

To summarize, each person, while doing their best to be polite according to their own cultural rules, would sound impolite and insincere to the other person. And they've only got as far as the greeting!

Chapter 7 Test Audioscripts

Section I Listening to a Conversation

Stan: What's the matter, Jenny?

Jenny: I was trying to get through to my bank. I really dislike those automated phone messages you get all the time.

Stan: You mean the ones where you have to listen and choose a number and press the right key?

Jenny: Yes . . . usually there's a list of choices and

at the end you just get another automated message. It's so frustrating . . . I prefer to speak to a real person.

Stan: I know it's frustrating sometimes, but I think it's a good idea. Just think how boring it is for people to answer the same questions all day long.

Jenny: That's true, but my question usually doesn't fit into any of the categories!

Stan: So what happens?

Jenny: They just put me on hold and I usually have to wait a long time . . . and . . .

Stan: Aha! So you just don't like waiting, is that it?

Jenny: Yes, I suppose you're right.

Section II Listening to a Lecture

My topic for today's lecture is differences between spoken and written English. And I'm going to group these differences under three main categories. These categories are: the medium of communication, grammar, and vocabulary.

So first of all, quite obviously, the main difference between written and spoken English is the medium of communication. Speaking and writing are two quite different ways of transmitting meanings. In spoken language, we can use stress and intonation to add meaning to our words. What about written language? Well, in writing you have to use punctuation—a question mark instead of a questioning intonation, for example. Or you can add words that convey mood, such as certainty or uncertainty. For example, in speech you might say *It* isn't *true!* but you might write *It is certainly not true!*, using an exclamation mark for emphasis.

The second category is vocabulary. If you are writing a note or a short email to your friend, then you might use some slang expressions or contractions. But in more formal written English, you should avoid slang and contractions such as *isn't* or *doesn't*. There is more frequent use of pronouns in spoken English. When you are speaking to someone, it is often quite clear from the surrounding context what you mean when you say *It's fine*. But when you're writing,

you need to be more specific and say if *it* means the weather, your work, the food . . . or something completely different.

The third category is grammar. In spoken English, people often use incomplete sentences. They stop and start and interrupt each other, and leave sentences unfinished. You might find mistakes in verb agreement, for example, because people change their mind in the middle of a sentence. In written English, however, especially formal written English such as business letters or academic essays, you have to use complete sentences, and mistakes in grammar are much more noticeable—so you have to be more careful!

Chapter 8 Test Audioscripts

Section I Listening to a Conversation

Joe: How was your birthday meal last night?

Maria: Fantastic! I'm crazy about Mexican food! How about you?

Joe: No, I don't care for spicy food.

Maria: How about Indian? There's a new Indian restaurant in town. It looks really awesome. Do you want to go there on Saturday?

Joe: Oh, no. I can't stand curry.

Maria: OK. How do you feel about Thai food?

Joe: I've never tried it, but how about just having steak and fries?

Maria: Why do you always want to eat the same thing?

Section II Listening to an Interview

Host: And today I'd like to welcome, Marietta Delfontini, the famous fashion designer who is going to tell us about her new line of environmentally-friendly fashion. Marietta, thank you for joining us today.

Marietta: My pleasure.

Host: To begin, could you tell us the meaning of the term *environmentally-friendly fashion*?

Marietta: Sure. Environmentally-friendly fashion refers to clothing that has been created in a way that is sensitive to the environment. In other words, it is made from natural materials, such as cotton or wool. It doesn't use nylon or polyester, for example, which are made from chemicals. And it uses natural materials that have not been produced using chemical insecticides or pesticides, I mean they are all produced organically.

Host: I see. And do you think there is a demand for this kind of fashion nowadays?

Marietta: Absolutely! Young people nowadays are very aware of environmental concerns. And they want to have fashion that responds to those concerns. Our new line will not only help to save the environment, but people who wear it will spread the message about environmentally-friendly fashion.

Host: In other words, by wearing your fashion, people will make the issue more popular?

Marietta: That's it exactly!

Host: There must be some things that aren't organic, buttons for example?

Marietta: Yes, that's true. We do make buttons from wood or from glass, but for those elements which cannot be made from organic materials, we re-use decorative accessories from vintage clothing, that is clothing from the 50s or 60s. It is contemporary clothing with a vintage twist.

Host: How is that good for the environment?

Marietta: Well, we think people are too quick to throw their clothing away. So we'd like to see more fashion that combines old and new to create an exciting modern look. I mean we're encouraging people to use their clothing for a longer time.

Host: Thanks very much, Marietta. We look forward to seeing your new collection.

Marietta: Thank you.

Chapter 9 Test Audioscripts

Section I Listening to a Conversation

Sally: There was an amazing story in the news today.

Jane: Oh yeah? What was it?

Sally: Well, it was about a little girl who had a heart transplant when she was just two years old.

Jane: You mean they gave her a new heart?

Sally: That's right. Believe it or not, they left her own heart inside her and just added the new one.

Jane: So she had two hearts?

Sally: Exactly.

Jane: That's so weird.

Sally: Well, now she's 12 years old and she's had some problems with the new heart so they took out the new heart and reattached the original one, which was still inside her. The most amazing thing is that the old heart had gotten better and now it works perfectly.

Jane: Unbelievable!

Section II Listening to a Lecture

It is a well-known fact that people have been searching for signs of life on other planets for many hundreds of years. Are we alone in the universe? Or are there other civilizations out there just waiting to be discovered? Only in the last few decades has it become physically possible for us to visit other planets. And today, I'm going to talk about some theories concerning life on one of our nearest neighbors—the planet Mars. How likely is it that there is life on Mars?

The belief that there may be life on Mars became popular in the 19th century when an Italian astronomer named Giovanni Schiaparelli observed lines on the surface of the planet which he called *canali*. This was mistakenly translated into English as *canals* and other astronomers thought that they might be evidence of the presence of water which would mean that life was possible.

Nowadays, with the use of much more powerful and accurate telescopes, it has been proven that these so-called *canals* do not exist, or in some cases, are dried-up water channels. But, although there may have been water on Mars in the past, there is no evidence of any water on the planet today.

Another source of evidence for life on Mars was the discovery of a meteorite, a piece of rock from Mars, which was found in Alaska in 1996. When scientists studied this meteorite, they found evidence of single-cell biological organisms in the rock. However, this evidence was contradicted by other scientists who say that there is no proof that this rock was ever in temperatures suitable for water, and that, therefore, it is impossible to say whether these organisms were ever alive.

The exploration of Mars in 2003 made the exciting discovery of evidence that there *has* been water on Mars in the past. So now the question is: How can scientists find out whether life has ever existed on Mars? Well, the obvious answer is that they'll have to get more samples of rocks. But, they'll need to get rocks from a site that will provide a good source of evidence. One possibility might be a dried-up lake, for example, where life may have existed even after life on other parts of the planet had disappeared. Another possibility is to obtain rock samples from the polar ice caps of Mars which have a temperature of minus 95 degrees Fahrenheit (that's minus 70 degrees Centigrade). Because of the lower temperatures, micro-organisms would be preserved for a much longer time and could still possibly be found.

These are some of the exciting questions being asked in the study and exploration of life on Mars. And the answers to these questions could tell us a lot about our universe and our world. Now what kind of questions do you have?

Chapter 10 Test Audioscripts

Section I Listening to a Conversation

Tina: Mike, are you busy on Saturday?

Mike: Why, what's happening?

Tina: It's my 21st birthday, and I'm having a small party. Can you come?

Mike: I'd love to. What would you like me to bring? Food, drinks?

Tina: No, that's OK, thanks, I think we'll have enough.

Mike: How about music? I have some really good dance music.

Tina: Oh sure, that would be great.

Mike: Are you doing something special, since it's your 21st?

Tina: Well, I think my sister's making a cake, and my boyfriend's bringing the drinks.

Mike: Could I bring some ice cream then?

Tina: OK, if you wouldn't mind.

Section II Listening to a Lecture

Host: As part of our course on the sociology of weddings, we're going to hear from an expert on the topic of weddings. I'd like to introduce our guest speaker today, Annette Cook. Annette is a professional wedding consultant. Today she is going to talk to us about weddings in the U.S.

Speaker: Thank you, Professor Jackson. And thanks for inviting me. Good afternoon everyone.

Well, the topic of weddings is a pretty broad topic and I thought I would try to narrow this down by focusing on the type of wedding that I'm typically involved in, and that is the big formal wedding. Why is it so important? I mean, why do people spend so much time and money planning a big wedding?

Almost five million Americans get married each year. And by the way, this number includes not only people who are marrying for the first time, but also people who are getting married a second, third, or fourth time. You may not know that the divorce rate for first marriages is about 50 percent, and there is a strong trend for divorced persons to have just as big or even a bigger celebration for their second (and even third and fourth) weddings. But to get back to the topic, why are big weddings so popular?

Of course, the main reason couples have a wedding celebration is to enjoy themselves and celebrate the start of their married life. But a wedding also has a symbolic meaning. It is a symbol of the couple's commitment to the relationship. Weddings are important for families, too. In our mobile and fragmented society, such family occasions are increasingly rare. Bringing families together, however, can also bring problems, of course, such as when there are family members who don't get along, or families of different religions or ethnic backgrounds who have different ideas about what the wedding should be like.

Before I forget, let me just mention that this is the time when a wedding planner can be *very* helpful. An experienced wedding planner can help to solve practical problems in a way that keeps everyone happy. Anyway, to get back to the topic . . . where was I? Oh yes . . . you can look at large weddings as a way for the two families to cooperate and get to know each other, and this will help provide a support network for the couple in their later lives.

Name _____ Date _____ Score _____

Interactions/Mosaic
Listening/Speaking Placement Test

Directions: Read these directions before listening to the recorded test.

There are four sections in this test, each with a different type of listening and questions. There are a total of fifty questions to answer. You will hear the test questions only once; they will not be repeated.

Sections:

1. Ten question items – after you hear each question, choose the best response. (questions 1–10)

2. Ten statement items – after you hear each statement, select the best conclusion. (questions 11–20)

3. Ten short conversations – after each conversation there is one question to answer. (questions 21–30)

4. Four longer selections – after each longer listening selection, there are five questions to answer about the listening. (questions 31–50)

Section 1 Listen to the question and choose the best response. **(2 points each)**

Example: (You hear:) Where's your sister gone?

(You read:)
(A) to Canada
(B) without her friends
(C) because she was late
(D) yesterday
Choice "a" is the best answer.

1. (A) tomorrow
(B) to visit his sister
(C) just this morning
(D) the train

2. (A) Yes, I must go there.
(B) About five hundred dollars
(C) I'll have a good time.
(D) A few days

3. (A) He's been once.
(B) She's been there for three months.
(C) No, she's still there.
(D) She was there as a child.

4. (A) It's not very fair.
(B) It takes an hour.
(C) It's two dollars.
(D) It's not very far from here.

5. (A) Yes, they can.
   (B) The bus stops near the theatre.
   (C) There is no way we could make it in time.
   (D) It's too bad we missed the eight o'clock show.

6. (A) It's a little too casual.
   (B) Yes, the pants fit.
   (C) They have three different sizes.
   (D) It's a bit tight.

7. (A) They prefer going to the movies.
   (B) I haven't really thought about it.
   (C) I have no references.
   (D) It's either black or white.

8. (A) I would be pleased if she finds a job that she enjoys.
   (B) My mother hopes she will go on to college.
   (C) I took her on a trip last year.
   (D) I want my legs to stop hurting.

9. (A) Yes, the doctor told me to start drinking it more often.
   (B) Yes, I needed something to eat.
   (C) No, I still drink milk every day.
   (D) Sorry, I don't have time.

10. (A) I'm sorry I was late.
    (B) I couldn't have come earlier.
    (C) Would you like me to come back in a while?
    (D) Sorry we left so late.

Section 2 Listen to each statement and then choose the best conclusion. (**2 points each**)

11. (A) Peter's lawyer likes his mother.
    (B) Peter likes his mother.
    (C) Peter is a liar.
    (D) Peter's mother is a lawyer.

12. (A) The flight arrived at 2:30.
    (B) The flight took off at 2:30.
    (C) The flight will arrive in an hour and a half.
    (D) The flight arrived at 1:30.

13. (A) Sixty students went on the sailing trip.
    (B) No students went on the sailing trip.
    (C) Only a few students arrived to go on the sailing trip.
    (D) Nobody signed up for the sailing trip.

14. (A) Judy has to plan something for her birthday.
    (B) Someone gave Judy flowers on her birthday.
    (C) Judy intends to do something special on her birthday.
    (D) Judy bought some plants as a gift.

15. (A) Peter is a fair player.
    (B) The match was relatively short.
    (C) Peter won the match.
    (D) Steve hit the ball fast.

16. (A) Mary was losing her eyesight.
    (B) John won the argument with Mary.
    (C) Mary forgot why she and John were arguing.
    (D) Mary and John argued because it was very hot.

17. (A) Gary preferred Robert to Peter.
    (B) Gary preferred Peter to Robert.
    (C) Robert liked Peter better than Gary.
    (D) Peter liked Gary better than Robert.

18. (A) It's time to plant things in the garden.
    (B) Soon it will be warm enough to start planting seeds.
    (C) You ought to visit the garden at the sea.
    (D) You should be considerate of the garden.

19. (A) The dinner was very good in general.
    (B) Dinner was at a restaurant.
    (C) Everyone thought the dinner was very good.
    (D) Dinner was very good every night.

20. (A) John's brother lives near the club.
    (B) John's brother owns the club.
    (C) John has never invited his brother to the club.
    (D) John's brother has never invited John to the club.

Section 3: Listen to each conversation. Answer the question you hear after each conversation.
(2 points each)

21. (A) It hasn't rained for many years.
    (B) It has rained an unusual amount this year.
    (C) It hasn't rained much here.
    (D) It hasn't rained this year.

22. (A) He thought the restaurant could have been better.
    (B) He agreed with the woman.
    (C) He thoroughly enjoyed the restaurant.
    (D) It was impossible for the restaurant to be nice.

23. (A) The wind hurt the man's house.
    (B) The wind hurt the woman's son.
    (C) Paint in the woman's basement was ruined.
    (D) Flood water damaged artwork in the woman's house.

24. (A) The man's brother is not strong enough to lift things.
    (B) The man's brother is not making any effort to find work.
    (C) The brother is unlucky.

      Ⓓ The woman is surprised the man's brother is still not working.

25. Ⓐ It's not unusual for him to play in hot weather.

      Ⓑ At an earlier time in his life, he played tennis in such weather.

      Ⓒ Playing tennis in hot weather uses up his energy.

      Ⓓ He's concerned about playing in the heat.

26. Ⓐ It's contradictory.

      Ⓑ She doesn't agree.

      Ⓒ She wants the man to look at the ducks.

      Ⓓ She's angry.

27. Ⓐ He's not planning to purchase anything.

      Ⓑ He doesn't need to get anything at this store.

      Ⓒ He doesn't agree about the prices.

      Ⓓ He doesn't like to buy cheap things.

28. Ⓐ The city nearly burned down.

      Ⓑ The mayor was rescued from a burning building.

      Ⓒ The mayor was hurt and moved.

      Ⓓ The mayor was criticized and left his job.

29. Ⓐ He thinks she should buy a large pizza.

      Ⓑ He thinks she should ask for extra mushrooms and cheese.

      Ⓒ He likes the mushroom and cheese pizza best.

      Ⓓ He thinks the pizzas are too big.

30. Ⓐ The judge was very sure about handling the case.

      Ⓑ The judge gave the man a severe punishment.

      Ⓒ The judge was difficult to understand.

      Ⓓ The judge couldn't decide the theif's punishment.

Section 4 Listen to each longer selection and answer the five questions for the selection. Listen to the first selection. Then answer questions 31–35. **(2 points each)**

31. What do you think T-A-L-K is?

      Ⓐ a radio station

      Ⓑ a TV station

      Ⓒ an animal rescue service

      Ⓓ a movie studio

32. What animals are missing?

      Ⓐ one dog and two cats

      Ⓑ two dogs and one cat

      Ⓒ two dogs and two cats

      Ⓓ one dog and one cat

33. Which of the animals were taken from a backyard?

      Ⓐ None of the animals

      Ⓑ All of the animals

      Ⓒ Oxen the German Shepherd

      Ⓓ Winston the wire-haired terrier

34. Who had a seeing-eye dog?

(A) Mr. Wilson

(B) Mrs. Lincoln

(C) Mrs. Thompson

(D) Oxen

35. What are the listeners supposed to do if they find one of the pets?

(A) Call the T-A-L-K phone line.

(B) Call the police station.

(C) Call the local animal shelter.

(D) Wait a week to call.

Directions: The following selection is a lecture in two parts. Listen to Part 1 and answer questions 36–40. (**2 points each**)

36. In what situation does this talk probably take place?

(A) nutrition class

(B) business or marketing class

(C) supermarket training

(D) a one-day seminar

37. According to the speaker, what is true about product placement?

(A) It's only important in supermarkets.

(B) The concept is hardly used in the United States.

(C) Children are not affected by it.

(D) It's an extremely important selling tool.

38. The speaker said that children often "pester their parents" in a supermarket. What does *pester* mean?

(A) nagging and begging

(B) petting or touching

(C) wanting candy

(D) grabbing food

39. What's the speaker's focus?

(A) product placement outside of the United States

(B) product placement both in and out of the United States

(C) product placement in the United States

(D) products you shouldn't buy

40. What specific examples did the speaker use?

(A) Candy was the only example.

(B) Candy was one of the examples.

(C) The examples were taken directly from the textbook.

(D) The examples would be on the test.

Directions: Listen to Part 2 of the lecture and answer questions 41–45. **(2 points each)**

41. What products did the speaker talk about?
- Ⓐ expensive products
- Ⓑ headache medicine
- Ⓒ tropical shampoo
- Ⓓ shampoo for oily hair

42. What did the speaker say about U.S. stores?
- Ⓐ All U.S. stores follow the same process for placing items on shelves.
- Ⓑ Most U.S. stores place pricey items at eye level.
- Ⓒ Many U.S. stores place inexpensive items at eye level.
- Ⓓ No U.S. stores place items at eye level.

43. What position was stated by the speaker?
- Ⓐ Inexpensive items are better than expensive ones.
- Ⓑ Expensive items are better than inexpensive ones.
- Ⓒ He didn't endorse inexpensive items or expensive ones.
- Ⓓ He doesn't like candy or shampoo.

44. What did the speaker tell the participants?
- Ⓐ They didn't have any homework.
- Ⓑ They had to get ready for a test.
- Ⓒ They had to do some research.
- Ⓓ They had to finish an assignment in class.

45. When does the class probably meet?
- Ⓐ Tuesday and Thursday nights
- Ⓑ Tuesday nights
- Ⓒ Tuesday mornings
- Ⓓ every other week

Directions: The following selection is a lecture. Listen to the lecture and answer questions 46–50. **(2 points each)**

46. What best describes folk wisdom?
- Ⓐ American folklore
- Ⓑ jokes
- Ⓒ sayings that give advice about life
- Ⓓ different means of expressing oneself

47. Which expression of folk wisdom is *not* mentioned?
- Ⓐ myths
- Ⓑ fairy tales
- Ⓒ songs
- Ⓓ poetry

48. What will the speaker probably focus on in the lecture?

- (A) humorous sayings
- (B) legends
- (C) songs of joy and sorrow
- (D) famous American Presidents

49. What source of folk wisdom will be used in the talk?

- (A) Abraham Lincoln
- (B) Mark Twain and Benjamin Franklin
- (C) students in this class
- (D) All of the above

50. Which is not mentioned about Ben Franklin?

- (A) He loved to eat and drink.
- (B) People admired his wit.
- (C) He took the bitter medicine.
- (D) He told others not to overdo things.

Interactions Listening/Speaking Placement Test Answer Key

Section 1

1. c 2. d 3. d 4. c 5. c 6. d 7. b 8. a 9. a 10. c

Section 2

11. d 12. a 13. c 14. c 15. b 16. c 17. b 18. a 19. a
20. d

Section 3

21. b 22. c 23. d 24. b 25. a 26. a 27. c 28. d 29. c
30. b

Section 4

31. a 32. b 33. d 34. a 35. a 36. b 37. d 38. a 39. c
40. a 41. a 42. b 43. c 44. c 45. b 46. c 47. d 48. a
49. d 50. c

SCORING FOR INTERACTIONS/MOSAIC LISTENING/SPEAKING PLACEMENT TEST	
Score	Placement
0–27	Interactions Access
28–46	Interactions 1
47–65	Interactions 2
66–84	Mosaic 1
85–100	Mosaic 2

This is a rough guide. Teachers should use their judgment in placing students and selecting texts.

Listening/Speaking Placement Test Audioscripts

Narrator:	Number 1. When did Steve get in?
Narrator:	Number 2. How much time will you have to spend in Boston?
Narrator:	Number 3. Has she ever been there before?
Narrator:	Number 4. How much is the subway fare?
Narrator:	Number 5. Should we try to get to the eight o'clock movie?
Narrator:	Number 6. Do you think that this jacket fits?
Narrator:	Number 7. What are your preferences in art?
Narrator:	Number 8. What are your hopes for your niece?
Narrator:	Number 9. On the way home from the doctor, did you stop for some milk?
Narrator:	Number 10. Couldn't you have arrived an hour later?
Narrator:	Number 11. Peter is a lawyer like his mother.
Narrator:	Number 12. Mary's flight was due at one, but it was delayed an hour and a half.
Narrator:	Number 13. Sixty students signed up for the sailing trip, but most of them failed to show up.
Narrator:	Number 14. Judy's got big plans for her birthday.
Narrator:	Number 15. Peter was beaten fairly quickly by Steve in the tennis match.
Narrator:	Number 16. In the heat of the argument, Mary lost sight of her original disagreement with John.
Narrator:	Number 17. Although Gary liked his uncle Robert, he was fonder of his cousin Peter.

Narrator:	Number 18. Considering the season, you really should plant the seeds in the garden before the frost.
Narrator:	Number 19. On the whole, the dinner was great.
Narrator:	Number 20. John's never been invited to the club by his brother.
Narrator:	Number 21.
Man:	The weather has been so hot this summer . . .
Woman:	And we haven't had rain like this in years.
Narrator:	What does the woman mean?
Narrator:	Number 22.
Woman:	The restaurant wasn't very good in my opinion.
Man:	I thought it couldn't have been nicer.
Narrator:	What does the man mean?
Narrator:	Number 23.
Man:	The storm sounded like it would blow the roof off my house.
Woman:	Wasn't it terrible? The flood in our basement ruined my son's paintings.
Narrator:	What did the storm do?
Narrator:	Number 24.
Man:	My brother is having a lot of trouble finding a job.
Woman:	What a surprise. I haven't seen him lift a finger.
Narrator:	What does the woman mean?
Narrator:	Number 25.
Woman:	Your serve. Whew. It's gotten very hot.
Man:	I know, but I'm used to playing tennis in weather like this.
Narrator:	What does the man mean?
Narrator:	Number 26.
Man:	The less I try to whack the ball, the farther it goes.
Woman:	Hmm, that's quite a paradox!

Narrator:	What does the woman mean?
Narrator:	Number 27.
Woman:	Richard told me about this store. He said they have the lowest prices in town.
Man:	You think? I don't necessarily buy that.
Narrator:	What does the man mean?
Narrator:	Number 28.
Man:	Did you hear that city hall almost burned down?
Woman:	Right, and then the Mayor was removed under fire.
Narrator:	What does the woman mean?
Narrator:	Number 29.
Woman:	How's the pizza here?
Man:	Good, by and large, especially the mushroom and cheese.
Narrator:	What does the man mean?
Narrator:	Number 30.
Woman:	That young man got 20 years for stealing a bicycle.
Man:	Hmm. The judge sure handed down a hard sentence.
Narrator:	What does the man mean?
Female Announcer:	This is the T-A-L-K "Lost Pet Watch." Tonight we are telling you about three missing pets.
	Blacky is a black-and-white kitten, six months old, who ran away from her owner, Mrs. Lincoln. Her house is next to the high school.
Male Announcer:	And then, Oxen, a large German Shepherd, is a guide dog for John Wilson who's been blind since birth. Mr. Wilson cannot get around without his dog. Oxen was last seen running through the Green Acres neighborhood. He's wearing a black collar and has a big scar over his left eye.
	Also, Winston, a wire-haired terrier, was taken from Mrs. Thompson's back yard. Winston is a prize-winning purebred worth about $3,000.
Female Announcer:	If you have any information, please call our studio at 1-800-PET-HELP. The police station no longer handles missing animal reports. The animal shelter's phone is broken and won't be repaired for a week.
	Stay tuned for news here at 103.7.
Narrator:	Part 1.
Male Professor:	This evening I am going to talk about product placement. Product placement is probably one of the most important concepts I will cover this semester. In the United States special care is taken when placing items in different parts of the supermarket. For example, candy is generally placed next to the cashier or check-out counter. This is because customers are often likely to grab a candy bar while waiting in line. Children, who are waiting in line with their parents, often pester their parents to buy candy for them. Another example has to do with the placement of expensive products.
	Oh – Let me turn that off......
Narrator:	Part 2.
Male Professor:	Now where was I... Right —
	Well, many stores in the U.S., not all, will place expensive products at eye level. Imported shampoos, for example, are placed at a level where they are clearly visible and people can easily reach for them. Please note that I am not supporting or endorsing cheap items over expensive ones. Before we end this evening, I want to talk about your next assignment.

Though you might not think of it as homework, I expect each of you to go to a large supermarket before next Tuesday to see where the over-the-counter medicine is placed. I look forward to hearing about your findings in a week.

Narrator: The final selection.

Female Professor: Hello, class. Today we're going to be talking about folk wisdom.

Every culture has many sayings that give advice about life. These sayings are part of what is commonly called "folk wisdom." Of course, folk wisdom is also expressed in other ways, such as myths, fairy tales, legends, and songs. Often, however, folk wisdom is shared in the form of short sayings about the best ways to approach life's joys and sorrows.

Today, we'll look at some of the humorous sayings of three famous Americans: Benjamin Franklin, Abraham Lincoln, and Mark Twain. Then I'll ask you to share some examples of folk wisdom from your own communities.

One characteristic of American folk wisdom is its humor. Humor makes the bitter medicine of life easier to swallow.

Ben Franklin was the first of many Americans to be admired for his humorous folk wisdom. Franklin himself loved to have fun. He liked to eat a lot, drink a lot, and be merry, but he always told others to practice moderation.